Advance praise for *Leading in the Top Team*

'The ideas here are critical for developing a company vision, especially one that is based on an aggressive growth strategy. As a CEO, I am using this book in very pragmatic ways. The detailed descriptions of the CXO roles, and how these are changing, help us greatly in selecting new members for the top team, in objectively appraising the contributions of CXOs, and in aligning the top team mind-set around our strategic goals, our processes, and our values.'

IGOR ALLINCKX
CEO, Sekisui Alveo AG

'This book provides valuable insight and practical ideas for anyone working within or alongside the SCM function of an organisation. It very clearly shows the linkage between SCM and business transformation, providing a mixture of traditional theory with forward-thinking ideas. Ensuring that SCM is recognised as a strategic differentiator is key, and this book provides a good framework on how that vision can be articulated and "sold" across an enterprise.'

LES BALL
Director of Supply Chain Management, EMEA Region, Eaton Corporation

'I really value the way this book describes the changing role of the CIO in the context of all the other CXO roles, and in particular, the way it brings to life the holy grail of IT and future role of the CIO – unlocking the full business value of all the information residing inside the enterprise.'

JIM BARRINGTON
Corporate CIO – Novartis International AG

'This book gives useful insights about the work of the CEO and other senior executives. Good reading for members of top level business teams, for those who support such teams, and for those who aspire to join them.'

TON BÜCHNER
CEO, Sulzer AG

'I believe that an effective finance function must work closely with the business in order to drive growth and manage risk in a balanced manner. The CFO chapter in this book provides excellent insights into the role of the chief financial officer, and the skills and qualities that are essential to fulfil this. Many aspects of the chapter resonate with my own experiences, in particular the recognition that strong leadership skills and focus on talent development are also fundamental to the CFO's mandate of protecting and enhancing shareholder value.'

RENATO FASSBIND
Chief Financial Officer, Credit Suisse Group

'The Chief of Marketing role is broad and complex, from day-to-day management of brands and portfolios, to long-term growth visions and innovation. But the most successful CMOs are the ones that engage the hearts and minds of the CEO and other functions to bring the total company closer to consumers and customers. This book describes the basics of doing just that.'

ALEX MYERS
Senior VP, Western Europe & Export / License, Carlsberg Breweries (Previously Senior VP, Sales & Marketing)

'A thought provoking hypothesis that emphasizes the systemic nature of the CHRO role whilst challenging the "right" to influence at the strategic level dependent on service delivery. It also highlights how crucial change skills are to any modern CHRO.'

GARY STEEL
Member of the Group Executive Committee, Executive Vice President, Head of Human Resources, ABB Ltd

'A practical toolbox for all CXOs and the CEO. This book provides invaluable insights on how to excel in the different roles and how to leverage mutual skill sets to succeed as a wealth creating team. Recommended for everyone from MBA students to CXOs, CEOs and board members.'

OERN R. STUGE
President Europe, Emerging Markets & Canada, Medtronic Inc.

'The brilliantly written chapter on the CCO challenge acknowledges the strategic role of corporate communications and its impact on a company's most valuable asset: its reputation. The chapter describes the multiple facets of the task of the CCO and the multiple skills a CCO should have. It also makes it clear that a business decision which cannot be sensibly communicated should probably be reconsidered – one reason more why the CCO should sit at the table where the decisions are taken and not wait outside until the decision has been taken to then just execute the communication.'

GABY TSCHOFEN
VP Corporate Communications, Barry Callebaut AG

Leading in the Top Team

CXO is the collective name given to that expanding class of corporate executives whose title begins with the word 'chief' and ends with the word 'officer'. *Leading in the Top Team* explores the leadership contributions required from the CEO, and from chiefs of other key business functions, including finance, marketing, sales, the supply chain, manufacturing, IT, R&D, HR, governance, communications and the strategic business unit. Leadership in each of these areas is examined by looking at its history, current challenges facing the CXO, how each function needs to work with other key areas, and likely future developments. The focus throughout is to provide practical advice based on the actions and decisions of real leaders in a range of roles and situations. This is an excellent book for giving business leaders, whether current or potential, an overview of the work of leadership and teamwork at the top level of the company.

PRESTON BOTTGER is Professor of Leadership and Management Development at IMD.

Leading in the Top Team

The CXO Challenge

Edited by

PRESTON BOTTGER

CAMBRIDGE
UNIVERSITY PRESS

CAMBRIDGE UNIVERSITY PRESS
Cambridge, New York, Melbourne, Madrid, Cape Town, Singapore, São Paulo, Delhi

Cambridge University Press
The Edinburgh Building, Cambridge CB2 8RU, UK

Published in the United States of America by Cambridge University Press, New York

www.cambridge.org
Information on this title: www.cambridge.org/9780521856324

First published 2008

Printed in the United Kingdom at the University Press, Cambridge

A catalogue record for this publication is available from the British Library

Library of Congress Cataloguing in Publication data
Leading in the top team: the CXO challenge / edited by Preston Bottger.
p. cm.
ISBN 978-0-521-85632-4
1. Leadership. 2. Management. 3. Industrial management. 4. Chief executive officers. I. Bottger, Preston, 1950–
HD57.7.L437553 2008
658.4′092–dc22

2007052883

ISBN 978-0-521-85632-4 hardback

Contents

Figures

Tables

Contributors

Gordon Adler	Former Chief of Communications and Public Relations, IMD, now Managing Director, Adler Way
Jean-Louis Barsoux	Research Fellow, IMD
Preston Bottger	Professor of Leadership and Management Development, IMD
Carlos Cordón	Professor of Manufacturing Management
Jean-Philippe Deschamps	Professor of Technology Management, IMD
Kim Sundtoft Hald	Former Research Associate, IMD, now Assistant Professor Copenhagen Business School – Department of Operations Management
Jonathan Lachowitz	Former Research Associate, IMD, now Managing Director, White Lighthouse Investment Management
Peter Lorange	IMD President, *The Nestlé Professor* – Professor of Strategy, IMD
Donald A. Marchand	Professor of Strategy and Information Management, IMD
George Rädler	Former Research Associate, IMD, now Program Director, Swarovski Academy
Leif M. Sjöblom	Professor of Accounting and Control, IMD
Ulrich Steger	Professor of Environmental Management, *The Alcan Professor of Environment*, IMD
Dominique Turpin	Professor of Strategy and Marketing, *The Dentsu Professor in Japanese Management*, IMD
Paul Vanderbroeck	Coach on IMD programs and Managing Director of PVDB Consulting

Editor's Acknowledgments

Many of the executives who contributed their views for use in this book asked that we not give their own names or the names of their companies. We fully understand and accept the need for confidentiality in these matters. While some contributors were happy to be named, we have simply taken the decision not to attribute names to any of quotations in any of the chapters. However, we do say 'many thanks indeed' to all the executive contributors, and to the many executives who, by participating in IMD programmes, have helped further our understanding of leadership in the contemporary business firm.

There were many dedicated people who made this book possible. My gratitude to them is very heartfelt.

President Peter Lorange and Deputy President Jim Ellert of IMD were constant in their support and encouragement during the book's preparation.

Jean-Philippe Deschamps championed the key idea of the book from the beginning and gave extraordinary encouragement throughout. Don Marchand came in at key stages with great confidence-boosting support as well as excellent strategic and tactical contributions.

The members of the technical team of research associates, writers, editors and typists were, in alphabetical order: Jean-Louis Barsoux, Vanessa Borradori, Mary Ann Bottger, Jochen Brellochs, Donna Everatt, Lynne Everatt, Anouk Frossard, Jeremy Kourdi, Jonathan Lachowitz, Beverley Lennox, Edwin Love, Lindsay McTeague, Ivan Moss, Michelle Perrinjaquet, George Rädler, Alexa Stace and Michèle Stoudmann.

Each one is due great thanks and recognition for his/her outstanding work.

PRESTON BOTTGER
Lausanne, July 2007

1 *Introduction – Leading within and across the functions*

PRESTON BOTTGER AND
JEAN-LOUIS BARSOUX

Leadership is the job of every member of the senior management team . . . The CEO is simply the leader of the orchestra – each section needs to contribute in its own way – for instance you have the leader of the string section, of the trombones, and so on. Clearly we should all be team players as well – but any CXO-level person should be leader, coach, and team player at different times. (CIO, global insurance group[1])

CXO is the collective name given to that expanding class of corporate executives whose title begins with the word 'chief' and ends with the word 'officer'. In this book, we present the critical leadership tasks that must be undertaken, and the methods used by CXOs in the functions of marketing, sales, finance, research and technology, supply chain, manufacturing, information technology, human resources, governance, communications, the business unit president, and the CEO.

Together these executives provide full coverage of the business capabilities required at the apex of the corporation.

Why CXOs?

This book is a response to requests made to us by many executives for a straightforward exposition of leadership *in context*.

The authors are professors and researchers at IMD, a leading global business school based in Switzerland. In our development programmes and field research, we are in continuous discussion with people whose responsibility is to get business results, short term and longer term. These people are also responsible for developing others who similarly must achieve results in the context of ever-greater business challenges.

We hear a wide range of descriptions and assessments of the complexities and uncertainties inherent in these challenges. One observation and request that we have heard increasingly in recent times is:

We are busier and busier. We know that clear-sighted and pragmatic leadership is necessary to keep our people from misspending their valuable time and energy. Actually, we need good leadership to help us all avoid going nuts at times! So now, please, take us back to basics: what is good leadership? There are many gurus offering idealistic formulas. But can we have the no frills version? And can you please answer that 'in context'? First, so that I can better see the implications in my own line of work. But also, so that I can see what all the other managers in the company are trying to do.

This would help us all better align our efforts to achieve better results, and remain sane!

The above is a compilation of comments made by many managers in a wide variety of companies and industries. Remarkably, we hear the same refrain from first-time managers, from MBA participants, from mid-level project and operations managers, and from senior executives, including CEOs. We have even heard it from seasoned board members who now realize that they need to refresh themselves about some of the details in the broad range of responsibilities of their company's executives.

In some cases, though it might seem strange, these very senior people in top governance roles must learn – for the first time – what some areas of management are actually all about.

This book is our response to this clear and present challenge of leadership development. The chapters document the tasks – and essential initiatives and responses to handle these tasks – that comprise the work of senior executives at the pinnacle of the company's core business functions.

The book is also a reaction to widespread calls for functional managers to take a company-wide view of issues. Management educators and consultants – and CEOs – constantly tell them: 'Look beyond your own backyard, get out of your silos, throw off your tunnel vision, and take a strategic perspective.'

This is a very common, and often useful, point to make to ambitious executives. But this piece of advice has an important twin that is often overlooked. To be influential beyond one's own turf, it is essential to be high-performing and high-contributing on that home turf.

The advice to become business partners and activists at the strategy level can encourage CXOs to take their eyes off the basics and can end up undermining their legitimacy as strategic contributors. Service functions should look to *serve* before they try to change the business.

The CXO's leadership credibility also rests on setting up processes that will continue to improve the technical capabilities of the function and help the firm to manage change. With these fundamentals in place, *then* CXOs can expect to contribute strategically.

Here, we tackle both sides of the challenge. We delve into what it is CXOs must do to make their own function work effectively – and explore how to knit it all together.

Audience

As the book developed, we found ourselves writing for three very distinct audiences and we could see them each using the book in different ways: business school students; mid-level and senior executives; and CEOs and boards of directors.

For MBA participants and upper-level undergraduates, who have not yet had the breadth of experience required to perform a CXO role, we provide a view across the entire leadership team. For many business students, the book will provide a greater understanding of the work of the corporate leadership team and the issues that top executives face each day. This sheds light on how and why CXOs perform their jobs in the way they do; something that often does not make sense to people with limited exposure to senior executives.

Secondly, the material in this book is useful for practising managers, including mid-level executives aiming to go higher and project leaders whose work often spans the various functional areas. It is also useful for line managers who aspire to make more sophisticated and high-impact contributions as leaders within the company. Even current CXOs can broaden their understanding of how to contribute within their function and what is expected of them at the top leadership table. It is equally important that executives gain a richer appreciation of what is expected of their colleagues in the leadership team. Armed with this broader perspective, managers can forge more powerful relationships with colleagues and play a more-productive role in their company.

Finally, for CEOs, business unit presidents and board members who are responsible for influencing the work of executive leadership teams, the book provides tools for assessing incumbents and candidates for the highest leadership roles in the headquarters staff. A clear understanding of the profiles, the job expectations and the functional skills needed to staff a CXO team can help CEOs and their boards make more-informed people decisions, and better assessments of their performance.

Leading in the top team: the CXO challenge

The book is divided into three parts. First, we lay out the imperatives that are common to all CXO jobs. Second, we examine the particularities of the individual CXO roles. Third, we consider how managers can find better ways of working together and integrating their efforts *across* the functions, to serve the larger corporate purpose.

Section 1: The business imperatives

A key theme of this book is that executives – bright and highly-experienced people – can sometimes get sidetracked from doing the obvious, the necessary things to do their jobs well. So we start with the essentials.

In section 1, we open with a broad view of leadership. Increasingly, it is necessary for companies to cultivate leaders at every level from CXO right through to front-line levels – project managers, team leaders and supervisors. They too must lead across boundaries, often without formal authority. They too must confront rapid change in business strategies, technology and work processes. They too must provide purpose, direction and focus for their employees in a context of high uncertainty.

The following leadership images are presented: the significance of the leader as wealth creator; the close relationship between leadership and strategy; the critical leadership methods of mission, process, structure and culture; and the central theme of the importance of quality-focus in the actions of the leader.

We then set out the two business imperatives that CXOs have in their overall wealth-creation mission: the management of talent and the management of learning. The themes are important enough to warrant their own chapters as they provide a basis for all CXO positions – and as such, are revisited throughout the book.

CXOs must master the use of talent and learning to ensure that their organization not only thrives today, but is also prepared for tomorrow's challenges.

Executives define talent in many different ways. In chapter 3, we introduce a framework by which to organize the CXOs' managing of their talent pool.

Seasoned executives observe that many students graduating from business schools expect that the bulk of their learning is behind them. However, people with a few years of experience in real business often observe that graduation from school marks the beginning of the learning marathon.

In chapter 4, we focus executive thinking on how to use learning management to maintain competitive advantages for their company. One of the key themes is the necessity to cultivate the habit of stepping away from the day-to-day work environment to regain perspective.

We then turn to the core of the book, which looks at leadership from the perspective of those who staff the top roles in the typical corporate headquarters.

Section 2: The CXO leadership challenge

Having discussed the key framing issues that must underpin the actions of any unit leader, section 2 documents the key tasks in each functional area, namely: marketing, supply chain, manufacturing, finance, technology and research, information management, human resources, governance and communication.

We start with marketing, because the entire business process rests on the identification and fulfilling of customer needs. The final role is that of the communications chief as this role provides a useful overview of the major stakeholders who must be informed of, involved in or influenced by the corporation's plans and activities.

Clearly these are not all the people that would report directly to the CEO, but in the interests of focus we have not included divisional or regional heads. On the other hand, we do address their concerns in a practical chapter on how the CXOs can provide better support to the heads of business operations.

The chapters in section 2 set out what successful CXOs do to ensure effective leadership within their respective functions. A combination of real-life examples and conceptual frameworks provide insights into both the overall challenges of the functional role and the everyday work of each CXO. Each chapter covers a similar set of themes, which include:

- The historical development of the CXO role;
- Current issues and trends;

- The critical tasks faced by the CXO, and the skills required to do the work;
- The role of the CXO at the top leadership table;
- Possible future changes in the CXO role;
- A purpose, direction and focus assessment of each CXO.

The purpose of this section is to highlight the contrasting realities of leading within each function. Each CXO confronts the same questions: What are my main roles and responsibilities? What do I have to deliver to the business units? What can I not afford to get wrong? What competing demands do I need to balance? What are the key constraints? Who are my internal customers? Which stakeholders require the most attention? Which matrices matter most? How will my effectiveness be judged? How can I have more say in the strategic direction of the firm? The same questions apply, but the answers to these questions differ significantly across the functions.

In short, differences in the purpose, direction and focus of each function lead to differences in outlook and leadership style. Section 2 shows how different CXOs inhabit different incentive regimes and 'thought worlds', reflecting the unique perspective, experience and priorities of each function.[2]

Section 2 concludes by exploring the often-tense relationship between CXOs and the line managers whom they must both influence *and* serve.

Section 3: The CEO and the leadership team – pulling it all together

In section 3, we present the challenges of integrating and aligning the contributions of all these functional areas, and then the methods to deal with these challenges. The critical roles of the CEO and the tasks of teamwork at the top level are examined in dctail.

First, we use a five-role model to explore the CEO's job and to consider which CXO positions provide good exposure to the various roles – but also to underline that the CEO job involves a very-substantive expansion of responsibilities. This chapter paves the way for a treatment of the CEO position along the lines of the previous CXO chapters.

Then, we explore the relations among CXOs as they strive to contribute to the firm's corporate goals. A key factor influencing the weight of each CXO's say in the strategic discussion is the ability to build alliances with, and to appreciate the perspective of, colleagues.

Observers of management – including academics, consultants and even board members – often bemoan the existence of 'functional chimneys', 'fiefdoms' and 'silos' that inhibit collaborative efforts within organizations. Often, these critics worry that clashes within the top management team are the result of politics, in-fighting and power-chasing among the CXOs.

The viewpoints presented in this section can help CXOs and their staffs to see beyond their own functional frames. We show how the various CXOs and their staffs view the business in different ways – for the simple reason that they are subject to very different concerns and constraints, choices and objectives and, critically, incentives. Understanding this range of perspectives is important for all CXOs, indeed any managers and professionals, who must engage in productive dialogue with colleagues in other functions.

We also consider the opportunities for and obstacles to improved co-operation across functional boundaries. We provide guidance by which managers can find better ways of working together and integrating their efforts across the functions, to serve the larger corporate purpose.

The concluding chapter reviews the leadership challenge of orchestrating the CXO team to deliver high-quality results in its ultimate mission of wealth creation.

Notes

1 G. Flood, 'Leading the way', *MIS UK*, 22 (1 April) (2004).

2 D. Dougherty, 'Interpretive barriers to successful product innovation in large firms', *Organization Science*, 3 (2) (1992), pp. 179–202.

SECTION I

The Business Imperatives

2 *The Leadership Imperative – Driving wealth creation*

PRESTON BOTTGER

It's my job to consider the long term. Most people in most jobs in the company don't think like that. They think about the day-to-day things – that's as it should be – so it's not at all obvious to them why the changes I think have to be made, have to be made.[1]

(CEO, global airline)

I sometimes see in leadership books and in reviews of these books a statement along the lines of: 'After decades of study, the phenomena of leadership are still not well understood.' This is a mistaken view.

Actually, a great deal is understood about leadership, and has been for a very long time. While it is certainly true that leadership is a vast and multi-faceted topic that finds different expressions in different situations, and can therefore be described and interpreted in many different ways, we can still make valid and fertile statements about 'what is leadership', even if there will never be a single-paragraph definition that will satisfy everyone.

The view of leadership that follows in this chapter is the author's personal statement. It will not be to all tastes. It distils twenty-five years of observation, engagement and scholarship, working closely with executives and listening to their views, as well as researching leadership across business, politics, the military, the arts, entertainment and sport.

Leadership and strategy are closely intertwined, in concept and practice. Both convey the related elements of desirable goals, the methods for pursuing them, and results actually achieved. Especially when we explore leadership in the business enterprise, as we do in this book, it is important to bear in mind this close relationship between individual leaders and the strategies they devise and employ.

A very general point to make about leaders is this:

Leaders are known by the goals and ambitions they express, by the results they achieve, and by their methods for achieving these results.

This chapter is presented in these terms. We look at leadership and strategy in terms of results to accomplish, and the methods for achieving them.

Later in this book we explore the specifics of leadership within the various functional areas of the firm – the work of the CXOs. The aim of the current chapter is to provide a general framework for leadership in business within which these later CXO examples provide details and particulars.

The intention in this chapter and throughout the book is to convey an overview, and some details, that readers can use to explore the following questions for themselves: What is my application of this to my own work? How does this apply to the leadership work that I am doing now, and must do, or will volunteer to do in the future?

Leaders must get results

Leaders in business must *create wealth*, short term and longer term. This can take many forms, but it starts with financial wealth. Business leaders must articulate and implement a theory of how the firm will make money given its position in its industry, and under given conditions of risk and speed of return on investment.

Financial wealth

This business theory must demonstrate why customers in growing numbers will repeatedly buy from the firm, and not from its rivals. It must spell out why customers will pay prices that significantly exceed the total costs of delivery and allow profits to be re-invested in pursuit of future results. It must be clear which existing capabilities this proposition is built on, and which future capabilities must be developed to sustain the advantage, and keep competitors at bay[2].

It is vital that CXOs – indeed as many leaders in the business as feasible – fully comprehend this theory, support it, and put it into action in their own spheres of influence. It is best when leaders at all levels are clear about how they can best contribute to the overall strategy. This way they can adapt and channel the efforts of their units into supporting the firm's economic model.

In extremely-competitive business situations, where profit margins are slim and under threat, the ideal but often-unattainable condition is that all employees, including the least paid, are fully aware of these key economic factors: who are the firm's key customers, and why; who are the firm's chief competitors; what is the role of each employee, at any level, in contributing to the firm's current projects for improving product and service quality, for innovating new products, and in reducing the total delivered costs of the firm's products.

The results might be achieved in the short term or the long term, but the results of leadership will be clearly noticeable and significant: wealth will have been created, so there will be new capital available that can be further deployed to create yet more wealth.

Non-financial wealth

Often, business leaders must also focus on creating non-financial capital – which could be called social wealth. Effective leaders create human and other social capital, in the form of greater abilities and capacities at individual, team and enterprise levels. For example, there is the nurturing of individual human talent, which is discussed at length in chapter 3. There is the endeavour to create structural and process capabilities for managing and learning, which we explore later in this chapter and in chapter 4. Also, there is the wealth that is embodied in high-level executive teamwork as described in section 3. These are all forms of social capital.

While some companies specifically reward executives for developing social capital, many do not. So it becomes an optional task for the leaders throughout the company whether they personally invest in the development of this less tangible wealth. Of course future generations of owners and employees will benefit from the creation of human and social capital, whether or not the leaders who created it are compensated for their achievements.

Social capital can also include public goodwill towards the firm and its offerings. This points to the topics of ethical and environmental impacts that sometimes conflict with economic goals. The social responsibility implications will vary across the different parts of the company: in finance, it might imply accounting probity, whereas for R&D it might mean designing products that are easier to recycle or produce less carbon dioxide.

The underlying point is that effective leaders make themselves responsible for wealth creation, which encompasses both financial and social capital. These are the desired *outcomes* of leadership. Now what are the *methods* for obtaining these results? To provide groundwork for detailed examination of leadership methods, we first explore the concept of strategy.

Leaders use strategies

Effective leaders form and implement strategies. Actually, we can say that strategy and leadership are two sides of the same coin.

What is a strategy? The word 'strategy' comes from Ancient Greek and means 'the art of generalship'. A strategy is what a general devises and puts into practice to achieve desired goals, by harnessing all the productive resources that can be accessed and mobilized by any means that the general has the personal capacities to bring under his influence.

Put this way, it might seem that strategy is the province only of the ultimate leader of the enterprise – the general or the CEO. And certainly the ultimate leader must devise and use an overall strategy. But this image of strategy is helpful at any level of leadership. Any person in any leadership role, however broad or however constrained, is well served if they act on the basis that to get desired or ordained results, it is necessary to identify, organize and mobilize all the relevant resources – people, money and other input factors – in pursuit of important goals.

It is also useful, and often essential, that a leader at any level of an enterprise understands the goals and methods of other leaders in the enterprise. In practice, of course, there is little time or direct incentive to try to understand others' strategies. However, for ambitious managers, it is very important to demonstrate their capacity to diagnose and implement helpful contributions to various components of the firm's overall strategy. It is this capacity for broader understanding and contribution that higher level leaders sometimes look for when they are assessing the promotion potential of people at lower levels.

To describe further the leadership-strategy connection, we now examine some details of business strategy. Then we explore the key components of leadership. In both cases, we will see that the essential task is to mobilize and organize *internal* assets so that the enterprise can thrive given its *external* circumstances.

Elements of a business strategy

There are many details to an effective business strategy, but in general terms such a strategy guides the firm[3]:

- In its dealings with its external environment, especially in its initiatives and responses to opportunities and threats presented by its shareholders and owners, competitors, customers, suppliers, new technologies, regulatory institutions, and various non-government organizations, including employee unions and community interest groups;
- In forming worthwhile goals and in making critical decisions, especially decisions which are not easily reversible, to commit resources to achieve these goals;
- In mobilizing the firm's strengths and managing its weaknesses represented by the capabilities embodied in its people, its structure, its processes and other assets, all to pursue these important goals that emerge from the context of external and internal opportunities and threats;
- In organizing internal activities and resources in pursuit of these goals – strategy includes forms of structure and particular processes to harness and guide the application of effort;
- In applying effort, especially in times of rapid growth or of instability, but also when external pressures are low, and when it is plain sailing – that is, strategy includes methods for energizing the system;
- In achieving a position of strength – that is, reserves of financial and social capital-by which to survive short-term setbacks; to develop responses to unforeseen and unforeseeable events, either those rich in positive possibilities or laden with negative threats; and critically, to permit the investments necessary to encourage adaptability and creativity for innovations which will ensure future revenues and profits;
- By doing all of this in ways that secure flows of money to repay investors the required returns on capital employed, as quickly as necessary, and to pay the employees of the firm, top to bottom, to keep them committed; and, to repeat for emphasis, to invest in innovations that will ensure that there is a future.

Looking at these elements, we see that a business strategy is a system of desired results and methods for achieving them, against a backdrop of factors in the external environment and internal capabilities. We now explore in greater detail the methods of leadership. All the while, we see that it is the work of the leader to 'do strategy', which covers everything from the long-term big picture, making major decisions about the commitment of large-scale resources, to handling key details on a daily basis.

Methods: mission, process, structure, culture

Leadership methods can be classified under four main headings: mission, processes, structure and culture. These are not in hierarchical order, nor are the topics described under each heading exclusive to that heading. There is some overlap and repetition, and not all aspects of leadership are contained within this framework.

These four methods are essential components of a system to get things done. They are useful for leaders in all areas and levels of the company. To achieve results, leaders must work on all four fronts.

The mission: purpose, direction and focus

To move people towards a goal, effective leaders propose a mission.[4] They must describe a future state that is attractive and exciting, and a pathway to get there, and transmit the optimism that it can be done.

The function of the mission is to energize and harness the contributions of all the people involved in the enterprise. It is what gets people excited and encourages them to work together in pursuit of a common, desirable goal.

To focus energy and to unify action, it is best if the mission is quickly understood, and is reinforced and repeated on a continuing basis throughout the firm. To embed the mission in the hearts and minds of employees, who have many other things to feel and think about, this clear and consistent repetition is crucially important.

Essentially, an effective mission statement provides a motivating, inspiring answer to the team member's question: 'Why care about product quality, speed, customer service and satisfaction, and shareholder value?' A desirable mission gives the individual a larger, attractive entity with which to identify and to which to contribute.

By articulating a mission, leaders bring purpose, direction and focus where these elements do not already exist, or are lacking in important ways.

Purpose

There is a saying: 'Without vision, the people perish.' Put positively, we know that many people are mobilized into action, and will sustain their efforts through difficult periods of setback and opposition, if they believe that their daily work is indeed assisting in the creation of, or the enhancement or maintenance of, something significant – financial and social wealth from which they and others will benefit.

But this is not only a top-level task. Leaders throughout the firm should be able and willing to answer the question: 'Why would our people devote their energy to implementing their own, perhaps minor, component of the firm's economic model?' It is clear that cleverly administered financial rewards are necessary to promote high performance. But many people work best if they can connect with, and see their own contribution to, a higher purpose.

What kind of purposeful mission gets talented people engaged and mobilized? There are several key components.

First, the mission must propose something that is rare and distinctive, if not unique: 'No one has done this before, ever. We will be the pathfinders.' Related to this, a powerful mission proposes a major stretch in performance and competence. 'It's going to be tough, but we'll handle all the challenges, technical and political.' Finally, a strong mission promises payoffs, both extrinsic and intrinsic, to the implementers and key stakeholders. 'This will be very worthwhile for all involved. If we do this well, there will be new career opportunities, bonuses, and we will all expand our professional toolkits'.

The element of purpose is what is often meant by vision and values. This is the big picture, the longer term, often not fully tangible, aspirations and goals that give people a sense of engaging in something significant, a worthwhile and attractive future state for which to strive. Values are 'what is important to us'.

The leader's task is to diagnose, articulate and then influence and facilitate others to see the larger corporate values, financial and social, and how individual and team efforts contribute to accomplish these.

The importance of an energizing and engaging mission, and of communicating this mission to others, is clear. The challenge is actually doing it. To maintain purposeful action, leaders must periodically guide or reorient people when they lose their way, perhaps due to over-work, too many setbacks, or too many successes.

Direction

The second element to consider is that of the direction provided by leaders. In providing direction, leaders make or facilitate choices about how and where available resources must be committed, to best serve the bigger purpose.

The leader must diagnose and articulate this purpose, and then influence and facilitate others in decisions on how to accomplish it, notably decisions on critical investments which will lock in certain patterns of major resource usage and managerial effort over long periods. Such decisions include which major projects to pursue, and which to avoid; decisions about expensive technology platforms; and decisions about methods and processes to be used for implementation.

Direction is determined by the decisions to which the company or unit is going to commit. Leaders, wherever they are in the company, need to be aware of the big resource decisions they are making or should be making, that once taken, are hard to pull back from. A major task in leadership is diagnostics: can one recognize a big choice when it is right under one's nose? Effective leaders orchestrate processes to ensure that the big decisions are diagnosed and resolved in good ways.

Often such decisions are not easily reversed, or indeed it is not possible to reverse them at all. Time and money have been spent, and there is no retrieving them. To accomplish significant goals, other goals must sometimes be abandoned. This can cause much disappointment, and resistance, as this is likely to mean that someone's aspirations are being blocked, partially or completely.

This is exactly the moment when the leader's personal decisiveness and ability to sell an idea, or to facilitate others in coming to a key conclusion, is vitally important: 'Yes, to fulfil the mission, we must commit to a particular course of action. In so committing, we are making investments of time and resources – tangible and intangible – to a certain direction, not another direction.'

Focus

Focus is the element of leadership that pinpoints those key details that must be handled correctly if big purposes are to be served.

The leader diagnoses, articulates and then influences and facilitates others in identifying the key details and success factors that must be 'nailed' to ensure high-quality execution and pay-off from the key directional decisions and investments, to serve the greater corporate purposes.

To get from A to B there are many things which might be done, but that are not essential. By contrast, there are some things that if neglected, significantly increase the probability of failure. This is a key aspect of leadership diagnosis: can you spot what must be done, which, if omitted, spells trouble? Leaders are there to remind people: 'Whatever else you do, make sure you keep your eye on this, this and this.' Daily attention to critical details in implementation: this is the leader's job, as much as expressing a grand vision.

One unproductive idea in contemporary academic discussions is that 'leaders only have to empower people and then all good things happen'. This is rather naïve and idealistic. What successful leaders do is implement ways of ensuring purpose, direction and focus. Effective leaders instil discipline and robust follow-up systems to make sure that team members deliver on deadlines and budget objectives, and they do so in ways that mobilize and energize people.

A leader must set up and manage processes to ensure that critical activities are getting done and that wealth is being created. Leaders at all levels need systems for information flow and decision making, for measuring performance, and for understanding the evolving interests of internal and external customers, and other external agencies. These processes are necessary to help keep people focused on the value drivers of the firm's economic model. We now examine operational processes more closely.

Processes

Operational processes comprise the activities – designing, making, selling, providing customer service – that put the firm's economic model into practice. The leader must determine which processes are needed to create outputs that customers will buy, that are distinctive or even unique, and that the competition cannot easily copy – and what must be done to sustain these competitive assets.

It is usual to distinguish two types of process: primary and support[5]. Primary operational processes are those activities which transform input factors, such as materials and human effort of various kinds, into outputs that are valued by customers. This applies both to the production and delivery of *services* as well as manufactured goods.

Underpinning these primary production processes are essential support processes. These are visible for example in the key staff functions of finance, accounting, marketing, human resources and corporate governance. These include a wide variety of activities such as: budget formation and administration, monthly reports, recruiting and compensation practices, sourcing of input materials, market research, advertising, brand management, selling, bidding, contract administration, project management, distribution, regulatory compliance, and ways of collecting payment from the customer and paying suppliers.

It is the leader's job to ensure that each component activity, primary or support, contributes significantly to the total value created by the complete process, and to the sustainability of value creation. This contribution will either be in terms of helping to differentiate the firm's products from competitors in quality, performance or image, or in reducing the total costs of production and delivery to the customer. That is, the key feature of all operational processes is that they help to create products of highest possible customer-value at least possible cost.

As we see in detail in section 2, CXOs take the lead in these efforts. For example, R&D drives the innovation of new products. The finance function can act to minimize the cost of capital employed across the firm's total set of activities. The accounting function can isolate sources of cost to aid their minimization. The human resources function contributes to differentiation by recruiting and developing people to staff the firm, and by devising motivating compensation practices. The marketing function contributes by identifying new opportunities through market research. The governance department helps in negotiating with regulatory bodies and key investor groups, and ensuring internal compliance requirements demanded by these parties. The IT function ensures that all of these processes are served by optimal flow of and access to high-quality information.

All of these tasks are best performed by processes which are designed to high standards. CXOs must ensure that primary and support processes within their functions are contributing to total customer-value. Of course, overall company performance is best served when leaders below CXO level are also contributing to process quality.

How can quality-mindedness be applied in managing the work of professionals and executives? There are several measures used in the management of manufacturing quality that provide useful metaphors. For example[6]:

First-run yield measures the capability of a process to get optimum results with just one run through the process. A low or poor yield means that the item, perhaps a decision, must be passed through the process a second or even third time. This gets expensive.

Through-put time versus value-added time measures the capability of a process in terms of the time, and hence other resources, that are consumed in adding features that contribute to true quality, which a customer might pay for, or which professional standards dictate are important.

Asset utilization measures the extent to which expensive resources, including executive time and office space, are actively engaged in value-adding activities as opposed to lying idle or doing things that would never be paid for by knowing customers, nor which add to professional standards.

More generally, the well-known total quality management (TQM) framework provides methods for analysing operational processes, identifying areas for improvement, and suggesting remedies. It is estimated that fewer than 20 per cent of TQM interventions have been successful. It is common these days to hear much cynicism about total quality management and other methods for improving process capability. But TQM and other methodologies, for example *re-engineering* and *six-sigma approaches*, have bought major gains when applied in ways consistent with key underlying principles.

The evidence is clear: such methods have positive results when certain key conditions are in place. These conditions are simple to specify, and hard to implement. They are:[7]

- Senior executives, starting with the CEO, must be seen to pay close attention to the practicalities and details of quality-process capabilities.
- This senior executive influence must reach to the front lines of production and service delivery, and to all points of the firm's investor, customer and supplier contacts.
- Decisions and actions must be based on the facts. Leaders must model diagnostic empiricism, learning from experience, and demonstrate follow-through to ensure actual process improvements as a consequence of learning.
- Front-line team members, those on the production floor, those delivering products and services to customers, those working with suppliers, those selling to customers, those in contact with investors and advisors to investors, all must be involved in ongoing learning and decision-making activities in company with senior executives.
- Senior executive time and attention must be devoted to ensuring that important and necessary information flow and co-ordination is occurring – at boundaries between units where such co-ordination will fail to occur if not closely managed.

These considerations move our examination of leadership methods to the next critical factor in the leader's tool-kit, that of structural design of the unit for which the leader takes responsibility.

Structure

In the simplest terms, the structure of a company, a unit or a team is the answer to: 'Given what we must do to thrive in our environment, who must do which specific tasks, and how is the work of many to be unified and goal-directed?'

The leader's task is to design and implement the best-possible structure, and then to handle the inevitable problems inherent in that structure, and deal with the tasks that are not addressed by the structure.

With an effective structure, the leader has designed and implemented a management system in which the right people have been assigned the right tasks, responsibilities and decision authorities, and in which these people reliably ensure free flow of useful information for the purposes of co-ordination and alignment of all the sub-units, and in which progress towards the overall corporate goals is a primary focus for all involved.

The structuring of an organization begins with an appreciation of the firm's position in its industry, its economic model, the required operational processes that will implement this model, and the culture. It then answers the question: 'How best to allocate responsibilities and authority to individuals and sub-units, and then coordinate all the pieces in pursuit of the overall goals?'

There are two key levels of structural design: basic elements and overall forms[8]. Design at the level of basic elements requires choices about: the location and legitimacy of decision authority in the network or hierarchy; the number of people or positions who report to a particular person or position, and number of levels in the hierarchy; the assignment of tasks and roles to sub-units, and co-ordination of these sub-units. Also important factors in structural design are choices about the degree of standardization of procedures, and degree of formalization of documentation.

Now, working with these basic elements, what overall form and *degree of each basic element* represent an optimal structure? The answer depends on the size and complexity of the firm, its products and its marketplace. Here are some brief illustrations.

The simple or entrepreneurial form has a boss (typically the owner-founder) and a number of people who revolve around and report directly to the boss. Each member of the company has some unique responsibilities and some which overlap with other people. There is little formalization and little standardization, and authority on all but minor operating decisions rests with the boss.

With greater size and complexity, there is the need for more specialization, especially in key functions such as accounting/finance, sales, production and human resources management. A firm organized along these lines is said to have a functional form.

Further scale and variety in product lines and greater geographic reach see the emergence of divisional structures which are essentially a number of functionally-designed units, often called strategic business units. These are typically focused on a product line or class of products and services, or a geographic region. These separate units are managed by a headquarters whose role can range from 'financial only' to broader corporate functions.

With massive scale and complexity a firm, such as an aircraft manufacturer or a global pharmaceutical company, typically uses a matrix form in which individual managers have responsibilities, and bosses, in at least two directions, for example function and project, or line of business and geographic region.

Each of these structural forms has distinctive strengths and solves certain problems of allocation and integration of effort. Also, each has certain weaknesses that leave problems unhandled – or even create them. It is the role of the leader both to design the structure and then handle the inevitable problems inherent in that structure.

Is hierarchy dead?

Over the past two decades, a recurring theme in the academic discussion of structure has been that 'hierarchy is dead', that specialization and role formality are defunct, that full decision authority should be placed at the front line, that spans of control must increase dramatically – twenty or 100 people reporting to you directly is fine – and that levels in the hierarchy must be decimated.[9]

Some versions of this view declare that hierarchical structure should disappear entirely, in favour of better alternatives, namely, loosely-coupled networks of teams. But this holds dangers for leaders.

One way of looking at it is that 'structure' is a technical term that refers to the *degree* of formalization, specialization, routinization, and levels of hierarchy, i.e. location of authority for decisions, and can vary from low to high.

Furthermore, there are no clear research findings that highly-structured organizations under all conditions are worse performers than those with low degrees of structure. In fact, more and more, managers report unnecessary and at times massive direct losses of human energy and great opportunity costs are incurred in structures that are underdefined.

Effective structures emerge in response to diagnostic questions such as:

For this company, given its position in its industry, with its sources of finance, with its particular customers and sources of supply, with its distinctive economic model and managerial capabilities, for the characteristics of the available labour force, given current and foreseen conditions, what are the right degrees of specialization and formalization for each class of activity? Where should authority be located for each class of decision? What is the optimum number of people or positions to have reporting to a particular person or position? Is effectiveness truly served by eliminating levels in the hierarchy?

In other words, the design of the structure must take into account the firm's environmental conditions, its goals, and the required processes and answer the question of how best to allocate tasks and decision authority to individuals and subunits, and then co-ordinate and unify all the pieces in pursuit of the overall goal? It boils down to the assignment of responsibilities and *reporting* relationships.

Co-ordination: voluntary lateral reporting – and managerial attention

Unfortunately, the notion of *reporting* has acquired a negative connotation in this current age of loose networks and empowerment. Reporting has become synonymous with control, obligation and 'telling the boss what you are doing and what you have done'. But beyond vertical interaction, reporting is also about horizontal exchanges. It implies telling colleagues what they might need to know, as well as what they want to know.

Getting people to talk to one another requires formal and informal agreements about who is responsible for what, and which people need to talk to one another and when, on what topics. The essence of this kind of effective co-ordination is that everyone makes a contribution – including calling people proactively, on the offchance that they need to know something.

This is why the topic of *co-ordination relationships* is critical. And it falls to the leader, when seeing that people are not talking to one another, to point it out and make sure that they do.

As we see in the next section, it is also the leader's responsibility to develop a culture where there is free flow of communication, both unbidden and unrestricted by higher authorities. But the communication aspects of culture are of course embedded with other factors in the company's culture. We now explore this topic in some depth.

Culture

Typically, leaders inherit a culture when they take over a team, a unit or a company. Cultures are notoriously difficult to change. After all, a culture comprises the accumulated habits from the past: 'We do these things, not other things, and we do them this way. That's our culture.' It is an effective way to resist change, to claim that certain behaviours are 'part of our culture'. These days, who can argue against that?

Well, leaders must often demonstrate that habits from the past are no longer productive, that in fact such habits might be destructive of financial and social capital, and that new habits are now needed.

Leaders can make themselves responsible for the culture. It can be a tool that they use to improve the attitudes and behaviour of employees and help people be more productive. Culture can also be an obstacle, in that leaders must work with the non-constructive and corrosive cultural practices that they have inherited.

Culture is analogous to the operating system upon which software depends. That is, culture rests on deep, often-unnoticed sets of assumptions and reflexive responses in absence of which nothing productive can occur. But if faulty, the operating system renders your software – and hardware – ineffective, even useless.

Here we take a very pragmatic approach to culture: the firm's success depends on people doing *what is necessary* to achieve results, short-term and long-term. But in many firms, a substantial proportion of what is necessary is not provided by the structure or processes: it is neither part of specified job roles nor is it explicitly rewarded by the bonus and promotion systems. So it depends on the culture – that is, in the spontaneous behaviour of people at all levels – to ensure that what needs to be done gets done.

Clearly, culture is a broad topic. We tackle it here from three different angles: the basics, quality, and dimensions of the social arena.

Culture: the basics

With what attitudes, values and behaviours do people approach their work and the human relationships associated with doing the work? The answer is seen in the organization's culture.

We said earlier that a mission can help focus human energy on the task by linking individual motivation to an exciting larger purpose. Does the mission engage people and get them to put their energies in the important tasks? Do people truly believe in the official vision and values, or do they see them as just more hot air from above? Again, the answer is seen in the company's culture.

There are many ways to describe culture, but there are several basic factors to focus on:

- What behaviours are permissible? What is rewarded, not rewarded, punished? What is discussable, what is taboo?
- More deeply, who decides what is permissible and discussable? This is the central issue of power, and who is permitted to participate in discussions of 'what is important'. Especially significant is the prevailing attitude to change, and to leaving the past behind.
- Are people ready to change the old ways, to move into the future?
- Is the conflict and sense of loss inevitably generated by change addressed, publicly or privately?
- What is the attitude to risk-taking? How heavy are penalties for failure? This is a critical factor because purposeful change necessarily involves risk-taking. If a particular path-goal combination has not been tried before, we do not know in advance if our methods will be successful.
- When things go wrong is it: 'Who's to blame?' Or: 'OK that happened, what do we do now?'

With these points in mind, the leader must assess whether the prevailing culture within the firm or the specific unit:

- Supports the economic model. Do people do what needs to be done? If not, what initiatives must the leader take?
- Supports effectiveness in operations and the flexibility required both for innovation and to make the structure work. If not, where to next?

Quality: how important for financial and non-financial results?
We discussed earlier the concept of quality when we examined processes. We now pick up the topic again as an aspect of the company's culture.

For leaders throughout the business, especially those without profit and loss responsibility, the quality concept serves as an essential performance metaphor for 'doing good things' to the highest standards and improving the contribution to total customer-value. It is the leader's task to instil an ethos of always improving the game and asking: 'How can this be done better?'

A quality focus in the firm's culture provides a shared language for all members to recognize, debate and decide on wealth-creating activities. For example, earlier we mentioned the concept of *first-run yield*. This measures the percentage of units that meet specification without rework or repair. Yet that image, from manufacturing, extends easily to aspects of the managerial decision processes: how many times do we have to go through something before we get it right?

Taking a quality perspective gets people focused on hard facts and effective, efficient actions. It provides methods for diagnosing upside opportunities and for reducing, if not eliminating, weak processes by which human energy and other resources are wasted.

A quality focus also promotes respect for data, for reality. Fact-driven discussions help to protect professional debates against possible fogging by personality weaknesses and clashes or turf-inspired blindness and deafness. And, they work against senior executives overruling more junior ones on the basis of their 'experience' or 'instinct'.

These protections promote the robust assessment of the significance of information and the benefits and costs of possible new courses of action. In turn, this assists decisions on where to make major investments of resources.

Critically, the respect for empiricism also helps ensure that bad news quickly works its way through the firm's information networks, and gets the attention it deserves. Leaders must continuously review existing projects and processes and either fix or discard those that have lost their significance in the creation of wealth.

Eliminating non-essentials provides more resources – time and human effort – to respond forcefully to unexpected threats or opportunities. It frees up team members' time and thinking processes, allowing people to remain vigilant, for fast responses when the unknowable happens.

Maintaining a quality-focus in the culture therefore encourages employees to direct their energies to creating value, and critically, to eliminate 'value-destroying activities'.

A quality-focus also enhances response speed by building up the firm's surpluses. The firm must have reserves of capabilities and assets that allow it to take a hit and then bounce back immediately. When individuals are worn down by crises and stretch periods, the appetite for productive innovation is much reduced. When quality is part of the collective mindset, the unit will be fresher, faster and more efficient in its daily current operations, and less often in 'catch up' mode.

Culture: four dimensions of the social arena

Leaders influence others by their own behaviour. How leaders act themselves in critical situations, and how they communicate with other people is a crucial medium of leadership. Leaders are role models for other people. The big question is: what kind of role model, what kind of example is being set when the leader 'does something'?

When the leader acts, others notice, and many either copy the leader with great fidelity; or at least they put on a good show of mimicry while pursuing other goals. Either way, what is crucial is the model provided by the leader.

If one seeks to provide leadership for others, it is essential to have a firm grasp of the key dimensions of human behaviour in organizations. The four dimensions described below are those given time-honoured attention by researchers in this field. These are: task-achievement, formality of role, interpersonal relationships, and power.[10] While they overlap in some areas, it is important to distinguish between them.

Using these four dimensions of culture, the leader can diagnose how people are using their energy in the company, what a better culture might look like, and what the leader might have to do to demonstrate more productive behaviour.

Task achievement dimension

In sustainable high-performance cultures, the leader demonstrates that work is worthwhile for its own sake. The leader shows how to contribute constructively by taking care of key details, and by attending to the broader purpose of the company. He or she creates a sense of shared credit with others for achievements, and also displays an obsession with learning from setbacks.

Sometimes, to move forward, leaders need to authorize people to take two steps back, to look for root causes and experiment with new methods.

This contrasts with some high-achieving cultures where there is over-dependence on success for 'feeling good'. If the leader does not react constructively to failure, it will tend to inhibit problem recognition – and when recognized may take a heavy toll on morale.

Similarly, when the leader pays insufficient attention to collective achievement (versus individual achievement), it can create an implicit pecking order. As discussed in chapter 20, this can make it difficult for the leader to achieve the necessary co-ordination.

We also see leaders whose basic commitment seems to be 'whatever works for avoiding failure now'. Inevitably, this leads to seat-of-the-pants decisions and random trial-and-error learning in operations, with little positive innovation.

Formality of roles dimension

Formality is often denigrated as being old-fashioned. And yet, there is the risk that, in dismissing formality, we throw out the baby with the bath-water, resulting in much random behaviour.

As role model, the leader must clarify boundaries between responsibilities, both horizontally and vertically. A good example is the topic of delegation and micromanagement. Does the leader make it clear where his or her responsibility stops, including pushing back on decisions that subordinates are trying to delegate upwards? And how disciplined is the leader about not encroaching on the responsibilities of subordinates?

Leaders can shape a constructive culture by ensuring that form serves function. They make sure that systems and procedures are designed by the people who use them, and all join in learning from others' successes and failures in handling complex tasks. When a system of formal roles works effectively, it is because members of the system are encouraged to contribute to its continuous updating and improvement, thus avoiding unnecessary conflicts and overlaps.

This contrasts with leaders who turn a blind eye when people bend or ignore rules, formal channels and procedures. They sometimes tacitly encourage them to do so, and so create unnecessary confusion. This also contrasts with cultures where leaders over-emphasize compliance with procedures, rather than accountability for quality and productivity. Form ends up dominating function, and people get tied up in red tape and swamped by unimportant detail.

Interpersonal relationship dimension

The leader can model an instrumental view of people, as resources for getting things done. The leader can also look to connect with and project a view of employees as valued members of the company's community, with individual needs and capable of making unique contributions.

Leaders must try to serve the right mix of individual and group needs, as well as the right mix of task and relationship behaviours. They must make sure that the 'need to belong' does not get in the way of discussing hard truths. They make it acceptable to confront differences in performance, talent and values by showing their own receptiveness to challenge and not only from their 'favourites'.

However, some leaders inhibit such discussions. In some cases, they are overly preoccupied with nurturing harmony, making it difficult to raise sensitive issues openly. Often the resulting harmony is only superficial, with an obvious price for task performance. In other cases, leaders are stiff with people and fail to elicit any sense of belonging; or else they work through side deals, resulting in relationships that are highly competitive and transactional. Everyone is a taker, with no givers.

The onus is on the leader to kick-start and maintain a culture where people are prepared to give, to the business and to each other. When we talk about the leader being generous, this does not imply indulgence or letting people get away with things. It means showing consideration, while expecting individuals to do their bit.

One CEO whom we observed made this expectation very clear at the beginning when he appointed his senior executives, by saying to his top team: 'This is business. Now, you want to be successful, and I want you to be successful. And I want to be successful. So let's all work together and be successful. And really I am here to help you, but please don't hide things from me or try to game me. I am here to push for and to contribute to our shared success, and therefore your success. But, if you mess around with the truth, and mess around with me, really there can be no room for you. This is not personal; this is business. Now, what do we need to discuss? Let's make sure we all understand the deal, then we can all get on with being successful.'

Power dimension

We do see leaders who are stewards and servants, exercising power for the good of the enterprise, for the good of each individual, and creating productive assets, financial and social, for the future. They influence others with unfailing respect for the individual. Of course, true respect sometimes includes helping people see their weaknesses. They mentor more junior people, giving responsibility in proportion to the subordinates' capabilities and readiness. They help people to find the confidence to take on greater responsibilities.

We also see leaders who create a culture based on power games. Money, power and fun flow to the fittest, and interpersonal rancour or anger at the 'lawless' system is considered bad form. The pattern of behaviour is 'scoring points' with clever wordplay. Wheeling, dealing and empire building are highly admired, if privately. Sophisticated political skill is necessary to get ahead.

There are extreme cases of tyranny and rule by fear. Some 'big guns' have established enduring power bases, and maintain them through exploitation of others' weaknesses and fear-mongering. The aim and use of power is for personal gain, with fear used in arbitrary and capricious ways. It is dog-eat-dog, and political fights are to the death.

In such cases of corrosive use of power, there are clear in- and out-groups, but it is not at all clear to the average player how to get 'in'. By contrast, in more-productive cultures, although leaders do not pretend that everybody is equal, they ensure that all members feel part of the same team.

Without minimizing the difficulty of changing a culture, the above dimensions represent continuums along which leaders can nudge the culture.

Your chosen sphere of influence

The framework presented above covers a vast amount of ground. Readers who are thinking that leadership seems to involve a massive array of responsibilities are absolutely right. Leadership comprises extremely complex sets of tasks. That is why not many people can do it effectively.

Here is an image of leadership that tries to convey the scale of the work, the purpose and the results:

> Leaders do, or cause to be done, all that must be done, and is now not being done, to achieve what we say is important. This applies to all types of tasks and relationships in all aspects of mission, processes, structure and culture.
>
> What is important is to create wealth, broadly defined, to permit investment in new rounds of enterprise to create even-more capital of financial and human kinds. With this creative process going on, there is more wealth and all that flows from wealth for more and more people.
>
> All this must be done in circumstances where new positive opportunities and negative threats are constantly emerging and are never fully predictable.

Section 2 of this book offers particulars to illustrate what this means in the various functions.

Of course, while leaders must pour great quantities of energy and focus into critical tasks, there are pragmatic limits to what they can do. So, it vital to select priorities against the realities of limited time, resources and pay-offs.

A significant challenge for leaders is this: many of their essential leadership contributions will never be recognized by those who judge, reward and promote them. So leaders have to decide for themselves: 'How big is the sphere of influence that I seek; what are those *optional* acts of leadership into which I will put my efforts?'

Notes

1 H. Kay, 'A very civil aviator', *Director* (August 1996), pp. 36–41.

2 An excellent exposition of competitive advantage is to be found in X. Gilbert and P. Strebel, 'Developing competitive advantage', in H. Mintzberg and J.B. Quinn (eds.), *The Strategy Process*, 2nd edn (Englewood Cliffs, NJ: Prentice Hall, 1991).

3 Based on J.B. Quinn, 'Strategies for change', in Mintzberg and Quinn (eds.).

4 Material in this treatment of *mission* is adapted from: J. Abrahams, *The Mission Statement Book*, (Berkeley, CA: Ten Speed Press, 1995), and R. Harrison 'How to focus personal energy with organizational mission statements' in R. Harrison, *The Collected Papers of Roger Harrison* (San Francisco, LA: Jossey Bass, 1995).

5 M.E. Porter, *Competitive Advantage* (New York: Free Press, 1985).

6 From unpublished documents prepared by Jim King, and personal communications.

7 T.C. Powell, 'Total Quality Management as Competitive Advantage: A review and empirical study', *Strategic Management Journal* (vol. 16, pp. 15–37, 1995).

8 D.S. Pugh and D.J. Hickson (eds.), *Writers on Organization* (Thousand Oaks, CA: Sage, 1996). Highly recommended is: Michael Goold and Andrew Campbell, *Designing Effective Organizations: how to create structured networks* (San Francisco: Jossey Bass, 2002).

9 For rejections of the claim that hierarchy is dead, see Elliott Jaques, *Requisite Organization: The CEO's Guide to Creative Structure and Leadership* (Arlington, VA: Cason Hall, 1989) and F.G. Hilmer and L. Donaldson, *Management Redeemed* (New York: Free Press, 1996).

10 Harrison, *Collected Papers.*

PUBLICATION DATE:	March 2008
ISBN:	978-0-87154-062-1 Paper

CONTACT:	Dana Adams Publications Russell Sage Foundation 112 East 64th Street New York, NY 10021 Phone: (212) 750-6038 Fax: (212) 371-4761 Email: dana@rsage.org

PAGES:	312
PUBLICATION DATE:	March 2008
ISBN:	978-0-87154-563-3 Paper
CONTACT:	Dana Adams Publications Russell Sage Foundation 112 East 64th Street New York, NY 10021 Phone: (212) 750-6038 Fax: (212) 371-4761 Email: dana@rsage.org

3 *The Talent Imperative – All CXOs must strengthen the company's talent pool*

JEAN-LOUIS BARSOUX AND
PRESTON BOTTGER

Finding, growing and holding on to great staff is every manager's responsibility, not only human resources. Just as it's every manager's job to comply with the law and not only the legal department's. (CHRO, oil company)

Too many line executives regard talent management as the responsibility of the firm's human resources department. While HR can provide the framework and advice on methods to ensure effective management of talent occurs, true responsibility for staffing and development lies with the unit heads.

We know from extensive research on exit interviews that people often explain their leaving the company by saying: 'My boss is not competent or capable of effective management.'

Weak management of talent – in the direct boss-subordinate relationship – leads to loss of high-calibre people before they reach the positions for which they are being groomed. Their high potential and skills are often lost by the company that has trained them. They can leave physically by switching companies, or check out emotionally and lose their drive and enthusiasm until finally they make a change.

This chapter considers the risks and responsibilities confronting CXOs as they nurture talent. The task of talent management is divided into manageable pieces by distinguishing different talent categories, between current and potential performance, and between talent for the company and talent for the unit.

We start by defining what we mean by talent, pointing out the dangers of viewing it too narrowly. We then show how CXOs are in the talent business. The following sections go through how they *must* be able to spot it, select it, develop it and retain it.

Defining 'talent'

When executives talk about business talent, generally they are referring to emerging or established leaders within the company. The accompanying image is often one of highly trained executives (many with MBAs and other advanced degrees) or very business-savvy individuals who shoot through the ranks, based on 'street-smarts' and consequent business results.

But this understanding of talent can be misleading and incomplete, particularly for CXOs.

It is *misleading* because it implies a kind of generic 'best and brightest' person, capable of slotting into any context and handling any assignment. In truth, no template works across all companies and all industries. A company staffed by only high-calibre 'Type A' personalities, is not always the best recipe for success. Balance among different types of talent is vital.

Astute CXOs maintain a broad and rich view of business leadership potential. They especially look at the nature of the candidate's experience and demonstrated results alongside the company's current and emerging needs.

Equating 'talent' with leadership potential is *incomplete* because other talent categories are essential for the success of the business model. We observe three categories of 'business model critical' employees:

- **The fast-trackers** Those who are earmarked for the CXO level positions or equally important roles in operations (e.g. the president of a business unit).

  Fast-trackers might start out in a particular function because of their educational background (for example, top engineers in production, elite arts graduates in marketing) or they might be on assignment in a particular function to round out their development.
- **The specialists** These are great individual contributors who work with their intellects and creative capabilities.

  Specialists are the researchers, accountants, engineers, lawyers, traders, designers, writers, trainers, software developers, auditors, buyers, sellers or consultants. Their output is often highly regarded in their particular profession and many receive regular calls from head-hunters.
- **The unsung heroes** They are middle managers, not destined for the higher reaches, but who 'keep the show on the road'.

Unsung heroes typically possess highly developed management capabilities and deep knowledge of key processes. They are repositories of the departmental memory and they provide stability as a key link between executives and staff.

These skilled middle managers often do a good job of developing the skills of subordinates and they possess a wide professional network inside and outside the firm. They know how to make things happen within the company and are adept at working within the system. These influential managers often toil in silence for modest rewards, and often without recognition from superiors, peers or more junior people. They are not especially mobile, making them easy to overlook, yet the role they play is irreplaceable.[1]

An incoming CXO must manage these three pools of pivotal staff and ensure that each works in harmony. They might have very different career trajectories but they are all critical to the effective execution of the business model.

To nurture these different talent profiles requires special attention to the challenges associated with each of the three groups. Before we look at these separate challenges, we first consider the common challenge of how CXOs can identify appropriate talent for their functions.

Identifying the talent

For busy CXOs, there are a number of 'must-dos' in identifying new talent. These are mostly driven by the need to find expedient solutions to unfilled positions. The essentials are outlined below:

Get organized, stay organized

CXOs must understand their own staffing requirements. They need a template, checklist or set of rules for seeing and evaluating talent. They need rich categories for spotting, assessing and assigning talent.

The company's generalized executive competency model can provide a useful starting point that can then be refined according to the specific needs of the function and the job.

For example, Figure 3.1 shows seven generic competencies that can help CXOs assess executive candidates. These are a compilation based

Figure 3.1: A diagnostic tool for selection

on our observation of typical executive skills used in many leading companies that are effective at diagnosing leadership talent.

The list is not comprehensive but these seven competencies provide a framework to help CXOs go beyond simplistic good versus bad judgments. They provide a model that enables interviewers to discuss in greater depth and breadth the relative strengths and weaknesses of several candidates.

We are not selling this set of competencies as a universal answer. But we do try to persuade executives to develop their own clear, multi-dimensional view of the capabilities required to staff their spheres of influence.

Engage with HR

CXOs should be in continuous dialogue with HR to secure critical hires from the top to the bottom of the function.

Firstly, CXOs can draw on HR's capabilities and expertise to sharpen their understanding of their own people requirements. For example, the CXO can get help in conducting a talent gap analysis.

Secondly, CXOs must understand their department's needs in depth and express this clearly to HR, especially where mid-career hires are concerned. This is why CXOs need an organized list of requirements as described above. For example, it requires that CXOs provide HR with regular feedback on the suitability of previous candidates as learned from first-round interviews.

Beware first impressions

Interviews, and other short-term episodes, are often poor instruments for predicting future performance.

In the first seconds of a meeting, interviewers typically form impressions about the candidate – good or bad. Unchecked, these views are quickly reinforced through selective observation and false attributions.

Early impressions, positive or negative, are highly influential on the interviewer's judgement. They can trigger self-fulfilling prophecies, with favoured candidates gaining in confidence and less favoured ones becoming defensive. The interviewer ends up seeing the very behaviour that he or she expected.

CXOs must be aware of their preferences and prejudices. They can offset their selection biases by asking questions whose answers could challenge their first impressions. While instinctive judgements can and often do lead to effective decision making, having the second opinion of other team members can often prevent a bad decision. When filling key positions, it is important for several interviewers to debate their impressions with one another, with the aim of breaking past poor judgements.

We see in many management books the admonition that executives should not employ subordinates who are clones of themselves. We add a caution to this piece of advice: there is nothing productive in recruiting people who cannot understand you or who oppose – actively or passively – your work objectives, or contest your methods for achieving those objectives. Yes, protect yourself in your areas of weakness, and get help from others whose strengths are different from yours. But also protect yourself from habitual rebels and your cultural enemies.

Look beyond the talk

Do not confuse the candidate's ability to talk with the ability to do.

It is easy to be impressed by a candidate's live performance. Verbal fluency and extraversion can easily be misread as focus, energy, drive and talent. A better bet, when looking for such qualities, is to check the person's track record to see the extent to which they have demonstrated these qualities in their past work activities.

Check references. Even though most candidates will give references who will only say good things, ask the following question: 'What is the one thing that you most dislike about the candidate?' The answer will tell you a lot more than a list of accomplishments. Everyone has their weak points; do not be afraid to get them out in the open.

Use the interview process to find out more about the *breadth* and *depth* of their experience. In judging a person's experience, one test for clarifying their role is whether the candidate previously worked within an existing system, modified the system or created a whole new system. Are they more entrepreneurial or better at improving something that has been created?

To discern managerial competence, the CXO must find out if candidates have initiated projects or headed them up; how many and what variety of people they have led; how they managed resources and deadlines; and what results they achieved, against what deadlines and other pressures.

Remember culture-fit

Beyond the candidate's technical ability to do the job there is the issue of cultural fit. This is equally important for the individual and for the organization.

To ensure a good match, the CXO must bc capable of assessing the candidate's values and personality vis-à-vis the company's culture.

Experience shows that selection decisions are often based on superficial signs of compatibility. CXOs must identify their own personal likes, dislikes and other biases that may influence their selections. In their enthusiasm for particular personal qualities, CXOs can fail to probe the shadow side of those same characteristics, as highlighted in Table 3.1.

Integrating mid-career 'stars' can be especially challenging in terms of culture-fit. For the CXO who is embracing change, this raises the dilemma between reinforcing the existing culture and introducing people who will 'add spice' and difference to the team. But again, beware of surrounding yourself with rebels and other corrosive types.

Developing talent

The key developmental challenges differ for each of the three talent categories previously identified.

The fast-trackers

Often known as *high-potentials* or *stars*, fast-trackers are often rotated quickly through several different functions to gain experience.

Table 3.1: ***Beware the shadow side***

The bright side	The dark side
Outgoing	Insincere, superficial
Intuitive	Judgmental
Dynamic	Impulsive
Assertive	Stubborn
Innovative	Unstructured, erratic
Unflappable	Detached
Imaginative	Unrealistic
Driven	Intimidating
Demanding	Intolerant, uncompromising
Single-minded	Abrasive
Perceptive	Manipulative
Conscientious	Obsessive
Reflective	Indecisive
Structured	Bland

The main challenge is to give them an appropriate assignment – one that stretches their competencies and at the same time allows the function to benefit and draw on the star's previous experience and current contribution of energy.

The department must get a meaningful contribution; the assignment should not represent a one-way gain. The assignment should also be for a period that is appropriate to the context, such as a full sales cycle or until a change is firmly embedded. Too often, high-potentials are rotated through assignments at set time intervals (e.g. six months), thus becoming experts at only one thing – starting new initiatives.

CXOs face a different challenge with their *hidden stars*. These are highly-competent junior individual contributors or managers whose skills have not yet been recognized more widely in the company. Developing junior people requires that they be surrendered to other functional areas and not imprisoned in the same job for too long.

While the loss of these high performers is likely to lead to a corresponding drop in productivity in a given department, it should be recognized as a net benefit for both the firm and the individual.

For a CXO, this sacrifice might be more-easily accepted under one or both of the following conditions:

- **The company recognizes the CXO's contribution** The CXO's own development plans, evaluation, rewards or opportunities reflect their efforts and success in nurturing subordinates.
- **Reciprocity** Even without personal incentives, a CXO will be more inclined to give up rising stars if other CXOs respond in kind – which means exchanging 'apples for apples', not exporting B players and expecting stars in return.

In the absence of these two conditions, the CXO can conclude that he or she is 'training the company' – that is, developing a disproportionate number of the company's leaders. The CXO's motivation for this contribution might soon wane without adequate recognition.

The specialists

Developing the specialists poses a different set of challenges. Some specialists might seek a move into management (often for better compensation) or be pushed into management when they surpass their peers in a given specialist field.

However, this transition is likely to succeed only if they have the talent for managing people, they have already received developmental experiences and they are accepted by their peers. Too often, the best specialist (e.g. software developer, engineer, scientist, accountant, etc.) is promoted to management for the wrong reasons – excelling at their specialty – rather than the right reason, showing high management promise.

Specialists often work in isolation from non-technical professionals, so they need to get used to working with peers in other disciplines – through secondments or participation in cross-functional teams. CXOs must be extra cautious when promoting specialists into management positions and recognize that they may need additional training and skill development.

They also need limited-risk exposure to managing people, for example, by leading a task force on a task with clear objectives and well-defined boundaries. As specialists they may have come to depend mostly on their own technical skills to meet objectives.

As managers, they will need to work through the efforts of others. This might call for preparatory training in tasks such as delegation, communication and making decisions when other people's interests conflict with their own.

Other specialists might not be interested in, nor cut out for, an executive role. The challenge with them is to keep them fresh and energized in their specialist role. This requires varying their assignments and giving them time 'off-line', perhaps in benchmarking visits to other firms in other industries, or participation in professional conferences – to retool, and expand and deepen their learning.

As an example, in one software company, Fridays are kept clear of major projects so that IT specialists can explore pet projects that have a shot at helping the company. In another firm, functional specialists are requested to partner up with colleagues from the business units to try to improve their big picture understanding and provide better support to the operations.

It is not easy to keep these specialists energized given the limited possibilities of rotation and promotion. Yet it is important to help them avoid the 'tunnel or cornered effect' that sees them become increasingly specialized and typecast – and incapable of switching focus or expanding their competencies without moving to another company.

The unsung heroes

This talent category presents two types of challenge to the CXO.

Perhaps the more difficult case is when people imagine their capabilities are greater than they really are. One of the generic tasks in managing talent is to deal with people when their hopes and aspirations are upset and, in effect, downgraded.

At some stage, ambitious and talented mid-level executives may learn that, in spite of their crucial past and continuing contributions, their bosses do not expect them to break through into the senior executive ranks. The challenge for the CXO is to help the person digest this setback. If this readjustment is successful, the CXO may be able to keep the person contributing at the same high levels as before.

The kind of effort required for managing a person's setbacks depends on the particulars. In some cases, the person gets the message quickly. In other cases, he or she must have it explained in detail, several times, and still will not accept the reality. The person can feel especially bruised if they have been 'strung along' by previous bosses who were anxious to get the most out of them. Some people are equipped to deal with such disappointments. Others can be very distressed.

Seeing high-flyers bypass them and specialists gain more recognition, the unsung heroes can start to feel undervalued. They can withdraw and start channelling more of their spare energy outside the firm. No one wins if they become cynical and bitter. Where they once served as enthusiastic agents for improvement, they can turn into passive (sometimes even active) resistors.

The CXO must pre-empt this loss of performance. To help talented executives come to terms with disappointment, the CXO can propose new developmental and learning challenges to keep them energized. Of course, they can also be rotated within the function, to give them a fresh challenge; but this course of action can only be used so many times. They can also be lent to other units or be put in charge of particular projects.

Ultimately, the best solution for all involved might be to encourage the employee, perhaps with some positive assistance, to broaden his or her horizons outside the firm. The CXO's challenge is to anticipate this situation rather than stumble into it – before talented individuals become toxic to their environment.

The second type of unsung hero is the person who has accepted the reality of their mid-level management career without the necessity of being told by others. Indeed, they are happy with the level of responsibility they have, and seek no additional responsibility and no additional pressure.

But still, the alert CXO will ensure that such a person remains fully engaged in the business. One useful method is to maintain and perhaps increase their involvement in the resolution of significant and complex issues, special projects that lie beyond their immediate job scope.

Working with the CXO to frame and resolve non-routine problems has a dual payoff. First, it is a sign of recognition to the mid-level manager that their input is valued. A primary driver of commitment to the leader, and to the firm, is that the person believes that, genuinely, their contribution is important to the company's progress.

Second, it extends the individual's experience. Over time, this also puts the CXO in a position to delegate more challenging assignments to the mid-level executive. The CXO may even deputize the person in certain forums as a sign of trust and respect.

This way, mid-level executives are not given decision responsibility beyond their desires or capabilities, but they make genuine and critical contributions to important tasks.

Preserving talent

Even if people excel in their jobs, it does not necessarily mean that they want to remain in the same position.

CXOs can lose talented people for different reasons. People who feel poorly managed, unrecognized, unchallenged or frustrated can be lost to the competition. Others may grow tired and simply lose their edge or their interest in the work. We now look at what CXOs can do to prevent talent bailing out and burning out.

Retention: bailing out

There are several aspects to retaining talented individuals. The CXO needs to let them know that they are valued and needs to be able to spell out the advantages of the current situation or company over other opportunities. To do this, the CXO has to develop an understanding of what matters most to each of the talented contributors and to show creativity in adapting to their needs. And finally, the CXO has to face up to the real reasons for resignations, in order to avoid repeating mistakes. We will consider these issues in turn.

Clear versus ambiguous message

The key to retaining talent is ensuring that individuals who are critical to the success of the business model know that they are valued. This is difficult to do without explicitly informing them of their relative status.

Clearly, this can also cause difficulties for those *not* in the talent pool and even more so for those *removed* from the talent pool. However, it has the key merit of making things clear.

In one very large US-based, but globalized, food and beverage company we know, the deal is made *very* explicit. Managers and specialists are asked if they would like to join the high-potential group. But to join this group, they must commit to doing a number of tasks, which are beyond normal expectations.

Those who fail to meet these additional requirements over the course of the year are simply dropped from the talent group. But their career within the company is not necessarily jeopardized. If, at a later stage, they adjust their priorities and want to rejoin the group, the company is willing to engage in that discussion. However, this is without any guarantee that they will be readmitted.

Also, there is no guarantee that, having rejoined the group and met the additional requirements, they will gain career advantage from it. They are simply putting themselves in a position to receive accelerated development and to be noticed.

The advantage here is that the process is transparent and can be openly discussed. It eliminates much of the intrigue, uncertainty and misunderstandings that can surround career discussions. It promotes a more-candid exchange regarding the nature of 'the deal' and how it suits the individual, and the company.

By contrast, we also know of other successful companies, both in the US and in Europe, in which the spotting and high-level mentoring of junior talent is essentially secret. This system appears to work. Any disappointment or cynicism among the non-select appears not to materially damage the business model.

The lesson here appears to be that the success of particular forms of talent management is conditioned by other factors in the governing business model.

The CXO as chief seller of 'the deal'

For each category of talent, it is the CXO's job to articulate what might be dubbed the 'employee value proposition'.[2] What does working for this company and, more specifically, working for this particular CXO, offer the person compared to other CXOs or companies?

For specialist talent, it might be the opportunity to be mentored by an eminent professional in the field. It could be the chance to work with state-of-the-art equipment – or to work free from the distractions of organizational 'rain', that is, the rules and politics associated with big-budget activity.[3] For managerial talent, it could be high-quality training, the types of projects or responsibilities on offer, or simply the winning spirit within the unit.

CXOs need to sell the basis of their competitive edge to retain talent – and that demands knowledge of what competitors can offer. This is a negotiation, a deal to be struck between the CXO (on behalf of the company) and the talented individual.

What about the non-negotiators?

Of course, highly-talented people are typically well aware of their worth, and are capable of negotiating for themselves in strong terms. But some talented people, notably specialists in technical areas, are deeply involved in 'doing the work', and find it difficult and even distasteful to bargain for conditions that suit them better.

So, instead of opening a negotiation with the boss, they simply leave for a new position in another company. There the grass appears greener and this approach certainly seems to involve less conflict than trying to improve their current situation.

This is a very special challenge for the CXO. First, do they even see this situation developing? Or, is the specialist's departure a big surprise? Second, if the CXO does spot the problem, how should he or she respond? How much effort should the CXO be willing to put into people who find it hard to argue on their own behalf?

One answer is simply dictated by demand and supply. That is, can the CXO quickly hire a qualified replacement? But another angle is this: has the CXO, as a nurturer of talent, actually put in the effort to coach the person, to pre-empt unexpected silent departures? Does the CXO legitimize the negotiation process and support the person in figuring out the logic of continuing to work for the company?

Therefore, the CXO must determine what matters most to those whom they cannot afford to lose, and provide it. Money is an essential part of the package. So is responsibility and a degree of freedom of decision-making authority. But money is sometimes overrated as a retention factor. If people are dissatisfied with the job and general conditions, money alone might not keep them in place for an extended period of time.

Soft benefits

Soft benefits can provide compelling hooks. These can include the possibility to renegotiate the terms of an employee's work-life balance, to redesign the job (to remove unwanted aspects), to broaden the skill base or to exercise more creativity.

For example, in investment banking, where mobility is very high, one company encourages its star analysts to establish home offices, so as to spend more time with their families. This practice is so appreciated that the company maintains outstanding retention rates despite paying up to 30 per cent less than competitors.[4]

Of course, prevailing HR policies may or may not assist the CXO in these retention efforts. Company policies – regarding compensation, rotation, training, flexitime, telecommuting, or the possibilities for expatriate experiences – can limit the CXO's range of options. Where this is the case, the CXO must engage with HR on how to push for policies that will help retain the productive and the talented.

Increasingly, the individual's commitment is to the boss, the team or the project, not the company. So it falls to the CXO to drive retention methods.

Investigating exits

Another key method for managing retention is to learn from exits. When CXOs lose talent, they should investigate the reason.

As one consultant observed:

> If a $2,000 desktop computer disappears from an employee's desk, I guarantee there'll be an investigation, a whole to-do. But if a $100,000 executive with all kinds of client relationships gets poached by a competitor, there is no investigation.[5]

It is easy to attribute defection to the person's ambition or pursuit of money. After all, people rarely leave for less money. But the reality is that it takes a lot of dissatisfaction with several factors before people choose to disrupt the status quo of their lives. CXOs who make mistaken attributions will probably repeat the same errors.

Knowledge of the reasons for particular departures can help CXOs anticipate who else may be thinking about quitting.

> In one Fortune 20 company, senior managers are asked to create what the company calls 'satisfaction grids'. These highlight the risk levels that the talent might leave the company. The idea is for bosses to analyse satisfaction levels, personal circumstances and critical career crossroads for the talent in their units – and to engage key people in discussion before they start actively investigating outside opportunities.

Exhaustion: burning out

Besides deserting the company, talented people can simply run out of steam. Here, we use the term 'burn-out' to mean that they grow bored, lose interest, lose their energy and enthusiasm for the job, and lose the drive to improve and innovate.

Fatigue factors

Burn-out can occur in all three talent categories. But what causes this mental exhaustion is likely to differ across the groups. With the fast-trackers, the problem can stem from frenzied rotation through developmental assignments that provide no real closure or sense of completion. Or it can derive from the feeling that 'I'm too important to do trivial work'.

For the specialists, the cause is likely to be one of excessive focus. The consequence of hyper-specialization is that the person will ultimately run out of new challenges in their domain. Yet, they have little possibility of transferring the skills and learning even to an adjacent domain.

For mid-level executives, who might well be survivors of several rounds of restructuring and fast-passing bosses, the strain might come from the sense that their contribution and handling of extreme pressure is not recognized by more senior executives.

Confronting such situations requires CXOs to consider two approaches: intervention and prevention.

Intervention

The individual's calibre and general competence is not in question. But their boredom and loss of motivation means that they are no longer the outstanding contributors they once were. Re-igniting the energy of talented individuals is no easy task, since they probably no longer want to do what they have been doing.

Thus, when the CXO considers what it will take to get them back on track, the challenge is to find and propose a fresh role; something that better corresponds to their personal abilities, desires and priorities. Because it involves a change of responsibilities, any intervention to remedy the situation is likely to be risky for the company and the individual.

It may demand a significant stretch into a new area or type of work, possibly requiring a hefty investment in training and development – but with no guarantee of success in the new area.

Clearly, for some individuals, it will be either too late or too costly to explore that investment. By the time the symptoms of burn-out appear, the options available to the CXO may be severely limited. The specialist has become too specialized, the manager is emotionally exhausted, and the star has lost the hunger to reach up a few more rungs.

If retention is not the aim, then the burnt-out employee can be offered a dignified exit and given the necessary support to rebound – both in recognition of their previous contribution and because remaining people in the talent pool will be watching closely how ex-talent is (mis)treated.

However, sometimes, there is no remedy. To find a way out of this situation, the boss (or rather the boss's predecessors) needed to act pre-emptively, two, five, or even ten years earlier.

Prevention

Bosses sometimes set talented people on a path where they end up running themselves into the ground or up a blind alley. Though vaguely aware of the risk, bosses often set those thoughts aside since a) the individual is delivering great results, b) the individual is not complaining, and c) the breaking point probably won't be reached on their watch.

For CXOs, it therefore takes foresight and empathy to head off a situation that might occur in the future and is unlikely to affect them directly. The boss's intrinsic motivation to manage a 'good deal' for the subordinate is crucial here. Often, there is no external punishment for the boss who burns out subordinates. Nor is there often explicit external reward for not burning out people.

CXOs looking to avert burn-out among their talented people must address three questions:

- **Who is at risk?** Prevention starts with taking stock of the talent within the unit, considering who is at risk and what could be done.

  Situations that should set off warning bells would include a rapid succession of high-intensity (or high-visibility) assignments without breaks; a prolonged spell in the same job; or systematic reliance on the same individuals to rescue troubled situations.

  CXOs should also be on the look-out for signs of overload. Perhaps some of their outstanding contributors are not as sharp or engaged as they previously were; or perhaps they continue to deliver results but are becoming very difficult for others to deal with.
- **Are they aware of the risks?** Often people collude in their own downfall – they do not read the warning signs. When asked about their work, they might use revealing qualifiers like 'It's still challenging, but it's not the way it used to be' or 'I'm enjoying myself, but the rush is missing'.[6]

  Talented managers may refuse to recognize the strain they are under, considering it to be an admission of weakness. For specialists, who are at the top of their game, the problem may be that they do not sense any need to diversify their skills or perspective.

  Thus, the challenge for the CXO is to help the subordinate recognize the risk. It may not be an easy discussion, since the employee may have little desire to change. This is particularly the case for specialists who often trade for too long on a particular strength because they enjoy it and because it gets results, not realizing that their narrow focus gives them no fallback position in the event of burn-out.

For both the CXO and the employee, the question is therefore, are they willing to put in some investment before reaching that point? And what kind and level of effort or sacrifice will it take?

- **What can we do?** Again, the measures that could help sidestep burn-out will depend largely on the talent category.

  For specialists it can involve more variety, putting them through developmental assignments that extend their expertise into adjacent areas – for example, as a trainer or seller. For stars, on the contrary, it might require less variety – a change of pace, a chance to replenish their energies and to reflect on where they are going. For mid-level management talent also, it can involve rotating them out of boring or potentially-exhausting positions.

  CXOs might explore even further the tailoring of jobs to the needs of individuals. The concept of 'job sculpting' refers to efforts to match people to jobs that allow them to express their deep-seated life interests. It is a method that can increase the chances of retaining talent.[7]

Of course, all these recommendations require that the boss views the talent within the function as people to develop, and not as resources to squeeze dry. Some executives regard the development of subordinates as a painful unrewarded duty. Others see it as the best way to serve their own purposes: getting greater leverage through the increased competence and greater loyalty from people who respond to 'the deal'.

A custodian of talent

When an executive takes on the job of CXO, he or she inherits a number of talented employees. Inevitably, these employees will be at different stages in their careers, as represented in Figure 3.2 – and will therefore have different needs in terms of development, coaching, stimulation, recognition and reassurance.

The challenge confronting the incoming CXO is to get the most out of the talent at his or her disposal – while at the same time helping employees to grow and making sure that most of them stay with the company.

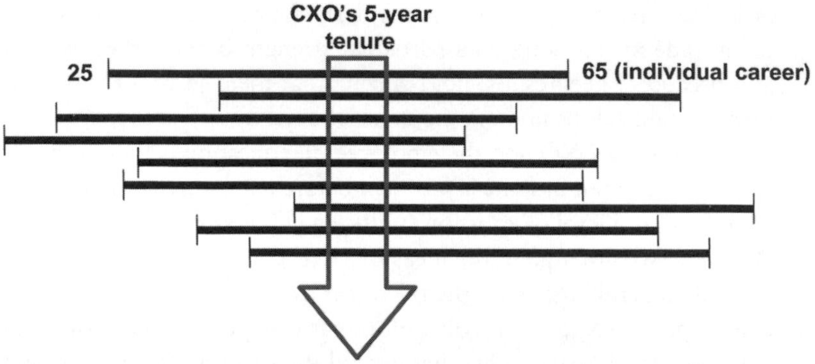

Figure 3.2: Talent over time

Here the CXO has the role of *custodian* – both of individuals' careers and of the firm's talent pool.

This role often poses a dilemma for the CXO who must try to reconcile the interests of his/her unit with the often conflicting interests of the individual and the firm.

What's in it for the CXO?

From a self-serving perspective, and assuming a three-to-five-year tenure in the job, the CXO would typically be better off by:

- Holding on to promising talent and not giving it up to the firm;
- Keeping specialists firmly focused on their forte and restricting their developmental opportunities;
- Misleading mid-level talent about their promotion prospects;
- Driving everyone relentlessly, without much care for the cumulative effects of psychological fatigue.

Given the pay-off of acting this way, why would CXOs behave otherwise? Why should they take on this custodian role? The answer is two-fold:

The career pay-off

In career terms, CXOs who establish a reputation as good developers of people are likely to gain standing within the firm – as net exporters of management talent. Companies are paying increasing attention to managers' talent development skills, through instruments such as 360-degree assessments.

Firms can go beyond the use of anonymous fill-out-forms instruments. In some companies, executives are being asked to state their views on their subordinates and colleagues in 'closed forums'. Information from such forums might not be generally broadcast throughout the company. But, important matters, such as the executive's willingness and capacity to develop the rising generation, are seen as important enough to be aired openly in certain group discussions.

Furthermore, some companies link senior executive compensation to the development of emerging leaders, and their attractiveness to other bosses.

The productivity payoff

In terms of attracting new talent, employees will want to come to work for them, precisely because of their reputation as good developers of people. Having first pick of the talent is bound to benefit the level of energy and performance within the unit.

Increasingly, we can expect that employee commitment will be to successful bosses, teams and particular projects, rather than to the company. If erosion of loyalty to the firm continues at the present rate, it will be harder for CXOs to nurture commitment and to drive methods for retention.

Indeed, CXOs might have to demonstrate that it is possible to have commitment to the work without loyalty to the company.[8]

Notes

1 Q. N. Huy, 'In praise of middle managers', *Harvard Business Review*, 79(8) (2001), pp. 72–79.
2 E. Michaels, H. Handfield-Jones and B. Axelrod, *The War for Talent* (Cambridge, MA: Harvard Business School Press, 2001).
3 R. Goffee and G. Jones, 'Leading clever people', *Harvard Business Review*, 85(3) (2007), pp. 72–79.
4 B. Groysberg, A. Nanda and N. Nohria, 'The risky business of hiring stars', *Harvard Business Review*, May (2004), 92–100.
5 S. Branch, 'You hired 'em. But can you keep 'em?' *Fortune*, 9 November (1998), pp. 47–51.
6 G. D. Parsons and R. T. Pascale, 'Crisis at the summit', *Harvard Business Review*, 85(3) (2007), 80–89.
7 T. Butler and J. Waldroop, 'Job sculpting: The art of retaining your best people', *Harvard Business Review*, September–October (1999), pp. 144–152.
8 P. Cappelli, 'A market-driven approach to retaining talent', *Harvard Business Review*, January–February (2000), pp. 103–11.

4 *The Learning Imperative – Going offline to improve performance*

JEAN-LOUIS BARSOUX AND PRESTON BOTTGER

The main constraint on improvement is not budgets so much as the relentless insistence on meeting short-term targets.

(CXO, international semiconductor manufacturer)

Within companies, learning has long been associated with individual training and development and seen as a responsibility for the HR function. But the demands for business improvement over the past several decades have made clear that learning must occur on-the-job in real time, and must involve teams and even large groups of people.

For example, by the 1980s, the total quality movement was playing a significant role in promoting a broader understanding that effective business learning is a *collective* endeavour. This approach stressed the need for continuous improvement and process enhancement implemented by people throughout the business system.

In the 1990s, learning practices were further enriched by the new concern with knowledge management. The IT function increasingly focused on ways of accessing and leveraging existing data and information within the company. Meanwhile the R&D, marketing and production functions were discovering how to learn from the organizing and technological capabilities of strategic partners and competitors.

Thus, the practicalities and challenge of learning have broadened and deepened in recent decades. The learning imperative has moved beyond the confines of HR training programmes to involve all functions. Learning – that is, application of results-from-experience and newly invented or borrowed methodologies – is essential at individual, team and company level.

Earlier focus on curriculum content and course design has given way to renewal and design of the business system – a broader scope. At top levels in the company, learning is now often regarded as a primary factor in competitive advantage and the responsibility of all, especially the CXO team.

Increasingly, unit-level leaders, particularly CXOs, are expected to be 'learning leaders', 'managers of systemic learning' and 'coaches'. They are expected to shape learning processes as well as manage the business performance of their functions.

CXOs are required to create opportunities for inquiry and exchange, and to raise the quality and practical impact of learning within their functions. They are expected to focus their learning methods on the requirements of the firm's business system – based on a valid understanding of how their function supports the company's business.

More and more, business leaders are seeking to improve pragmatic learning, individually and collectively. They *know* they should be driving it. They *want* to find and implement better ways of working and delivering business results. They *want* their employees to feel engaged.

The problem is *how*? Learning does not just happen spontaneously. It takes time and effort. It must be legitimized and managed. It takes sustained commitment of resources, especially executive time. The task for CXOs is to embed learning *in the culture*. This chapter shows how.

A model of learning

Learning is the process through which the person, team, and larger organization acquire new knowledge and develop new methods by which to adapt successfully to the changing environment.

This requires two types of learning. One is the accumulation of knowledge, essentially facts and techniques. The second, and often more critical, is the capacity to see things in new and more robust ways. This helps the members of the company make better sense of the reality they face.

There are many models of how individuals and units can learn. Some are *content*-based, proposing a number of interrelated building blocks to develop organizational learning. The 'five disciplines' approach is a prime example.[1] Others are *process*-based. These prescribe a sequence of steps that will lead to learning. An example is the classic 'scan-interpret-act' cycle.[2]

The model of learning we describe here is process-based. Like many other models, it applies equally at individual and at unit level. Additionally, it has the advantage of highlighting why *useful* learning is so difficult.

Figure 4.1 below represents an *ideal* learning cycle. The *action* phase is where most executives spend the vast majority of their time. They are driven by the demands others place on them and are following through on commitments already made.

Very few individuals can make major steps in learning while they are busy doing. To learn – that is, to see things differently, to get new ideas and to develop new methods – most executives need time-out from their regular activities. Only then can they *reflect* on what has been happening and what is likely to happen if they remain on their current course.

They can assess whether their expenditure of energy and time is adding up to desirable results. They can check if their environment is changing, and if so, what new challenges or opportunities are opening up.

They can begin to ask:

What should my new priorities be, if I am truly to accomplish what is both desirable and feasible?

The outcome of this reflection phase is a *new perspective*. That is, there are insights into new possibilities, and the productive applications of new knowledge and techniques. There is a fresh view of the challenges facing the team and the type of changes that are needed in terms of ways of thinking, ways of doing, and in methods for accomplishing results.

This opens the path to *decisions* about how to proceed differently and with greater scope for improved wealth creation. For example, in terms of resource allocation, the executive must determine what allocation of time and energy should be put into what issues and when.

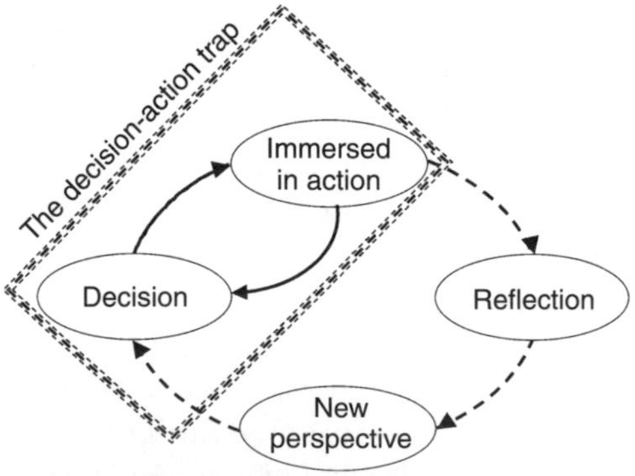

Figure 4.1: The learning cycle

Such decisions lead back to the action phase, in which the new learning, especially the new methods and practices, are enacted, and higher quality results are obtained.

The challenge for CXOs is to lead their teams through this learning cycle.

But the majority of executives we observe are immersed exclusively in action and decision making. They have difficulty taking themselves and their teams offline to engage in deeper and potentially more productive learning. They find themselves floundering between decision and action, in a succession of quick fixes and incremental adjustments. The urgent drives out what is important.

It is a rare executive who can see things differently or get new ideas when vigorously oscillating between these two poles. As shown in Figure 4.1, we call this the *decision-action trap*.

We now focus in more detail on the four steps in the cycle, and examine how CXOs can break out of this rut and enhance their team's learning capabilities.

From action to reflection

We saw in chapter 2 that true leadership includes, but goes beyond, refreshing existing processes and practices. It also entails *creating* new good things and *eliminating* bad things. Both of these tasks are difficult if not impossible when in the thick of the action.

Over time, most people, even high-level professionals and executives, can become fully absorbed by their everyday activities. They lose sight of the big picture, the 'reasons why', and the necessity for upgrading their 'methods how'.

Periodically, they should stop and ask themselves the key questions:

- What are we trying to do?
- What have we learned?
- Is what we are doing taking us in the right direction, with the right benefits at the right costs?

CXOs who are stuck in the decision-action cycle might be running a very efficient operation and delivering exactly what is expected of them. Their bosses and customers are happy. There is no pressure to think or do differently. They do not see the potential benefits of stepping back to re-evaluate their team's priorities and practices.

The danger they face is not seeing that their business environment is evolving in ways they have not anticipated. Having painted themselves into a corner, the only way to survive may be through expensive and painful change.

Re-assessment is always easier when there is great dissatisfaction with, or danger, in the current situation. The basic questions are: how can CXOs engage in reflection and re-assessment *before* they *must*? What can they do to develop the *hunger* for learning within their teams?

Three practices, discussed in more detail below, can help.

Imposing time-outs

The first habit to overcome is that of executives not making time for learning, except in response to crises or a direct command from above. Ongoing preoccupations and everyday emergencies result in postponement of opportunities for reflection. Or, they are tacked on to other forums as a kind of afterthought, a 'nice to have if we get to it'.

But the pressures of the moment will always win out, unless CXOs reserve time in advance and make sure that it is fixed in everybody's schedules.

Another reason that CXOs do not make the time for reflection is that they do not *see* the need for it. Sometimes this is caused by *overconfidence* in the team's current purposes and methods. Or, it is the result of *ignorance* of what could be done better or differently. The next two points address these failings.

Sharpening the discomfort

Often, the challenge is to puncture the complacency of successful teams and functional units. We observe some successful CXOs who accomplish this by ensuring that a loud voice is given to key stakeholders who rely on the units' outputs.

Of course, different functions must look to different stakeholders to discover where they are falling short.

For example, R&D might have much to learn from customers, especially dissatisfied ones. For marketing, dealerships and retailers can offer rich information on where improvements are necessary. Meanwhile manufacturing can question suppliers, and finance can get feedback from external financial analysts, and accounting firms.

Core service functions, such as IT, communications and HR can ensure they get similar criticism by canvassing *internal* clients, including other CXOs. Critically, they should question line managers in the revenue-earning parts of the business.

The underlying necessity is to create strong mechanisms that force the unit to focus on information about itself that might otherwise be screened out.

A good example of this comes from a computer manufacturer. To collect complaints about the company's products and services, it established a scanning unit to monitor messages posted in chat rooms and Usenet forums.

As the CEO put it:

It's a whole new form of feedback. It's not just noise to us.[3]

Regular streams of such information help to create more receptiveness to learning. And more importantly, it injects purpose and focus into the learning.

Learning from others

Often, stakeholders – such as suppliers and customers – can provide valuable diagnosis of *what* needs improving. But typically they will not be able to say *how* to improve. To access ideas for improvement, CXOs can tap into various sources, including experts or leading-edge customers.

Benchmarking against top performers is perhaps the most widely used stimulus to learning. CXOs can learn from companies that are good at what they do. The range of benchmarking possibilities starts with companies in the same industry. For example, an auto manufacturer might create a learning partnership with a big supplier, say, a tyre manufacturer.

CXOs who believe they are already on the leading edge within their industry, might look to unrelated industries for companies with outstanding practices and processes.

For example, GE managers made benchmarking visits to FedEx, which has exceptional customer service.[4] Nike and Disney both examined the distribution system at L.L. Bean, the catalogue giant.[5] And Cisco benchmarked the Bellagio hotel resort in Las Vegas to learn about its fully integrated online HR system.[6]

CXOs might look even further not only in search of replicable processes, but also for inspiration.

For example, in the search for productivity improvements at General Mills, a food manufacturer, technicians were sent to watch the pit crews servicing cars at racetracks. Reportedly, they were so inspired that they developed new methods that sliced the changeover time for a plant line from five hours to twenty minutes.[7]

Now, there are cases where CXOs can become obsessed with practices in other firms and other industries. In doing this, they overlook the possibilities for benchmarking right under their noses – in other units *within* their own company.

In fact, this phenomenon is described in frustration by many executives as:

If only our firm knew what our firm knows.

This expresses the results of two separate but frequently related problems. One is the view that others 'out there' can do it better than our people.

The second is perhaps an even greater challenge: that is, to share the results of expensive experience, namely successes and failures, with others in the firm who might be competing for the same promotions, recognition or perhaps scarce funding in the upcoming budget cycle.

From reflection to new perspective

Obviously, these outside stimulants can generate learning only if there is receptiveness. By contrast to the example above, insights from external benchmarking projects might be rejected on the basis of 'not invented here'. That is, useful ideas might be dismissed because 'our business is different' – without further consideration of the potential benefits.

Now, when a system is set up to deliver a certain capability, and is successful, it develops momentum of its own. Much of the ensuing behaviour of members of the system is driven by habits, unexamined methods developed for yesterday's problems. Intellectual and emotional rigidities set in that may reduce openness to other approaches.

Learning and new ideas can threaten established routines, skill sets and formal or informal hierarchies. It can challenge values and assumptions that individuals and groups do not even realize they hold. Existing 'theories' are critical determinants of what people see, hear, believe and can imagine.

There are two obvious ways that CXOs can reduce such resistance to learning. Firstly, they can coach people to put their existing assumptions or preconceptions into 'neutral'. This requires proactive shaping of a fruitful learning context. Secondly, they can encourage people to express their ideas. This often requires the CXO to be a model or example of productive learning behaviour.

Shaping the learning context

The context in which learning discussions take place will strongly influence the content and output of such discussions.

At the simplest level, there are questions such as:

- Are we on-site or off?
- Downtown or country setting?
- What's the dress code?
- What's the agenda?
- Does the boss speak first, last, or not at all?

Typically, the actual workplace is a counterproductive setting for thinking beyond the boundaries of existing work patterns. Even if interruptions are eliminated, the associations with everyday work tend to inhibit the questioning of accepted assumptions and cherished beliefs.

A new physical environment can stimulate different views and assessments of what is working, and what is not. It helps break out of set ways of assessing what is important, and it often forces team members to interact with one another in different ways. It influences the degree to which people feel inclined to let go of prior assumptions about ideas, and critically, to let go of prior assumptions about their colleagues.

Reshaping the context also requires setting fresh expectations about the purpose of the meeting. It is useful to set clear guidelines for what is expected of participants in the discussions, and how this is different from what is considered 'normal'.

Important questions to be addressed include: What will be the general mode of conducting the discussion, the degree of openness and risk taking, the kinds and levels of conflict that will be encouraged, and the role of the CXO in the meeting: chair, moderator, or equal participant with an external person acting as facilitator?

These signals indicate that the normal rules are to be suspended – and help to distance the discussion from every-day activities.

A good example involved an incoming telecom CXO who took his direct reports for a weekend meeting at a hut in the Swiss mountains.[8] Besides the low-stress ambience, the rationale for choosing that setting was that the hut had no technology facilities. This broke the prevailing 'PowerPoint culture', which usually encouraged formulaic and narrow responses to challenges and opportunities.

Modelling productive learning behaviour

Perhaps the best way for CXOs to drive and support others' learning is to demonstrate their own commitment to learning.

How do CXOs best show this? They legitimize time-outs from immediate work-tasks by talking about learning, by expressing odd and way-out ideas, by reporting on what they learned at conferences or outside meetings. They show their keen interest in cause-effect mechanisms, not just when things go wrong, but also when they go right.

CXOs can also demonstrate their capacity to re-examine and modify their own views, especially by showing openness to challenging ideas. More significantly still, learning-obsessed CXOs acknowledge when they change their minds. And they are prepared to discuss the factors that explain why.

Sometimes the U-turn is a response to changes in the environment and sometimes it is the aftermath of a bad decision. Either way, they do not try to disguise it. Instead, they use the event to demonstrate adaptation to external changes, failures and errors.

Consider the example of the CEO of a biotechnology company. He made the mistake of pursuing a potential blockbuster drug too aggressively, even when the initial results were not very positive. He recognized his personal failure to say 'stop' in time. But more importantly, he agreed to have the case written up and taught in the company's own leadership development course.[9] Though embarrassing, he used the setback to demonstrate his commitment to learning.

By their willingness to acknowledge mistakes and stand corrected, CXOs can send powerful messages to others about their desire to engage in healthy debate. In doing so, they help create a limited-risk environment for others to admit errors, to float creative and possibly productive ideas and to keep learning.

From new perspective to decision

The reflection phase should lead to a fresh perspective, or vision, as it is often called. Concretely, what does a fresh perspective or vision look like? There are three key components.

- First, it proposes a breakthrough idea, more than just an incremental improvement, something that is rare and distinctive, if not unique.
- Second, it represents a major stretch, but it remains doable – both politically and technically.
- And third, a lot of people, especially the implementers and key stakeholders, stand to benefit from it in major ways.

With these characteristics, the new perspective refreshes the sense of *purpose*. It serves as a unit-level *vision*, an attractive future with the right pay-offs.

Now the reason for reflection is not simply to gain a new perspective. The aim is to be more effective in action. It is to make sharper decisions about how resources are allocated, and to create greater wealth by such investments. Resources for investment include individual time and energy. They also include unit resources, notably financial funds.

Many visionary ideas remain just that: ideas. The sense of purpose captured by the new perspective needs to be translated into action. And that requires what might be called major 'platform decisions'. These entail significant commitments of resources that establish the new *direction*. These commitments allow the CXO to move beyond vision – to ensure traction.

There are two major barriers to follow-through. One concerns the resources available to make this work. The second has to do with the fear of committing significant resources to a particular course of action. Let us look at each in turn.

Securing the necessary resources

To pursue opportunities for improvement, managers need resources. Of course, this implies a certain degree of discretionary funds and time. Restricted financial funding often precludes experimentation when results and success are uncertain. In such cases, the CXO can contribute by securing funding. But beyond that, improvement initiatives also draw on the key resources of executive time and energy.

Many executives feel too stretched by the sheer number of their ongoing projects, task forces and change initiatives, to add another to the portfolio. They simply do not have the spare mental capacity to contemplate another improvement effort. They are too busy just getting through the day, to divert energy to working on the processes for tomorrow.

To harness and focus human energy, and other key resources, leaders must diagnose and then strip away activities that have lost their significance.[10] Often, business leaders will focus on improving existing operations and pushing new initiatives. But they devote little attention to reviewing projects and activities that should be discarded. To focus on more value-adding activities, something has to be stopped.

Prototyping

The second major factor that can inhibit new action is the risk of taking a big bet on an uncertain outcome. 'Quick prototyping' is a way through this problem.[11]

Of course, prototyping is often associated with products, but it applies just as well to processes. For example, a marketing team can run small-scale trials in test markets and HR can experiment at a pilot site with a new ways of evaluating performance.

Prototyping is an antidote to the energy-sink of being paralysed by high stakes. It enables the transition from thinking to productive action without deploying major resources in an irreversible way. It also generates knowledge and feedback that allow people to focus on unresolved questions and to refine their approach.

This incremental method reduces the uncertainty and risks associated with 'big bets'. In this respect, the 'decision' stage is often the first in a series of learning loops that might (or might not) eventually lead to a full-scale roll out, with the associated commitments of resources.

Cycles of rapid prototyping help individuals and units to accelerate their learning – provided that there is an effective evaluation mechanism, and that feedback is frequent and informative. One approach to capturing the learning from experiments is to use a form of after-action review.[12] This is built on four simple questions:

- What did we plan to do?
- What actually happened?
- Why did it happen?
- What are we going to do next time?

The prototype might fail and the initiative might then be abandoned. But the lessons from this failure can guide the next round of prototyping, and show the way to next steps to robust final solutions.

From decision to action

Pushing through these commitments into everyday action is what allows the CXO to align purpose, direction and focus (as discussed in chapter 2). Of course, this is easier said than done.

Typically, it is a major challenge to embed learning into everyday action routines. This is true even when there is widely-shared acceptance that a new approach is worth pursuing. Four tasks are critical to ensure implementation.

Realigning

The new approach might clash with existing systems. In particular, when implementing improvements, it is important that HR and communications practices follow suit. This is to avoid the old and perennial trap of 'rewarding A, while hoping for B'.[13]

A typical error is to introduce a new system whose success depends on greater collaboration among people within the function – while leaving in place an evaluation system that ranks people against one another and a compensation system that rewards individual performance.

Unlearning

Even if the systems are aligned, old routines and practices might continue to prevail. The new method is not etched onto a blank slate. There is a previous etching – and for the learning to be adopted, that previous logic must be 'unlearned'.[14] This requires the discarding of old routines and practices, the re-thinking of cause-and-effect relationships and consequent new courses of action.

The elimination of old procedures to make way for new knowledge and methods can also be labelled 'organizational forgetting'.[15] CXOs can facilitate this process by reconfiguring reporting structures, changing decision processes, and updating reward systems to break down entrenched habits. CXOs can also encourage new behaviour through personal recognition or other soft incentives.

Persisting

It takes time and significant effort to regroove behaviour and make it stick. CXOs must help people appreciate the deep level of work that is required and the necessity for persistence. If people assume that change is easily achievable, the first big setback can take the wind out of their sails.

Measurement problems can make it difficult to gauge progress or to know whether the improvement project is working. Again, there is a danger of regressing to old habits when new ones appear not to have the desired impact. In particular, CXOs can find that their relationships with other units or functions become strained, as the new pattern of interactions disturbs the other units' set routines. Others might try to drag the CXO's unit back to the old ways.

To secure the support of other units, it is often necessary to sell them the benefits and necessity for new methods. It is usually necessary to show the other units how they too will *benefit* from the new approach.

Influencing

The cycle is brought to a close when the improvements are achieved and the new knowledge is shared convincingly with others – both internally and externally.

What is the payoff for passing on the lessons to others, in ways that actually impact what they think and do?

First, it helps to embed the learning. Passing on the knowledge forces the CXO and other executives to articulate what they have learned so that others can apply it and perhaps extend it. In the process, the passers-on can also make the knowledge more usable for themselves. Teaching is an excellent way to learn.

Second, there is greater likelihood that the new routines will be maintained if other units are kept informed of on-going progress and the clear benefits.

Third, the discussion with others of new lessons and effective practices provides an opportunity to gain an external perspective on what has been achieved – and what might have been done differently.

And fourth, sharing can trigger further learning opportunities. The exchange of learning, knowledge and energy between the unit and its environment recharges the batteries and provides a stimulus for the next round of learning.

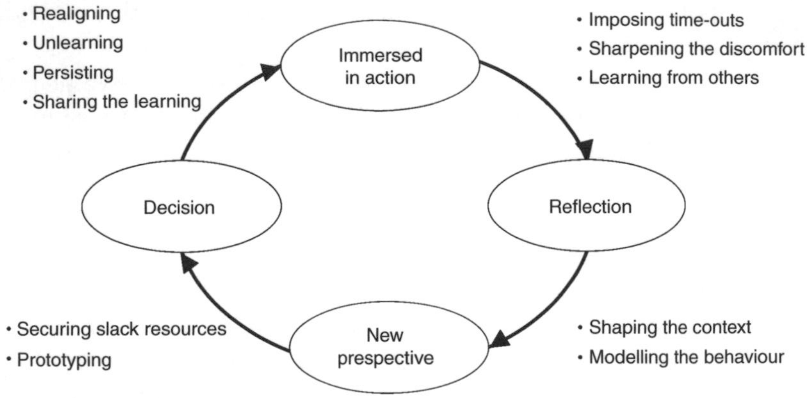

Figure 4.2: The learning cycle comes full circle

Full circle

In many companies today, there is wide acknowledgement that an effective learning culture represents a critical competitive advantage. Executives see the importance of reflection and the capacity to generate new perspectives. The chief challenge for CXOs is 'doing it'. How to get out of the decision-action trap?

As summarized in Figure 4.2, the learning cycle presented here acknowledges this practical difficulty and proposes some countervailing measures. The purpose is to provide CXOs with an alternative to *ad hoc* and costly learning that *might* derive from unexamined experience, or the traumatic learning that is driven by crisis.

Once exposed to this framework, some executives go on to implement their own version of the process. They take a disciplined approach. They consciously take control of their time-outs rather than waiting for circumstances to present a lull in the action (which rarely happens). As one executive conceded:

> I hate these [retreats] being in my diary because I know I can't afford the time. But when I get here, I wish we did them more often.

Other executives tell us:

> I really know what you mean, but I can't. I'm actually too busy to give myself that kind of luxury. Besides, I'd have trouble explaining it to my bosses.

Our response is this: ultimately, it is a matter of how much this method can reduce your pain!

How long do you think you can carry on like this? Maybe you'll get by for a couple of years or even more. But is it sustainable for the next one to three decades? If you do not take charge of your own learning, who will do it for you? And how will you stay fresh and energized over the decades to come?

The CXO's job is to attend to all facets of the unit's value chain. This requires spending time on selling one's ideas, on developing networks, on shaping perceptions and on influencing others. It requires spending time to improve production processes, striving to deliver everything that is expected of the function. It also means investing in R&D, that is, spending time on the development of new capabilities.

The capacity to learn – to be able to see one's options from a new perspective, and then to devise and implement methods for advancing towards worthwhile goals – is the key to the unit's short-term productivity and its thriving over the longer term.

Notes

1 P. M. Senge, *The Fifth Discipline: The Art and Practice of the Learning Organization* (New York: Doubleday Currency, 1990).
2 R. L. Daft and K. E. Weick, 'Toward a model of organizations as interpretation systems', *Academy of Management Review*, 9 (2) (1984), pp. 284–95.
3 C. Fishman, 'Face time with Michael Dell', *Fast Company* 44 (2001), pp. 82–88.
4 D. Brady, 'The Immelt Revolution', *BusinessWeek*, 28 March (2005), p. 64.
5 K. Kane, 'L. L. Bean delivers the goods', *Fast Company*, August/September (1997), pp. 104–10.
6 W. Breen, 'Full house', *Fast Company*, January (2001), pp. 110–14.
7 J. Forster, 'The lucky charm of Steve Sanger', *Business Week*, 26 March (2001), p. 67.
8 P. Bottger and G. Rädler, 'Leadership at TDC sunrise', IMD case IMD-4-0278 (2004).
9 P. Hemp, 'A time for growth', *Harvard Business Review*, July/August (2004), pp. 66–74.
10 J.-F. Manzoni, 'How to institutionalise dissatisfaction', *EBF: European Business Forum*, Spring, 21 (2005), pp. 81–83.

11 D. Leonard–Barton, *Wellsprings of Knowledge* (Cambridge, MA: Harvard Business School Press, 1995).
12 D. A. Garvin, *Learning in Action: A Guide to Putting the Learning Organization to Work* (Cambridge, MA: Harvard Business School Press 2000).
13 S. Kerr, 'On the folly of rewarding A, while hoping for B', *Academy of Management Journal*, 18 (4) (1975), pp. 769–84.
14 R. A. Bettis, and C. K. Prahalad, 'The dominant logic: retrospective and extension', *Strategic Management Journal*, 16 (1) (1995), pp. 5–14.
15 P. M. Holan, N. Phillips and T. B. Lawrence, 'Managing organizational forgetting', *Sloan Management Review*, 45 (2) (2004), pp. 45–51.

SECTION II

The CXOs: Within the Functions

5 *The Chief Marketing Officer – Creating, delivering and communicating value to customers*

DOMINIQUE TURPIN AND GEORGE RÄDLER

This chapter first traces the development of the marketing function over the past fifty years. Then, following a survey of current and emerging developments in global markets, the authors identify three key roles for the contemporary CMO: technical specialist, customer advocate and strategic contributor. The tasks facing the CMO in these roles are examined in detail. To round out this exploration, the chapter then sets out the important factors in the CMO's relationships with other key CXOs. In conclusion, the authors look ahead and suggest that the effective future CMO will continue to focus on differentiation of products, building and exploiting brands, and getting the company's culture, perhaps even more critically than the structure, to express the value of responsiveness to the customer.

The role of the chief marketing officer

Marketing cannot concern itself simply with brand identity guidelines, good television commercials, and rising awareness scores. Marketing is about building new businesses, divesting unprofitable ones, and leading customer-focus across the organization. (CMO, global food company)

In many product-driven companies, the marketing strategy is the company's strategy. It is the job of the chief marketing officer (CMO) to keep the company on a growth path, delivering customer value and creating shareholder wealth.[1]

Corporate growth is under constant threat. The tectonic shifts that erode competitive advantages are similar across industries: commoditization, decreasing loyalty rates and power shifting towards distribution partners. There is a never-ending drive to cut costs, increase sales and introduce innovative products.

The CMO must anticipate and exploit the markets, and simultaneously lead the organization and influence the other CXOs in supply chain, technology and information systems, in order to maintain margins while delivering value to the customer.

The CMO function, often with another title or combined with other executive responsibilities, continues to gain in importance and scope. The CMO must change with or ahead of the market, exploit new technologies and be in tune with constant social changes.

Many CMOs are still heavily involved with traditional marketing roles such as managing product lines, channel selection, and promotion management. New realities, however, require that they also be firm-wide drivers for the design of systems that produce and deliver the right products and services to customers. As such, CMOs must also be participants in the development of corporate strategy and understand the intimate links with suppliers and customers. To do so, they need a sound understanding of the company's business system, the customer and the company's position in the value chain.

CMOs guide the company in assessing customers' needs. They must drive the firm to produce goods and services that satisfy those needs more completely than any of their competitors. In addition, they must weed out unprofitable products and the systems that support them, and be on the lookout for strategic acquisition targets. Marketing is a never-ending process of assessing needs and potential opportunities, as marketing decisions affect competitors and customers' reactions.

The CMO's role today is larger and more encompassing than in the past. While traditional models such as 4Ps or 5Cs are useful (see next section), the marketing cycle has to include new, more sophisticated inputs and models; and the speed of business moves faster with every passing year.

Likewise, traditional measurements such as unit sales are no longer a sufficient scorecard; there is an ever-increasing demand for real-time accurate data on products, profitability and the competition. In fast-moving consumer goods industries, CMOs have to pay attention to how retailers such as Wal-Mart or Carrefour measure performance using product rotation, profitability per metre or cubic foot, consumer retention, and so on.

Increasingly, a growing number of CMOs are measured more on the return on marketing investment. Although it is still difficult to measure the impact of a communication campaign, CMOs will continue to be pressured by other CXOs and the board of directors on how marketing investments affect the bottom line and other functional areas. Many companies have awakened to the reality that, after several years of multi-million dollar ERP implementation, their system still does not deliver the information they need to make decisions. Information management and measurement remain key challenges.

The evolving role of marketing

Over time, the job of the CMO has evolved from a narrow tactical function riding the sales wave of favourable post-war demographics, to a much broader and more strategic position. In the 1950s and 1960s, marketing was primarily responsible for stimulating demand. Industrialized countries were still recovering from the effects of World War II and increasing sales year after year was relatively easy. The marketing manager was mainly responsible for the sales and physical distribution of the company's products.

In the 1970s, marketing's role broadened to include what became known as the 'Ps', or the marketing mix. This was about what *product* to sell at what *price*, in which *place* (meaning the distribution channels through which the product would be sold) and how to communicate with customers, *promotion*. CMOs began to speak in terms of brand positioning, product extensions, pricing promotional strategies (everyday low prices vs. episodic high/low prices), and advertising spending allocation. Later, marketers added the concept of *positioning* to their vocabulary, a key concept that can be summarized as 'telling customers what to expect from the product or service offered'.

In the 1980s, more importance started to be given to new strategic aspects, such as understanding *competition*, new *customer* and *consumer* trends, *channel* evolution, *costs* and the new economic *context* (referred to as the five 'Cs' in marketing literature[2]). Because of slow economic growth in the late 1980s, it became increasingly important for marketing to work with other functions to rethink the entire value creation process. CMOs formed new collaborations with the plant, R&D, human resources management, administration and management control. These collaborations helped to ensure that scarce resources were used in ways that enhanced value to the consumer.

Downsizing, cost cutting and re-engineering eroded the CMO's influence in the early 1990s. As businesses focused on various change

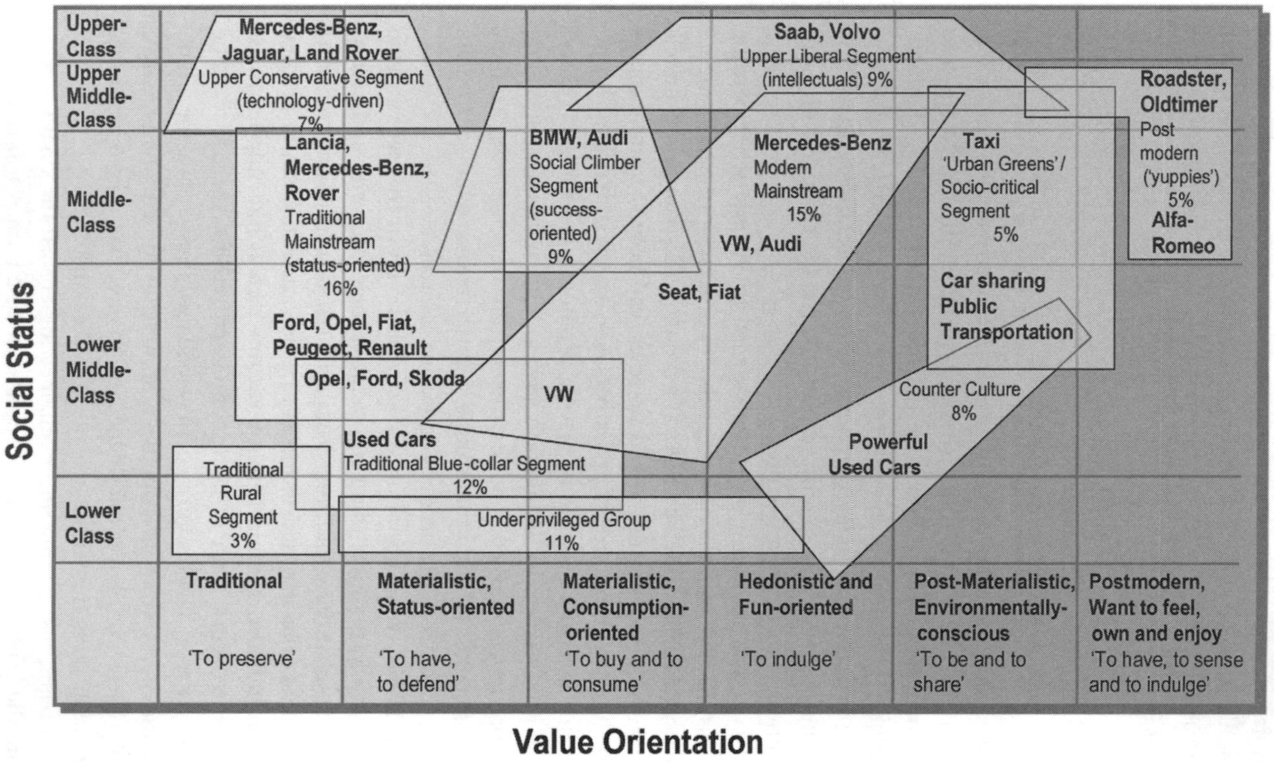

Figure 5.1: Car industry segments
Source: Marketing Systems Essen, Eurosensor by Impulse/ Sigma

initiatives, customer interaction was no longer a top priority and resources were scarce. However, by the late 1990s, the competitive landscape once again shifted radically. Customer focus suddenly became the key to success not only for marketing but also for the entire organization.

The current context

Globalization has meant that manufacturing technologies and information have spread around the world, breaking down many perceived borders.

The existence of a global marketplace allows low-cost producers on one side of the world to supply markets everywhere. Consumers have an unprecedented level of choice. If a brand does not offer their preferred size, shape, colour or price point, they will find another that does. This explosion of choice makes managing brands profitably much more complicated.

For example, according to the CMO of a large German automotive manufacturer, the car industry could be classified into eight clusters up to the mid-1980s; by the late 1990s there were already around twenty-seven. Figure 5.1 highlights the available segments in the car industry.

In addition to the explosion of choice, the widespread adoption of the internet (and related technology/IT developments), as well as the lowering of the cost of publishing and finding information, have been the most noticeable contributors to this competitive shift. The internet has become an important new sales, promotion, and distribution channel, as the growth of firms such as Amazon.com, eBay or iTunes indicates. The revolution in *business intelligence* and *decision models*, made possible by breakthroughs in computing technology, has been equally important, although less conspicuous.

Technology has enabled CMOs to break segments into the size of one. Through the combination of various databases, marketers use business intelligence to profile customers and tailor offers to them. For example, supermarkets can now automatically print coupons for competitive products, banks can make better offers in less time by looking at various customers' accounts, and emails arrive in customers' inboxes based on the products they purchased online.

The CMO must also deal with the growing importance of developing countries (not only China, but India, the Middle East, Eastern Europe,

South America and other parts of Asia and Africa). New-found discretionary income is another major new trend; trying to predict the next emerging market is a challenge.

Executives see the advantages of getting into these markets early but they are also aware of the risks in shifting scarce resources away from competition in core markets and spreading their organizations too thinly.

Purchasing behaviours also differ widely in the developing world. Coca-Cola can sell a Coke at a price locals can afford – but not a bottle. The solution: West African vendors open the signature bottle and pour the beverage into a plastic sachet that the customer takes away with them. The bottle goes back to the bottler.

Mobile phones exist in the developing world where there are no traditional land lines, cutting distances and speeding up the flow of information. However, instead of one person owning a phone, there is a network of mobile phone 'operators' in villages around the world who enable people to use the phone for a call only when needed, rather than having to buy the phone and pay for a monthly subscription.

Technology, whether it was the introduction of Ford's assembly line or the lightning-fast speed of information flow on the internet, continues to bring new challenges and rewards to the role of the CMO. The wide availability of data and information, the development of 'emerging markets' and the explosion of consumer choice are all challenges that the CMO must master. In addition to the changes brought about by technology and globalization, there are other new sources of cost and competitive pressures[3]:

- Commoditization;
- Consolidation;
- Retail and distribution market gorillas;
- Margin erosion (hence the need to grow);
- Customer focus on value;
- Competition through service.

The road to success for the modern CMO is through a landscape which is changing. Many companies have not even defined the role of the CMO at the executive level, although most US *Fortune 500* companies now have a CMO.

However, the title remains less common than other CXO positions in the top executive team. For example, 98 per cent of US *Fortune 1000* firms have a chief executive officer, 91 per cent have a chief financial officer, and 83 per cent have a chief human resources officer.[4]

CEOs of those *Fortune 500* firms who have CMOs say that they need someone who does more than what is conventionally expected of a manager of marketing. Their view is that the CMO must not only guide the business through the marketing management process but must also be an active owner of the company's strategy. Next, we explore three traditional types of CMO roles.

The roles of the chief marketing officer

Based on working with many global companies, we have identified three general CMO types: specialists, customer advocates and strategic contributors. Each reflects different CEO expectations, as well as different capabilities and responsibilities of the CMO and his or her team.

- The specialist CMO focuses on the bottom line. Understanding customers and wealth creation are the most important elements because customers are the route to profitability and enhanced shareholder value. This means that those customers who are not profitable or who undermine the value of the business are closely monitored and rejected if necessary.
- The CMO as customer advocate has a cross-functional orientation that does not only pay lip service to 'a customer-centric' organization, but drives it throughout the culture. This CMO understands how all aspects of the organization interact and more importantly how they benefit and impact upon customers. He or she works to make the whole organization greater than the sum of its parts, as far as the customer is concerned. This means consistently collaborating with peers across the organization and driving cross-functional improvements in delivering customer value.
- Strategic contributor CMOs operate at a higher level and drive the strategic direction of the business. In this role, they operate at the highest level of the firm and may delegate the more operational aspects of marketing.

The CMO's job description can vary greatly from one company to the next. The CMO's major responsibilities are set and constrained by three key factors: the firm's business model, the CEO's attitude towards marketing and the skills of the CMO. For example, if the business model features one or a few strong core brands, the CMO can wield considerable influence both inside and outside the company.

CMOs working in diversified companies with many strong brands tend to find it more challenging to wield their 'corporate' influence in the field. Diversified product companies tend to have strong brands and brand managers, making the brands themselves seem larger than the company.

One imperative remains constant across the CMO types: the need to keep the firm on a growth path. But the contribution of the CMO, whether as marketing specialist, consultant or strategic contributor, is a key factor for the CEO and aspiring CMOs.

The marketing specialist

Marketing is a core function for almost every firm. As a marketing specialist, the CMO is responsible for the traditional marketing responsibilities:

- Customer analysis
- Segmentation and differentiation
- Pricing
- Advertising and promotion
- Forecasting sales
- Distribution
- New product development
- Brand management
- Customer retention

Of course, the specialist CMO must build and lead the marketing team. The team must demonstrate a service-oriented mindset and be technically strong in the key marketing functions listed above. While the marketing specialist should be an excellent manager, the high-level strategic requirements of the job are limited. The CMO as marketing specialist is the default role, a role that is well illustrated by the content of traditional MBA textbooks.

Integrating traditional and innovative marketing technology

While marketing responsibilities have remained constant in the specialist role, technologies have changed dramatically. To improve tracking of marketing return on investments, many large companies are spending more money on addressable media: online events and promotions, email campaigns, hosting web logs (blogs) and other creative uses of new technology combining both online and offline media.

Success in new media campaigns is boosting the role of online advertising. It is no longer a novelty in a CMO's arsenal but a necessity that must be well integrated into the traditional marketing system.

Spending on internet advertising increased to US $9.1 billion in 2004 – a 25 per cent increase from 2003 – and strong growth has continued in 2005 and 2006. For some industries, the internet has emerged as a powerful communications and distribution channel, increasing sales, strengthening brands, improving customer service and helping consumers make better choices. It is also leading to more competition as prices and product information become globally transparent.

CMOs are rethinking their marketing systems and revolutionizing the way their companies do business as information availability is a double-edged sword. Even CMOs who manage many of the world's largest brands (whose firms dominated the use of traditional media) are using the internet extensively.

For example, Procter & Gamble has placed the web at the centre of an extension of one of its biggest brands – Tide Coldwater. Viral and interactive marketing through the company's website enables visitors to sign up for product samples and email their friends. Visitors are informed about product features and an interactive calculator can be used to see how much money they can save by washing in cold water. A media-rich email campaign (with video, interactivity and impressive graphics) can reach thousands of consumers for a fraction of the cost of traditional media.

Decision models are another analytical tool which the marketing specialists use to exploit customer data. Examples include: market response models, market entry models, new product models, advertising models, and sales-force allocation models.[5]

While some tools may be traditional, companies' business models and specific challenges are not; the CMO must be able to adapt. The following is a traditional process and an effective framework for the marketing specialist's role:

The marketing management process

Five main steps in the marketing management process:[6]

1. Market research

Research is the starting point. It determines how the firm positions itself and its products, and how it sells. Research also determines the firm's product and financial strategy.

Research means recognizing buyers' specific needs, preferences and perceptions. The most successful firms have the greatest understanding, insight and actions based on knowledge.

2. Segmentation, targeting and positioning

Research is likely to have identified several market segments. The firm needs to prioritize efforts in each segment. The firm then assesses its core competencies against each segment and decides which will bring the greatest success. This process of targeting ensures that the firm's resources are focused. The company then positions its product, making the product's benefits and differentiation clear to customers. The complete positioning is the value proposition.

3. Tactical marketing

Tactical marketing supports the product's position and relies on the tools of the marketing mix: the product, its price, the mechanisms used to make the product available (also known as 'place') and promotion. The marketing mix is valuable for informing, reminding and persuading the target market about the product's availability and benefits.

4. Implementation

Marketing implementation is about linking with other departments and companies in key business processes. R&D, purchasing, manufacturing, marketing and sales, human resources, IT and finance all need to combine for the company to keep delivering to the customer.

5. Control

Marketing's role is to help each function to work as part of a learning organization, ensuring everyone knows their role in delivering customer value. This involves collecting comments from the market, analysing results, making timely adjustments and controlling information flow.

Measurement challenges facing the marketing specialist CMO

Demands for greater accountability have forced CMOs to focus on new metrics.[7] Marketing executives are pressured to demonstrate a return on investment (ROI) despite the inherent challenges in measuring marketing effectiveness.

Renewed focusing on metrics often pushes the CMO into a tactical orientation. Producing short-term results can come at the expense of long-term market development. Managing expectations is a key success factor in the CXO team. It is important to ensure that the long-term strategy is not sacrificed to demonstrate quick returns.

Many marketers often use metrics such as brand awareness rather than financial measures to show value added to the company. Marketing ROI is generally more complex to calculate than financial ROI, but is a necessity with the pressures on costs. Relationship-based industries such as financial services tend to use awareness and image-related forms of measurement. Industries with limited customer relationships in which marketing differentiates commodity products (such as food) rely on market share, growth and profit metrics.

Although these forms of measurement are valid, their value can be misunderstood by other senior executives who are used to looking at financial results. The communication gap involving metrics is understandable. However, the gap can be bridged by encouraging a stronger measurement culture in marketing and the alignment of other contributors in the organization to produce valuable marketing information.

Developing an effective marketing capability requires the CMO to use clear metrics and demonstrate marketing's ROI. Educating colleagues around the executive table on the usefulness and limitations of the measurement facilitates a balanced approach and, when well managed, can provide the CMO with credibility and influence.

The leadership role of the marketing specialist

The marketing specialist faces three key challenges in the role as leader:

Ensuring differentiation

Differentiated products and brands can simultaneously increase revenues and shareholder value. Market segmentation and the marketing mix remain important and must be complemented by a more insightful, strategic view.

Developing distribution channels

Large corporations typically rely on the strength of their brand to ensure distribution. However, in both consumer and business markets, distribution channels are changing, distances are shrinking and more products are being delivered based on electronic ordering. Branded producers may find that their influence on the market is diluted or undermined if they fail to collaborate and innovate with their distributors.

Providing an effective, central marketing function

The final leadership challenge for the CMO is to balance local and central marketing activities. Many organizations suffer from having too much of one approach and not enough of the other, and poor collaboration between the two. The key challenge is to define clearly the roles and responsibilities of central and local teams; and to make sure the two work together.

The customer advocate

It is the job of customer advocate CMOs to know the customers, to know their needs, wants, 'headaches', and their willingness to pay for the next innovation. CMOs in this role must also ensure that the company is aligned to deliver. They must be experts on how brand characteristics interact with the marketplace. They share this knowledge as *consultants* to the rest of the firm.

Like the marketing specialist CMO, customer advocate CMOs have a centralized marketing function, to ensure consistent application of brand standards. They also provide alignment between divisional plans and overall corporate direction, spreading best practices around the company. They play a larger role than the marketing specialist.

Another strategic role of the customer advocate is making difficult decisions on portfolio rationalization. An expanding brand portfolio increases product complexity across the entire value chain, which increases costs dramatically. Effective portfolio management is a bottom-line activity, meaning that it must be justified to the CEO and CFO. Once the CMO has buy-in from the CEO and CFO, the portfolio strategy must be reconciled with agendas in other functions, where the CMO must integrate with other CXOs.

The CMO must work productively with business units and suppliers, and persuasively with the top management team. Marketing strategy is elevated to the executive table. The CMO must ensure consistency and clarity from the executive level on all aspects of marketing communication.

To excel, the customer advocate must work closely with the CEO. The CEO is the leading advocate of the brand but requires the expertise of an effective CMO. The customer advocate also needs allies in the field. Making business unit managers marketing heroes can accomplish this. Two vital resources are necessary: money and talent.

The customer advocate CMO can drive the corporate agenda with these two resources. By having a discretionary central budget and a team of marketing experts, both of which can be used to support specific operations in the field, the CMO can exercise considerable influence in driving the company's strategy while assisting operations.

Successful customer advocates are strong in both creative and technical tasks. They must be self-confident, politically-aware operators with the interpersonal skills to lead. They must also be able to manage the detailed aspects of the role with a broad, strategic and cross-functional view.

Challenges facing the customer advocate

The primary challenge facing the customer advocate is developing a customer-focused organization. The CMO needs to articulate and implement a clear and common vision for customer focus throughout the organization, not only in marketing. Several questions are fundamentally important in this task.

- Who are our customers and our customers' customers?
- Why do they buy from us?
- How are we better than the competition?

The answers to these questions determine the culture of customer focus; they must be highly visible in the organization and only periodically validated and revisited.

Marketing competence must be developed throughout a customer-focused organization. Education is a fundamental. Attraction, selection, retention and reward of employees based on customer-focused behaviours are necessary. Establishing real customer focus requires change and empowerment at lower organizational levels.

Customer focus is most likely to be achieved when accompanied by an intense commitment from the chief executive and the entire CXO team. Consistency and commitment of the management team to building a customer focus will be measured over several years and requires sustained effort.

Marketing strategy inevitably crosses functional boundaries. A customer-focused organization facilitates effective implementation of strategy by ensuring consistency at every point that a customer touches the firm. As the CMO of a bank put it, his work is to:

> Break down the silos across our distinct lines of businesses, ensure an integrated, consistent customer experience and help drive innovation.

The leadership role of the customer advocate

Providing solutions – not selling products

More than ever before, customers are impatient and less and less loyal. Product quality is taken for granted; one mistake and the customer can be lost for life. Choice, customization and simplicity are expected. Businesses must move from selling products to providing solutions. The customer advocate CMO must lead.

Adopting a collaborative approach

Chapter 7 on the CSCO highlights the need for the head of operations to collaborate closely with marketing. This is to ensure that the whole value chain, which extends outside the organization, serves the customer. The CMO must convey, to everyone involved, what the customer wants and how these needs should be met.

Rationalizing and strengthening brands

Organizations can easily fall into the trap of providing short-term sales inducements or acquiring brands, rather than building existing ones to be even stronger. The challenge of rationalizing and strengthening brands falls primarily to the CMO. Wealth creation is sometimes achieved by shrinking rather than growing.

The strategic contributor

Strategic contributor role

CMOs as strategic contributors are partners with the CEO; their responsibilities extend beyond marketing. They drive the corporate growth agenda and are actively involved in strategic acquisitions and overall company strategy. To be effective in this role, CMOs must be both analytic strategists and creative marketers.

The best CMOs are tenacious and positive change-drivers with strong convictions about their products and extreme personal stamina. Such a strategic position requires these qualities. The strategic contributor CMO must have earned and must maintain the respect and trust of the CEO and executive peers.

When there is company-wide agreement that the company's brand assets need a watchdog, the CMO is well positioned to become a strategic contributor. This is often the case with companies that have a single, valuable global master brand.

These CMOs are often supported by enthusiastic CEOs who are themselves 'born marketers' (such as Steve Jobs at Apple, Nicolas Hayek at Swatch, and Carlos Ghosn at Renault/Nissan).

The CMO and corporate strategy

The central role of the strategic contributor is to ensure that marketing helps the CEO's decisions about corporate strategy. To do this, the strategic contributor CMO focuses on three questions:[8]

What business are we in?

Choosing the right portfolio for the business is imperative. This choice invariably relies on an assessment of two issues: market attractiveness and the firm's competitive strengths. The Boston Consulting Group portfolio matrix, developed nearly four decades ago, which segments business lines based on these criteria, is still used in some companies for portfolio rationalization. However, many firms prefer to apply their own specific rules – Jack Welch, for example, insisted that GE's product companies should be globally first or second out of any market they competed in.

What value do our businesses add to each other, and which are the most significant relationships between our business units?
The company's operations, resources and structure need to be assessed in terms of how well they benefit customers and create value. The CMO is central in making this assessment. An effective corporate marketing team will provide fresh insights into the coherence of the firm's portfolio. Moreover, the CMO is well placed to identify areas for improved economies of scale.

What is the role of the corporate centre?
Parent companies may choose to become active in their portfolio firms or leave them to conduct their own business. The extent of involvement by the centre is an increasingly significant issue for major businesses. Opportunities to co-ordinate activities between businesses have been enhanced by technology, leading many firms to rethink their entire business structure. Getting the right mix between what is managed centrally versus locally is a key strategic choice. Getting the answer wrong can lead to a lot of corporate disruption, animosity and loss of productivity, as well as loss of credibility of the CXO team.

The extent of a corporate centre's involvement in local businesses depends on whether there is a 'parenting advantage'. This, in turn, depends on whether the corporate centre has unique capabilities, resources or access to stakeholders that can help individual business units. The CMO's view of potential cross-brand strategies, product coupling, and more offers essential insight into these business structure decisions.

Challenges facing the strategic contributor

Like the marketing specialist, the strategic contributor is challenged to quantify the benefits of marketing activities through metrics. In addition, three challenges face the strategic contributor:

- Building a broad view of the business;
- Driving an integrated marketing plan;
- Providing in-house expertise;

Building and articulating a broad view of the business
The ultimate mandate of the marketing function is to deliver growth profitably. Therefore, the CMO must analyse, anticipate and interpret

business trends coming from the market, competitors and internal sources (i.e. innovation team). The CMO needs to communicate these trends and related insights to influence the strategic direction of the firm. This process can be especially complex in multinational firms. There may be hundreds of business units located around the globe, each producing a wide range of products for dozens of target market segments with widely diverse needs and wants. In addition, information availability remains a key challenge.

How do CMOs broadly understand the dynamic, complex and highly competitive environment in which their company operates? Some best practices:

Be alert to technological developments
For example, Polaroid was not alone in being caught unprepared for the move from processed to digital film.

Define the market as customers do
Seize opportunities to satisfy customers' expressed and unexpressed needs. For example, in 1980 IBM viewed the developing personal computer industry as being defined by hardware. IBM adopted Microsoft's operating system as standard on a non-exclusive basis – and ceded dominance of the software market forever. This mattered because customers want software applications, not just hardware.

Monitor current and potential competitors
The airline industry is one example of poor insight in this area. Established airlines largely failed to combat the emergence of low-cost competitors in the US, Europe and Asia. Businesses from travel agents to booksellers have similarly underestimated the impact of internet competitors.

See the emergence of new channels of distribution
For example, Dell's direct sales strategy took its industry by storm and continues to outperform peers.

Understand the political, legal, economic, social, cultural and ethical context of each market in which the firm is operating
For example, Royal Dutch/Shell was slow to appreciate the impact across Europe of the disposal of the Brent Spar oil platform. The

firm's brand and revenues suffered as a direct result of failing to understand the ethical concerns prevailing in its European markets.

Sometimes, the outcome of a broad vision is that CMOs have to take a risk. They promote the big ideas that can have a fundamental impact on the fortunes of the company. CMOs balance the current company direction while guarding against complacency and competitive threats. In the view of one CMO:

> Marketing needs to figure out how to balance the big, innovative ideas with the sustaining ideas.

Driving an integrated marketing system

Integrating a marketing strategy into the corporate strategy means combining many diverse elements to support the company's vision. This can be complex. As a result, strategy changes should not be made too often. Decisions may meet one customer's or one operational need but not another, implying trade-offs and causing conflict. The CMO must find common ground for the entire company to support the overall strategy.

The CMO typically retains many marketing functions in-house, such as sales support, customer service and field marketing, and co-ordinates an array of outsourced activities. Depending on the size of the company, the industry and the competencies of the firm, advertising, direct marketing, public relations and research are commonly outsourced. However, the CMO should never permit the outsourcing of essential, core marketing activities such as the 'Cs analysis'. This is what one exasperated executive referred to as 'outsourcing our brains'. The CMO also needs to be aware that the strategic value of various marketing functions can shift over time.

Integrating and implementing a new marketing strategy can be contentious. Senior marketing executives are often in charge of different channels inside the organization, and battle over budget and operating control. The proliferation of technology increases the complexity of marketing and market research. Therefore, integrating traditional marketing tools with online and other technology-enabled tools is a major challenge.

The CMO's job is to accelerate growth using all available resources and tactics. Confusion can occur between what might be labelled marketing *tactics* and marketing *strategy*. The distinction between tactics and strategy is crucial in its potential effect on the organization or the value proposition. Materially changing either the organization or the value proposition elevates the discussion into the realm of strategy.

Once the strategic direction has been set, it is the CMO's responsibility to ensure that it is implemented through the professional marketing team and strategic partners.

- Is the marketing team equipped to handle the implementation?
- Is the team supported by external partnerships?

The CMO must also ensure that the organizational structure, competencies and incentives are in place to deliver marketing's mandate. The effective CMO communicates realistic expectations regarding strategy to both the peer executive group and the chief executive, and delivers on those expectations.

Providing in-house expertise

The CMO is positioned as the firm's customer expert and champion. This task is complicated by rapidly-changing consumer dynamics, high customer turnover, low loyalty and retention rates, and a fast-paced competitive environment. Even a small percentage change in customer retention can have a material impact on sales and profitability. Consequently, the CMO needs to understand motivations underlying customer behaviour.

In maturing markets where customers have plenty of choice, their needs often go unarticulated. Customer insights are derived from four areas:

- Analysing qualitative and quantitative research;
- Understanding customer and technology trends;
- Assessing customer relationship management (CRM) data;
- Empathizing with customers and considering their situation and needs.

Asking naïve questions and watching customers use the product is often the first step. Logitech, a manufacturer of computer peripheral products, is known for having teams of engineers and marketers spend hours observing how customers use products. This helps them to innovate in valuable ways. The results have been new products such as the wireless computer mouse and a one-touch remote control for TV and peripherals.

The astute CMO both broadens and narrows the market, viewing the consumer landscape from various perspectives. For example, a soft drink marketer might expand the frame of reference from cola drinks to all beverages or narrow it to flavoured colas.

Redefining the market may highlight opportunities to be assessed against the firm's capabilities. An expanded market definition may point to brand extension opportunities, the launch of a new product or the acquisition of a company.

The strategic contributor CMO needs to ensure that market research provides insights into customer needs and that the organization can create wealth from these insights. Well-defined market research is a sound investment when it helps the firm either avoid costly strategic blunders or exploit opportunities. Research information needs to flow easily around the company, getting to the right people at the right time.

The leadership role of the strategic contributor

Encouraging radical innovations that drive the market (and not vice versa)

Many organizations want to be market driven, meaning they aspire to respond attentively to customers. This contrasts with the best organizations that *lead* the market. This is much harder to accomplish. It requires the CMO to help the organization understand its customers in as much detail as possible and deliver innovative solutions based on market understanding.

Radical innovation often requires that firms anticipate their customers. The development by 3M of the Post-it note is such a case. Nobody waited for a request for a new product called the Post-it note. 3M simply used its understanding of its customers and its research to deliver an innovative, profitable product.

Transforming the business

The strategic head of marketing needs to be a skilled, versatile operator, equally able to support the CEO, peers and business unit managers. This must be done creatively and analytically, a challenge in large complex companies.

The CMO must also keep the organization constantly aware of and focused on the market. To accomplish this, the CMO will need to transform and strengthen the organization by focusing on some, or all, of the aforementioned challenges.

The strategic contributor CMO is, on an evolutionary scale, currently the highest level role that a CMO plays in a company.

Next we will discuss some of the CMO's key relationships and give some insight into the future of the CMO.

The CMO's key relationships

CMOs, regardless of the role they play, need a good understanding and working relationship with colleagues across the business. CMOs are often brought in from the outside to be change agents in the company. Sometimes this structural modification can cause internal friction. Successful CMOs recognize this and undertake early initiatives that produce measurable results whenever possible. It is important to build alliances and gain influence with other CXOs.

The CMO and other senior executives

The CEO, CFO, CIO and CTO have typically been the chief marketing officer's main interactions. The chief of operations and CMO need to collaborate to ensure a consistent customer experience. The head of HR needs to provide reward and education systems that foster a customer-oriented approach. The CMO's work also affects the HR department; strong brands help recruitment.

The CMO relies on two-way communication with R&D to provide new, differentiated products that are valued by customers and come quickly to market.

The chief financial officer

The CFO has three key responsibilities that the CMO can directly or indirectly influence:

- Delivering a steady, predictable cash flow;
- Growing revenues;
- Increasing wealth creation/shareholder value.

A good relationship with the CFO requires that the CMO understand the impact of marketing strategy on profit. The CFO can be particularly valuable in helping the CMO to develop and record marketing metrics. These metrics help to ensure a sufficient return on investment from marketing activities. In turn, the CMO provides a plan for a systematic investment in marketing. Such plans enhance cash flow and reduce risk.

The chief technology officer

Many great innovations are developed in-house with, at first, little customer input. Remember that no customer ever asked openly for the development of a Post-it, an iPod, a DVD or an energy drink such as Red Bull. Once a great new product concept is born in the lab, making sure that the product is relevant to the customer target market and that its value is properly communicated must become a common objective for both the CTO and the CMO.

Constant dialogue and co-ordination between the marketing team, the technical people and the sales force are essential to a successful product launch. Too many product ideas born from a technology perspective end up in the graveyard of 'great innovations', never reach the consumer or die right after their introduction on the market.

The reasons for such failures are most often linked to poor internal communication between the various corporate functions: lack of a product champion, poor sales force incentives, wrong marketing mix, or the belief that the 'right' product will sell itself! Transforming a great technology breakthrough into a meaningful value proposition for the customer target, defining the right marketing mix and ensuring proper feedback from the market place to the various functions of the company are key success factors in any product launch.

The chief information officer

A CMO's involvement with IT differs from business to business. In some cases, the involvement extends no further than overseeing content on the company's website. In technology-based firms, by contrast, the CMO and CIO work hand-in-hand to build the company brand. Google, one of the most recognizable brands in the world, does not have an advertising agency yet still enjoys extremely high customer loyalty thanks in part to the hand-in-glove operation of IT and marketing.

The CIO provides marketing with information systems that deliver integrated, accessible market information. The CMO's role is to ensure that the accuracy of this information, notably about customers and competitors, is maintained on an ongoing basis.

The chief executive officer

A CMO is most effective when he or she reports to the CEO with expectations that are aligned with the CEO's priorities. According to a recent survey, however, this rarely happens. The Conference Board's 2004 survey of the *Top Ten CEO Challenges*[9] lists the top four chief executive priorities as:

- Top-line growth (52 per cent);
- Speed, flexibility, adaptability to change (42 per cent);
- Customer loyalty and retention (41 per cent);
- Stimulating innovation (31 per cent).

According to a 2004 survey, the typical marketing unit's focus is tactical and disconnected from the CEO agenda. For example, 83 per cent focused on branding guidelines and 52 per cent on counselling business units and sharing best practices. Only 46 per cent of marketers reported driving growth as an area of focus.[10]

Fewer than half of respondents shared a focus on the same issues as the CEO. This difference in agendas causes dissatisfaction with the role and performance of marketing. According to a June 2004 survey of CEOs, 35 per cent said that their marketing organization needed improvement. Only 18 per cent said that they were very satisfied.[11]

Expectations must be set jointly to avoid non-aligned agendas between the CMO and the CEO. These include agreeing shared priorities and outcomes. If priorities are not shared and the CMO is left unsupported by the CEO, failure is virtually assured. The CMO also needs support from the CEO to build and maintain a customer-focused organization. In return, the CMO provides marketing support and insight, shaping and influencing the firm's strategy. The CMO is also well placed, as a result of his or her closeness to the market, to lead certain new initiatives and transformational activities.

Let us now try to anticipate how the CMO role will evolve.

A look ahead

If the history of marketing has anything to tell us about its future, it is that the discipline will continue to get more advanced, complex and demanding. Many of the fundamentals will stay the same, but the speed of business will require new methods, new tools and faster and more-efficient execution to win the marketing battles of the future.

A leading book entitled *Beyond Traditional Marketing*,[12] and written by a number of IMD faculty, explores in depth how the role of marketing will change in the future. Some of the key insights are highlighted below:

- Differentiation remains the key to producing a marketing strategy that will build sustainable advantages for a company.
- Branding will remain the ultimate differentiation factor.
- A brand is more than a product; it is also about the people who execute the strategy.
- Developing a passion internally for a brand is vital to an organization, since at the end of the day only people help to differentiate products, make customers loyal, enable premium pricing, and reinforce internal commitment and organizational identification.
- A key to effective market sensing is to get all parts of the organization to focus on delivering the value proposition to the customer.
- Values and behaviour are more important than organizational structure.
- The real role of marketing is to support the CEO in driving customer responsiveness, measurement and simplicity.
- There are four broad guidelines for management:

  1. Look beyond structural and organizational solutions to enhance customer responsiveness.
  2. Translate the business's value proposition into a simple mandate that all employees can understand.
  3. Design a simple decision-making governance mechanism to enhance organizational speed.
  4. Learn to discriminate between customers who complain in the hope of getting something extra from those genuinely aggrieved because the company has failed to deliver on their promise.

Based on some of the insights above, what changes can we expect to the role of the CMO? As Figure 5.2 highlights, the challenge continues to be refining the role of chief marketing officer as the *strategic marketer*.

The CMO of tomorrow needs to be capable of dealing with a more complex environment and to engage the entire organization to focus on customers. New technologies and analytical techniques will provide the tools to make this possible. For example, associative rule mining has been used in retailing to discover that customers tend to purchase beer and diapers together on Thursdays.[13] Such surprising results can yield big pay-offs for firms that can exploit them.

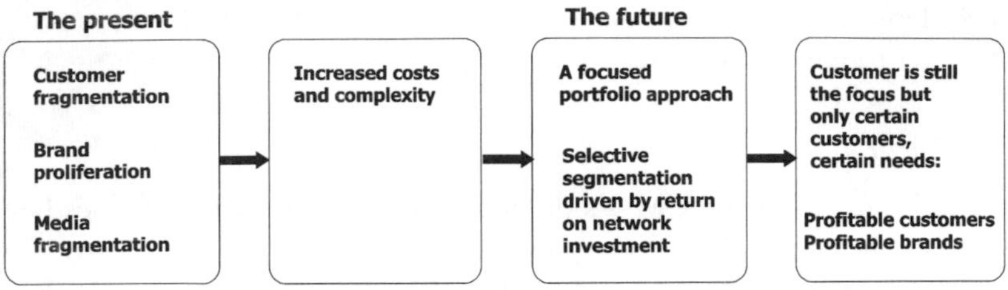

Figure 5.2: From the present to the future

As business lines become more complex, we can also expect marketers to become more specialized. Clothing manufacturers will have clothing marketers, technology firms will have technology marketers, and international firms will have international marketers. The marketer's job will be to understand and exploit changes in the marketplace; as markets become more distinctive, so too will the role of the marketer.

Finally, CMOs will need to grasp the big picture of the business. They will need to combine the functional and industry experience of the customer advocate, the tacit knowledge and implementation focus of the specialist, the high-level view of the strategic contributor and expect it all to move faster and become more competitive in the future.

Assessing the role of the CMO

The following questions provide a starting point when assessing the role of the CMO.

Purpose

1. What are the CMO's priorities and how could these be developed? Is his or her role primarily to:
   - Be an efficient administrator of marketing and a source of advice?
   - Influence and persuade people, championing the customer?
   - Be a change agent, excelling at analytical and creative tasks and leading the way the organization thinks about customers?
2. Does the CMO have ***credibility*** by being well informed, and balancing his or her contribution to strategic as well as technical issues?
3. Does the CMO's contribution extend beyond the marketing function, demonstrating ***relevance*** and benefiting the company's business activities as a whole?

4. Does the CMO ***influence*** the company's culture and attitude to customers, and the way it works?

Direction

5. What guides the CMO's decisions and what techniques does he or she employ?
6. Does the CMO operate the marketing infrastructure to serve the business? How could this be improved?
7. Should the CMO do more to:

   - Differentiate products and brands?
   - Provide solutions – not simply sell products?
   - Develop distribution channels?
   - Adopt a collaborative approach with other heads of operations?
   - Rationalize and strengthen brands?
   - Encourage radical innovations that drive the market?
   - Provide an effective, central marketing function?

Focus

8. Is the CMO focused on the details necessary to develop the marketing function's contribution to the business?
9. Are there adequate measures in place to assess marketing's return on investment?
10. Do front-line people dealing with customers receive adequate support? Are they sufficiently informed and empowered?

Notes

1 Various points in this chapter were taken from the following sources: P. Kotler, *Marketing Management* (Upper Saddle River, NJ :Prentice Hall, 2003); N. Kumar, *Marketing as Strategy: Understanding the CEO's Agenda for Driving Growth and Innovation* (Boston, MA: Harvard Business Press, 2004); P. Hyde, E. Landry and A. Tipping, 'Making the perfect marketer', *strategy+business* Special Report Winter, Booz Allen Hamilton 2004; D. Branscum, 'Outer limits', *CMO Magazine* (February 2005); D. J. Dalrymple and L. J. Parsons, *Basic Marketing Management* (New York: John Wiley, 1995).

2 R. Lauterborn, 'New marketing litany: 4P's Passé; C-words take over', *Advertising Age* (October 1, 1990), p. 26.

3 K. Kashani (ed.), *Beyond Traditional Marketing: Innovations in Marketing Practice* (Chichester: John Wiley, 2005), pp. 4–9.
4 Hyde et al., *Making the Perfect Marketer.*
5 G. L. Lilien and A. Rangaswamy, *Marketing Engineering: Computer-assisted Marketing Analysis and Planning* (Victoria, BC: Trafford, 2004).
6 Kotler, *Marketing Management.*
7 R. Shaw and D. Merrick, *Marketing Payback: Is your Marketing Profitable?*' (New York: FT Prentice Hall, 2005).
8 Kumar, *Marketing as Strategy.*
9 E. V. Rudis, *CEO Challenge 2004: Perspectives and Analysis*, The Conference Board, Report Number: R-1353-04-RR (November 2004).
10 ANA/Booz Allen Hamilton Marketing Organization Survey (2004).
11 *CEO Magazine* (June 2004).
12 Kashani (ed.), *Beyond Traditional Marketing.*
13 I. H. Witten and E. Frank, *Data Mining: Practical Machine Learning Tools and Techniques* (San Francisco, CA: Morgan Kaufman Publishers, 2005), p. 27.

6 *The Chief Sales Officer – Sell, sell, sell!*

JONATHAN LACHOWITZ AND
PRESTON BOTTGER

The chief sales officer (CSO) is part of the CXO round table when sales and sales growth are of such importance to the company that the executive function of marketing is divided into CMO and CSO. The CSO's primary focus is top-line growth, at any cost. However, the CSO cannot ignore strategy and profitability, two key tension points between sales and marketing. Having a CSO is sometimes a short-term decision when sales growth is a new key item on the CEO's agenda. Often, market share growth on a global scale and head-to-head competition with key competitors is to be expected and the CSO's job is to keep sales growth at the top of the corporate agenda.

In this chapter, the authors explain how the CSO's role is distinct from that of the CMO and focus on how the CSO works within a global organization's top leadership team. They explore the CSO role in different types of companies, B2B vs B2C and the challenges the CSO faces working alongside colleagues in the CXO team.

The role of the chief sales officer

As the executive vice president of sales, I am responsible for worldwide sales of products in over a dozen divisions. We have a diverse set of products, mainly for end consumers, but we sell mainly to doctors, hospitals and governments, and recently we have been losing market share to some of our key competitors in both big-pharma and the generics. Motivating our sales staff of over 1,000 employees and communicating a single vision from the headquarters is one of the key challenges I face. The top line of the company's P&L is mine, and I have only a couple of key measurements on my scorecard, sales growth, market share growth and, well, to some extent profitability too. I am constantly at odds with the heads of R&D, marketing, manufacturing; we are our biggest enemy when it comes to sales growth and if those guys could just straighten out their departments, we could sell even more . . . (CSO of a global pharmaceutical company)

The chief sales officer has a very clear primary role increasing revenue growth, a key driver of wealth creation. The CSO's main objective, while perhaps the easiest to understand and measure among all of the CXOs, is also riddled with tactical challenges. The CSO may be responsible for one sales force globally and organize and drive objectives from the headquarters, however this model is not common. More likely, the CSO is responsible for a number of different sales forces in different geographic areas, within different product lines and perhaps in many different business units.

How is the CSO able to focus and ensure that the sales force is acting in concert with the rest of the organization?

There is one clear answer: the CSO must have an ownership stake in the marketing strategy of the company. The successful execution of any marketing strategy in a company that has a significant sales force relies on a coherent understanding and buy-in from the sales executives. It is only by having an ownership stake in the success of the marketing strategy that the CSO can balance the short-term sales growth objectives with long-term strategy execution.

The following two case studies serve as examples of the important link between sales and marketing:[1]

Case study 1 – The missing strategy

A manufacturer of mobile communications equipment was losing market share in Europe because of a lack of a coherent marketing strategy. The firm's seven national sales subsidiaries had traditionally enjoyed considerable management autonomy within broad financial controls exercised by its headquarters. At any one time, this sales-oriented organization was pursuing seven 'sales strategies' in as many national markets. Headquarters' marketing policies – in such vital areas as end-user market selection, pricing and whether sales emphasis should be on standard product or customer-designed systems – were thus overshadowed by the immediate sales considerations of individual subsidiaries. In the battle for market share their competitors flourished, having the advantages of well-structured regional marketing strategies. In effect, the firm was paying dearly for lack of an effective transition from the strategy produced at headquarters to the national sales action.

Case study 2 – The uniformed sales force

A reputable US manufacturer of medical diagnostic equipment was having great difficulty in penetrating the European market with its computer tomography scanners, sold to hospitals and clinics. Their product was positioned at the top of the market for technical excellence, faster patient through-put and excellent after-sales service, but was losing sales to its less-advanced European competitors. Alarmed, the management investigated a sample of lost sales, and discovered that buyers were ill-informed about the company's product features and were also over-sensitive to its high list price. The investigation showed that this was a response to the preoccupation of the sales force with the equipment price (hence they were offering repeated and ever-increasing discounts off the list price), and their neglect of selling arguments in the areas where the product had a clear edge over the competition. Something essential had been lost in the transition from strategy to selling.

In each case the execution of the sales strategy at the tactical level was not aligned with marketing strategy and the business results suffered. In each case the role of the CSO at a high level should have been clear; however, there was no coherence at the executive level and no translation to the tactical level. The CSO in each case would have benefited from remembering and communicating the differences between sales and marketing.

The role of marketing is to select the target markets. Once these targets are selected, marketing also determines which products should be offered, the appropriate pricing, how and where the products are to be distributed and in what way the products and company are to be promoted. The sales force is one element, albeit a very important one, of the overall strategy, through the direct method of promotion. When moving from marketing strategy to sales force implementation, it is vital to remember two things:

1 Effective sales managers (who understand and buy in to the marketing strategy) are essential.
2 Strategic decisions are not made by the sales force.[2]

CSO roles in different types of organizations

CSO roles differ significantly from company to company. While at the strategic level this does not change the CSO's objectives, it does have an impact on lower level strategic choices and the interaction with the other CXOs. CSO positions can broadly be classified in the

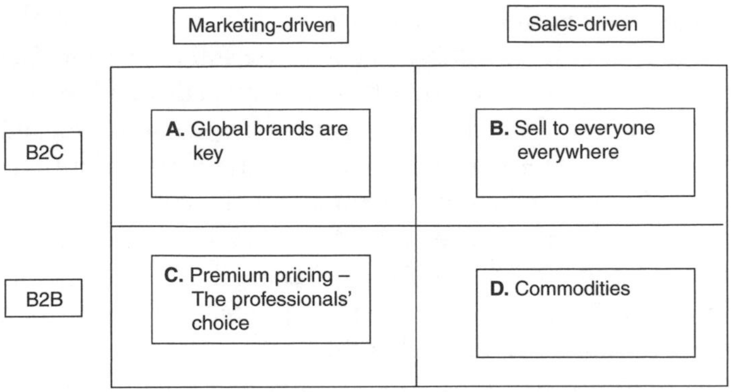

Figure 6.1: Company types

following matrix: within companies that are either driven by marketing or driven by sales, and where their product markets are mainly to other companies or to consumers (see Figure 6.1).

Global brands are key

A good example of where the marketing department seems to run the company would be Proctor & Gamble. The sales force is really secondary, the company is well established and mature. In this type of company, the CSO position may be new, to try to divide the power of a strong CMO into two separate positions or to give the sales force a higher standing in the company. The CSO will likely have a weaker role than the CMO and will have to work hard to influence strategy.

Sell to anyone and everyone, anywhere and everywhere

The sales force is the most important part of the company. Historically this has been much more common than Box A. Here the marketing department is likely to be small and centralized, often in the corporate headquarters. In this case the CSO is likely to be very powerful. The company may have had years of relatively-high growth or may be in a high-growth phase. The company will tend to be younger and less mature. Here, the sales force is often still a maverick organization, which may be exactly what was needed to fuel the high growth. The CSO has often risen from the ranks as one of the most successful salespeople; this may or may not translate into being a constructive member of the CXO team.

Premium pricing – the professionals' choice

In the B2B arena, marketing and brand names are still important. The audience is much narrower, but product and service quality and perception are still important. The marketing department is still powerful and may use the influence of government, lobbyists, the press, and trade shows and publications to shape opinion about the company's products. In this case, the CSO, like in group A, is still a somewhat weaker role than the CMO (if the CSO position exists at all). The CSO's role is often very 'process' and tactic-oriented; the products are often good or very good to the point that they sell themselves. If this is the case, the CSO may be more focused on customer care, after-sales service or merely efficient order processing.

Commodities

This is a cut-throat market where volume is key and the sales force will need to be aggressive and knowledgeable. Sales opportunities here are becoming less frequent, more complex and larger, while the competition is fierce.[3] The marketing department may be small or non-existent. The CSO knows his role: volume, and sell, sell, sell. Marketing strategy is often a secondary consideration since not one day of selling can easily be missed. The CSO has to make sure that the sales force is large enough to cover the markets and to fight off the competition, which is likely to be intense.

The CSO's role, perhaps more than any of the other CXO positions, is likely to be defined as a function of the company's place in its market, relative to products, customers, geography and the competition. While the focus of sales growth, in line with the marketing strategy, is clear, it is at the tactical level that the CSO's role becomes more a function of its position. An in-depth discussion of tactics is beyond the scope of this book, but the following section on sales management policies will help the practitioner start to organize his or her tactics around sales management policies.

Once the CSO, the CMO and essentially the CXO team agree on marketing strategy, then the CSO can focus on driving the sales organization for both revenue growth and achievement of the company's strategic objectives. Here then, the CSO must focus exclusively on sales management policies.

The role of sales management policies is to guide other sales executives and the sales force in the following key areas[4]:

- The organization, reporting lines and supervision of the sales force;
- The recruitment, retention and promotion policies;
- Training, education and management of the culture;
- Compensation and reward systems;
- Key performance measurements.

The CSO is responsible for the design and implementation of effective sales management policies. A full understanding of and buy-in to the company's marketing strategy are essential. This will ensure that the desired outcome that the company expects from the sales force – measured not only in sales growth but also through other indicators such as profitability, market share, market share growth, segment growth, and so on – can be achieved and that all of the executives and the sales force are clear as to the direction the company is headed.

By designing sales management policies and implementing them in line with the marketing strategy, CSOs will be able to demonstrate that they are both team players and effective leaders.

The CSO's leadership role

Providing direction and focus

Shareholders demand it, the CEO demands it, the financial markets expect it, even the employees and customers are highly aware of it: of course we are talking about revenue growth. It is one of the most-widely-recognized financial figures, especially by non-finance people, such as salespeople. Many companies are measured by it, and even *Fortune* magazine celebrates it with its annual rankings of the Fortune 500 US and global companies by sales.

So again, the CSO's key measurement statistic is clear, sales are X this year and everyone expects sales to grow, not to decline. CSOs are caught in a never-ending cycle of demand for growth and so they must deliver. Where the CSO's job is more than just a sales-level benchmark and a targeted growth multiple, is in the translation of marketing strategy to sales management. The CSO is the top sales executive and must provide the direction and focus of the marketing plan in order to design effective sales management policies.

CSOs often come from the ranks of top salespeople in the company, so while they must talk and act as a corporate officer, it is unlikely that they will give up their salesperson personality completely. In this respect, if the company has a sales culture that caters or panders to the top salespeople, rewarding them in lavish ways for selling more and more of the company product, an executive who meddled too much with the incentive systems would be most unpopular. The view would rather be that the meddling should focus on what needs to be done to earn the rewards such as six-figure bonuses, all-expenses paid holidays, recognition throughout the company, and so on.

Ensuring efficiency and effectiveness

On the other hand, the focus on sales growth and rewarding the top salespeople does not place enough emphasis on how the selling process has matured over the past decades. Sales and marketing, in their usage of data and information, have matured and started to work more closely together in many companies, towards the same goals. CSOs now must make sure that their HR policies are designed to attract and maintain the right type of salespeople for their organization.

CSOs must also ensure that the sales force is focused beyond just a sales target, towards the details, where a marketing analyst lives. The sales force needs structure, with processes in place that ensure that they know what the company expects from them, and when spending more time and effort on some customers or potential deals is necessary.

Education and shared success stories are also important. Executive education courses are expanding rapidly as companies ensure that their sales executives understand company strategy and the necessity for 'all that corporate stuff'. CSOs are actively involved in fostering a culture of shared success and open communication; and as is often the case with a sales conference, lots of fun remains too!

Building a winning team

Finally, the CSO, as a leader, is charged with building a winning sales force. From time to time this may mean 'right-sizing', scaling up or down, finding people with different types of experience and ultimately making sure that the right people are in the right place at the right time to sell the company's products. Increasingly, technology is playing a role in the sales process, often eliminating or dramatically reducing face-to-face interactions between buyer and seller.

The increased use of technology in some cases will mean smaller sales forces; in other cases it will mean a different profile of sales representative is needed. Regardless of the changes being made, people will still be involved in many sales transactions for decades to come and, as such, the CSO will still bear responsibility for building a winning sales team.

The CSO's challenges

One of the key challenges of the CSO is to bridge the gap between sales and marketing, not only as an individual, but for the entire sales organization. Sales and marketing often don't 'speak the same language', but to operate both efficiently and effectively, they must, otherwise success is left to chance. One of the most effective ways to bridge this gap is, as stated earlier, to ensure that the CSO has some degree of ownership in the marketing strategy. For the sales organization as a whole, a comprehensive understanding of the marketing strategy, is more necessary than a thirty-slide PowerPoint file that is sent around on email or posted on the company website.

The relationship between the sales and marketing departments needs to be managed. The CSO and CMO should not expect it to happen automatically, even if the two executives have a good line of communication. While traditionally the sales department's role was to sell and work with customers and the marketing department's role was to handle everything else in the marketing mix, the world is now changing. The CSO and senior salespeople must be prepared to be actively involved in working with marketing to jointly make key decisions on branding, distribution, pricing, advertising and other key elements that traditionally were decided in marketing's ivory tower[5]. The roles of sales and marketing are blurring, emphasizing that the CSO must feel ownership of the marketing strategy.

If the CSO regularly has to reconvene his or her sales executives and sales force to re-explain the marketing strategy, perhaps this is a sign that something is inherently wrong at the marketing level. We have seen many companies that reinvent their strategy as a part of their annual cycle, and design course after course so that the 'people' will just 'understand' the latest iteration of strategy from HQ. Marketing strategy does not need to be overly complex or sophisticated to be highly effective; but it does have to be relatively easy to execute, the stage at which many a brilliant plan has failed. This point is important because so much time is wasted and confusion generated by the desire of the 'corporate types' to educate 'the field' on marketing strategy when in fact the strategy itself is fundamentally flawed.

The CSO's role is to make sure that the job of selling in his or her company is clear. This starts at the contact point between the company and the customer. The key determinants to having a clear sales task are defining:[6]

- Which customers?
- Which products and/or services?
- What activities are the sales force expected to do (and not do)?
- What are the key internal interface points between the sales force and other parts of the company?

Having a clearly defined selling process is absolutely vital. While the CSO and the headquarters may be in charge of making this happen, the groundwork must be done out in the field, involving key customers, salespeople and any organization that touches the sales process.

Another key CSO challenge is making sure that the sales force is properly designed. The following questions[7] should be discussed:

- How many sales forces should the company have?
- How should they be organized: reporting lines, geography, etc.?
- How should a sales representative (or team) be educated? What skills are needed in the room to close the sale?
- How are borders (between reps and sales forces) determined so as to reward people properly, encourage competition, but discourage in-fighting?

At the operational level, once the marketing strategy and selling task are clear, and the proper organizational design has been completed, the CSO's job is still not finished. There also needs to be a proper measurement system in place, with key performance indicators that go deeper than just total sales volume. A proper sales measurement system will also encompass key pieces of information that feed into systems that support marketing (including measurements from both inside and outside the company) and human resources (for compensation and development purposes).[8]

While the CSO will spend a great deal of time shaping an effective sales organization and working with the marketing department, there are of course executive-level challenges. A CSO's role within the executive team is to ensure that the marketing strategy is sound before it gets communicated to the sales organization. This is vital. Embedded in the challenge of bridging this sales and marketing gap are the relative positions of the CMO and CSO, when they are both at the same level, reporting to the CEO.

In organizations with a strong CMO, the CSO will often have to fight to keep a seat at the executive table. It is well known, through the eye of any marketing executive, that sales is just a subset of marketing and in any case, their job is to execute, not to think. The CSO must have broad enough experience and knowledge of how marketers see themselves to be an effective defender of sales at the executive level. The CSO must show the CEO and others how occupying a seat, at the ever-more-crowded executive table, brings value to the organization. CSOs are often well spoken and used to selling; selling their right to remain at the table may be one of the toughest deals they close.

In companies where the CSO is stronger than the CMO, the CSO's challenge may actually be to focus more on the long-term strategic thinking that marketing brings to the table. If the CSO is the twenty-year sales veteran who has sold everything and anything to everyone, then changing his or her mindset to think beyond the latest target may be significant. But it is absolutely vital in order to play an appropriate executive role. The CXO team is charged with the task of balancing long-term and short-term objectives and the conflicts this embodies often show themselves in the sales vs. marketing arena.

The CSO and their colleagues on the CXO team

Much of the chapter has focused on the relationship between sales and marketing and the CMO and CSO. This section will focus on the relationship between the CSO and some of the other CXOs.

One of the less-obvious but most-important relationships for the CSO is with the CHRO. Managing the sales force and designing and implementing effective sales management policies will often require a significant amount of work and deal-making with HR. The sales force, more than most functions in the company, will often push the boundaries of the generally-accepted ways of doing business in the company. Due to commissions and bonus schemes, the top salespeople may be paid more than many of the CXOs; this will certainly be a point of contention.

In order to secure a sale, a sales representative may make promises or engage in actions that the company's attorneys or CGO would frown upon, not to mention how governments or regulatory bodies would react. With the big rewards of having a high-performing sales force, comes the risk of problems and bad publicity. Managing the conflicts and contradictions inherent in this part of the business will again often require executive attention. Here, a thoughtful CSO should engage the help of the HR department to ensure that sound policies are designed that not only encourage the right wealth-maximizing behaviour of the sales force, but also the right cultural and ethical behaviour to match the culture that the company is trying to foster.

Depending on the products, and if the company does their own R&D, the CSO will often interact with the chief technology officer (CTO). For many products, the sales force gets requests for technical features that customers would like to have. The CTO and the CSO both have an incentive to ensure open communication among their staff. In many companies, having an organized way for the sales force to have a say in what the R&D people are working on (and reasonable information on the current status and expected release of new products) brings a great deal of synergy to the organization. Likewise, the sales force may be a good reference point for the R&D group to help prioritize where their time and money are spent.

The CSO will often have a tough relationship with the chief supply chain officer (CSCO) and/or chief manufacturing officer (CMO), especially if promises for product delivery dates and product specifications are not met. The salesperson is often the front line of contact not only to take orders, but to hear about problems. The CSO will certainly let the CSCO and CMO know if their departments are not satisfying customers' requirements.

Finally, the CSO will often have a CFO to contend with. The CFO, in this role, will often oversee and control the amount that the sales department inevitably spends in the name of 'entertainment' and other selling expenses. The CSO will not only have to justify that selling expenses are at a reasonable level, but that expenses are in line with corporate policy, accounting and otherwise. It is often through sales channels and budgets that are loosely controlled that trouble can arise over the improper spending of company money.

The role of CSOs in the CXO team is often a lively one. They can be the hero or the scapegoat from one month to the next and have the possibility of being the best friend or worst competitor of any of their CXO colleagues. A 'dynamic' sales personality, if well channelled and controlled, can be a force for progress around the CXO table; if not, it can be a source of disruption. It comes down to the incumbent CSO, as well as how much latitude is allowed by the CEO.

The future of the CSO's role

The CSO role and the question of whether it is really needed at the CXO table face an uncertain future. Large companies will almost always have an executive in charge of sales, but they may not be needed at the CXO level. One main argument for that is that sales is a subset of marketing and the CMO should have an executive in charge of sales reporting to him or her, but not as part of the CXO team.

If the central marketing function is well run by the CMO, and marketing and sales communicate and work well together, then the above view that having a separate CSO will make the CXO table more crowded than it needs to be, is correct.

However, in some companies and in some situations, having a CSO for a certain time period makes a lot of sense. When a CEO wants or needs to drive sales growth as one of the company's top objectives, having an executive focused only on sales at the CXO level can be very effective. If two large companies merge and there are two distinct sales forces that, when merged, will likely cause considerable challenges, having a CSO from the executive team who is the ultimate decision- and policy-maker during the transition phase can send a powerful message and help to resolve the post-merger challenges. Finally, if the CMO is in too weak a position to be effective on a global basis, having a CSO to assist with promoting the marketing agenda and company strategy is necessary.

The CSO position is in decline. Given the choice of having a CXO-level marketing executive or a CXO-level sales executive, it makes sense in most companies to choose the marketing executive as it should be marketing strategy that drives sales, not the reverse. In choosing to have or retain a CSO, the CEO should assess whether there is room at the top for this role and what deficiencies there are in Marketing that require a CSO on the top executive team.

Assessing the role of the chief sales officer

The following questions provide a starting point when assessing the role of the chief sales officer.

Purpose

1. How effectively does the chief sales officer:
   - Manage the process of revenue growth?
   - Retain and reward high-performing sales staff?
   - Foster a culture of education and sharing of best practices?
   - Use customer feedback and information technology strategically?
   - Balance short-term sales growth targets with priorities from marketing: namely strategic priorities and profitable sales growth?

Direction

2. Effectiveness – does the CSO do and say the right things? Is he or she a model of corporate citizenship, making it clear that while sales growth is important, so too are corporate ethics. Does the CSO foster teamwork whereby the sales force is seen to work as a team with the rest of the company or is the sales force considered a maverick organization?
3. Efficiency – does the CSO do things at the right cost, balancing the needs and understanding of the overall company objectives? Is there a sales process in place so that the right amount of time is being dedicated to the right customers and sales opportunities?
4. How well does the CSO combine and balance top line revenue growth with the company's overall strategic direction and priorities? Is the CSO able to wear several hats and balance CXO and sales responsibilities?

Focus

5. How well does the CSO build and develop a winning team? Is there good communication between sales and marketing, do they support each other and understand each other's goals and roles? Could some of the CSO's team members ascend to CXO roles?

6. Do the compensation and reward systems drive the right performance from the sales staff from both a sales growth and ethical standpoint?
7. Does the CSO effectively manage performance and support corporate objectives and initiatives – again, managing by example? Or do they defend the way that 'their' sales force does things and look at their people as an exception and not having to follow corporate? Is the CSO a team player?
8. Does the CSO hire team players with high capacities – people who work with other functions and the corporate headquarters as well as other salespeople?
9. Is the CSO able to voice his or her opinion to the CEO? Is the CSO respected by CXO colleagues even during disagreements with marketing and about company strategy? Is the CSO a strong leader who could go further?

Glossary

B2B
B2B is short for 'business to business'. It tends to be used in reference to a wide variety of interactions between two different businesses, in a commercial sense and is often referred to in a sales exchange and juxtaposed to B2C, see below.

B2C
B2C is short for 'business to customer'. It tends to be used in reference to a wide variety of interactions, between one business and the end customer who is an individual rather than a business entity, in a commercial sense and is often referred to in a sales exchange and juxtaposed to B2B, see above.

Big pharma
The top twenty to thirty pharmaceutical companies in the world. These companies generally have revenues of several billion dollars a year, are present internationally in the US, Europe and Asia, and generally have fully-staffed units for R&D, marketing, sales, manufacturing and regulatory compliance.

Top line

This refers to the top line of the income (profit and loss) statement of a company. The top line is normally gross revenues before any deductions of costs, expenses, overheads, etc.

Notes

1 K. Kashani, 'From strategy to sales', *Management Decision*, 25(4) (1987), pp. 10–11.
2 Kashani, 'From strategy to sales', p. 11.
3 B. P. Shapiro, A. J. Slywotzky and S. X. Doyle, 'Strategic sales management: A boardroom issue', Harvard Business School 9-595-018, (Rev. 6 May 1998), p. 1.
4 Kashani, 'From strategy to sales', p. 12.
5 Shapiro, Slywotzky and Doyle, 'Strategic sales management', p. 12.
6 Shapiro, Slywotzky and Doyle, 'Strategic sales management', p. 9.
7 Shapiro, Slywotzky and Doyle, 'Strategic sales management', p. 11.
8 Shapiro, Slywotzky and Doyle, 'Strategic sales management', pp. 13–15.

7 *The Chief Supply Chain Officer – Designing and managing lean and agile supply chains*

CARLOS CORDÓN AND KIM SUNDTOFT HALD

The challenge for the operations function is to produce high-quality goods and services on time, at minimum cost while responding to shifting market demands. This requires understanding and management of the whole supply chain from beginning to end. Executives responsible for operations in both manufacturing and service businesses face similar challenges in supply chain optimization.

As outsourcing has increased and companies co-ordinate with customers and suppliers, the importance of operations management has progressed rapidly. In this chapter the authors outline the developments that have lifted the role of the senior operations officer into that of the chief supply chain officer (CSCO), and discuss the challenges faced today and those of the future.

The operations management task

Our objective today is to deliver the products and services our customers require on time, with perfect quality and at a minimum cost. Whether we make them ourselves or not is irrelevant for the customer.

(VP Manufacturing and Sourcing, pharmaceuticals company)

Operations is responsible for producing the goods and services that the company sells. This function must orchestrate effective planning, organization and control of all the resources and activities necessary to manage the supply chain from beginning to end (see Figure 7.1). In today's business world, efficient supply chain management is necessary to remain competitive and profitable. Underperform, and customers and shareholders will punish you.

Management of the supply chain and transformation of business processes are two main areas of operations management's responsibility. Managing the supply chain encompasses the process from the supplier's internal operations until end-customer delivery. Transformation

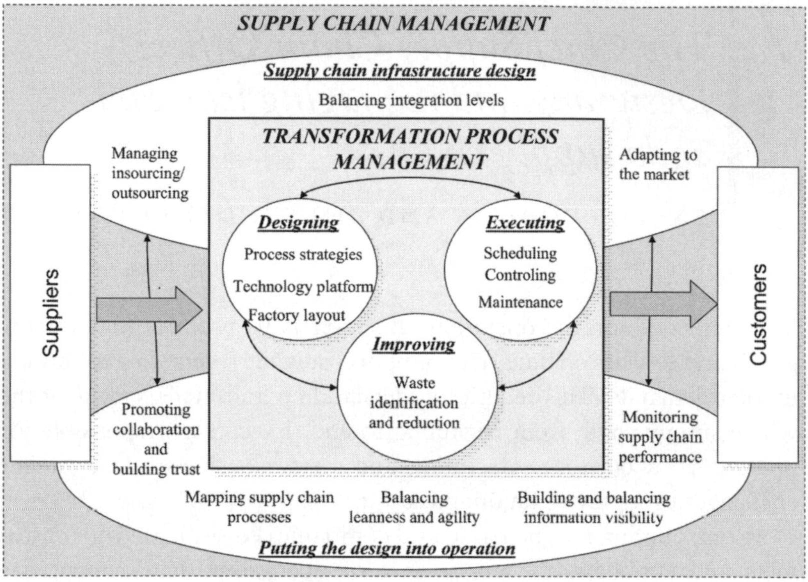

Figure 7.1: The operations management task

process management more narrowly focuses on the optimization and management of internal production activities.

Supply chain management is the more senior and established of the two roles. The effective integration of both internal and external operations is a key competitiveness driver in every company. Designing, refining and implementing new processes are key supply chain activities. Supply chains often develop in layers over time, through expansions, mergers and product changes. Managers often inherit a patchwork; creating a supply chain from the beginning is a luxury.

Designing supply chain infrastructure involves three main strategic activities. The CSCO's team is constantly searching for efficient solutions to improve **the flow** of material, resources and information. Secondly, they carefully consider which activities to perform **internally, rather than outsource**. Balancing the **integration levels** within the company's infrastructure is a third key strategic activity.

Progressing from design into operation involves five main activities:

1 Mapping and managing supply chain processes;
2 Building and balancing information visibility;

3 Promoting collaboration and building trust;
4 Balancing the dual targets of leanness and agility;
5 Monitoring and reporting on supply chain performance.

Business transformation focuses more on tactical and operational issues. Its aim is to optimize production and to support supply chain strategy and design. Business transformation involves three main activities: design, execution and continuous improvement of internal processes.

Effective process design requires clearly defined deliverables: what are the key inputs, outputs and interactions or connection points with other processes? Designers must balance efficiency and flexibility. Executing internal operations is about maintaining reliable processes and minimizing supply chain interruptions. Finally, process improvement focuses on identifying opportunities for waste reduction and efficiency gains without a comprehensive re-design. A continuous feedback loop of key process measurements is imperative to improve quality and reduce costs.

Operations management is both complex and challenging. It is the backbone of many companies and must remain both solid and flexible. Effective operations managers require advanced skills in design and execution. Clear alignment with business strategy is vital. For CSCOs to deliver a winning (high-quality and profitable) supply chain, they must harness the business imperatives described earlier in the book: leadership, talent and learning.

In the following sections, we explore the historical role of operations management. We track the progression from senior operations manager to today's chief supply chain officer, a key member of the company's executive leadership.

The emergence of the senior leadership role – chief supply chain officer (CSCO)

To understand the role of today's CSCO it is useful to have an overview of the many historical initiatives that have influenced operations management thinking. These include the MRP (materials requirements planning) systems in the 1980s, total quality management and just-in-time manufacturing that became popular in the early 1990s, and lean manufacturing and re-engineering in the late 1990s. Today, efforts to improve demand and supply chain management remain widespread. Each phase has contributed to the quest for an optimal balance between value and cost as companies strive to remain competitive.

Most manufacturing companies have historically placed a strong internal emphasis on the plant or factory. Operations only became 'noticed' when there were disruptions to production and supply: e.g. strikes, disasters, raw material shortages or quality problems. In the words of a retired pharmaceutical CEO, the focus of the operations officer in the past was to 'cause no problems'. That is, deliver the product when needed, with the required quality, at a reasonable cost. The supply chain often played a back-seat role to the more publicly noticed sides of the business such as marketing, sales and finance.

Until the 1970s, the senior operations officer was either the factory boss, or the boss of the factory bosses.[1] Typically, senior operations officers were engineers or administrators in charge of planning the construction and operation of their companies' productive assets. They tended to progress through line jobs in the factory to the top of their function.

Increasing competitiveness and the dropping of trade barriers led to the need for business innovation in many companies. The improvement programmes of the 1980s and 1990s changed the focus of the role from *maintenance* of operations to *improvement*. Business leaders realized that producing higher quality and lower-cost products with less waste and inventory in the supply chain was strategically more valuable. Effective end-to-end supply chain management was the answer. Consequently, companies recruited more senior operations officers from quality and process improvement backgrounds.

Then companies began the march towards outsourcing, driven by the quest to contain costs, and enabled by technology improvements. Integration of operations with customers and suppliers started to become more common. Consequently, operations' focus widened from looking at the manufacturing line to encompass all the activities from supply through to customer service.

Historically, the senior operations officer was responsible for making the plant run efficiently. The role matured. Integration now meant working with many partners both inside the company and externally.

Senior operations officers with backgrounds in planning, logistics and purchasing become more prevalent. There were two reasons for this change in scope:

1 The need grew for greater co-ordination and integration within the supply chain.
2 There was more emphasis on sourcing because procurement costs could represent up to 80 per cent of total product costs for some businesses.

The CSCO was now responsible for making sure that each of the supply chain partners fulfilled their roles – inside and outside the company. Today's executives must focus on supply chain integration. They incorporate the entire supply chain into a larger and seamless system. Partners in the supply chain must be able to work both independently and together. Optimization of performance must occur at both the company and individual levels.

The changing scope of the senior operations officer role is evident in the titles used. Some examples include supply chain director, supply chain vice-president or senior vice-president of purchasing. From now on we will refer to the senior operations officer as the chief supply chain officer (CSCO).

The CSCO has partially evolved from the chief manufacturing officer role (CMaO). While the CMaO role has also evolved independently (see chapter 8), it was previously characterized as being reactive and inward looking, optimizing operations inside the factory and focused on cost. Today's CSCO has evolved beyond this into designer, manager and steward of the entire supply chain (see Figure 7.2).

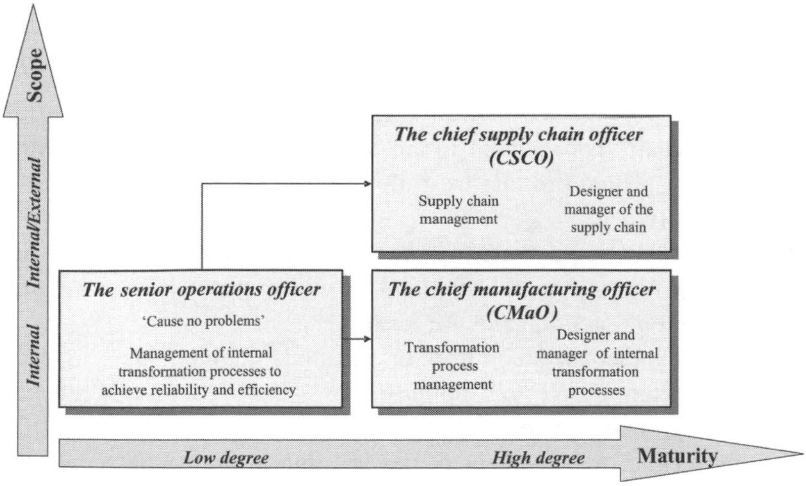

Figure 7.2: Changes in the role of the senior operations officer

The CSCO as designer and manager of the supply chain

Traditionally, companies have viewed themselves as independent entities, competing with other companies in order to survive and create wealth for their shareholders. Today's successful CSCOs have had to adopt another way of thinking.

This new philosophy recognizes that while wealth creation remains important, each member of the supply chain has an effect on the performance of the others, the overall supply chain and the ultimate end-customer. Long-term survival is at stake; partners must be chosen carefully. Competition is no longer company versus company, but supply chain versus supply chain[2]. It is important that this viewpoint is apparent in all aspects of the CSCO's management of the supply chain.

> Ninety per cent or more of the decisions I make today involve our suppliers in some aspect or another. They are either caused by them or they certainly affect their operations. Realizing this fact, I constantly train myself to think about the wider picture when I make decisions. (Supply Chain Vice-President, manufacturing company)

Ultimately, the CSCO is in charge of managing the set of processes that enable a firm to supply products and services. How can today's CSCO succeed in the complex job of optimizing a supply chain from beginning to end? In addition, what are the most important functions and competencies needed in order for the CSCO to succeed? These are the key questions that we answer in the following sections of this chapter.

First, we take a closer look at what supply chain management (SCM) means. Some of the most-used definitions have proven to be the most valuable:

- Supply chain management is the effort involved in producing and delivering a final product from the supplier's supplier to the customer's customer.[3]
- Supply chain management is the integration of business processes from end user to original suppliers, providing products, services and information that add value for customers.[4]
- The simultaneous integration of consumer requirements, internal processes and upstream supplier performance is commonly referred to as supply chain management.[5]
- Supply chain management is the integration and management of supply chain organizations and activities through co-operative

organizational relationships, effective business processes and high levels of information sharing to create high-performing value systems that provide member organizations with a sustainable competitive advantage.[6]

As these definitions indicate, the successful CSCO must employ a wide range of leadership styles to manage complexity. Most important, the CSCO must be process oriented, and focused on finding the right balance of integration in the supply chain.

The ***process-oriented*** CSCO views internal business processes as part of the broader inter-organizational business process chain. The CSCO must identify the key supply chain processes and set strategic and measurable targets for process improvements. This may require small-scale changes or complete process redesign. ***Integration*** is another key concern. Effective CSCOs know that a truly integrated supply chain does more than reduce costs: it creates value through increased speed and agility in operations. The company, its supply chain partners and its stakeholders can profit from this value.[7]

Different companies choose different levels of integration in their supply chains. The CSCO is responsible for assessing the gap between current and desired levels of integration. The CSCO must then co-ordinate with the other CXOs in business process implementation and overall company strategy. The level of integration in current operations can be assessed using a four-stage model[8] (see Figure 7.3 below).

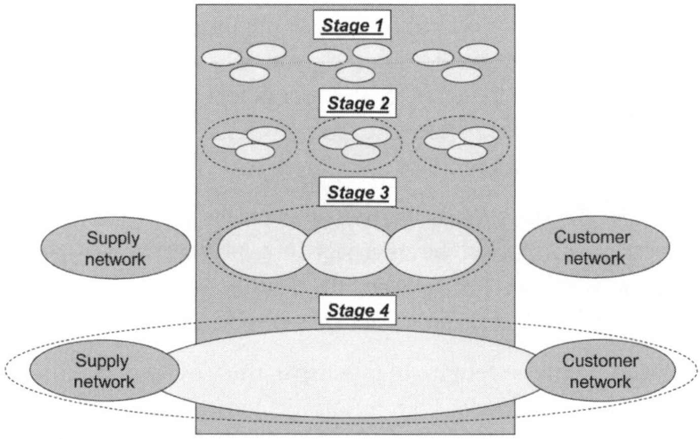

Figure 7.3: A four-stage categorization of supply chain integration

1 At the most basic stage, all internal and external activities and functions operate independently from their respective environments.
2 At the second stage, each of the internal functions acts as an integrated whole.
3 At the third stage, the company operates as one seamlessly connected system or unit.
4 At the fourth and most advanced stage, the company and its supply chain partners work as an integrated whole.

Assessing current and future levels of integration alone is not enough. To succeed, the CSCO must contemplate the following questions:

- What should we outsource and what should we insource?
- What functions should be centralized or decentralized and where should centralized operations be located?
- What benefits can we reap by integrating with customers and suppliers?
- What risks are associated with higher or lower levels of integration?
- What tools can increase the level of integration between our company and our supply chain partners?

In the remainder of this chapter, we look to answer these important questions faced by the CSCO. First, however, we will look at the top-line design challenges. Then we will take a closer look at how the CSCO puts the design into action.

The top-line design challenges faced by the CSCO

CEOs in an expanding list of industries are including supply chain management on their strategic agendas. As more and more markets transform into commodity markets, customers perceive little difference between the products offered. Therefore, companies are turning to their supply chain as a way to differentiate themselves from their competitors.

We are very involved at every level. We are the ones driving all the margin planning and execution for the company. Right now, we are engaged in helping our salespeople win. We know exactly how what we are doing affects the company.

(Supply chain president of a leading US electronics company)

In order for the company to remain competitive, the CSCO must ensure that the supply chain is a key differentiating factor. He or she must constantly seek to design and manage a lean and agile supply chain that supports the company's overall strategy.

The CSCO must be proactive in identifying opportunities for the CEO, thereby influencing the overall company strategy. The CSCO must also be reactive by designing and running a supply chain that supports the overall strategy, and co-ordinating activities with the other CXOs. As more companies embrace business process thinking, traditional roles are threatened. Responsibilities at the CXO level are changing with some companies migrating from functional organizations to process organizations in assigning responsibilities.

But how can and should the CSCO design a supply chain that matches the overall company strategy? What is the optimal supply chain design? Which parameters should be the guiding principles in designing the supply chain?

It is important for the CSCO to search for the answers to these questions when faced with the top-line design challenge. Successful CSCOs have found that exploring the following three areas is useful in coming up with the most focused answers:

1 Learning about and adapting to the market;
2 Managing insourcing/outsourcing decisions;
3 Balancing integration levels within the supply chain.

Learning about and adapting to the market

Most companies lack a framework for deciding what type of supply chain is best suited to their different products and services. The effective CSCO creates competitive advantage by designing supply chains that meet the needs of the end market while making sense in light of company strategy.

The first step in designing a supply chain is to consider the type of product sold. There are two broad types of products and services – functional and innovative.

Functional products and services are standard and tend to have many substitutes. They satisfy basic customer needs (businesses or end consumers). The demands for these products and services tend to be relatively stable in an industry. However, individual companies can experience big variations due to competitive factors. Functional products often have long life cycles.

The frequent introduction of new features differentiates innovative products and services from their competitors. Therefore, the operations function does not have a long demand history on which to base a forecast; the supply chain must be adaptive. The demand for new products and services is often unpredictable and unstable. The life cycles of innovative products can be short. Some innovations migrate to become functional products by creating a new market or extending an existing one.

Companies producing commodities typically have a higher proportion of functional products. Other industries, such as high-tech and fashion, compete primarily with innovative products and services.

The well-informed CSCO realizes that the game of competition changes depending on whether the company is producing a functional or an innovative product. Designers of supply chains must consider the product's characteristics; one size does not fit all (see Figure 7.4).[9]

When a company's products or services are primarily functional, the top priority in the supply chain design should be efficiency. When its products or services are primarily innovative, the supply chain should be designed to be responsive.

As one supply chain vice-president of a global hearing-aid producer expressed:

> For our new and innovative products, our top brands, it's in the first half year of their market life, before our competitors catch up, that we earn all our money. Being flexible, fast and responsive in our supply chain operations in this stage is, therefore, of major importance for us.

In summary, the first step for CSCOs in the high-level design of their supply chains is to adjust to the product. It is necessary to explore and understand which goals the company must pursue for each of its

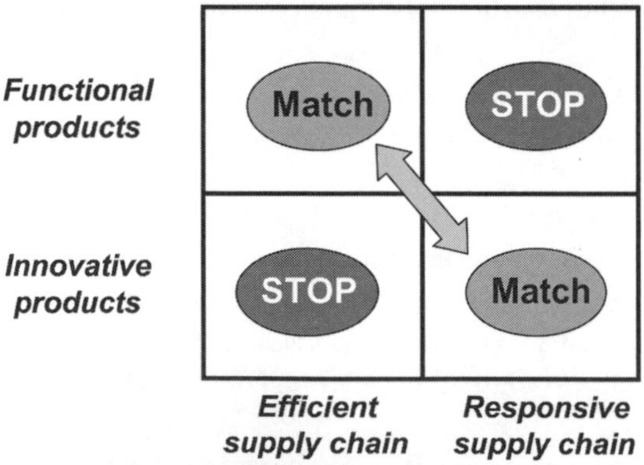

Figure 7.4: Linking product and service characteristics to supply chain design

products and services. The CSCO must decide whether efficiency and cost, or responsiveness and time compression, are the main drivers for each supply chain.

Managing insourcing and outsourcing decisions

The next key design challenge faced by the CSCO is deciding what to insource or outsource. Numerous studies suggest that there are many benefits associated with outsourcing: it can reduce costs, improve asset efficiency and increase profits. However, deciding which activities a company should outsource is complex and often involves a considerable amount of risk.[10] There is a great deal of evidence that many companies get things terribly wrong when outsourcing, with costs increasing and quality deteriorating.

The CSCO must realize that, when production or services are outsourced, responsibility for quality, customer satisfaction and even cost remains in their domain. When it comes to decisions about what to outsource, the CSCO should take care not to outsource the wrong things, i.e. the company's core competencies.[11]

> There is a question about whether or not to outsource, and at the moment our approach is not to outsource when the management of the activity can be considered core. However, some activities we consider non-strategic, and here we have a good reason to outsource if we can lower costs.
>
> (Senior vice-president of purchasing, large European retailer)

The CSCO must regularly assess where the company makes the greatest contribution to the overall success of the supply chain and hence the company. To do this, the CSCO must evaluate the competencies and capabilities of all the organizations in the supply chain. An effective learning and sharing culture throughout the chain is vital.

A structured process must be in place when managing sourcing decisions (see Figure 7.5). Financial considerations must support the decision to outsource. However, emotions are often at the base of decisions, which can cause intense internal fighting. The CSCO must counter this with a long-term and rational perspective that takes capabilities and long-term risks and opportunities into account. The CSCO must be keenly aware of internal politics; many walls and empires are bound to fall as the company continues to modernize its supply chain and business processes.

Financial-based considerations:

	Outsourcing	Insourcing
Cash flow	+	-
Cost	(+)	(-)

Operations-based considerations:

	Outsourcing	Insourcing
Visibility/Control	-	+
Flexibility	+	-
Complexity	-	+

Risk-based considerations:

	Outsourcing	Insourcing
Investment	+	-
Appropriation concerns	-	+

Figure 7.5: Financial, operational and risk-based factors give the CSCO input into the insourcing/outsourcing decision

A good insourcing versus outsourcing decision should cover at least four main areas:

1 Financial considerations, often driven by the CEO or CFO;
2 Operations-based considerations that should be raised by the CSCO;
3 Risk-based considerations that should concern both the CEO and CSCO;
4 Political considerations: managing expectations around the CXO team.

Financial considerations, which include cash flow and production costs, can often favour outsourcing. However, total cost issues can go both ways.

Operations-based considerations, such as visibility, quality control and the complexity of interacting with a supply chain partner (which can result in slower reaction times), will often favour keeping activities in-house. On the other hand, considerations such as flexibility and capacity will favour outsourcing. Michael Dell reinforced this when he explained why Dell had been able to grow so much faster than its competitors:[12]

Suppose we have two suppliers building monitors for us, and one of them loses its edge. It's a lot easier for us to get more capacity from the remaining supplier than to set up a new manufacturing plant ourselves. (Michael Dell, founder and CEO of Dell Computers)

Finally, the CSCO must consider risk-based factors. If the activity or production task involves a considerable investment, outsourcing may decrease the transaction-specific investments and risk for the company. On the other hand, if the activity involves proprietary or sensitive content, suppliers might start up their own, similar and competing activity. This is an argument for keeping the activity inside the company.

As companies focus on their core activities and outsource non-core functions, their success increasingly depends on their ability to control and influence the whole supply chain. This leads us back to the issue of integration. Effective CSCOs realize that they need to look at the sourcing decision and its consequences in conjunction with how to balance the level of integration within the supply chain.

Balancing integration levels within the supply chain

Balancing integration levels within the supply chain is critical. The CSCO must first promote internal integration. Then, as supply chains span organizational borders, it is essential to build bridges with external supply chain partners.

A key role of the CSCO is to enlist suppliers and customers in an effort to develop products faster and to reduce manufacturing costs. The question is: how can this be achieved? The CSCO needs to decide what level of integration is required for each link in the chain and then identify and apply the tools to reach the desired level. Again, an effective learning and communication environment throughout the supply chain is vital.

What level of integration and management to apply?

The first step in integrating externally is to identify and assess key customers and suppliers. It is inefficient to integrate all the links in the supply chain: more integration is not necessarily better. A balanced approach is more effective as integration is a dynamic process that requires adjustment over time.

The task of allocating company resources, such as service to customers and development to suppliers becomes crucial. The CSCO orchestrates this allocation by communicating company principles directly to his management team. Indirect communication is also important through the way in which company strategy, company values and procedures that support such internal resource allocation are communicated.

There are three important links to consider when allocating a company's supply chain resources.[13]

1 ***Managed process links*** are those that the company judges important to integrate and manage. Typically, these links have a significant impact on the performance of the company. An example would be servicing a large customer, or a supplier delivering scarce or proprietary products or competencies.
2 ***Monitored process links*** are links that are not as important, and where the company does not need a high degree of integration. It is still important that these links be integrated and managed appropriately. They should be monitored on a continuous basis.
3 ***Non-managed process links*** are links that the company is neither managing nor monitoring. The CSCO and his or her management team do not find these links critical enough to allocate resources to them.

The company has a limited pool of resources. The decision of what the company should not manage and monitor is as important as what they should manage and monitor. Key customers and suppliers will suffer if too many resources are allocated to less important customers, suppliers or functions. A non-optimized and underperforming supply chain will undermine company profitability and the ability to adapt to future changes in the business environment.

How to integrate the supply chain

There are three major alternatives for the CSCO to drive and balance integration in the supply chain. It is important that the CSCO adjusts the levels of use according to specific supply chain or sourcing strategies.

- ***Information sharing*** is the first option. At this stage, data and information are openly exchanged between the company and its supply chain partners. Specifically, the CSCO fosters the sharing of demand forecasts, production schedules, promotion plans and/or shipment schedules. However, the partners receiving the information have no influence. Their only option is to adjust operations to fit. Integration and information sharing can and should be enhanced in the supply chain with information technology. Later in the chapter, we discuss this in more depth.

- ***Co-ordination*** is the second alternative. At this stage decision rights are delegated to the best-positioned supply chain member, or combination of members. Vendor-managed inventory (VMI) systems are an example of a system used at this integration level. In VMI systems, suppliers receive information on customer inventory levels and forecasts of expected future demand. Suppliers decide when and how much to deliver to fit with internal operations and customers' requirements.
- ***Collaboration*** is the final stage. Establishing common goals and building organizational linkages are completed. Participating members share the risks, costs and gains. Work shifts upstream or downstream through outsourcing. Resources are redeployed, consolidated and shared between members of the supply chain. A discussion of how to promote collaboration and build trust occurs in more detail later in this chapter.

Putting the design into operation

In this section, we look at how the CSCO puts the supply chain design into operation. The CSCO must focus on five key areas to implement the design:

1 Mapping and managing supply chain processes;
2 Building and balancing information visibility using IT;
3 Promoting collaboration and building trust;
4 Balancing the dual targets of leanness and agility;
5 Monitoring and reporting on supply chain performance.

Mapping and managing supply chain processes

Both practitioners and academics have proposed several different sets of standard supply chain business processes. The supply chain operations reference model (SCOR-model), proposed by the supply chain council, is widely practised in US and European companies.

The SCOR-model gives standard descriptions of management processes and a framework of relationships to connect them. The model also suggests metrics to measure performance and best-in-class supply-chain management practices for each of the identified processes.

The principle of the SCOR-model is describing the processes in increasing levels of detail. This allows the CSCO to use the level of sophistication required at the time of adoption. The SCOR-model identifies five core supply chain processes (see Figure 7.6).[14]

- ***Plan*** is the process that balances aggregated demand and supply to develop a course of action which best meets sourcing, production and delivery requirements.
- ***Source*** is the process that procures goods and services to meet planned or actual demand.
- ***Make*** is the process that transforms products into a finished state to meet planned or actual demand.
- ***Deliver*** is the process that provides finished goods and services to meet planned or actual demand. Typically, this process includes order management, transportation management and distribution management.
- ***Return*** is the process associated with returning or receiving returned products for any reason. This process extends into post-delivery customer support.

The strength of the SCOR-model (and other similar models) is the standardized format and terminology to facilitate communication between the different supply chain partners. CSCOs need to focus on the critical supply chain processes that enable them to satisfy customer needs. The SCOR-model is a useful tool for benchmarking, designing and reconfiguring the supply chain to achieve desired levels of performance.

Building and balancing information visibility using IT

The activities carried out in the supply chain are often scattered across companies and geographies. The supply chain's information platform is the glue that binds the supply chain together. A significant role for the CSCO is to set priorities for the use of information systems in operations.

> I can't think of one single aspect where we don't use software to manage our supply chain operations. It starts from the moment our customer places the order on the internet until it's delivered to them. Once in a while we learn how dependent we are on them (i.e. the IT systems), it's when 'something happens' in the IT-department and the systems we use break down. I remember especially one incident, right after implementing our new ERP-system. At that time we were not able to deliver products out of our main inventory location for three days, it was nerve breaking and it nearly killed us.
>
> (Supply Chain Director in mid-sized European-based consumer goods company)

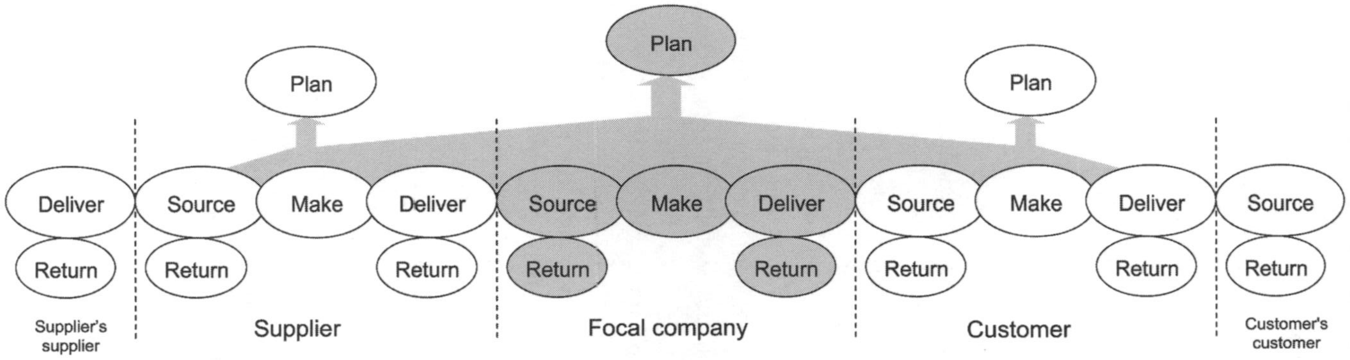

Figure 7.6: The supply chain operations reference model

A few of the considerations that the CSCO must deal with when converting to electronic supply chain management (e-SCM) are:[15]

- What are the key functions of the IT systems both internally and externally?
- How can the use of standardized software make the supply chain more efficient and responsive?
- Where are the optimal points for information exchanges?
- Where are the shortcomings in information visibility and availability?
- What are the best solutions to enable collaboration in real-time?

A traditional and important role of IT was to aid efficiency by assisting the automation and standardization of business processes. However, the CSCO must also use IT as an enabler of visibility and integration in the wider supply chain. This is especially true inside the factory walls. Chapter 8, which looks at the role of the chief manufacturing officer (CMaO), discusses this in more detail.

When used properly, IT systems foster information sharing, co-ordination and collaboration. They can also be vehicles for adjusting the levels of integration and visibility in supply chain processes as discussed previously.

Enterprise resource planning (ERP) systems (e.g. SAP or Oracle) have made information accessible to a wider community both inside and outside a company. This integrated and real-time platform is a prerequisite for moving a company to a stage 3 category of integration (see Figure 7.3). Even today, most ERP systems focus on integration within the company.[16] It is the CSCO's responsibility to expand the scope of the IT platform beyond company borders.

Several different solutions can facilitate information sharing. For example, electronic data interchange (EDI) facilitates the exchange of information, formats and standards enabling better sharing and coordination. Other solutions, such as advanced planning systems (APS), are supply chain planning tools. They assist companies in building and executing the optimal allocation of resources across the supply-chain.

Another distinction is between systems that promote long-term relationships and systems that foster short-term, transaction-oriented, price-focused relationships (i.e. e-auctions and e-marketplaces).

The CSCO wears many hats when it comes to the link between IT and putting the supply chain design into operation. The CSCO plays a key role in integrating and streamlining information exchanges between and among all of the partners in the supply chain. Finally, it is critical that the CSCO co-operates with the CIO to integrate supply chain issues into the wider IT platform of the company.

Promoting collaboration and building trust

As we mentioned previously, external supply chain partners have traditionally seen each other as adversaries. Business improvement initiatives have fostered an increased focus on core competencies and improvement in cost, quality and time. The resulting trend, which has led to an increase towards outsourcing, makes it essential for the CSCO to build relationships with key customers and suppliers.

Who are the key customers and key suppliers? Successful CSCOs understand the segmentation of supply chain partners. Each customer and each supplier is placed into a segment according to how much they contribute to the overall supply chain and company performance. To suit the competencies and value provided, the resources and commitment to each relationship needs adjusting.

For instance, it can make sense to build deep relationships with suppliers of critical components or if a product has a very small group of suppliers. On the other hand, minimal time and effort should be spent building relationships with suppliers that deliver standard components and no other obvious improvement to the supply chain. The CSCO must design strategies and structures that promote thinking strategically about trust relationships. This is a challenge that evolves over time. Supply chains are regularly consolidating through merger and acquisition (M&A) activity. This presents a risk that the new larger entity will demand the favoured conditions previously offered to one of the merging partners. The CSCO must be cautious.

Moving a supply chain relationship from a power game to a trust game can be difficult. It requires a management style that fosters a co-operative attitude towards business partners.

Working to increase the mutual attraction between the buyer and supplier has become a valuable trust-building technique. Toyota and Honda have come a long way in this regard compared to their US competitors Ford, GM and Chrysler. As the CEO of one supplier and a senior executive from another supplier put it:[17]

Honda is a demanding customer, but it is loyal to us. American automakers have us work on drawings, ask other suppliers to bid on them, and give the job to the lowest bidder. Honda never does that.

Toyota helped us dramatically improve our production system. We started by making one component, and as we improved, Toyota rewarded us with orders for more components. Toyota is our best customer.

From these two quotes, we can see that loyalties, recognition, tough performance-based rewards and inter-organizational help and learning all play key roles in building strong collaborative relationships between buyers and suppliers.

Output from our research indicates that in order to build a company's collaboration and trust through attractiveness, the effective CSCO must work with the purchasing director to understand and promote the supply chain partners' perceived comfort, dependence and relationship expectations.[18]

Balancing the dual targets of leanness and agility

We explained previously that successful CSCOs could create competitive advantages by designing and implementing supply chains that match market demand. But how does the CSCO put into practice the idea of distinguishing between functional and innovative products?

We have already discussed how efficiency and responsiveness play important roles for functional and innovative products. In order to connect these roles with the adjustment of supply chains to different product and service types, we need to introduce the concept of balancing the dual targets of leanness and agility.

- Leanness means developing a value stream that eliminates all waste, including time, and ensures a smooth and predictable output.
- Agility means using market knowledge and the virtual company to exploit profitable opportunities in a volatile marketplace; flexibility is built into the system.

Lean supply chains are suitable for functional products and services. CSCOs competing with lean supply chains must focus on quality, lead times and service levels as market qualifiers, and focus on cost as market winners (see Figure 7.7). Lean supply chains are also often referred to as the Toyota production system. It was Toyota that first

Agile supply	*Quality* *Cost* *Lead time*	*Service level*
Lean supply	*Quality* *Lead time* *Service level*	*Cost*
	Market qualifiers	**Market winners**

Figure 7.7: How to build and manage lean and agile supply chains[19]

adopted this way of thinking and even today it is Toyota that executes it to perfection.

Agile supply is suitable for innovative products and services. CSCOs competing with agile supply chains must focus on quality, cost and lead time as market qualifiers, and service levels as market winners (see Figure 7.7). The supply chain must be adaptable and flexible. However, this type of supply chain is most useful in markets dominated by short life cycles. In such market situations it is not a question of running a smooth and predictable operation, but rather of being capable of accelerating and decelerating production and supply. Companies operating in the technology sector should adopt an agile supply chain. Here Dell is an example of a company running an agile supply chain to perfection. However, companies outside the technology sector, competing on speed, such as Zara in the fashion industry, have demonstrated the power of an agile supply chain as a competitive weapon.

Leanness and agility are nothing without the integration of suppliers. As demonstrated by both Toyota and Dell, running both of these strategies to perfection implies that suppliers must be organized in fully integrated supplier networks.

In some cases, it is possible to combine the two approaches within the total supply chain setup. Decoupling points should be positioned to best suit the need for responding to a volatile demand downstream. These points must also provide level scheduling upstream from the marketplace (see Figure 7.8).[20]

To promote a different focus on quality, cost, lead time or service levels in different parts of the supply chain, the CSCO must design supporting performance measurement systems that are accurate, timely and trusted.

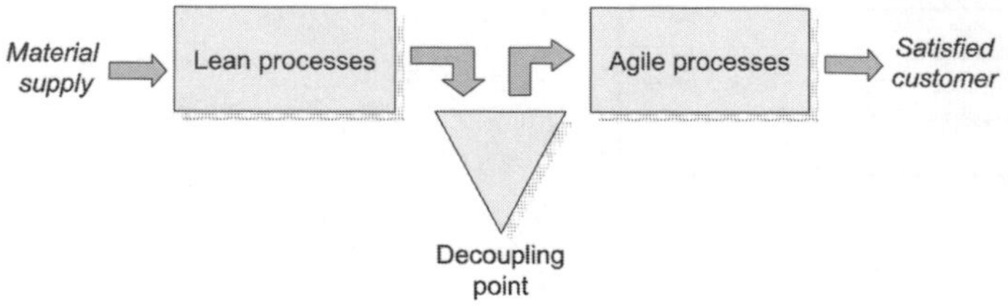

Figure 7.8: Combining lean and agile supply chains to achieve competitive advantages

Monitoring and reporting on supply chain performance

The final area to be explored is how the CSCO monitors and reports on supply chain performance. This is a crucial step in achieving success for the CSCO and the operations function. Monitoring performance in a structured way provides the information needed to make the necessary adjustments, and achieve an optimal supply chain operation.

Performance measurement systems are a valuable management tool for the CSCO. They provide the necessary guidance for converting design decisions and strategies into action and helping the CSCO and the CXO team to answer some of the following key questions:

- Are we on the right track?
- What are the causes behind the effects?
- What can we do better tomorrow?
- Where are the weak spots in the supply chain that cause delivery problems and excessive inventory levels?
- Where do we want to focus our attention to optimize the current operation?
- What are our priorities?

It is not an easy task to design and use such performance measurement systems. If not used properly, they can be costly and do more organizational harm than good. Therefore, it is critical that the CSCO takes great care in designing them.

Traditional financial accounting measures, like return-on-investment and earnings-per-share, are output oriented and give little guidance about the underlying causes behind them. In fact, they can be misleading when the CSCO is looking for opportunities for continuous improvement and innovation.[21] When used alone, they are a dangerous route to follow for the CSCO who is managing supply chain processes. A shrewd CSCO will form a strong partnership with the CFO in order to combine financial and operational measurements.

New measures and systems are required to manage the operations function and the supply chain. The CSCO must integrate these measurement systems so that they are linked, consolidated and in alignment with the overall company chain strategy. This means that the CSCO must communicate goals and expectations derived from the overall strategy to his management team.

The CSCO must also provide a measurement infrastructure in which the performance of different supply chain subprocesses and functions is visible to the other functions and processes, both internally and externally.

Finally, in order to make behavioural changes, the CSCO should work with the CHRO to link supply chain success and performance to individual bonuses and other types of recognition.

The future of the CSCO leadership role

Continuous economic, technological, political and social changes characterize today's business environment. To cope with these changes, companies, supply chains and people must respond by adjusting the way they operate. Change in business has become inherent; it is up to business leaders to manage and master their changing environment and keep both their skills and their company at the leading edge.

Operations tends to be the function under the most pressure to adapt; but it is also the most difficult to change because of the major investment involved. It is important that the CSCO play a key role in this adjustment and modernization process. Successful CSCOs are constantly searching for and forecasting future trends, seeking to improve the flexibility of their supply chains. Our research indicates that the most prominent emerging external trends for supply chains will be:

A continued geographical expansion of markets

Due to developments in political systems and infrastructures, more and more market barriers will disappear; others will appear. This will force many companies to think globally and locally at the same time. This means that the CSCO must focus on designing a flexible and adjustable supply chain infrastructure that can operate equally well both globally and locally. Historically this applied only to large businesses, now many small and medium-sized businesses must also think globally.

Continued customer pressures for individualized solutions

Customers will continue to demand individual solutions that fit their unique needs. In the future, customers will demand and get increasing opportunities for configuring the products and services delivered to them. This means that supply chains must be both flexible and responsive, and encourage customer involvement.

Building partnerships based on innovation, flexibility and speed

Some industries in the past, and even some today, focused on supplier partnerships that improved cost and quality. Tomorrow's fast-changing markets will shift the focus to partner selection and relationship management based on innovation, flexibility and speed. Teams and partnerships will form and disband as opportunities present themselves and then disappear.

Building modularity into the supply chain

Product modularity will be the basis of many supply chain strategies in the future. By building modularized products, supply chains become more responsive and innovative, i.e. divided into subsystems or modules. Tasks performed in the supply chain will go from sequential to parallel. Different companies can take responsibility for separate modules and a reliable product will result from the collective efforts of the supply chain.

Managing product developments and introductions faster

We are moving from a world in which the big eat the small to a world in which the fast eat the slow. This certainly applies to product development and introduction. Supply chains will continue to move away from long periods of stable production. Short and changing product runs and new product introductions will grow in frequency.

More frequent product updates and introduction will characterize future supply chains. This means that the CSCO must build a supply chain centred on new product development and capable of quickly accelerating and decelerating in recurring cycles.

Advancement in and integration of information and communication technologies

New and evolving business applications, combined with the explosive growth of the Internet, will continue to have a dramatic impact on the way that companies operate and interact. Managing these opportunities requires the development of a new set of skills and capabilities. The need to develop systems, processes and practices that support real-time sharing of information between trading partners is likely to be one of the most challenging areas in the next decade.

Environmentally sound supply chain management

Pressure on companies is mounting to take more responsibility for their environmental performance and the social implications of their trade. The movement to enhance regulations on hazardous goods, recycling, disposal and green packaging of products are but a few of the demands that have arisen from the increasing concern for the environment. Many companies also see green (money) by being green (proactive about environmental concerns); becoming more energy efficient, recycling waste and having a good corporate image can all help the bottom line. Demands to be socially and environmentally conscious will almost certainly increase in the future.

Since supply chains are integrated systems, environmental problems are intrinsically linked to the management of the chain.[22] The company must take a serious interest in what its suppliers, and the suppliers' suppliers, do to minimize pollution and run a socially responsible production. The CSCO must prepare for potential problems and opportunities both up and down the chain. The CXO team must formulate policies and strategies accordingly to deal with significant shifts not only in the market place but also in government policies and public opinion.

Handling reverse logistics

The liberalization of return policies, a growing emphasis on customer service, and the reuse of parts and packaging as part of environmentally sound supply chain management will result in an increased backward flow of goods through the supply chain. This in turn will put pressure on the need to manage reverse chains as an integrated part of the supply chain.

For the CSCO, managing reverse logistics can present an enormous challenge. Supply chain infrastructure and supply chain software solutions are often only concerned with bringing products and services downstream to customers. In this challenge, there are also great opportunities for keeping costs down and building customer loyalty.

In conclusion, the future of the CSCO leadership role is challenging. It will continue to grow in importance. The role's impact will make or break a business. Therefore, CSCOs must adopt flexible, adaptive, open, innovative and integrative leadership styles. They must increasingly work across the internal and external functions and processes in the supply chain. Many CSCOs will be promoted to the CEO role with their broad internal experience and external relationships.

Assessing the role of the CSCO

The following questions provide a starting point when assessing the role of the CSCO.

Purpose

1. How well does the CSCO articulate a clear, compelling vision and strategy for the supply chain?
2. Is the CSCO's purpose to do better things (transformation), or to do things better?
3. Is this purpose clearly understood, accepted and welcomed by customers, employees, the CXO team and partners?
4. Is the purpose of the IT system in use in operations to automate or to enhance communication, coordination and collaboration?

Direction

5. Does the CSCO adopt a process-oriented management style?
6. Does the CSCO understand the importance of internal integration and promote it?
7. How well does the CSCO balance integration levels in the supply chain?
8. Is the CSCO proactive in providing input to the overall company strategy?

9. How well does the CSCO cope with outsourcing issues?
10. Does the CSCO understand how the supply chain can be designed to match market demands?
    - The distinction between functional and innovative products and services? The distinction between lean and agile supply chains, and how they can be implemented?
    - Does the CSCO understand how IT can be used in balancing integration levels in the supply chain?
11. Have all of the important supply chain processes been mapped?
12. Does the CSCO understand and apply the following four principles needed to enhance profitability? How well does the CSCO:
    - Deliver customer value?
    - Focus on improving processes?
    - Build a culture of curiosity and experimentation?
    - Ensure that simplicity beats sophistication?

Focus

13. What is the scope of management? Is the CSCO predominately concerned with internal operations or are the operations of supply chain partners also a major concern of the CSCO?
14. Which performance measurement systems are in use? Are they integrated?
15. Does the CSCO diagnose, articulate and then influence others to ensure that the operations function delivers to the customer? In particular, does the CSCO display:
    - A constant quest for improvement?
    - Visionary thinking and active communication?
    - An ability to develop and engage people?
    - Respect, flexibility and openness to new ideas?

Glossary

The Supply-Chain Council
The Supply-Chain Council is an organization and community for those specializing in supply chain management. It was set up in 1996 and by 2005 had close to 1,000 corporate members.

Upstream

In supply chain management, upstream denotes the part of the supply chain flowing from the supply network, that is, from the suppliers' supplier to the company.

Downstream

In supply chain management, downstream denotes the part of the supply chain flowing from the company towards the customers in the end consumer market.

Life cycles

Product life-cycles are the time intervals in which a certain product or service produced by the company is distributed to the market. When life cycles are short, this means that the company constantly has to develop and introduce new products and services on the market to satisfy the needs of customers. On the other hand, when life cycles are long, this means that the company can focus more on operating an efficient and stable supply chain.

Benchmark

Benchmark in a supply chain context often means that a company compares its own performance in operations to that of its competitors to achieve best-in-class processes.

Decoupling point

The decoupling point is the point in the supply chain at which the customer's order penetrates. At this point, the order-driven flow from customers and the forecast-driven flow from the company and its suppliers meets. Typically, the physical evidence of the decoupling point is a main stock point from which the customer's orders are supplied.

Core competence

A core competence is a bundle of skills and technologies that enables a company to provide particular benefits to customers.

Just-in-time manufacturing

Just-in-time (JIT) is a management philosophy conceived by Toyota in the 1980s. The main principle in the philosophy is continuous and forced problem solving. In the production area delay times and inventory levels are kept at a minimum since the philosophy is that unnecessary inventories and delays mean inefficient use of resources and further hide underlying problems.

Top-line design

Top-line design challenges focus on supply chain strategy development and infrastructure design. It is top-line, since this group of operations management designs sets the frames inside which the rest of the operations management design tasks have to fit.

Notes

1 For more on this role, which still exists, although with changes in focus and outlook, please refer to chapter 8, which describes the role of the chief manufacturing officer (CMaO).

2 M. Christopher, 'Logistics and supply chain management – Strategies for reducing cost and improving service', *Financial Times* (Pitman Publishing, 1998).

3 Supply-Chain Council, chainorg/Resources (2002), available at: www.supply-chain.org/Resources/faq.htm.

4 D. M. Lambert, M. C. Cooper and J. D. Pagh, 'Supply chain management: Implementation issues and research opportunities', *International Journal of Logistics Management* 9 (2) (1998), pp. 1–19.

5 K-C Tan, V. J. Kannan, R. B. Handfield and S. Ghosh, *International Journal of Operations and Production Management*, 19 (10) (1999), pp. 1034–1052.

6 R. B. Handfield and E. L. J. Nicholds, 'Supply chain redesign – Transforming supply chains into integrated value systems', *Financial Times* (Prentice Hall, 2002).

7 H. L. Lee, 'Creating value through supply chain integration', *Supply Chain Management Review*, September/October (2000), pp. 30–36.

8 G. C. Stevens, 'Integrating the supply chain', *International Journal of Physical Distribution and Materials Management* 19 (8) (1989).

9 M. L. Fisher, 'What is the right supply chain for your product?', *Harvard Business Review*, March–April (1997).

10 P. Jenster, H. S. Pedersen, P. Plackett and D. E. Hussey, *Outsourcing – Insourcing: Can Money be Made from the New Relationship Opportunities?* (John Wiley and Sons, 2005).

11 C. K. Prahalad and G. Hamel, 'The core competence of the corporation', *Harvard Business Review*, May–June (1990), pp. 79–91.

12 J. Magretta, 'The power of virtual integration: An interview with Dell Computers' Michael Dell', *Harvard Business Review* (1998), pp. 72–80.
13 Adapted from D. M. Lambert and M. C. Cooper, 'Issues in supply chain management', *Industrial Marketing Management*, 29 (2000), pp. 65–83.
14 Adapted from SCOR Version 7.0 overview.
15 D. F. Ross, *Introduction to e-Supply Chain Management – Engaging Technology to Build Market-Winning Business Partnerships*, CRC Press LLC (2003).
16 C. Cordón, C. and T. Vollmann, 'Building a smarter demand chain', *Financial Times*, 22 February 1999.
17 J. K. Liker and T. Y. Choi, 'Building deep supplier relationships – HBR spotlight, The 21st century supply chain', *Harvard Business Review*, December (2004), pp. 104–113.
18 C. Cordón, K. S. Hald and T. Vollmann, 'Managing attraction in customer-supplier partnerships', working paper Lausanne: International Institute for Management Development (2005).
19 R. Mason-Jones, J. B. Naylor and D. R. Towill, 'Lean, agile or leagile? Matching your supply chain to the marketplace', *International Journal of Production Research*, 38 (17) (2000), pp. 4061–4070.
20 J. B. Nalor, M. M. Naim and D. Berry, 'Leagility: Integrating the lean and agile manufacturing paradigm in the total supply chain', *Engineering Costs and Production Economics*, 62 (1999), pp. 107–118.
21 R. G. Eccles, 'The performance measurement manifesto', *Harvard Business Review*, Jan/Feb (69) Issues 1(1991), pp. 131–137.
22 'Why social responsibility matters – An interview with Anthony Nieves, senior vice president of purchasing and supply Hilton Hotels Corp.', *Supply Chain Management Review*, September (2004), pp. 46–51.

8 *The Chief Manufacturing Officer – Process execution, improvement and design*

KIM SUNDTOFT HALD

The leadership of the manufacturing function comprises design and management of transformation processes. The focus must be on creating value for customers and shareholders. Ensuring efficiency and effectiveness in current operations is vital.

This chapter distinguishes the role of the chief manufacturing officer (CMaO) from that of the CSCO. It then explores the CMaO's executive role as it has evolved from an execution-oriented mode of management to one that is more strategically focused. The new CMaO needs to master platforms of transformation technologies and production philosophies and excel as an internal integrator.

The role of the chief manufacturing officer

It's hard to keep up with all the new stuff these days. Just a few years ago I knew every technology available in our area, but today this is no longer the case. I haven't slowed down; it is the pace of change that has accelerated. Sitting on top of this development, knowing what's out there in terms of new technology and operations principles and being able to assess what can be of use to us is the new competitive frontier. We need to find out how to excel in this area.

(Chief of manufacturing with twenty years' experience in the role)

The CMaO occupies the tactical and operational territory just below the chief supply chain officer (CSCO). This chapter extends and complements chapter 7 on the CSCO; in many companies the two roles are combined. The author focuses on the key elements that make up a CMaO's responsibilities, as distinct from those of a CSCO. The differences between the two roles are also briefly discussed. The focus here is less on historical elements of the CMaO position (which are covered extensively in chapter 7) and more on specific roles the CMaO plays as a member of the CXO team. Finally the technological tools available to the CMaO in executing his or her role are explored in some detail.

Where manufacturing and engineering expertise are of strategic corporate value, the CMaO is often a member of the CXO team. Interaction with the CEO and other company executives is vital to keep manufacturing strategically aligned with the rest of the organization. Before focusing exclusively on the role of the CMaO, it is important to explore the differences between the two senior supply chain management functions in the company, the CSCO and the CMaO.

With the emergence of supply chain management philosophies and best practices in the 1990s, there was a need for a CSCO, someone who could think strategically and see the whole supply chain from beginning to end. Today the CSCO is primarily responsible for integrating the aggregated supply chain processes into a larger co-ordinated system.[1] The core production and transformation expertise is therefore left in the hands of the CMaO.

The main task of the CSCO is to set up the supply chain infrastructure. It is the CMaO's job to optimize functional performance. The CSCO fosters co-ordination and integration internally and between the company and its supply chain partners. Thus the CSCO acts as creator of high-level physical and managerial structures. In doing so, he or she is integrator, designer, proactive improver and strategy developer.

The CMaO, by contrast, executes within the supply chain infrastructure. The role is focused on optimizing the core transformation processes in three major areas: design, execution and improvement (illustrated in Figure 8.1). The CMaO coordinates with other internal and external entities to achieve this objective, but the main focus remains internal to the company.

Thus the CMaO is a process designer, process improver and process executor. The CMaO does not formulate strategy but, rather, executes strategically. The manufacturing processes, whether designed for cost efficiency, speed, quality and/or flexibility are in alignment with company objectives. In the next three sections, each of the 'process' roles is discussed in more detail.

The chief manufacturing officer as process designer

Challenges from global competitors during the past two decades have prompted companies to focus on designing (or redesigning) best-in-class

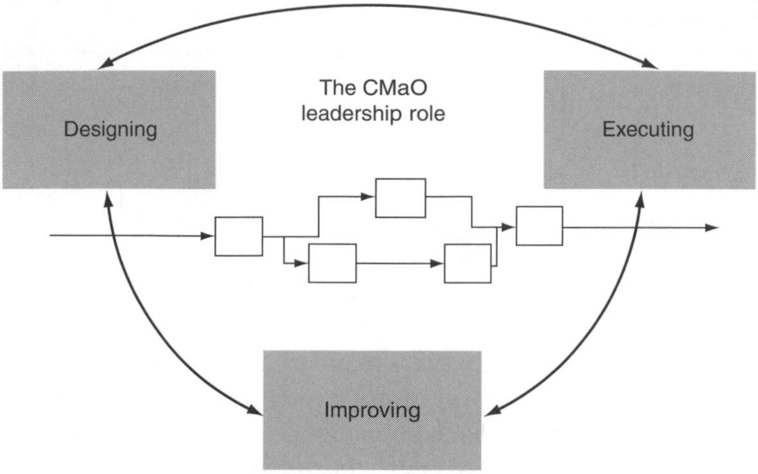

Figure 8.1: The CMaO leadership role

processes. This is to ensure maximum return on investments in equipment, employee capabilities, technology and other elements of manufacturing infrastructure. As a response, practitioners and academics have developed increasingly sophisticated methods for designing these transformation processes. This section gives an overview of how the CMaO leads process design within the factory walls – the first of three major leadership functions.

With the proven success of the Toyota Production System[2] and the emergence of the just-in-time philosophy in the late 1980s, the link between process design and the improved efficiency of manufacturing operations became increasingly clear. As part of the technological revolution, different production technologies aimed at improving the transformation process were developed. This resulted in the emergence of the 'technology platform' as a managerial issue.

Globalization, sophisticated design philosophies and the technological revolution all made developing the 'right' design process more complex. This became a major focus for the CMaO, and a range of diverse but interrelated questions now required the CMaO's attention:

- What strategy should be used to transform resources into goods and services?
- How should the factory floor be designed?

- What production technology should be implemented?
- How should the available IT be used in the planning and control process?

Designing process strategies

As a first step in designing the transformation process, the CMaO must consider which process strategy to adopt. This strategy is the map that transforms resources and raw materials into goods and services in a way that meets customer requirements and product specifications. Process design must support company, market and product strategy.

Process design choices are strategic decisions for the CMaO. Depending on his or her level of autonomy, the decision is often co-ordinated with the CSCO to match the overall supply chain strategy for the organization. Some of the key elements that need to be considered are cost, time, quality and flexibility. However, to achieve process excellence, it is best to choose and focus on two of these four elements, as trying to achieve them all would leave the process mediocre at all of them.

For each new product manufactured in the factory, the CMaO must proactively co-ordinate with research and development, product development and marketing. Gathering information on both flexibility requirements (range of product variety) and forecasts (production volume estimates) early in the development cycle is crucial. This simplifies process strategy choices and enables mobilization of the required production capacity.

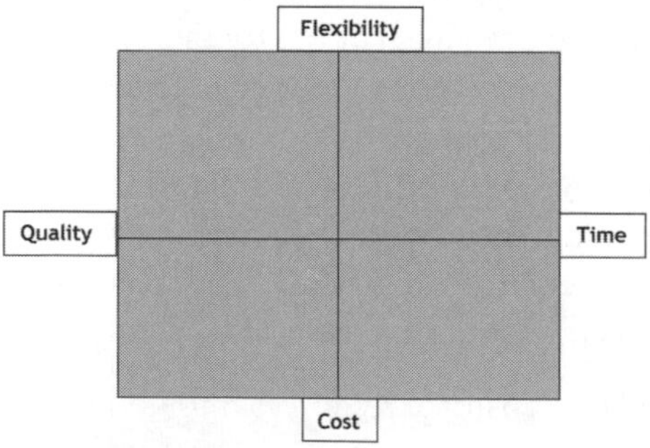

Figure 8.2: Process design – decision map

Knowing the long-range plans of the CEO and the CSCO is essential for the CMaO. Research and development, new product introductions, capital investments, facility locations and expansions must be analysed and absorbed within the capacity structures of the factory. What does the future hold? Do current capacity capabilities match future requirements? How can more flexibility be built into the current capacity platform? These are a few of the strategic questions that the CMaO needs to analyse.

Drawing the factory layout

Before deciding on the design of the factory floor, a detailed layout of the physical transformation grid within the factory walls is necessary. Because of the nature of the investment involved, this is a decision or cluster of decisions that may determine the transformation capabilities of the factory in the long run.

Layout design involves the CMaO deciding on a number of trade-offs. These include dimensions such as capacity requirements, flexibility concerns, space allocation, and non-value-adding movement, quality of work life and employee behaviour.

To illustrate the link between the layout decision and employee behaviour, consider the following scenario:

Due to short-term restrictions on expansion, a computer manufacturer was forced into operating two extra production lines in the same facility. When analysing the situation later, management discovered that communication between operators had improved and that work-in-process inventories were reduced. What could explain these unintended but positive consequences?

Because of the limited space, operators were closer to one another. This proximity allowed each person to see more of the production line. Working more closely facilitated team member communication. The workers could tell one another about problems and opportunities for improvements, which fostered an environment of teamwork and knowledge sharing. Furthermore, no floor space was available for work-in-process inventory, making the workers change their behaviour to eliminate excess inventory.

The above scenario demonstrates how factory layout decisions can be important. The decisions are often complex and require the full attention and leadership of the CMaO.

Three well-accepted layout principles in manufacturing organizations are product-oriented, group-oriented and process-oriented.

Product-oriented layouts

In product-oriented layouts, transformation equipment is dedicated to products with specific configurations. The advantage of this approach is its ability to produce in large repetitive volumes. Its major drawback is its inflexibility and the risk of investing in equipment dedicated to products that begin to lose market share. When designing product-oriented layouts, management's goal is to create a smooth, continuous flow of production. The key metrics are high average utilizations of equipment and personnel. Such decisions are often called line balancing.[3]

Group-oriented layouts

These production layouts are similar to product-oriented ones, except there are several small flow lines. Each flow line is dedicated to one or a few products. Each line has a self-managed group of workers (the focused factory), with sub-managers responsible for each work-cell. The U-shaped form of these systems means workers are physically closer to one another and to more machines. This proximity gives the workers the opportunity to work on more than one process, so they need skills in a variety of areas. This type of layout is the one most often proposed in the just-in-time philosophy.

Process-oriented layouts

In process-oriented layouts, products or components are moved to different job-shops according to their specification. The advantage of this approach is the flexibility it allows in customizing products or services. Its major drawback, however, is its inability to effectively produce large volumes. When designing process layouts, the most common tactic it to arrange work centres to minimize the cost of material handling.

Designing the technology platform

Technology has had a significant influence on production. Even today, after the first wave of 'the technology revolution', it is still considered to be the major change factor in production management.

Production technologies aimed at improving efficiency directly, by automating the transformation process and increasing its flexibility, are called computer integrated manufacturing (CIM) systems. CIM systems are the technology platform of the organization. They automate and link the core manufacturing processes to design and warehousing.

A CIM system typically contains many types of advanced manufacturing technologies (AMTs). The AMTs or the CIM system may be connected to form stand-alone islands of automation or archipelagos of automation (i.e. partially-integrated or fully-integrated systems).[4]

Managing the level of integration in the CIM system is important for the CMaO. There will be different risk, cost and flexibility profiles for the factory, depending on the extent of the connections of the sub-technologies on the platform. These profiles must be adjusted to the overall supply chain strategy of the organization.

With CIM, it becomes possible to:

1 Automate the core transformation processes;
2 Control and inspect subassemblies;
3 Automate storage and movement of parts;
4 Integrate design and redesign tasks into manufacturing.[5]

The main elements in each of these groups of CIM technology are discussed below.

Firstly, AMTs, aimed at automating manufacturing, are focused on the core component fabrication and assembly processes. The focus is on using technology to replace or complement manual operations. Some of the core technologies in this group include:

Computer numerical control (CNC)

This technology is the basic mechanism that brings machinery to life. It automates machine operations via coded instructions located on the machine's own computer and memory platform. CNC is the control component in robotic structures. This type of electronic control of machinery:

- Increases transformation speed by reducing changeover time;
- Decreases quality mistakes, and thereby waste, by increasing precision;
- Increases flexibility due to ease of programming.

Robotics

Robots are flexible machines that have the ability to hold, move or grab items and perform human-type operations. They function through electronic impulses that activate motors and switches. Robots are built from three interlinked structures: the mechanical structure; the power structure; and the control structure. Initially robots were used for heavy, unpleasant and even dangerous work. Later the emphasis was on eliminating monotonous jobs, automation and cost saving.

Secondly, AMTs aimed at controlling and inspecting the transformation processes and intermediate components are concerned with increasing the reliability of these checks. They further automate the often monotonous and repetitive tasks involved in this process. With AMTs it has become possible to convert a previously discrete control process into a continuous one. In some instances it is even possible to merge control and inspection as a seamless integrated part of core manufacturing processes. Some of the core technologies in this group include:

Process control
This type of technology combines IT with sensor equipment to monitor and control physical processes in the factory. It is particularly applicable in determining and controlling temperature and pressure in chemical operations. Additionally, process control technology is useful in measuring microscopic tolerances in electronic and other types of high-tech industries.

Vision systems
Here video technology monitors and inspects processes. This type of technology is particularly applicable in situations where visual similarity is a key quality driver.

Thirdly, AMTs aimed at automating storage and movement of parts are focused on the automation and optimization of processes normally characterized as waste or non-value-adding to end customers. Some of the core technologies in this group include:

Automated guided vehicles (AGVs)
These electronically guided and controlled carts are used to move materials between core transformation processes or between production and storage.

Automated storage and retrieval systems (ASRS)
These computer-controlled systems allow components to be automatically placed in or taken from designated locations within the warehouse.

Fourthly, AMTs aimed at integrating design into transformation assist with designing products and processes. The use of technology in this area results in the blurring of organizational boundaries between product development and core manufacturing processes. The technologies in this group include features for improving engineering, testing through simulation and documenting specifications. Some of the core technologies include:

Computer-aided design (CAD)
Using this interactive graphic image system, products and processes can be designed in three dimensions. Changes and redesigns can be done quickly without much additional cost.

Computer-aided process planning (CAPP)
This technology aims to combine design parameters with processing codes. In this way, CAPP links design, engineering and manufacturing processes.

As a result of the number of options involved in computer-integrated manufacturing, managing the technology platform can be complex. Therefore, successful CMaOs require capabilities to initiate and lead technology implementation. However, they also need to understand that introducing new technology in the transformation process may be disruptive and must be balanced. They must consider a range of factors, including current technology platforms; the maturity of the technology; the risks involved; and possible payback scenarios.

Mapping planning and control into the available IT infrastructure

Advanced software has improved the planning process considerably over the past two decades. Today running material requirement planning on thousands of product components is done automatically overnight. This would have been impossible just a few years ago.

It is often assumed that the functionality of information systems follows the requirements of the production planning and control procedures in companies. This is often the case only when the planning and control software is customized. In practice, most companies implement ERP-systems where the production planning and control functionality is more or less predesigned. It is therefore crucial for today's CMaO to know the possibilities and limitations of this off-the-shelf software.

ERP represents a comprehensive software approach to supporting decisions associated with planning and controlling the business. In well-integrated organizations, the ERP system is often the only planning platform. In this way, both supply chain and factory planning visibility are increased. Production becomes linked to external partners (both customers and suppliers), internal functions (i.e. procurement) and other areas in the organization. Therefore, the factory is no longer an isolated system, but integrated in the supply chain.

Although having a single integrated system platform is one way to move a business forward, it brings new challenges for CMaOs. They must secure the planning and control platform and ensure that data are timely. This involves gathering information about the current status and exploring the possibilities of the existing IT systems. Here, the CMaO must co-ordinate with the CIO.

The chief manufacturing officer as process improver

Today, to meet the pressures of globalization, my CEO expects our internal transformation processes to be leaner than ever. What does this mean for me? As the main person responsible for eliminating all types of waste in the factory, the real challenge for me is to drive my employees, foremen and supervisors to see this waste elimination effort as more than discrete projects, but rather as an ongoing challenge, as a burning platform.
(CMaO of global hearing-aid company)

This section takes a closer look at the second of the three main roles of the CMaO – that of process improver. Today this role is closely linked to the notion of leanness, as indicated in the quote above. Continuous improvement methodologies are built into advanced process designs.

Striving for continuous improvement in transformation processes should be a cornerstone for every CMaO. But what exactly does improvement mean in this context? In a transformation environment, improvement translates into the elimination of non-value-adding activities, i.e. the reduction of waste, the increase in quality and a decrease in time. In a normal transformation environment, seven different types of waste can be identified:

- Performance of processes that are unnecessary or are simply 'wrong';
- Rework that is required to fix mistakes;
- Waiting time – people and machines are in excessive 'down time';
- Motion – operators must make unnecessary movements;

- Conveyance – parts or products must be moved over excessive physical distances to reach the next stage in the production process;
- Excess raw materials – more materials than necessary available at a given time;
- Faster processing speed than necessary – which leads to excess finished goods inventory.

These factors add no particular value, but do add costs; therefore, they should be reduced or eliminated where possible. However, because they are interrelated, attempts to eliminate one waste area can make another worse. Therefore, improvement efforts must be co-ordinated, and will often tie back to process redesign. The CMaO leads the attack against all types of waste throughout the factory.

The CMaO must ensure that activities are co-ordinated and optimized. As it is not possiblie to do this alone, the CMaO's main challenge is to install mechanisms and procedures to heighten employees' focus on proactive continuous improvement. Education is paramount.

Employees must be trained in process thinking and to identify waste. Building a culture that embraces change and improvements, that moves decision authority lower in the organization and that rewards exceptional performance is part of the CMaO's mandate. Thus, the CMaO must drive the implementation of infrastructures that ensure adequate training of new personnel and performance-related pay. Likewise, employees and management who block improvement initiatives and protect the status quo should be reassigned or removed. The CMaO has a vested interest in working with the chief human resources officer.

Over the last two decades several managerial philosophies have been introduced to support continuous improvement efforts in transformation processes. Lean manufacturing,[6] total quality management (TQM),[7] just-in-time (JIT) and six sigma are some of the best-known ones.

Lean production, for instance, encompasses a wide variety of management practices, including just-in-time scheduling (Kanban), work teams, cellular manufacturing and supplier management. The core idea of lean manufacturing is that these practices can work together to create a streamlined system that produces finished products at the pace of customer demand, with little or no waste.

Adopting lean thinking means '*learning to see – learning to identify waste*'. One of the main tools in 'learning to see' is mapping the value stream. This task normally involves two activities. First, a detailed understanding of all current operations is documented and made visual. This is achieved by mapping all the main activities that are involved in producing selected products. Second, the resulting *value stream maps* are analysed to see where each of type of waste can be eliminated; and where necessary processes are redesigned to be more efficient.

Process design and improvement are two key activities for the CMaO. However, a significant part of the CMaO's job revolves around managing the manufacturing processes. Executing the process design, consistently and regularly are covered in more detail in the following section.

The chief manufacturing officer as process executor

My main goal is to support our organization in promoting customer satisfaction. As chief of manufacturing I think that the best way I can achieve this is to push for a culture of reliability. We need to think and breathe reliability in everything that we do.

(Chief of manufacturing in a US food producer)

In the pursuit of reliability, two functions of the CMaO as process executor are most important: planning and controlling.

Planning is and always has been crucial for reliable day-to-day operations in the factory. This entails keeping processes stable, running production as close to zero defects as possible, and ensuring that all delivery schedules are met. Secondly, controlling is important to ensure that larger goals are met and, where necessary, to take corrective action.

Previously both planning and control were centralized. The CMaO participated in and often performed the different tasks involved in these processes. Today, however, successful CMaOs promote a performance measurement culture, empowering employees at all levels of the operation to be proactive improvers. Consequently, the successful CMaO today often concentrates on measuring high-level strategic trends, rather than performing specific tasks himself. Delegation in a measurement culture is imperative.

Also, as a result of extensive developments in software for manufacturing planning and control, planning processes have become highly automated. Standard functionality, similar to what is included in enterprise resource planning (ERP) systems, dominates IT solutions for manufacturing planning. These trends have shifted the CMaO role away from core planning activities. Instead the CMaO works on influencing high-level strategy and bridging strategic planning with operational plans at the factory level.

CMaOs are challenged to answer the following questions as a central part of their role as process executor:

- How to translate, influence and adapt to the overall supply chain plan?
- How can current factory capacity and requirements be matched with the delivery and capacity plan?
- What to measure? What not to measure?
- What control and performance measurement systems to use?

The next two subsections explore in more detail the role the CMaO plays in planning and controlling the transformation process.

Planning the transformation process

The first responsibility of the CMaO acting as process executor is to set factory-specific targets and communicate them to both internal and external customers.

The CMaO coordinates meetings to develop the main supply chain plan. Depending on the type of organization and the dynamics of the market which it serves, these meetings can take place from once a week to once a month. Here the CMaO must act as a negotiator on behalf of the factory, trying to make its current capacity and capability fit with the global strategy of the company.

The CMaO must also initiate updates to the capacity plan. This includes determining the nature, quantity and timing of production and capacity in the intermediate future.[8] Here the CMaO meets with the foremen and supervisors from the different departments in the factory. Together they decide on the intermediate production plan and on which capacity adjustment strategies to use.

When matching capacity to supply chain requirements, the CMaO must consider and decide on a number of alternatives. The following questions need to be addressed:

- Should the size or composition of the workforce be changed?
- Should subcontractors be used (using suppliers as capacity buffers)?
- Should inventories be used as capacity buffers?

In taking overall responsibility for the planning process in the factory, the CMaO is the gatekeeper, balancing the high-level strategies and long-term plans of the CEO and CSCO with the short-term order processing capacity and capabilities of the factory. Success in this task depends on the CMaO's skills as an information processor and negotiator.

Controlling the transformation process

The second responsibility of the CMaO acting as process executor is to orchestrate the day-to-day control of current performance against factory targets. The objective is twofold. First, the CMaO must reconstruct the image of performance as it is experienced by both internal and external customers. Next, he must identify areas in current operations where corrective action needs to be taken. Finding what to measure and how to measure in order to report and improve operational performance are often not trivial. Those organizations that are new to this way of thinking often end up measuring too much or measuring the wrong things.

Performance in terms of quality, delivery and cost is normally measured as part of the control task[9]. To control quality, statistical process control (SPC) is often used. It is a methodology for monitoring processes to identify what causes variation and signalling the need to take corrective action.

To control delivery performance, several different kinds of measures can be tracked and reported on a continuous basis, including product lateness (delivery date minus due date), average lateness of orders, average earliness of orders and/or percentage of on-time deliveries.

Finally to control cost in manufacturing processes, practices such as target cost management (TCM) and total cost of ownership (TCO) can be applied. TCM, originally developed by Toyota, is a practice designed to ensure that the manufacturing costs of products are controlled at a level less than end-product market prices minus acceptable profit margins[10]. TCO is a cost-control method increasingly used by manufacturing companies to identify all costs incurred throughout the life cycle of equipment, including acquisition and installation, operations and maintenance, and end-of-life management.[11]

The future role of the chief manufacturing officer

In view of the turbulent history of operations management, the prediction of future changes to the role of the CMaO is a difficult task. However, based on the outline of the main roles and responsibilities of the CMaO in this chapter, we can predict several trends and speculate on how the role will evolve.

In the past, the role has evolved mainly due to external pressures. These include customers' changing demands which lead to increasingly shorter product life cycles and individualized products; requirements and requests for environmentally safe production; and progress in production technology and IT.

The CMaO's job will also continue to evolve, from the role of a reactive executor to a more complex and strategic role within the CXO team. The CMaO's future responsibilities will still focus on the three key areas:

Design

Design of both physical and managerial processes will continue to be a key CMaO responsibility in the future. The process design task will continue to increase in complexity. New production technology will be introduced and new thinking will evolve in operations management philosophies, factory layout configurations and automation levels. Efficient and responsive design, as well as redesign, will become inherent to the CMaO's future role.

Improvement

Although the focus on continuous improvement is not a new endeavour, the last two decades have witnessed the introduction of a range of management philosophies to facilitate the task. Understanding and driving implementation of one of these philosophies within the factory walls is and will continue to be important.

Execution

A new understanding of the CMaO as executor has emerged. Unlike the old role, where the focus was on centralized planning and control, the new role concentrates on sensing and interacting with other internal functions. Establishing a decentralized measurement culture and managing portfolios of IT software for manufacturing planning and control are key elements for the future.

In conclusion, the CMaO role will continue to evolve from overseeing continuous improvement to *continuous design*. Organizations and teams will form and disband as needed; efficiency and performance on the key elements of cost, quality, time and flexibility will separate the wealth creators from those who do not survive. The future of the CMaO role will lie in *production platform management*. Successful CMaOs will contribute by applying advanced manufacturing technologies and managerial production philosophies in their efforts to optimize customer and shareholder value.

Assessing the role of the CMaO

The following questions provide a starting point when assessing the role of the CMaO.

Purpose

1. Is the purpose to **execute,** to **improve** or to **design** best-in-class transformation processes?
2. Is the purpose aligned with the overall organizational strategy of the CEO and the overall supply chain strategy of the CSCO?
3. Does the CMaO act consistently and communicate the main purpose of the functions to internal and external employees and customers?

Direction

4. How well does the CMaO understand and perform the role as internal integrator and communicator?
5. What is the relationship between the CMaO and the other organizational officers?
   - Can these relationships be improved?
6. How are tasks allocated between the CSCO and the CMaO?
   - Does the CMaO report to the CSCO or directly to the CEO?
7. Is the CMaO able to influence decisions made in other functional areas that have an impact on factory operations?
8. Does the CMaO delegate responsibility to supervisors and foremen, promoting empowerment of workers?
9. How well does the CMaO understand and perform the new role of platform management?
   - Does the CMaO understand and master portfolios of new production technologies and what they can do for current operations in the factory?
   - Does the CMaO understand and master new management philosophies and what they can do for current operations in the factory?

Focus

10. Does the CMaO understand and articulate how the function can bring value to internal and external customers through its roles as executor, improver and developer?
    - Are customer requirements and priorities investigated?
    - Are factory transformation processes aligned with these requirements and priorities?
    - Is an adequate control and performance measurement process in place to ensure that customer requirements are met?

Glossary

Enterprise resource planning (ERP) systems
ERP systems are designed to improve an organization's planning and the way that its business processes function. The advantages can be significant savings in time, costs and human capital as previously vital but labour-intensive tasks such as planning, tracking and co-ordinating are automated.

The disadvantages arise from the inability of the systems to meet comprehensively the evolving needs of an organization, and the way that they are used and maintained.

JIT
Just-in-time (JIT) is a management philosophy conceived by Toyota in the 1980s. The main principle of the philosophy is continuous and forced problem-solving. In the production area, delay times and inventory levels are kept to a minimum since the philosophy is that unnecessary inventories and delays mean inefficient use of resources and further hide underlying problems.

Six sigma
Six sigma is a disciplined, data-driven approach and methodology for eliminating defects in any process in the organization.

The transformation process
The set of linked activities that together with the resources used combines raw material and components into finished products and services.

Notes

1 For a detailed description of this leadership role please refer to chapter 7 of this book.

2 See, for example, T. Ohno, *The Toyota Production System* (Cambridge, MA: Productivity Press, 1988), or S. Shingo, *Non-stock Production* (Cambridge, MA: Productivity Press, 1987).

3 See, for example, T. K. Bhattacharjee and S. Sahu, 'A critique of some current assembly line balancing techniques', *International Journal of Operations and Production Management* 7(6) (1987).

4 For another segmentation of advanced manufacturing technology, see for instance Goetsch (1990) where the CIM wheel of the Society of Manufacturing Engineers (SME) is described: D. L. Goetsch, *Advanced Manufacturing Technology* (New York: Delmar Publishers, 1990).

5 H. Sun, 'Current and future patterns of using advanced manufacturing technologies', *Technovation* 20 (2000), pp. 631–641.

6 For further information see J. P. Womack and D. T. Jones, *Lean Thinking: Banish Waste and Create Wealth in Your Corporation* (New York: Simon & Schuster, 1996).

7 For further information see B. G. Dale, *Managing Quality*, 4th edn (Oxford: Blackwell Publishing Ltd., 2003).

8 For further information see T. E. Vollmann, W. L. Berry, D. C. Whybark and F. R. Jacobs, *Manufacturing Planning and Control for Supply Chain Management*, 5th edn (Maidenhead: McGraw-Hill/Irwin, 2005).

9 For an overview of control methods for manufacturing see for example B. H. Maskell, *Performance Measurement for World Class Manufacturing: A Model for American Companies* (Cambridge, MA: Productivity Press, 1991).

10 R. Cooper and R. Slagmulder, *Supply Chain Development for the Lean Enterprise – Interorganizational Cost Management* (Cambridge, MA: Productivity Press, 1999).

11 J. Heilala, J. Montonen, and K. Helin, 'Selecting the right system – Assembly system comparison with total cost of ownership methodology', *Assembly Automation* 27 (1) (2007).

9 *The Chief Financial Officer – A capital position*

LEIF SJÖBLOM

The central importance of the CFO derives from two main roles. Firstly, ensuring that the company has sufficient funds to implement its investment and growth strategies, and secondly, promoting the most efficient use of those funds. Shareholders expect the CFO to 'keep the house in order'. This means the CFO needs the confidence of the investment community as well as employees. Professionalism, leadership skills and integrity are essential.

In this chapter, the author explains how the finance function has evolved. He explores the purpose of the CFO – to enable the optimal use of capital to maximize shareholder value – and describes how the CFO role is developing and the skills needed to succeed.

The role of the chief financial officer

Any successful CFO has to be a damn good businessman who also knows how to count.[1]

As CFOs, we have an obligation to respond to [external pressures] with sound advice for our fellow business leaders. We are responsible for creating concrete measures to protect and maintain good, balanced corporate governance – not just compliance. We have an obligation to demonstrate integrity and sound business principles.[2]

A company's destiny is so closely linked to its financial performance that the CFO is an influential member of the executive team. The CFO can be particularly powerful in companies that are under-performing and in industries with high financial risk. For example, the CFO plays a key strategic role in firms such as oil companies that are exposed to volatile commodity prices and exchange rate risks. As the public face for the financial impact of strategy and performance in the financial markets, CFOs are often in the spotlight. The investment community scrutinizes their words and actions very closely.

The CFO must ensure that sufficient funds are available for day-to-day operations and that these are allocated efficiently when implementing the company's investment and growth strategies. From the shareholders' perspective, the CFO controls and promotes the most profitable uses of these funds. These two roles are interdependent, since achieving and developing strategy depend on the optimum use of resources and securing additional finance.

General Motors and the evolution of the finance function

The foundations of the 'modern' finance function were established in the 1920s, most notably in the DuPont Corporation and in General Motors (GM). GM was the most successful company of its time. Within thirty years, CEO Alfred Sloan led the company to become the world's largest corporation. GM's decentralized and entrepreneurial business model proved to be superior to the centralized and efficiency-driven business model of Ford. The enormous success of GM influenced many other companies, leading them to adopt similar management systems.

Like many major innovations, the financial systems at GM evolved out of necessity. GM was a forerunner in organizational design, with Business Units (BU) organized around specific customer segments. The organization was decentralized so that day-to-day operating decisions could be made close to the market and customers.

Unfortunately, this structure placed the company in jeopardy. Inventory control was poor and capital expenditure exceeded what the company could afford. There was no clear picture of how much cash the company had or where it was located. As Sloan commented: 'The weak divisions threatened the existence of the strong ones, and the strong ones themselves were operated more for their own than the corporation's interest.'[3]

GM's response to this crisis was to develop a forecasting and planning system. It was the model for many of the financial reporting systems that we find in most corporations today. Starting with a sales forecast, production plans were prepared to match expected demand. Production levels determined inventory levels and capital expenditure.

This planning system ensured that spending was related to market demand and was based on what the company could afford. It ensured that capital was not wasted and that the company would not run out of cash. These internal process developments were essential to manage growth and risk effectively and to optimize the use of resources. Today, budgets and planning systems remain vital means of ensuring orderly operations.

The forecasting and planning system ensured the short-term survival of GM, but not its future prosperity. GM needed to improve its operational efficiency. 'No-one knew, or could prove, where the efficiencies or inefficiencies lay,' Sloan admitted. It was not obvious what financial systems were needed or how they should be implemented in a decentralized organization. In Sloan's view: 'If we had the means to review and judge the effectiveness of operations, we could safely leave the prosecution of those operations to the men in charge of them.'

The limiting resource that needed to be optimized was capital. This led GM to develop a Return on Capital concept to evaluate divisions and to provide appropriate funds. The system, known as a DuPont tree (see Figure 9.1 below), integrates finance with operations. It clearly shows how individual operating decisions affect the P&L and balance sheet, and ultimately drive the rate of returns. The DuPont operating

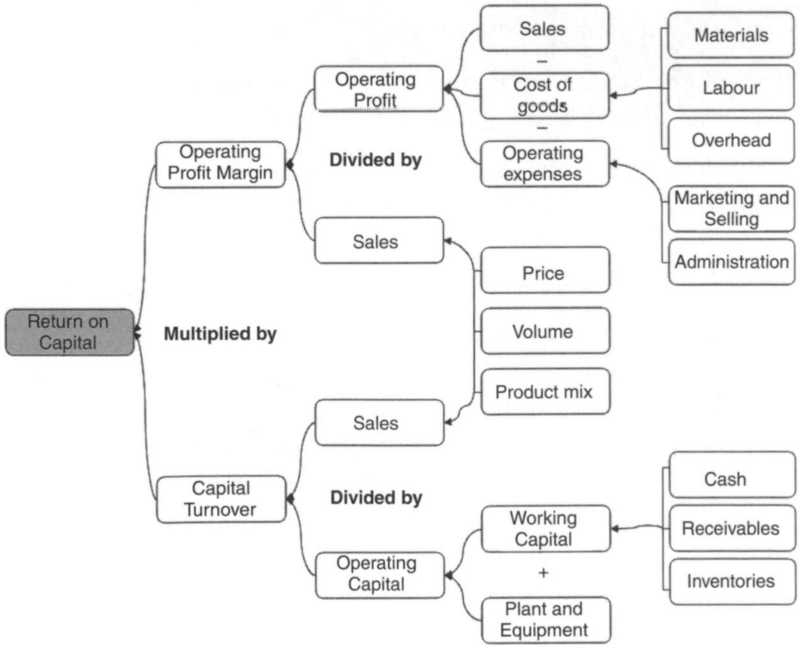

Figure 9.1: DuPont chart

capital (OCT) and return on capital (ROC) trees, provide an effective project and company analysis framework that highlights business performance and allows for effective benchmarking between projects, business units and companies.

If one can see how all the facts in the business individually bear upon a rate of return, one has a penetrating look into the business. (Alfred Sloan)

GM introduced other revolutionary concepts, including shareholder value. Although Alfred Sloan valued what he termed 'a quantitative basis for sound decision making', GM was not driven solely by financial considerations. For many years, it was a very pragmatic company, with finance used as a tool to support operations and strategy. The objective of the financial control system was to make things visible. It was also valuable for communicating and considering information. In Sloan's view: 'The figures did not give automatic answers to problems. They simply exposed the facts with which to judge whether the divisions were operating in line with expectations.'

The financial management mindset

Although the finance function is now more complex, the mindset and concepts of GM's financial systems can be found in many organizations.

- The decentralized business model still dominates – particularly for companies which rely on being close to the final customer. This requires some centralized co-ordination and this, in turn, depends on effective financial systems.
- Forecasting and planning systems (most notably budgets) are used to set targets, control spending and assess performance. They also play a governance role by providing a framework for reporting to shareholders, the board of directors and regulatory authorities. Finally, they have an internal role, supporting decision-making by quantifying the financial implications of operating decisions.
- Allocating capital to business units based on expected returns optimizes its use. The CFO plays a key role in reviewing and approving investment proposals.
- Finance is a support function that must be integrated with operations: it cannot exist in a vacuum. It must effectively balance between business control and allocating capital for growth.

- If the 'house is in order' and the company delivers what it promises, it is easier and cheaper to find investment funds for future growth strategies.

The purpose of the CFO

Enabling the optimal use of capital to maximize shareholder value

Many people perceive the CFO as the shareholders' champion. The CFO's overarching goal is to enable, control and promote the most profitable uses of a company's capital. This encompasses everything from tax planning to corporate communication and is focused on the generation and use of capital. This goal is achieved by measuring how well capital has been used and determining how it should be deployed in the future.

The CFO has been called the modern day Janus – the Roman god of beginnings and endings – with one eye on the past and the other on the future.

The eye that is on the past is focused on internal and external reporting, and internal controls. It also ensures that systems and processes are in place to support decision-making and satisfy regulatory requirements. The forward-looking focus is on value added activities such as strategy formulation, risk management, value chain analysis and planning. The CFO is also focused on allocation decisions such as capital expenditure, and mergers and acquisitions. The CFO's role in investor relations and governance blends reporting performance and setting future expectations.

The purpose of the CFO is capital optimization within a strategic context that combines the future and the past. This touches every corner of the organization and all aspects of financial management. How does one tackle such a massive mandate? A good place to start is to break the mission of the CFO down into its component parts (see Figure 9.2).

There is no such thing as a 'typical CFO'. Different companies and industries have different requirements, and different people have different styles. Before we assess the similarities, consider the following three examples illustrating the typical daily activities of three different CFOs (see Table 9.1). Despite these differences, there are several similarities in the purpose of the CFO.

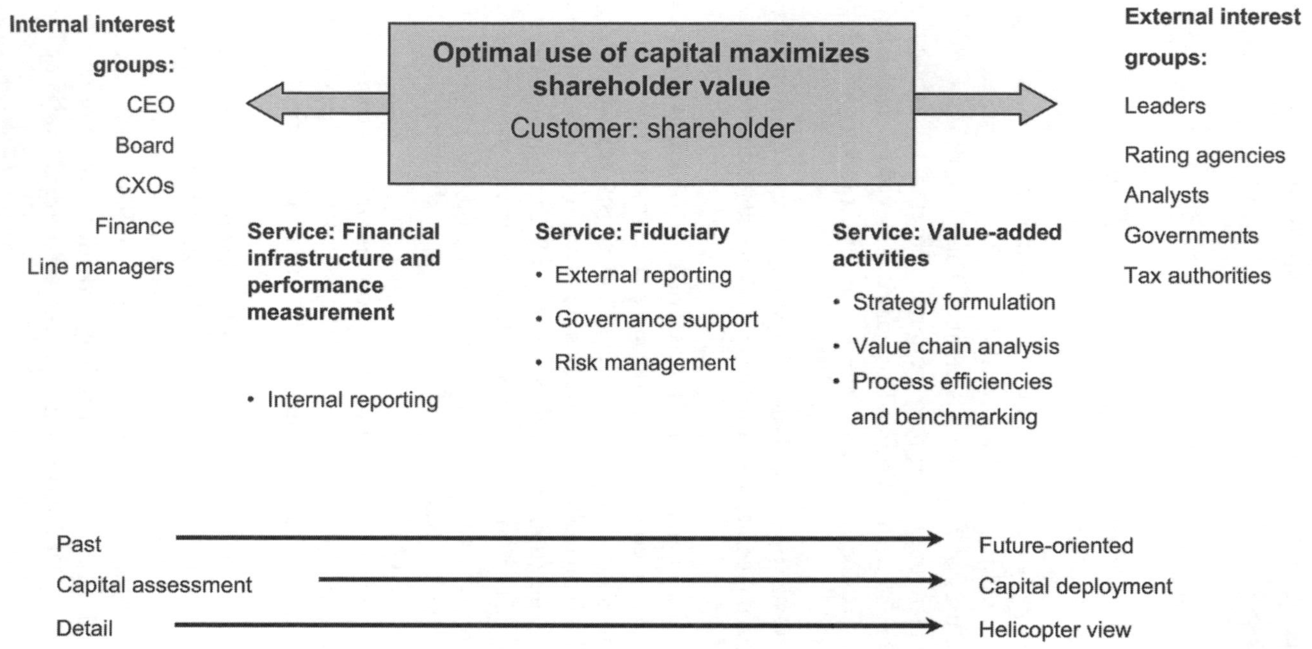
Internal interest groups:
CEO
Board
CXOs
Finance
Line managers
Optimal use of capital maximizes shareholder value
Customer: shareholder
External interest groups:
Leaders
Rating agencies
Analysts
Governments
Tax authorities
Service: Financial infrastructure and performance measurement
• Internal reporting
Service: Fiduciary
• External reporting
• Governance support
• Risk management
Service: Value-added activities
• Strategy formulation
• Value chain analysis
• Process efficiencies and benchmarking
Past
Future-oriented
Capital assessment
Capital deployment
Detail
Helicopter view

Figure 9.2: Pillars of CFO purpose

Table 9.1: ***A day in the life of a CFO: Three examples***

CFO of a major European chemical company

Key areas	Classical tasks	Key success factors
Investor relations (30%)	Contact with investors and competitive monitoring	Efficiency
Strategy	Participate in and support company direction	Customer orientation
Control, accounting and compliance	Bookkeeping, reporting, generating information	High degree of knowledge and expertise
Mergers and acquisitions	Driving the M&A process	Speed and accuracy
Treasury	Financial flow management, financing/investing/hedging	People development
Information technology (IT)	IT infrastructure management, IT financial system, support	Change management

CFO of a major industrial company (moving from classical CFO tasks to less traditional ones)

Key areas	Typical tasks
Reporting	Assessing where we were, where we are, where we are going
Benchmarking	Analysing and sharing best practice among group companies
Strategy	Quantifying data and ideas, scenario planning
Proactive catalyst for change	• Convincing BUs of the need for change • Providing support • Avoiding complacency

CFO of a major technology company

Key areas	Tasks
People (30%)	Organizing, developing people
Supporting internal customers (30 %)	Supporting senior staff, leadership planning, undertaking strategic initiatives
Control (30%)	Getting the numbers: notably revenues and margins
Customers (10%. 'Only 10%')	Presentations, process support

Financial infrastructure and performance measurement

A company's financial infrastructure (for example, invoicing) is often taken for granted, but without it a company would soon vanish. These day-to-day activities need high accuracy and reliability, but must also be cost effective. This is a legal requirement for fiduciary purposes (reporting to external stakeholders) and is necessary for assessing and evaluating performance (internal stakeholders).

One-third of a CFO's time can be spent on 'getting the numbers and reporting where we were, where we are and where we are going'.

Fiduciary

The administrative burden has increased following changes to the legal requirements of external reporting and basic legal compliance, particularly with the passage in the United States of the Sarbanes-Oxley Act in 2002. This was at least partly triggered by the scandals at Enron, Tyco and WorldCom. Ensuring good investor and media relations is an important task, absorbing 30–50 per cent of a CFO's time. This task cannot be delegated. Investors and financial analysts expect the CFO and the CEO to be the public figureheads of the company.

In the era of renewed emphasis on corporate governance, CFOs and their boards must satisfy themselves that they have sufficient and effective governance mechanisms in place. A CFO is increasingly in the spotlight to assess and manage quantifiable and non-quantifiable risks (people, natural disasters and industry changes). This is known as 'enterprise risk management'. In extreme cases, CFOs may also find themselves a target, being called into legal proceedings when there have been cases of fraud or gross mismanagement at the company.

Value-added activities

Typical value-adding activities include providing business support, benchmarking and the quantification of strategic options and scenarios. CFOs may even be called upon to meet with important customers or help to close important deals. In many companies, CFOs take an active part in developing and leading corporate strategies, especially mergers and acquisitions. CFOs must apply a strategic outlook to their role in order to succeed.

The views of three CFOs highlight different attitudes to the challenge of creating shareholder value:

A company has no right to exist for the sake of itself – we must create value for our shareholders. But that does not mean I am a supporter of EVA (Economic Value Added). It is gone, and nobody misses it. Instead, we concentrate on simple things that really drive value.

It is a key aspect of our mission. However, it should not be the single goal for any company. We need balanced, sound aspects of growth – market share, customer satisfaction, employee satisfaction.

It is not perfect, but there are no good alternatives in a market economy. The Enron case showed that one can go too far, but that is not a reason to reject Shareholder Value thinking.

The CFO's leadership role

Providing direction and focus

The quest for increased efficiency affects every company. In many situations, the finance department feels that it has to take the lead. We need to walk the talk and start by cleaning up our own activities. If we are inefficient and inaccurate, we cannot then demand that the rest of the organization is efficient and accurate.

Many companies operate in a highly competitive environment, with increasing pressure to deliver value to shareholders. The CFO is expected to drive increasing efficiency. To demand that others be efficient, the CFO must also run a tight finance function; outsourcing and the use of shared service centres is on the rise.

Finance can be evaluated using two criteria:

1. Effectiveness: doing the right things. Financial infrastructure, reporting and fiduciary services need to be accurate, reliable and timely. The tolerance for errors is very small. Also, providing value-added services increases operational excellence and drives strategic direction.
2. Efficiency: doing the right things right. Providing timely and high-quality services at the lowest possible cost is essential. As one CFO commented, 'Efficiency is a must. If the cost is not right, we can't justify our existence – we might as well outsource the finance function.'

Efficiency versus effectiveness is echoed in both the mission and vision of the finance function. Consider the mission and vision of the finance function of five CFOs, described in their own words:

- 'Efficiency in execution';
- 'Efficient processes in place to support internal customers';
- 'High level catalyst for operational excellence';
- 'To create a dynamic finance organization that drives strategic direction';
- 'Financial management to ensure the survival of the company' (a CFO facing a major turnaround situation).

Ensuring efficiency and effectiveness

Efficiency is a prerequisite for effectiveness. The CFO is expected to be involved in value-added activities. Therefore, processes must be streamlined to free up time for the CFO to add value.

For example, Cisco Europe has streamlined its internal processes. It has implemented a paperless, fully automated, web-based financial transactions system where all information is available in real time on the desktop. This results in lower transaction costs and in decision-making that is faster and more transparent.

According to Cisco's CFO: 'We used to spend 65 per cent of the time on transactions and 35 per cent on value-added activities. Today we have reversed that relationship.' An additional benefit is that Cisco can use its system as a showcase for potential customers, contributing to its position as a leading IT infrastructure provider.

Many people have realized the benefits of streamlining processes to provide timely information. For example, Ciba Specialty Chemicals can consolidate over 150 legal entities worldwide and provide complete financial statements, signed by the auditor, by 20 January. By 4 February, the annual report is mailed to the shareholders. 'This allows us to look ahead, to spend time on value-adding activities rather than basic compliance,' says CFO Dr Michael Jacobi. This process is implemented internally on a monthly basis, freeing up valuable time.

To make even more time available, the budget process was also streamlined. Although many companies employ an extensive and time-consuming bottom-up budgeting process, the final budget is often inaccurate.

'Nobody wants a budget,' Dr Jacobi explains. 'We used to spend many man-years on the budgeting process, and toward the end of the year 70 per cent of the management attention was on the budget figures, with little time left to care for the customer. Still, when the budget reached the top management, it was never approved without adjustments: the board of directors adds 10 per cent here, cuts 5 per cent there, and so on. And then the politics start. It is not a very motivating process and it consumes enormous resources.

'Clearly we still need to set targets, but there is no need for an overstructured approach. Target setting is top-down and very high level: sales growth in local currency, EBITDA and free cash flow. For strategic control purposes, we use a five- to seven-year forecasting horizon. For more tactical decisions we provide timely monthly information (actual versus last year) and quarterly outlooks.'

Building a winning team

The CFO cannot do all the work. Delegation and teamwork are a key to success. This is highlighted by the view of one CFO: 'There is no way you can get away with just being a boss in today's flat organization. If you are not able to perform in a team, you will have to leave.'

The CFO must build the team, shape the culture and articulate the vision to focus the team's energy and build commitment.

Moreover, recruiting and developing people is an area that needs particular attention. In the past, finance professionals were recruited and promoted primarily on technical skills. Today, finance needs to be integrated with operations and the rest of the organization. Therefore, finance professionals should also be recruited for their ability to work in a team.

The two examples in Table 9.2 highlight the importance of teamwork skills.

Surprisingly, IMD's research indicates that many CFOs do not motivate staff through high salaries and bonuses. Many CFOs feel they can pay salaries that are slightly below market rates, provided that there are professional challenges and opportunities to develop skills. Table 9.3 below indicates the motivational drivers of finance professionals at the same companies mentioned in Table 9.2.

A consistent theme is an emphasis on performance. 'If we want to instil a performance mindset in the organization, we first need to walk the talk in our organization,' said one CFO.

Table 9.2: *Recruitment criteria for finance professionals at two companies*

Company 1	Company 2
• Technical skills, analytical skills, ability to digest complex issues • Is the person a good team player? This is assessed in three unstructured interviews. • A unanimous decision is required before a person is hired.	Culture fit is the key criterion – all other skills can be developed: • Empowered, self-sufficient person (no time for babysitting) • Perceived as a great team player, able to liaise with other groups. • Adaptability to a changing environment

Table 9.3: *What motivates people*

Company 1	Company 2
• Success and clear direction as a company • Professional challenges • Reputation • Geographical moves (international assignments) • There is not a lot of financial emphasis – salaries are in line with the market	• A good culture – and the CFO can reinforce the culture • Communication is strong: – Clear goals and initiatives – Celebrate success • Bonuses ('which we unfortunately cannot pay for the moment') • Development – Training – Job rotation

We used to have a reputation where the central finance organization was the place to spend a sabbatical. This is something I have changed completely. Today, headquarters has a reputation for working much harder than the business units.

Emphasizing performance has implications for dealing with non-performers. One CFO's approach is that non-performers just have to go.

You need to be very clear about how you handle difficult situations; you need to think a lot about it. You need to be very open, very blunt. But you also have to make sure that the exit is friendly and on good terms. It must be face-saving.

Difficulties with staff are unpredictable, consuming time and energy. Within finance, professionalism, integrity and credentials matter to a higher degree than in other functions. The best defence against underperformance is to assemble a strong team, create a strong, positive culture, and let people do their jobs. Encouraging continuing education internally and externally is also very important.

Relationships with other senior executives

The CFO and the business unit (BU) head

The role of the controller is to measure and report accurately what is happening in the business so that correct decisions can be made. The role is not to interfere with the business.

One of the key tasks of the finance function is 'controlling' – traditionally perceived as the policing function. The modern CFO views 'controlling' as providing insight rather than oversight. Today's definition of controlling is twofold:

- To provide accurate and timely information in a transparent way;
- To help managers execute.

As one CFO said, 'Controlling is mainly business gap analysis. You need to ask the question: Why does a BU not perform according to expectations? For internal or external reasons? And then act on the information.'

There is a clear segregation of responsibilities between managers and finance. The controller is not Big Brother watching the managers. The controller supplies information and the BU manager makes business decisions. One CFO defines the controlling process as:

- Setting clear objectives and communicating them (often top-down);
- Providing timely and accurate information ('monthly closes');
- Participating in regular meetings between business unit heads, CEO, CFO and HR to discuss results and to exchange information.

Excessive controlling or micro-management is not possible due to its excessive costs. Instead, control systems have to incorporate a certain amount of trust. Cisco's real time information system is one example.

According to Cisco's CFO, 'The control is still there, but we have greatly simplified everything . . . The system is based on trust. For example, expense reports are submitted online and are approved by simply pushing a button. About 10 per cent of the reports are randomly audited. Because of this, all information is now available in real time on the desktop, which means more transparent and faster decision making.'

Not every CFO has the same experience. 'Unfortunately there are times when I feel I have to play devil's advocate,' commented one CFO. 'Politics is part of any meeting, and some people put their self-interest before the corporate interest. For example, there is a natural excitement for making "sexy" acquisitions. Someone must be able to put on the brakes and question whether we really are creating value. My job is to make sure we don't overpay.'

The CFO and the CEO

In the view of one chief financial officer: *bad chemistry between the CFO and CEO is a recipe for disaster.*

The importance of financial performance means that many CFOs are powerful. While CFOs do not actively strive for power, some become 'deputy CEOs', involved in every business decision. In several companies, being CFO is an effective route to becoming the CEO. This is not always a good situation. Finance should be a support function, providing specific expertise, but is not necessarily an executive function. To paraphrase several CFOs, 'The CEO is in charge of the business. With a strong CEO, the CFO is a pure support function. But the CFO has the right to voice his opinion.'

CFOs are increasingly involved in strategy and presenting a united front to the investment community. Therefore, a close and harmonious partnership between the chief executive and CFO is essential. However, this relationship should not be *too* harmonious. In the post-Enron era, boards expect the CFO to provide a perspective on the business that is independent of the CEO. Further, to maintain professional integrity, CFOs must feel free to express their opinion and stand their ground.

The CFO and the board of directors

Ten years ago I tried to raise some issues with the board, and nobody wanted to listen. Today, if a CFO came to the board and started to bring things up, the board would be worried about the legal ramifications of not listening.[4]

Boards are more accountable than ever before and they have a symbiotic relationship with their CFOs. Each relies on the other for information, oversight and validation. This relationship has become more robust: contact is more frequent and intense, and responsibilities are more explicit. Under the USA's Sarbanes-Oxley Act and for those within its sphere of influence, power has shifted in favour of the board. In particular, the audit committee has a significant role, hiring the external auditor and being formally linked to internal audit staff.

Despite this increasingly active role, board members are largely outsiders who rely on knowledgeable and trustworthy insiders. Whereas past CFOs may have dumped financial data on the board and fled, they now provide the analysis that allows directors to be comfortable with the numbers. This requires a degree of tact, educating without seeming to educate those for whom finance is not a first language. Unsurprisingly, the CFO's communication skills were rated third, after integrity and independence, in a survey of directors' views.[5]

Between rubber-stamping and crossing swords lies a healthy middle ground in the relationship between the CFO and board. As one board member we met said: 'We trust, but verify'.

The CFO and other CXOs

The CFO's contribution to the management team is primarily that of a strategic financial advisor. This involves translating the management team's activities into business cases by quantifying the financial impact of initiatives.

Some companies use the CFO's expertise and mindset to change other parts of the organization. One CFO of a pharmaceutical company mentioned his involvement in rethinking the governance of the research and development process: 'My role is to impose a certain discipline. Finance people are used to having milestones and performance indicators, and that is the mindset we need in research and development to continue to be successful.'

In some companies, the relationship between the CFO and CIO is particularly strong. Some CIOs even have direct reporting lines to the CFO. This is due to several factors, including a natural intertwining of the roles. Most company-wide information systems eventually feed the financial reporting systems; upstream accuracy is vital for efficiency. There is a need to develop complex, integrated systems to support the financial information infrastructure. This also combines with a need for financial scrutiny of most IT projects.

The future of the CFO role

The CFO has always been in a delicate position, trying to balance internal and external stakeholders in the best interest of the corporation. These challenges are likely to increase, rather than decrease, in the future. Also, the CFO will need to combine a high tolerance for working with ambiguity and coping with significant personal stress.

The external environment drives much of the increased pressure. The economies of Europe and North America are not growing, but as one CFO said, 'People still expect salary increases.' So, too, do shareholders, who are becoming increasingly demanding and less willing to accept performance that was sufficient in the past.

Effective administration and efficiency: doing more with less

Companies are expected to do more with fewer resources. Furthermore, the CFO is expected to lead by example. This leads to outsourcing, off-shoring, reduced headcount and very low tolerance of non-performers. As fewer resources are expected to produce more, the CFO of the future will not succeed without achieving significant improvements in efficiency. Building and maintaining efficient teams is a key success factor.

Since the mid-1990s, a main source of efficiency improvements in finance and other support services has been the 'shared services' concept. Instead of duplicating support services in many countries, resources are pooled centrally and shared by several legal entities. Transactional processing services such as invoicing and accounts payable, call centres and sales and customer services are examples of shared services.

The main drive behind shared services is cost savings. However, there are additional benefits. For example, by creating a critical mass, a company may be able to attract and retain more talent. This is very important in a function where competition for highly competent employees may be a limiting factor.

Shared services centres have a dark side too. Often, cost savings never materialize, internal politics render the new centre ineffective and service levels drop dramatically. Combine this with high staff turnover due to the repetitive nature of the work and wage competition from other multinational shared services centres. Establishing a truly cost-effective shared services centre with exceptional performance is not a project for the faint of heart.

The external regulatory environment (notably the USA's Sarbanes-Oxley Act) is another trend that has increased many companies' administrative burdens. Even worse, many CFOs find themselves dragged into meetings with other managers to examine every contract that has a potential legal or accounting implication.

The strategic side of the CFO's job is by no means becoming easier. The CFO's strategic role is twofold. He must spot opportunities or weaknesses, and allocate capital and resources more effectively. There is a growing demand from BUs for financial support and risk management. However, the natures of risk and uncertainty are very different, and much less predictable, in today's world. For example, few people would have considered the impact of terrorist attacks on the business before 11 September 2001.

A further consideration, which can put considerable pressure on the CFO, is that today's CFOs are often public figures, particularly in the financial community. Shareholders and the non-stop business television and print media are looking for someone who is articulate and charismatic, but above all has a steady hand. Even the slightest tremble may be enough to lose the confidence of the investors.

Since the CFO is not in a position to do everything, success requires exceptional leadership and communication skills.

Leadership qualities

The leadership requirements of the CFO of the future are many and varied, but there is one about which there can be little debate: the ability to build confidence and trust. These are vital for successfully working with the financial community and external stakeholders. However, the same confidence and trust are equally important when working with the CXO team and internal stakeholders.

Since the CFO is not able to do everything alone, confidence and trust in his or her people is also essential. So, too, is a vision for the finance function, ensuring that it is aligned and capable of pursuing that vision.

However, several elements need to be in place before that can be achieved.

Integrity and credibility

Integrity, more than any other skill or personal quality, can make or break a CFO. It is also something that may require significant management courage to preserve. Since they still remain the 'guardian of the profit,' CFOs must have the courage to voice their opinion. They may even need to stand up to the top management team (including the CEO) if necessary.

The CFO must also lead by example. This means running an efficient department and insisting on high standards of performance from members of the finance team.

Although the CFO is rarely involved in the details, finance is a highly specialized profession where the credibility of the top executive requires a mastery of technical skills. This is not restricted to accounting and finance skills. It should also include a sound understanding of the legal and regulatory environment, a high degree of IT literacy and a complete understanding of the business strategy.

Operational understanding and a service mindset

Credibility and ability to add value come not only from technical finance expertise. They also result from a solid understanding of the business issues and how finance can add value. This was noted eighty years ago, when Alfred Sloan argued that finance was a support function that must be integrated with operations.

This view is highlighted by one CFO: 'There is no use having a CFO just putting numbers into a five-year plan . . . without an understanding of the business.'

Unfortunately, the increasing technical complexity of finance has tended to result in a functional 'silo.' Encouragingly, there is now a trend where many CFOs have prior operational exposure.

Communication skills, relationship skills, empathy and personal energy

The true test of a CFO comes during difficult times, and many companies have faced or will be facing increasing hardship. CFOs unanimously cite communication skills as the main requirement when the department or company is going through tough times.

The CFO is a networker, both with external stakeholders and with the management team. The CFO must manage the dual role of 'guardian of the profit' and of business partner. This means providing support without kowtowing, and providing direction without arrogance.

The role of the CFO during difficult times

CFOs involved in restructuring their organization single out communication as their top priority. It is the key reason for their success. Communication skills and personal energy are increasingly recognized as being vital to successful leadership.

An industrial company that went through a major turnaround emerged at one-third of its original size. The CFO cited this as a major achievement, attributing his success to 'open and frank communication, good chemistry with the people, treating people fairly and managing the process fairly . . . not just cold dismissing'.

One CFO had to close down an IT centre in Spain. He knew the immediate risk was that people would leave, particularly the ones he wanted to keep. People were informed that they had jobs for the next two years, but in the longer term the operation would be moved.

The CFO commented: 'The key is good, frequent communication. You need to be very open and honest and very frank about how you see the changes and what will happen . . . you need to get people involved, keep them busy with projects that make sense. It is also important to celebrate success, for example the end of a project. Not just to give them the bad news.'

Michel-Marc Delcommune, CFO of MOL, the national oil and gas company in Hungary, implemented shared services and then completely outsourced these services to a third party. This involved the separation of more than 400 staff. Many had been with the company their entire working lives and had not adapted to the competitive environment of Hungary in the 1990s.

Mr. Delcommune used a 'road show' concept, similar to the one for investors, to tour different sites and explain the projects. By using a hands-on approach, he convinced employees that they would be treated fairly. More importantly, he helped them to address the question: 'What will happen to me, personally?' This proactive communication style was a major reason why the project succeeded.

In essence, the best CFOs are people who, by viewing financial performance through the lens of operational know-how, can decipher what the market is telling the company. They can recognize and understand what is driving or inhibiting success. Furthermore, they can enable the organization to transform that knowledge into a workable strategy. Such an undertaking requires that the CFO apply his or her full repertoire of skills to become a key strategic player.

Assessing the role of the CFO

The following questions provide a starting point when assessing the role of the CFO.

Purpose

1. How effectively does the CFO:
   - Ensure that the company has sufficient funds to implement its investment and growth strategies?
   - Promote the most efficient use of funds?
   - Measure how well capital has been deployed in the past and determine how capital should be deployed optimally in the future?
   - Lead the finance function, satisfying the requirements of internal and external customers?

Direction

2. Does the CFO provide transparent real-time information for internal decision-making and for governance purposes, without interfering or distracting the business?
3. Effectiveness: Does the CFO do the right things? Is the CFO's work and that of the finance function accurate, reliable and timely? Does the finance function add value to the business and how could this be improved?
4. Efficiency: Does the CFO do things at the right cost? In particular, does the CFO lead by example? Does the CFO provide systems that reduce the cost of the basic activities and free up time for value-adding activities?
5. How well does the CFO combine operational excellence with dynamic support for the company's strategic direction and priorities?

Focus

6. How well does the CFO build and develop a winning team?
7. Does the CFO effectively manage performance – again, managing by example?
8. Does the CFO hire team players – people who work with other departments as well as other people in the finance function?
9. Is the CFO able to voice his/her opinion to the board and CEO?

Glossary

Sarbanes-Oxley Act

The US Congress reacted to the highly publicized bankruptcies of Enron and WorldCom by enacting the 2002 Sarbanes-Oxley Act. Sarbanes-Oxley is almost entirely concerned with strictly enforcing the latest generally accepted accounting principles (GAAP).

Shareholder value

Shareholder value is based on the view that a company should aim to maximize its value to shareholders. The concept of shareholder value works from the premise that a business only adds value for its shareholders when equity returns exceed equity costs. Shareholder value analysis (SVA) is focused on long-term profit flows, and so the analysis requires a long-term perspective.

Acknowledgments

I am grateful to Michael Jacobi, Etienne Hoepffner, Michel-Marc Delcommune, Nour Avrany, Jesper Brandgaard, Markus Brechbühl, Bruno Allmendinger and a number of other CFOs who prefer to remain anonymous for the opportunity to discuss their leadership challenges. Any opinions expressed in this chapter are purely my own.

Notes

1 S. Wehrwein, 'The changing role of the CFO', Knowledge@Wharton, May (2002).
2 P. Currie, CFO of the Year in Canada, in his acceptance speech, March (2004).
3 See A. P. Sloan, 'My Years with General Motors', *Currency* (1996), (first published in 1964).
4 J. Graziano, CFO of Apple Computer, quoted in *CFO Magazine*, March (2005).
5 Survey conducted by *CFO Magazine* and the National Association of Corporate Directors.

10 *The Chief Technology Officer – Corporate navigator, agent of change and entrepreneur*

JEAN-PHILIPPE DESCHAMPS

The CTO function has its origins in both research and development (R&D) and engineering, but the scope of its responsibilities and influence vary widely across companies and industries.

The author describes how today's challenge is to strike the right balance between the central steering of technology and its operational decentralization to serve the company's businesses well. The CTO focuses on effectiveness (doing the right things) and efficiency (doing things right), but at the same time, looks to the future to identify and acquire new technologies and competencies. He/she is expected to deliver new products and processes that will create and sustain the businesses of the future and contribute directly to the company's growth and value.

The challenge for many CTOs is to change the traditional mindset in R&D, opening people to accept and integrate new technologies from outside and encourage inter-disciplinary cross-fertilization.

The CTO used to be a specialist resource within the top management team, but should now be recognized by management colleagues as a full partner in strategic discussions. For that to happen, the CTO needs to earn his/her colleagues' respect by displaying business acumen and leadership.

Chief technology officer/chief research officer: A common origin in the R&D function

I am the first person with that title [CTO] in our company. Before that, I was heading R&D in one of our four business units and most of my time was spent supervising projects for my unit and managing our large development staff. Why did we set up this CTO function? I guess to build bridges between our R&D units and learn to work together on shared technologies. We must not reinvent the wheel and, most importantly, we need to look beyond our own courtyard to identify and secure those new technologies that will change the name of the game in our business for years to come.

> But honestly, my job is still far from being well defined and I still have to find out what my priorities should be in the eyes of my top management colleagues. I also need to work out how I am supposed to interface with my former R&D colleagues, who now report in dotted lines to me while continuing to receive their marching orders from their business unit VPs . . .
>
> (Newly appointed CTO of a medium-sized high-technology company)

Only recently has the role of chief technology officer (CTO) or chief research officer (CRO) emerged in the executive team. (NB: Despite the different titles and roles, elaborated below, we use both terms in this chapter.) Previously this CXO function was indistinct from the traditional role of head of R&D or engineering. The change can be traced to two factors. One is the growth of large, multi-product, multi-business and multi-technology corporations in the 1970s. The second is the realization that technology is a critical asset that needs to be competitively managed with a long-term perspective.

The first factor originates in the evolution of corporate organizations from a functional hierarchy to a business unit approach. This trend spread like wildfire in the 1970s. The organizational disruption often led to the dismemberment of large, integrated R&D centres and the creation of focused strategic business unit (SBU) labs. By breaking up R&D into smaller units and making them report to dedicated business leaders, CEOs hoped for a more business-responsive R&D. However, they soon realized that decentralization risked fragmenting resources, loss of shared creativity and a gradual duplication of competencies. Many former R&D chiefs suddenly found themselves with neither staff nor labs under their direct supervision. In many cases, these senior technologists were asked to co-ordinate R&D competence across organizational boundaries with a small central staff. Some kept the R&D acronym in their title, becoming vice-president R&D or R&D director.

The second driver of the changing CTO function was the rapid appearance of new technologies in the 1980s and 1990s. Industries were revolutionized; companies broadened their technology portfolios. For example, engineering, plastics and digital electronics revolutionized the car industry, and molecular biology and biotechnology changed traditional chemistry-driven drug development. The emergence of these new technologies forced companies to reassess their technology strategies and build new competencies. Many traditional

R&D labs did not immediately master many of the new technologies. This reinforced the need for senior technologists on the top executive team. And thus, the CTO became the guardian of the company's long-term technological competitiveness.

Today, most large technology-intensive companies have appointed a CTO. This trend is also increasing in medium-sized companies. CEOs are assigning a member of their top executive team to represent the company's scientific and technical functions on the board of management. However, their titles and functions vary widely between companies.

CTO/CRO: a common interest despite different titles

Differences between CTOs and CROs stem essentially from the way they define their discipline and choose their process emphasis.

- CROs tend to see their world as science-driven. They focus on the research and discovery process. Creating and exploiting knowledge and new science and technology-based businesses commercially fuels their drive. CROs are found in research-intensive industries such as pharmaceuticals, medical technology, advanced electronics or specialized chemicals. They carry a variety of titles, e.g. vice-president science and R&D; scientific director; corporate research officer; research vice-president, and so on. Some of them have an even bigger title: CEO – research.
- By contrast, CTOs talk and think more often in terms of technology, i.e. applied science, with a focus on developing new products or manufacturing processes. They traditionally concentrate on technical choices and management processes: i.e. technology forecasting, road mapping, audit, development, outsourcing, sharing and deployment. CTOs are typically found in the electronics and information technology industry. They are appearing in other industries too, with titles like chief technology officer, senior vice-president technology, and corporate technology director.

The boundary between these two titles remains blurred, as many executives straddle the two types of function. Whatever their titles may be, CTOs and CROs are generally expected to fulfil four core responsibilities:

What are your job responsibilities today?

	Direct line	Dotted line
• Innovation process management	59%	32%
• Knowledge management	41%	32%
• New, tech-based, business development & venturing	36%	27%
• Corporate central research organization	27%	41%
• Divisional or SBU R&D organization (CTOs)	27%	50%
• Quality management	27%	32%
• Information technology/informatics	23%	45%
• Intellectual property management	23%	55%
• Technology and operations support management	18%	45%
• Manufacturing process innovation	18%	50%
• Engineering management	14%	59%
• Decentralized corporate competence centres	9%	64%

Source: IMD CTO survey, 2000
(N = 30)

Figure 10.1: CTOs' & CROs' line versus staff responsibilities

Supervise R&D activities and guard intellectual property (IP)

This often entails a combination of line and functional responsibilities with an emphasis on functional integration. Some CROs will be hierarchical supervisors of all central or corporate R&D labs. This is often the case with CROs from the pharmaceutical industry. Other CROs serve mostly co-ordination, alignment and stimulation functions. They have very limited line responsibilities, particularly regarding divisional or business unit labs. (see Figures 10.1 and 10.2).

Manage the deployment of scientific and technical staff

The top executive team usually views the corporate CTO as the high-level human resource officer of the scientific and technical staff. Though they may not have a hierarchical relationship with their staff, CTOs are usually responsible for hiring staff and overseeing the allocation of senior personnel.

The rotation of scientists and engineers from central labs to business unit labs – and as often happens in Japan, from labs to plants – is important as it ensures that R&D staff are exposed to the reality of business. It also creates vacancies for new scientists with cutting-edge competencies.

One of my most difficult jobs is to convince some of my most senior research managers that they should leave our corporate organization to join one of our business units. These

Area of CTO/CRO responsibility	% listing item* 5 yrs ago	% listing item* today
Innovation process management	55%	91%
Intellectual property management	36%	77%
Divisional or SBU R&D organization	45%	77%
Knowledge management	50%	73%
Decentralized corp. compet. centres	41%	73%
New, tech-based bus. dev't/venturing	41%	64%

Source: IMD CTO survey, 2000
(N = 30)

* direct line + dotted line responsibilities

Figure 10.2: The growing scope of CTOs' & CROs' responsibilities

people, often, have stopped doing R&D work. They just manage others and, at one point in time, it is in their and the company's interest that they should move to the business side so as to leave room for new talent and allow me to maintain a flatter central R&D organization. (CTO of a large electronics company)

Allocate corporate funds to strategic R&D programmes

These can be high-impact programmes designed to pioneer a new technology, catch up with competitors or launch a new activity between or across divisions or business units. This role includes monitoring whether funds are used effectively and nurturing projects until they come to fruition. This portfolio role, even for those with limited line responsibilities, is one of the most powerful ways to influence the company's research and technology strategy. CTOs in Japanese technology-intensive companies derive most of their top executive influence from this particular role.

In our company, the bulk of our technology and R&D investments are in the hands of our business units. They decide where and how to spend their R&D resources. As a result, we have tended to favour incremental product-line extensions. It is to overcome that risk that I have set up a budget for corporate-funded high-risk/high-impact projects. This allows me to ensure that we are going to work in new areas that our business units would not want to pioneer alone. (Former CTO of a global engineering company)

Advise CEOs, boards and top management colleagues

Educating CXO colleagues on scientific and technological issues is a classic role for the CTO. Some companies still use their CTOs primarily in this limited, non-executive function. They are the 'experts', pulled out to be consulted on critical technology choices, then sent back to their labs. But, in today's technology-intensive environment, this expert function is often insufficient. Executive management needs people who understand the strategic implications of technology choices, the strategy of the company and the impact of technology on the bottom line.

The changing role of the CTO/CRO: from managing to leading

For decades, R&D and its senior managers have been shielded from short-term business pressures. That view of the world is changing rapidly. The evolution of global markets and technologies, the growing complexity of companies and the increasing pressures to increase shareholder value force the CTO to consider short-term results. Market and financial expectations for top and bottom-line numbers are now passed on to technology chiefs. Increasingly, CTOs are being asked to contribute directly to the company's growth and profit. Long-term tracking of R&D projects and their profitability is another challenge the CTO has to master.

These pressures are causing CTOs to shift their emphasis from managing functions, people and assets to leading a transformation. This shift means instilling a sense of purpose, direction and focus in all technical departments. Aligning scientists and engineers with the company's strategic direction helps to build cohesion and increases the probability of the company's success.

However, despite this trend towards a more strategic involvement in company affairs, CTOs will always be judged on the company's overall R&D effectiveness. If there are few new products in the company's pipeline, CTOs will not be credible as full partners at the strategy table. R&D must be seen to be efficient with time and money and effective by introducing competitive new products and features. In short, the CTO's credibility hinges on R&D's results. To hold a seat at the executive management table, CTOs must earn the respect and trust of their colleagues in their functional area.

Instilling a sense of purpose in the role of science and technology

In the past, like most of my colleagues – all young scientists out of university – I joined that company's R&D group as I would have joined a postgraduate research position, attracted by the prospect of working on exciting new technology, travelling to attend scientific conventions and becoming famous through widely published new discoveries.

Well, that is long gone, I am afraid. Today, as CRO, one of my first jobs is to make our staff more market and business-oriented. We have to justify our existence and the funds the company invests in research. My business colleagues look to me and to research as the source of new technologies that will make them win. They also expect us to invent and deliver the new products and businesses that will make us grow as a company. My job is to deliver results and I am evaluated on the perception that my board of management have of whether I am bringing a satisfactory return on R&D investments! (CRO of a global electronics company)

Pressures for growth and performance generally trigger a renewed sense of purpose and urgency at all levels. Sitting at the top of their scientific and technical community, CTOs will be expected to get ready for a quantum jump in the contribution of R&D to business success. Having climbed the ladder through R&D management, their traditional emphasis was on functional efficiency. As they reach the CXO team, this aspect of their job declines in importance. But their role as guardians of the company's long-term scientific and technological competitiveness is rapidly expanding.

This substantial change in management agenda and emphasis is clearly highlighted in an opinion survey conducted by IMD among CTOs and CROs from leading international companies. These senior executives were asked to list their priorities in the past five years and the ones that would retain their attention over the next five years.

Among the eight broad challenges proposed, the majority indicated a declining importance for two traditional aspects of their job (see Figure 10.3):

- Organizing R&D for a global world: spreading R&D resources to tap scientific brains and operate in all parts of the world.
- Organizing for technology management: traditional R&D organization issues, technology funding and technology management processes.

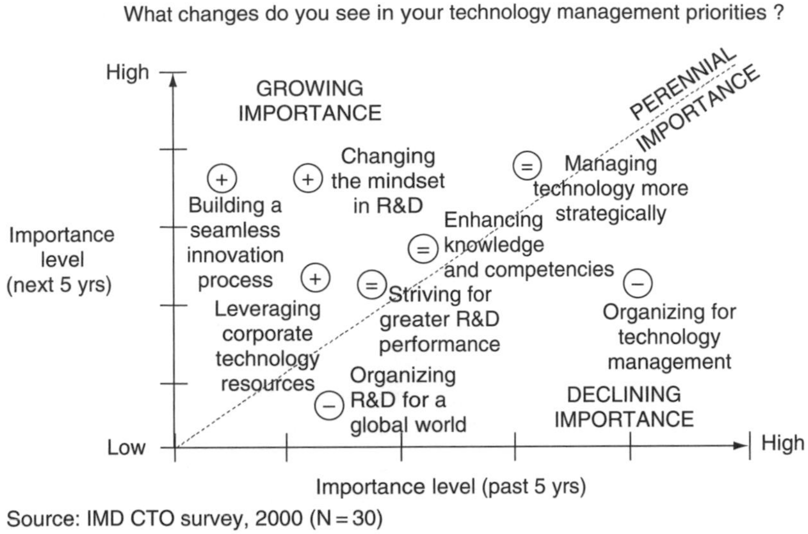

Figure 10.3: The changing agenda of the CTO/CRO

In contrast, the survey highlighted a continued emphasis on three perennial strategic missions:

- Managing technology more strategically: linking technology and business strategies more effectively, particularly for the long term.
- Enhancing knowledge and competencies: focusing on creating, using, sharing and protecting knowledge, as well as discarding irrelevant knowledge.[1]
- Striving for greater R&D performance: improving the contribution of R&D to business success, essentially through a more-strategic project selection.

These important aims call on leadership skills to a larger extent than on organizational or managerial abilities.

Finally, three priorities appeared with an increasing brightness on their radar screen, all relating to the CTO's ability to transform the organization, which requires strong leadership qualities:

- Change the mindset in R&D by introducing a stronger business focus and a more acute sense of urgency among the scientific and technical community.

- Build a seamless innovation process: communicate and work more effectively with other functions, for example marketing or manufacturing.
- Leverage corporate technology resources: a greater attention to technology in-sourcing and outsourcing to capitalize on the specific strengths of technology partners.

Providing a sense of direction in science and technology

> One of my important missions was to ensure that our company stayed abreast of, and used, all those new technologies that are radically altering the way we develop drugs.
>
> For years, I was the advocate and promoter of combinatorial chemistry, high-throughput screening techniques and bioinformatics. When these had been reasonably mastered, we embarked on boosting our knowledge of genomics and proteomics to be able to benefit fully from our partnerships in those domains. The search for new technologies is an unending quest in the pharma industry.
>
> (Former CRO of a large drug company)

Perhaps the most challenging part of the CTO's job is the expectation to provide the board and top executive team with clear directions on where and how much to invest in science and technology.

Deciding on the appropriate level of R&D spending – generally expressed as a percentage of sales – is one of the most debated top management issues in technology-intensive industries. CTOs are, inevitably at the centre of that debate. The R&D budget, whatever the method used to make it look rational, is ultimately the CTO's responsibility. Investment allocation in R&D will reflect:

- A *vision* of where and how technology will shape the future of the business and create opportunities;
- A management *ambition* level regarding the risks it is willing to take in introducing new technologies;
- A *faith* in the power of science and technology to out-perform or out-innovate competitors.

Formulating a vision for technology

The CTO has a decisive role to play in bringing about management's vision, ambition and faith regarding technology. That process, which can

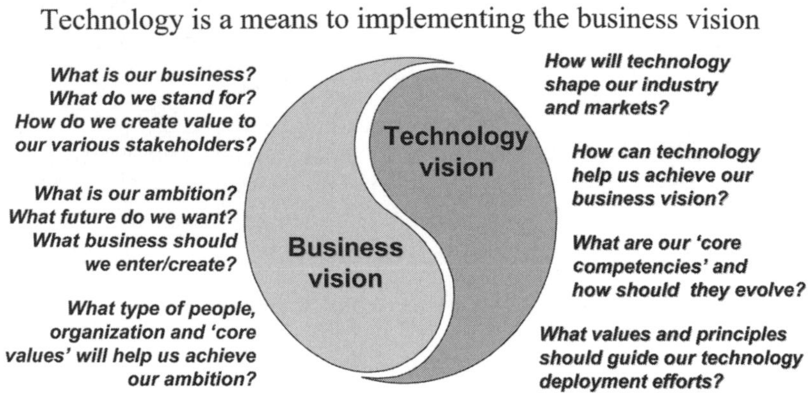
Technology is a means to implementing the business vision
What is our business?
What do we stand for?
How do we create value to our various stakeholders?
What is our ambition?
What future do we want?
What business should we enter/create?
What type of people, organization and 'core values' will help us achieve our ambition?
Technology vision
Business vision
How will technology shape our industry and markets?
How can technology help us achieve our business vision?
What are our 'core competencies' and how should they evolve?
What values and principles should guide our technology deployment efforts?

Figure 10.4: The interdependence of technology and business visions

be called 'technology visioning', is similar to what process management teams use to sharpen, reorient or renew their business vision. Specialists[2] claim that a company vision is composed of two linked facets:

- A picture of an 'envisaged future', highlighting a desirable future state of the company, and how it wants to be perceived by its stakeholders;
- A 'core ideology', stating what the company stands for vis-à-vis its stakeholders and the values it promotes.

This is sometimes distilled into a short policy statement that is communicated to the outside world.

The same process applies to technology, which is a means of implementing the business vision (see Figure 10.4). Normally, the business vision will drive the technology vision. However, in technology-intensive industries, the reverse often happens.

Through a process of technology visioning, the CTO should provide a sense of direction to the company's R&D efforts. There are generally two sides to it, a 'harder' side and a 'softer' side (see Figure 10.5).

Envisaging the future regarding technology (the 'harder' side of a vision)

Envisaging the future entails defining the scope of the company's technology coverage and identifying competencies that are critical for the company to master. It is up to the CTO to recommend which areas of R&D should be investigated, developed and grown (or pruned). The

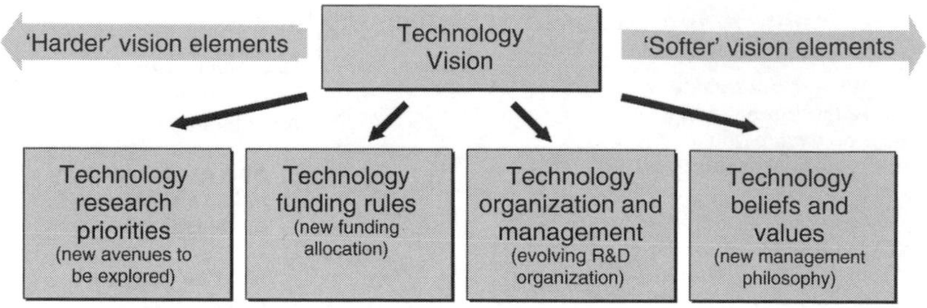

Figure 10.5: The 'hard' and 'soft' elements of a technology vision

CTO also plays a key role, along with the CFO, in recommending and justifying the funding level for future investments.

Envisaging the future also means defining the role of technology in the company strategy. Cisco Systems Inc. provides a good example of the link between business and technology visions. The company's vision – becoming the preferred internet-enabling company and total solution provider on the basis of its product superiority – has rapidly been translated into a clear technology vision and a serial technology acquisition strategy (a strategy that was only viable when the company's stock price was high). The company has learned how to select technology targets carefully, acquire them rapidly and integrate them immediately. Its vision has been translated directly into action.

A company will never be able to maintain a technological lead from only its own resources. The CTO must ensure the organization is open to using the best technologies, regardless of the source. It is often less expensive to license or acquire a new technology than to develop it in-house. In fact, it is not uncommon for companies today to post technical challenges online and receive bids from other companies to fulfil some of their technological needs. A striking example is given by Procter & Gamble with its 'connect and develop' strategy. P&G's CEO, A. G. Lafley, mandated that 50 per cent of the company's innovations should come from outside. The strategy was not to get rid of Procter & Gamble's researchers, but to better leverage them. From about 15 per cent in 2000, the proportion of external innovations had thus risen to more than 35 per cent in 2006, and 45 per cent of the initiatives in the company's product development portfolio have key elements that were discovered externally. This strategy has already led to a dramatic increase in R&D productivity and innovation success rate.[3]

Developing a core ideology regarding technology (the 'softer' side of a vision)

Some CTOs have gone beyond envisaging the future. They have formulated and promoted policies, behaviour, beliefs and values about technology and a guiding framework for its deployment and management. For example, at 3M, technical managers know that the technologies deployed belong to the company and not to their business units. Everyone in 3M's technical community is expected to practise the values derived from such a belief: a systematic sharing of technologies across labs and business units – an elusive goal in many corporations.

The softer side of a technology vision deals with changing working behaviour and the mindset about technology in the organizations. Clarifying this ideology and getting it adopted is one of the key leadership roles of the CTO. This includes:

- Establishing and building a consensus of beliefs and values within the company's scientific and technical community;
- Making these beliefs and values explicit, for example in the form of a 'technology charter' (see example in Figure 10.6);
- Getting the technology charter endorsed by management and communicating it widely among R&D's business partners;
- Designing and running a program of change to embed the new behaviours into day-to-day lab reality (see Figure 10.7).

A final aspect brings us to one of the fastest-growing areas of concern captured in the CTO survey: changing the mindset in R&D. The nature of the new mindset is typically company-specific. In companies with a strong central R&D function, the objective of the change programme is often to make the staff more responsive to business demands. R&D is expected to be flexible to business demands; to be cost-conscious and pay close attention to the speed of development. In other companies with a strong growth objective, such as Dow Chemical Co. and Royal Philips Electronics, the efforts may focus more on entrepreneurship and new business creation. In the pharmaceutical industry, CROs will often promote a more effective collaboration between research centres, both within the company and with external technology partners (for example

Charter outline

- The fundamental role of technology in business success and the nature of the company's innovation challenge, i.e.:
  - The roles of proprietary versus non-proprietary/outsourced technologies;
  - The relative importance of technology forecasting versus market sensing;
  - The rules concerning technology ownership, usage and accountability;
  - The proper time horizon of the company's technology investments.
- The strategic management of technology and the role of chief research or technology officers, i.e.:
  - The level of enforcement of technology synergy across businesses;
  - The policy regarding technology outsourcing, partnering or venturing;
  - The role of CTOs as business 'supporters' versus new business 'creators';
  - The power and intervention authority of divisional CTOs.
- The particular role, function or mission of the central research organization versus divisional R&D units, i.e.:
  - The contribution of research and appropriate level of R&D decentralization;
  - The role of research in developing new competencies and businesses;
  - The mission of research in attracting, developing and transferring talent;
  - The attitude of research regarding technologies falling outside business priorities.
- The internal organization of the Research Centre, its funding and the evaluation of its output, i.e.:
  - The merits of organizing along 'disciplines' versus ' technology platforms';
  - The relative importance of corporate versus business unit funding;
  - The measurement of research's output in terms of value created;
  - The policy regarding sub-critical and peripheral research activities.
- The management of human resources in technology (hiring, performance evaluation, career management), i.e.:
  - Preferred profile and breadth of skills of incoming scientists and engineers;
  - Rotation of scientists between research and development centres;
  - Involvement of R&D leaders in strategic business management issues;
  - Focus of R&D staff evaluation (R&D output quality versus business success?)

Figure 10.6: Charter proposed by the CTO of one of the world's leading chemical companies

with smaller associated biotech firms.) Regardless of their focus, these programmes tend to require continuous attention by the CTO or CRO. Changing the mindset of the people working in R&D is not an easy or short-term task.

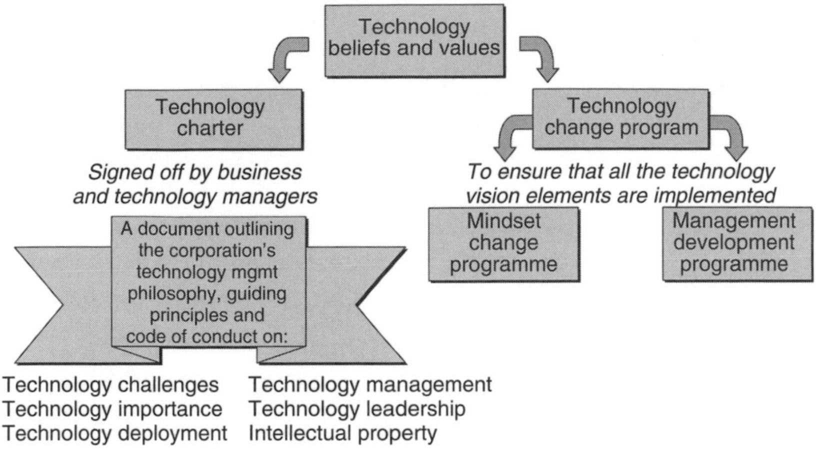

Figure 10.7: Grounding shared technology beliefs and values

Enforcing a sense of focus on technology

Our CEO is very much concerned by the fact that many of the technologies and competences that we are deploying are becoming very mature. They are not giving us much competitive advantage anymore.

So, I have started investigating opportunities for outsourcing some of our traditional R&D activities, in the same way as we started outsourcing part of our operations and services. The idea is to free resources so as to invest more in new competences to support our drive in nutrition. (CRO of a global food company)

As future-oriented leaders, CROs will be expected to guide the company and align the technological focus with the company's strategy. Being accountable for the long-term technological competitiveness of the company, CTOs or CROs often have the following formal responsibilities in their job description:

- Identify technologies that have the highest competitive impact on the company's businesses today. Identify technologies that will or might replace existing methods and be disruptive to the entire business or industry.
- Audit the company's competitive technological position in a realistic and objective manner. Analyse opportunities and threats that might result from major technological strengths and weaknesses.

- Contain the risk of technology fragmentation. Ensure that enough resources are devoted to the company's most-vital technologies, even at the expense of reducing investments in less-critical areas.
- Invest in new critical technologies ahead of time (but not too early). Choose investment strategies that reduce risks to an acceptable level while maintaining flexibility.
- Outsource non-essential technologies that waste resources and do not offer any particular competitive advantage. Outsource in a way that guarantees access to key technologies needed to remain competitive.

Each item highlights one of the most-fundamental roles of the CTO/CRO, and one that requires a lot of courage: *make choices and focus*.

Andy Grove, the charismatic chairman and former CEO of Intel Corp., recognized that choosing to focus all his company's resources on microprocessors and abandoning memory development and fabrication was perhaps the most difficult decision in his career.[4] Despite the predicted growth in demand for computer memory and Intel's competitive position, Grove realized that he could not grow the memory business in parallel with the promising microprocessor business. At stake was the risk of Intel becoming a mediocre competitor in two businesses. The fabulous growth of the company shows how inspired (or fortunate) this decision was to focus on microprocessors, a domain where Intel now claims a leading technological position.

Not all companies have to confront dilemmas of such magnitude. Nevertheless, the need to focus on certain technologies with its corollary – the abandonment or outsourcing of other technologies – is widespread.

The delicate task of identifying candidates in the two categories – technologies to be acquired and developed and technologies to be abandoned or outsourced – clearly belongs to the CTO. But the task does not stop with that identification. The most-critical part of a focused technology strategy is implementation. Two significant challenges need to be addressed in implementation:

- How to acquire and deploy new knowledge time- and cost-effectively. To deal with this issue, the CTO will often recommend strategic acquisitions or partnerships. Here, leadership skills will be tested because the new technologies (and often the associated people) have to become established in the 'new' organization. Grafting new knowledge onto a somewhat-sceptical R&D organization is not easy.

- How to phase out less critical technologies without losing competitive advantage. This issue is even more delicate. Technologies equate to knowledge and knowledge resides in people. Abandoning a hitherto important area of knowledge often means losing key people. Not all scientists and engineers can be easily retrained, and sometimes the objective is to reduce headcount and internal costs.

CTOs must be acutely aware of the danger of demoralizing staff. Averting that risk without giving up on the company's overall objectives is another strong test of this CXO's leadership capabilities.

The emerging role of 'corporate entrepreneur'

Traditionally in our company, corporate R&D was there to develop and master the technologies needed to support our businesses. When we realized that our business units could not bring us the growth our shareholders expect, then we decided to change the focus of our corporate R&D centre. It is still to support current business, but it has also the mission to open new territories and generate new business.

This is why we have started a program to boost the entrepreneurial spirit of our scientists and we created a special group responsible for following up on promising project ideas with a business creation potential. (CTO of a global chemical company)

In a growing number of mature companies, CTOs are expected to leverage the company's R&D resources to create new business. A priority for the CXO team in this 'post-re-engineering' period is to build new 'legs' for growth.This emphasis on new business creation has led to a variety of innovative management practices.

At Bayer Group, Philips and Mitsubishi Chemical Corp., management demands for new business creation have been translated into new corporate R&D funding policies and criteria. Pure exploratory research is maintained, but at a lower level than in the past. Considerable efforts and corporate funds are devoted to strategic research initiatives, i.e. innovative projects capable of generating new business streams. Other companies, such as Motorola, have introduced a systematic search for technology-based business opportunities in their road-mapping process. Business and technology reviews, led by cross-functional teams including CTOs, focus on trends and developments that point to new opportunities. They can trigger requests for corporate funding and new business development initiatives of significant size and risk.

Finally, a growing trend is that CTOs are increasingly encouraged to build a corporate development group of their own. Many variations exist in this area. At Hewlett-Packard, the CTO has set up a small strategic group, as part of their corporate labs, to study and pursue new business creation opportunities. Other companies have set up R&D-funded new business incubators of their own. These organizations are responsible for pursuing opportunities until they can be transferred to existing business units or spun off as separate ventures. DuPont was an early adopter of this incubator concept with its 'commercial demonstration group'. Their incubator reported directly to the CTO. At Motorola it was called Motorola New Enterprises.

Such emphasis on new business creation is not universally recognized (or successful in creating value) at a time when many companies are under pressure to focus on their core business. Corporate entrepreneurship may not appear prominently on the CTO's current job description, but this is likely to change. As a consequence, a new set of responsibilities may be added to the traditional CTO's job description:

- Review and change R&D funding policies and criteria to ensure adequate resources are allocated to strategic initiatives. Lead the development of new businesses, not just the enhancement or protection of existing ones.
- Set up processes, build partnerships and promote attitudes that will lead R&D to systematically evaluate new technology-based business opportunities.
- Participate actively in the creation of a corporate development group to pursue new opportunities.
- Coach infant businesses throughout their early lives on behalf of the CXO team. Ensure high-potential projects are quickly entrusted to business-oriented project leaders.
- Build partnerships between the company's business units and R&D to support the new business ventures. Help them set up as independent organizations or integrate into the existing business.

The message is loud and clear: the CTO and CRO positions are gradually becoming the 'CIO' or chief innovation officer. The new mission is to lead the company towards new opportunities for growth. If the dual role of all senior executives is to 'master the present' and 'pre-empt the future'[5] the CTO and CRO has always been expected to favour the latter part of the job. Increasingly, however, the CTO is expected to go even further – to create the future. This means fostering an organizational climate for innovation. The CTO must breed future 'innovation leaders'[6] who will lead projects and build businesses. Innovation leaders can be characterized by:

- An extreme level of openness to external ideas and technologies;
- A mix of 'emotion and realism' or 'creativity and discipline';
- An acceptance of risks and ability to learn from failures;
- The courage to stop – not just to start – things;
- The ability to build and lead winning teams.

Facing the challenge as part of the top executive team

My job as a CTO cannot be defined as easily as that of my senior colleagues from Finance or HR. Since we have decentralized all our R&D resources into our divisions, I am not running a department any more. I am simply influencing other people's decisions.

My degree of influence is fundamentally dependent on how my boss – the CEO – and my divisional colleagues look at it and how they trust my judgement. As long as our current CEO and our Divisional VPs are not very 'technical', they let me have a lot of responsibility and freedom in technology-related decisions, but that could change with a new CEO. (CTO of a medium-sized engineering company)

In the top executive team, CTOs often maintain a privileged relationship with the CEO where the company relies heavily on technology and innovation. But the main day-to-day relationship of the CTO is with divisional presidents or business unit heads, whom they must both support and challenge.

CTOs' primary role is to support the company's businesses. They manage corporate R&D resources and budgets, build partnerships with external sources and provide strategic guidance on technology. But at the same time, they will often find themselves in a challenger role vis-à-vis their CXO business colleagues. This situation often arises when the CTO's colleagues are tempted to take shortcuts or underinvest in new technologies in their quest for short-term results. Non-technically trained business managers may underestimate the strategic significance of certain technologies.

Years ago, as digital electronics was emerging, it took me a lot of time and effort to convince my colleagues not to close a small lab we had in that area. That lab was building knowledge in digital signal processing but it was not directly productive because our products were still based on analogue technology.

My colleagues viewed that little team as an expensive overhead item that they wanted to cut. My reaction was: 'Over my dead body!' Today, they could not imagine what would have happened had I not protected that lab.

(Retired CTO of a large electronics company)

The relationship of CTOs with other members of the CXO team will typically be less intense and less ambiguous. Sometimes there will be friction and overlap with the chief information officer when the two functions coexist at the top management level. The CEO should clearly define the boundaries between the chief technology officer and the chief information officer in order to minimize potential conflicts. One challenge the CTO (usually with the help of the CEO) faces is to help their executive management colleagues understand that the CTO role has changed in at least four key areas:

- **Positioning** From being a *specialist resource* within the senior management group, the CTO is increasingly becoming a *full member of the top executive team*, sharing in key business decisions, not just technology ones.

  This broadening of horizons is bringing about a dramatic change in perspective. The CTO's loyalty is no longer oriented towards R&D or the scientific community, but towards company stakeholders and management colleagues. This change is putting pressure on CTOs to become credible business partners, sharing the same understanding of business dynamics and the same vocabulary as their management-educated colleagues.
- **Scope** From managing a *functional slice* of the corporation – R&D and technology – the CTO is increasingly being asked to steer a number of critical *business processes* involving numerous other functions.

  Typical examples include the innovation process from idea and technology to market and the new business creation and venturing process. Additionally, because so many technologies come from outside the firm, the partnering, or supplier-management, process can also fall under the CTO's realm.

  Another challenge for CTOs to master is to steer cross-functional management teams and negotiate trade-offs between conflicting technological and business objectives.

- **Objective** From developing and optimizing the use of corporate assets – both technological competencies and R&D funds – the CTO is increasingly asked to deliver tangible *output*. Introducing winning new products and processes, and sustained growth and value to customers and shareholders is an expectation of the job; not a stretch goal.

  This change in expectations is again putting pressure on managers, who may have started work in an environment in which management expected R&D to justify its efforts, but not its results.
- **Emphasis** From managing *hard issues* (i.e. technologies), the CTO is increasingly being asked to focus also on *softer* ones. Managing changes in culture and mindset, teamwork, communications and motivation, not just inside the labs but also across functions, is another new challenge.

  This change in emphasis is making new demands on the traditional management skills of the CTO. It clearly calls for a greater and broader sense of leadership.

A unique leadership profile

Ultimately, your success is going to be linked to your personal credibility, both vis-à-vis your scientific and technical staff and with your management colleagues. This credibility has to be rooted in your competences, of course, but it goes beyond. You will be credible if you have a vision, make the right choices and walk the talk to make it happen.

But for our type of function, success is also linked to your sense of pedagogy and force of persuasion in both directions. You need to be pedagogic and persuasive with your scientific and technical staff, to align them with our long-term business objectives and bring about interdisciplinary and cross-functional collaboration.

But you need the same qualities to influence your top management colleagues in the way they think about technology and deploy it for business advantage. Maybe CTOs need a special form of leadership! (CTO of a global telecommunications company)

In summary, aspiring CTOs need to exhibit the following important characteristics:

- They must exhibit leadership talents. This chapter has highlighted what it really means for these high-ranking science and technology executives to instil a sense of purpose, direction and focus. Leadership is about aligning their technical community behind the company's vision and objectives and building a commitment for change.

- To qualify for the job they must be credible as senior executives, scientists and technologists to both technical and business colleagues. Their credibility will reflect a successful career in R&D and at the interface between R&D and the business.
- They also have to be well connected, able to network with external sources. They must demonstrate business acumen and be able to put science and technology into a strategic business context. They must have a track record of 'delivering the goods', bringing results in a competitive field.
- Aspiring CTOs need a number of personal qualities. They need a high level of tenacity to fight their classic enemies: fragmentation of effort across businesses and labs; orthodoxies and the resulting distorted view the company will have of the future; short-sightedness made worse by ignorance, and over-specialization.[7]

  They also need passion to inspire and sell projects to their colleagues. They have to be able to teach colleagues how technology affects the business. Finally, CTOs also need a fair amount of diplomacy to ensure that the right decisions are made and supported.

Assessing the role of the CTO

The following questions provide a starting point when assessing the role of the CTO.

Purpose

CTOs/CROs have always been expected to develop and optimize technical competencies and R&D funds. Today, they need to raise a new sense of purpose within their staff, reminding them continuously that they are accountable for contributing to the future growth of their company through winning new products and processes.

Direction

CTOs/CROs have always been expected to help their company manage and optimize their technology portfolio. Today, their mission is, more than ever, to pre-empt the future by identifying and investing in critical new technologies that will sustain the businesses of tomorrow. CTOs/CROs are becoming business entrepreneurs!

Focus

CTOs/CROs have always been expected to be the guardians and promotors of their companies' competencies. Today, their priority is to ensure that they focus their internal resources on core, i.e. differentiating technologies while encouraging their staff to be open, accept and leverage external technologies.

These renewed senses of purpose, direction and focus call for a higher level of leadership of the CTO/CRO as a full member of the top management team.

Notes

1 Refer to K. Ichijo, *Strategic leadership for managing knowledge-based competence of a corporation*, paper presented at Strategic Leadership Conference, IMD (August 2004).

2 See: J. C. Collins and J. I. Porras 'Building' Your Company's Vision', *Harvard Business Review*, September–October 1996, pp. 65–77.

3 L. Huston and N. Sakkab, *Connect and Develop: Inside Procter and Gamble's New Model for Innovation, Harvard Business Review*, (84) No. (3) (March 2006).

4 A. S. Grove, 'Why Not Do It Ourselves – The Memory Business Crisis And How We Dealt With It Is How I Learned The Meaning Of A Strategic Inflection Point', *Only the Paranoid Survive*, (New York: Currency Doubleday, 1996), pp. 81–97.

5 D. F. Abell, *Managing With Dual Strategies: Mastering the Present, Preempting the Future*, (The Free Press, 1993).

6 Refer to J. Deschamps '*Innovation and Leadership*', *The International Handbook of Innovation*, ed. L. V. Shavinina (Elsevier Sciences, 2003), pp. 815–31.

7 Refer to: Y. Doz, 'The CTO as Entropy Fighter – An Action Agenda', paper presented at the 4th Conference on Global Issues of Technology and R&D, Management Centre Europe, Brussels, June 1995.

11 *The Chief Information Officer – Achieving credibility, relevance and business impact*

DONALD A. MARCHAND

Information can be described as data endowed with relevance and purpose. It is through information about customers, competitors, operations and products that business value is created and performance improved. Effective usage of information is essential for executives to manage their companies and for businesses to create value.

In this chapter, the author explains that the CIO's role and significance are growing and evolving quickly. The challenges facing Chief Information Officers are explored in detail: developing the credibility of the IT organization, reorganizing IT to meet business priorities, and finding new ways for information to add value.

The role of the chief information officer

> I feel my biggest challenge is to establish the credibility of the IT organization and function among the business unit managers of our group. Job one is to manage the IT investments and resources of the group in a cost-efficient and effective way, to deliver on our promises and commitments, and to move beyond being IT 'mechanics' to enablers of process and business change.
>
> (Newly appointed CIO of a global industrial products group)

What is unique about the CIO role? What business contributions could CIOs make to their company's success? Should the CIO be accepted as having a strategic leadership role or is it purely operational? The answers to these questions have become much clearer as organizations recognize the potential impact, significance and cost of information.

In the past, it has often been unclear whether the CIO role was simply another label for the head of information technology. The role was often seen as someone simply to keep the systems up and running and to get the best prices possible from the IT vendors. We will argue that the emergence of the CIO role represents a new and more lasting change in a senior executive position.

The development of the CIO's role resulted from an increasing awareness that information needed to be managed. Information was recognized as an important resource in much the same way as people, financing and materials. This required managers to plan, budget, evaluate and use information efficiently and effectively.

This shift to treating information as a major *resource*, a potential competitive advantage, required a structural change in the organization. A new definition of the CIO's function was needed. The CIO's expanded role would be to act as the focal point for managing information resources and computing, telecommunications and office technologies. IT was no longer solely a support function, although internal services remained important. Now, information had to be managed similarly to finance, HR and even product inventory. Data turned to information runs through its own supply chain. Information and Information Systems used strategically can enhance wealth creation.

This new function called for a different breed of manager – one capable of understanding the management of information and IT in the context of the business's priorities and challenges.

The role therefore evolved with a decided bias on *defining* the IT function. The only information that really counted was 'data' that could be automated in some form. Other forms of information, such as those that were less structured, informal or paper based, were considered valuable only if they were suitable for digital conversion.

Consequently, IT progress was linked directly to technological progress, and the CIO title conveniently merged with the IT role. Technological development helped to define and influence information management. CIOs could then ride the waves of technology in the IT industry, confident that their seat at the senior management table would be strategically relevant.

The journey from cost control to business value

In the late 1980s and early 1990s, the CIO role was clearly influenced by the trend towards re-engineering business processes, with an eye on downsizing and cost control. This was the first time the job of the CIO was associated with process improvement. One guru of the re-engineering movement argued that companies were 'paving the cow paths' if they were not rethinking, eliminating and simplifying their business processes *before* introducing new software and database applications.[1]

However, during this time re-engineering and cost control became closely associated, with many companies using re-engineering to explain downsizing. Consequently, IT would focus on automating processes to improve productivity, with the focus on cost control and increased efficiency. The role of the CIO was to enable the process of re-engineering and restructuring while keeping the cost of IT under control. In many companies, the CIO became allied with those who advocated 'rightsizing' and the use of IT for cost control and standardization of processes.

The dominant themes of controlling costs and rationalizing resources with IT continued in the 1990s and they combined with a focus on standardizing IT systems. The CIO concentrated on helping to control the growing costs of IT, as companies placed personal computers, laptops and the supporting infrastructures in the hands of an increasing number of employees. Companies also adopted standard IT infrastructures for email and data communications and used outsourcing to consolidate IT services.

The CIO in this era was a powerful enabler, helping companies to streamline, standardize and contain the total cost of IT. Again, the CIO role was closely allied with that of the CFO. Since cost control and providing adequate IT services were the key operating themes, you often saw the CIO reporting to the CFO before getting a direct reporting line to the CEO.

From the mid- to late 1990s, three major developments influenced the CIO role:

1 The rise of the Internet and the emergence of e-commerce and e-business.
2 The need to prepare for Y2K and the new millennium by changing basic software systems.
3 Development of Enterprise Resource Planning (ERP) and Customer Relationship Management (CRM) systems as 'solutions' to the challenges of supply chain management, financial control and customer focus.

During this era, the role of the CIO developed in two directions. First, the CIO could create value by focusing on 'e-enabling' through the Internet, intranets and extranets. Although e-projects were generally separated from the IT function with specialized staffs and budgets, CIOs were called upon to support these projects and transform the company's IT infrastructure.

Second, as the IT industry began to offer powerful applications for ERP and CRM, there was a move to automate business processes. This affected all major processes, from finance to order fulfilment, logistics, manufacturing and sales. The convergence of Y2K with these new ERP and CRM systems then led to an unprecedented boom in the IT industry as companies migrated their legacy systems in advance of the new millennium.

For the first time, the focus on cost control was supplanted by a focus on 'driving the business with IT.' During the late 1990s, the CIO took on a more prominent business role because of the size of IT investments and because their scope extended throughout core activities.

However, during 2000 the e-business bubble, dot.com hype and inflated stock market valuations came to a swift end, under the impact of the economic downturn coinciding with 9/11 in 2001. Similarly, in 2002 and 2003 continued sluggishness in the global economy meant the growth cycle of IT investment and the focus on e-projects and ERP and CRM systems slowed down significantly.

Senior executives lowered their expectations about what 'e,' ERP and CRM could achieve and the big question became 'What is the business value of IT?' CIOs returned to their roots of cost control, standardization and rationalization of IT resources, but with a twist.

Business leaders increasingly challenged the assumptions underlying the investments they made in ERP, CRM and 'e' initiatives. Also, they were less willing to invest in new IT deployment driven by the technology industry without a clearer view of business benefits. For the first time, the CIO was being challenged to deliver business value and control costs *at the same time.*

The questions that senior executives ask tend to focus on where IT's business value really lies and how it will deliver competitive advantage and ultimately enhance shareholder wealth. Business leaders realize that IT is available to every firm in their industry and the result is a 'competitive necessity' rather than a competitive advantage. So, the new question is: does IT matter?[2]

The quest for business credibility, relevance and impact

The CIO's quest for a business leadership role addresses three questions (illustrated in Figure 11.1).

Figure 11.1: The CIO leadership role

- How can the CIO effectively and efficiently manage the IT organization and resources to deliver value?
- How can the CIO enable managers to deploy and use IT in their business units most effectively?
- How can the CIO become accepted as a member of the senior management team, shaping the business strategy and capabilities needed for enhanced performance?

Manager of IT resources and operations

The CIO's most basic responsibility is to be an effective leader of the business's IT resources. Given the continuous changes in technology, aligning the IT function with the structure and processes of the business can be very challenging. It requires attention to seven key activities.[3]

1 *Governance of the IT function*, which requires action in two areas. Firstly, organizing the internal functions to serve the business. Secondly, involving managers and functions in decisions related to IT priorities, projects and investments.
2 *Operating the core infrastructure and related services*. These activities are the commodity service end of the IT organization, simply 'keeping the lights on' or 'fixing the plumbing.' Network availability and the responsiveness of services are key criteria when measuring performance.

3 *Managing the applications portfolio supporting business processes.* Companies have a combination of applications embedded in various versions of software, and these require regular changes and updates. This may be because of obsolescence, new user requirements or, more likely, software developments that make previous versions expensive to support.
4 *Recruiting and managing IT skills, expertise and people.* For the CIO, the people side of IT is a major issue. This is because skills vary with changing technologies and with decisions to insource or outsource specific processes and services.
5 *Developing and retaining IT project management skills.* This is a major source of concern for CIOs. In most companies the number of IT projects that fail, run over budget, run over schedule or simply underdeliver, has far exceeded those that are delivered on time and on budget and meet the needs of users.[4]
6 *Managing the suppliers of IT services and products.* As the IT industry has grown in size and scale, the influence of vendors on decisions about services, products, projects and investments has grown as well. For many CIOs, decisions about what vendor(s) to select can be career enhancing or career ending.
7 *Measuring and managing the company's IT investments.* How well does the company manage IT expenditure – is it getting value for money?

Today, companies spend most of their IT budget on applications and services that are 'necessary to operate' and 'essential to compete'. The challenge for the CIO is to decrease the amount spent on the 'necessary to operate' by gaining efficiencies and standardization, while investing in applications which provide a real advantage and build new capabilities (see Figure 11.2).

Assessing how well a company spends money on IT means asking three key questions:

- *Are we spending more or less on IT than other companies in our industry?* Total IT spending as a percentage of company revenues has been the benchmark measure of IT since the 1970s. Although researchers have failed to find a correlation between IT spending and business performance, this measure has continued to dominate executive discussions of IT performance. This is because it is easy to understand and compare across companies.

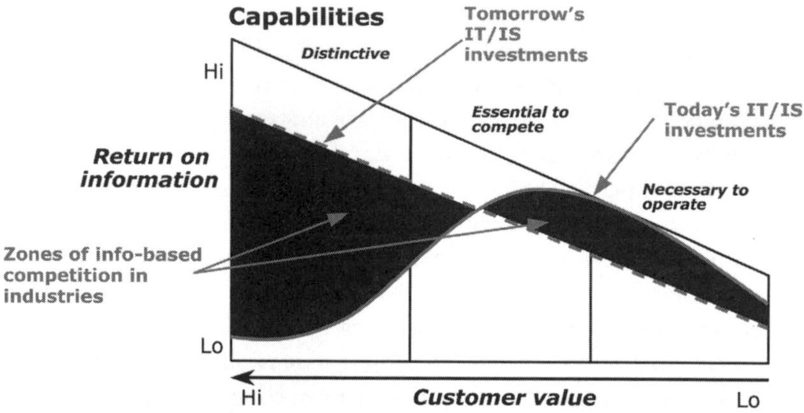

Figure 11.2: Competitive value of tomorrow's IS/IT investments

- *What business return are we getting from our IT investment?* This question is a source of continuing debate between business managers and CIOs, largely because it is so difficult to answer.

  The impact of IT investments on the business has often been difficult to trace, especially when these investments involve changes in IT support and information for decision making. Also, the answers have been calculated in terms of forward-looking projections of return on investment (ROI) that are then not evaluated after projects are completed.
- *What proportion of company IT investment is spent on applications and services that are:*

  'Necessary to operate' the business, such as general ledgers and payrolls?

  'Essential to compete' with other companies, such as ERP and CRM?

  'Distinctive' business capabilities, such as business intelligence and market knowledge that give the company an advantage over its competitors?

CIOs' leadership role depends directly on their credibility for effectively managing IT resources, providing high levels of internal 'customer services' and consequently contributing to the company's success.

The CIO's responsibility can be summarized as: *'Spend less; follow, don't lead; innovate when risks are low, and focus more on vulnerabilities, not opportunities.'*[5] These directions may seem conservative, but they represent the CIO's first leadership challenges when building credibility with colleagues.

The CIO as an enabler of business change

We have spent the last seven years reinventing our company through acquisitions and divestitures to be a leading speciality chemicals company. As CIO, I have spent two years realigning IT strategy and resources with our new business units and reducing the duplication of hardware, networks, software, data and IT people. We are just entering the stage when we can enable business changes by deploying and using IT and information resources effectively in our twenty-two business units. The challenge is not if, but how we will do so. (CIO of a global speciality chemicals company)

In addition to managing IT resources and operations, the CIO must direct IT-enabled processes and projects. This involves close collaboration with managers inside the company and with customers, partners and suppliers outside. The CIO also needs to contribute to the effective use of information and knowledge in business units by developing appropriate information, people and IT capabilities.

This requires an understanding of how IT and process changes affect behaviours and information practices in the company. It also requires the CIO to guide changes in business processes, information, people and IT.

Managers are confronted with frequent changes in their business and market conditions and these require shifts in three areas:

- The design, re-design and continuous improvement of business processes;
- The use of management information, especially external market and competitor intelligence;
- How people are expected to use information about customers, products and services across the company.

If employees' use of information and IT is a key concern of CIOs and business managers jointly, how should this issue be addressed?

For many years, the emphasis of change management has been to deploy an IT project and hope to change the behaviours associated with the way information and IT are used. IT, in the form of ERP and CRM systems, could be used as an agent for 'business change'. This was done by forcing changes on employees who had no choice but to *adjust* their work habits and information practices to fit the new processes and systems.

What made this view even more compelling for business managers was that 'there was no going back'. For IT people, this view of IT-driven change made their efforts noble, yet relieved them of the inevitable resistance and reactions of affected users.

For business managers, this approach became a convenient way to introduce changes. Bring in IT and process changes and people are forced to adjust. In other words, you have made changes without taking direct responsibility for them. Moreover, if the projects did not achieve the desired results over time, then IT and process management people could be blamed.

A second approach to the challenge of 'change management' recognizes the need to consider people and organizational adjustments when IT changes take place.

In this case, project managers assess the impact on those people most directly affected by the projects and any training needs. They make business managers aware of their responsibility to proactively manage the change *after* the 'go live' date. Although the intentions are good, execution can typically fail for three reasons:

- *IT and process change projects (such as ERP and CRM) tend to consume the available time and resources of the project team.* Often, to meet deadlines and budgets, project managers cut the training and other initiatives that occur at the end of projects.

  The result is often that the project goes live without adequate focus on the human adjustment required to use the new processes and systems. After going live, the project teams declare victory (often with a big party) and are disbanded, with little attention to how the new systems and databases will be subsequently used.
- *People's use of information and IT in the new process does not receive adequate management attention or resources.* Business and IT people move on to other projects, devoting little or no attention to how the new systems should be used. 'Out of sight and out of mind' seems to characterize this situation.

  In addition, since these projects typically affect front-line people and middle management, senior managers are largely unaware of the behavioural and information practice changes that their subordinates face in their daily work.

  Managers tend to assume that workers should accept process and IT changes. They attribute a lack of acceptance to inevitable human resistance to change. What is clear is that neither CIOs nor business managers place much value on increasing the use of these systems and databases after the project has been deployed.

- *The use of information and IT by people affected by changes and new systems is largely invisible to the CIO and business managers.*[6] IT projects and investments are typically the most visible factors. Business managers and CIOs often devote up to 90 per cent of their attention to planning and initiating IT projects.

  Some managers and CIOs naïvely seek to solve business problems with IT by thinking that these problems will go away if they implement new 'IT solutions.' For example, many companies invested in CRM systems to solve a lack of 'customer orientation' among their employees.

  What many managers failed to understand was that CRM systems have to be accompanied by behavioural and cultural changes in the ways people use information and IT. Senior business executives, to the company's peril, have often not understood, measured nor managed these 'soft factors' effectively.

  In contrast, our research suggests that only 25 per cent of the business value of IT and information is linked to deployment and investments, whereas 75 per cent is linked to 'soft factors' relating to people's use of information and IT.[7]

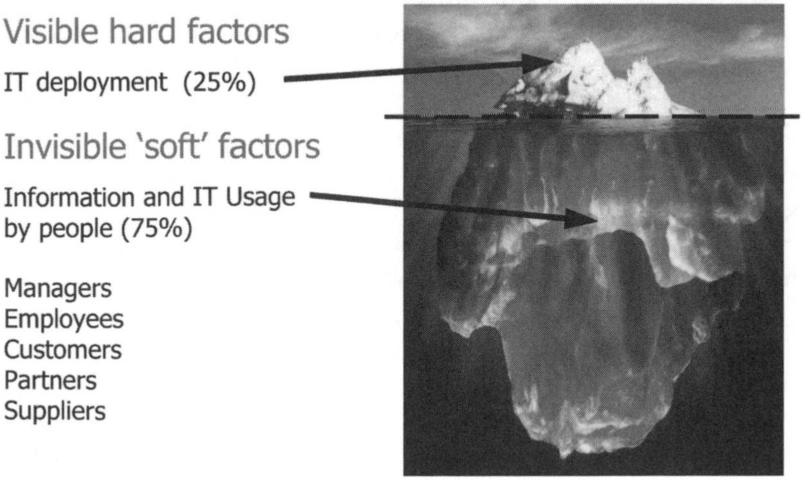

Figure 11.3: The business value of IT > deployment of IT

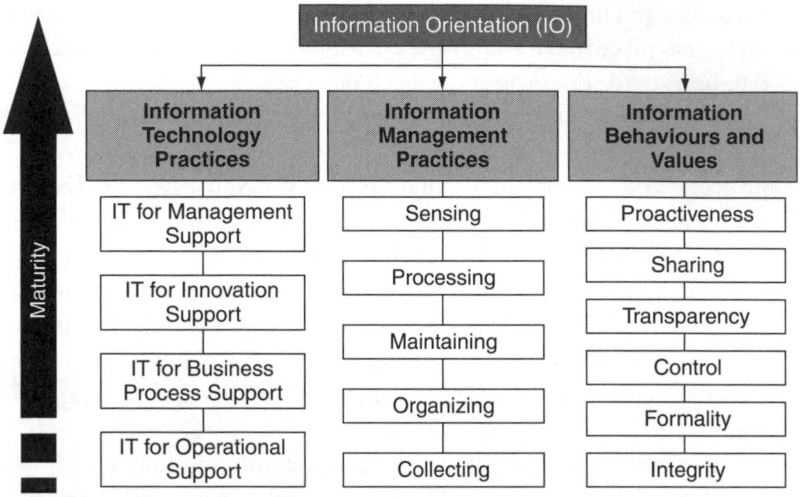

Figure 11.4: The information orientation maturity model
Source: D. A. Marchand. W. J. Kettinger and J. D. Rollins, *Making the Invisible Visible: How Companies Win with the Right Information, People and IT* (New York and London: John Wiley and Sons, 2001).

Clearly the business value of information technology is a vital business issue. Many managers and CIOs devote 90 per cent of their attention to IT investments and deployment that account for only 25 per cent of the business value of IT and information. The use of information and IT receives much less managerial attention. Consequently, much of the potential value in improved use of information and IT may be largely lost.

How can CIOs help managers drive business performance by changing the way people use information and IT? Research at IMD demonstrates that managers increasingly see the value of information and IT as going beyond technology to the knowledge and capabilities of their people. This encompasses the human behaviours and values related to how information and knowledge are used.

It also affects information management practices – the way information is sensed, processed, maintained, organized and collected. We call this the information orientation (IO) of the company (Figure 11.4).[8]

We have shown that managers believe their employees' use of information and IT is linked to business performance. Because the IO maturity of a company can be measured, managers and CIOs can explicitly evaluate their company's progress in developing information capabilities.[9]

Although CIOs control how IT is deployed, they do not control how it is *used*. CIOs must work with business managers and other members of the CXO team to exploit the business value of information and IT usage over time. Consequently, they can target the 75 per cent of the business value of IT that resides primarily in the soft factors. To have the greatest impact on a business, the CIO must have a place on the CXO team.

Strategic business player and part of the senior management team

When I became CIO, I inherited a credible and cost-effective IT organization in the eyes of business managers. The real challenge for me now is to build on this credibility, making sure that our business units compete with information, IT and people. I also need to provide leadership among my senior executive colleagues for how IT, information and our people can be used to deliver future growth. Being a recognized player on the management team is a must for meeting these challenges.

(CIO of global pharmaceuticals company)

The third dimension of the CIO leadership role is the least tangible but the most important. The CIO has to be a genuine player on the senior management team rather than a functional bystander. Gaining the acceptance of senior managers usually requires that the CIO fulfil three high-level requirements (see Figure 11.5).

Figure 11.5: The CIO leadership role – Key performance criteria

1 The CIO must earn ***credibility*** by managing IT resources and operations effectively. If CIOs cannot efficiently deliver IT services and systems, then their claim to membership is severely limited.
2 The CIO's contribution must extend beyond the IT function to demonstrate ***relevance*** to the company's business activities. The value of information, people and IT as essential elements of the company's operating model must be emphasized.[10]
3 The CIO must be able to have an ***impact*** on the company's mindset, actions and business. This can be done by positioning information and IT so that other team members view it as contributing to their business success.

Achieving these criteria results in a self-sustaining 'virtuous' cycle, with business credibility leading to successful and relevant changes. This, in turn, cements the CIO's contribution as a strategic business player with a major effect on the success of the business. However, the converse is also true. Failing to achieve these criteria leads to a downward spiral of ineffectiveness and frustration. Chief executives have not been shy about replacing CIOs who presided over IT disasters or who fail to meet the expectations of the CXO team.

The CIO must also pass what we call the golf test. Other members of the team must perceive the CIO as being the kind of person the CEO would invite to join them on a golf day, when the emergent strategy and decisions that will affect the company or business unit will also be discussed. Is the CIO included in informal team discussions and activities to shape key decisions?

Clearly, not all senior management teams play golf, but most have some informal 'test' which determines inclusion or exclusion from their informal deliberations. It is critical for success that the CIO passes this test.

The rise or fall of the CIO is dependent on how well these conditions for acceptance and inclusion on the senior management team are met.

Influencing the business strategy: moving from good to great

Although some CIOs earn their inclusion in the senior management team, they are not always able to influence how that team leverages information and IT capabilities. Effective management of IT deployment and the IT function obviously matters.

Companies must deploy IT at least as effectively as their competitors and as efficiently as possible. However, the company's managers should also seek to align IT with their business needs. Settling for sound IT deployment without simultaneously focusing on how information is used runs the risk of failing to optimize the business value of IT.

Ironically, for business managers to leverage the full value of IT they need to focus on the effective use of information, people and IT in their business *first*. Only then can they align IT deployment with their strategies and capabilities. This important change in management mindset is required so that linkages between information capabilities are embedded in the way business is done.

Companies such as Dell, Wal-Mart, Frito-Lay and CEMEX have built their businesses on customer, market, product and operational information.[11] The competitiveness of these companies arises from the way their managers deploy and use their information, people and IT capabilities to develop performance.

They strive to extract 100 per cent of the business value of information and knowledge by continuously improving their information, people and IT practices. They not only capture the 25 per cent of business value from IT deployment; they also go after the 75 per cent resulting from effective use of information by their managers, employees, customers and partners.

The CIOs in these companies share a senior management mindset about the effect that information, people and IT practices can have on business success. They see their role as influencing the business strategy and model. This allows their companies to create advantages in using knowledge and information that competitors cannot easily replicate.[12]

By linking the deployment and use of information and IT to business capabilities, these CIOs position themselves as fully contributing members of the CXO team. They build on their credibility and relevance gained by executing the other two dimensions of CIO leadership (managing IT resources and enabling business change) to achieve maximum business impact.

Furthermore, they give the senior management team the opportunity to break free from the cycle of competitive necessity. This is achieved by exploiting aspects of IT and information management that are the most difficult for competitors to imitate.

Avoiding disorientation: information orientation at work

A growing number of companies have implemented major IT projects using the principles of information orientation.

For example, a European banking group transformed its struggling branch-based retail banking business into one of the most successful banks in its market within 1,000 days. This was accomplished by getting the right information to people in the branches, enabling them to successfully cross-sell their products. The bank kept its new customer relationship project simple by providing their customer representatives with:

- An easy-to-use and intuitive IT interface;
- Clear information about customer segmentation, product selling targets and company performance information;
- Incentives that created an open culture, emphasizing teamwork and action.

Similarly, a small Latin American commodity business became one of the largest global players in its market by successfully deploying and realizing the benefits of technology. Executives admit that the transformation of their business was based on a cultural change. This required a new emphasis on meeting commitments, using information to develop new ways of serving customers, and developing information-centric processes that increased operational efficiency.[13]

The future of the CIO leadership role

The CIO role as it has evolved over the past twenty years is focused on deploying IT and controlling costs. The ambition to develop the CIO's role to enable companies to leverage information for greater wealth creation and knowledge remains largely unfulfilled.

In many companies, CIOs have opted for the first dimension of the CIO role (managing IT resources), thinking that it was the most achievable and politically safest. However, their contribution to the other two dimensions (enabling change and being a strategic business player) has been marginal at best. What needs to be done?

- *Develop (or rebuild) the credibility of the IT organization quickly.* Credibility in executing the role buys time but is not sufficient on its own. There is no substitute for the next step: adding business value.[14]

- *Move beyond the positioning of IT as a 'competitive necessity' and connect information and IT capabilities with the company's strategies and goals.* As IT becomes a simple competitive necessity, the role of the CIO as head of the IT function may be diminished.

  Some business managers have answered the question, 'Does IT matter?' with a resounding '*No!*'. They believe IT provides no real basis for competitive advantage and should be managed as an efficient cost centre. The CIO's task is to prove that important though this is, IT can provide much more value to the business.
- *Influence the perceptions of other members of the senior management team.*[15] As individuals, CIOs must build credibility and relevance so that other senior managers accept and welcome their contributions. As team members, CIOs must move beyond IT deployment and cost control to demonstrate the business impact of using information, people and IT capabilities. However, business impact is conditioned by whether other senior managers will work with the CIOs to leverage information capabilities in their activities and permit CIOs to be fully contributing members of senior management teams.

It is clear that in many companies today, the future of the CIO role is dependent not just on the qualities of incumbent. It also relies on the belief of senior managers that having a CIO as a business colleague is valuable and contributes to their business unit or company. However, the history of the CIO role in many companies is not pretty. Whether the future role of the CIO rises above the tide will depend on how business managers and CIOs work together to realize the benefits of deploying and using information in their businesses.

Assessing the role of the CIO

The following questions provide a starting point when assessing the role of the CIO.

Purpose

1. What are the CIO's priorities and how could these be developed? Is their purpose primarily to:
   - Manage IT resources and operations?

- Support business improvements by ensuring the effective use of information and IT?
- Influence the business strategy, moving the organization as a whole from good to great?
- Has the CIO established ***credibility*** by managing IT resources and operations effectively?
- Does the CIO's contribution extend beyond the IT function, demonstrating ***relevance*** and benefiting the company's business activities as a whole?
- Does the CIO ***influence*** the company's culture, mindset and the way it works?

Direction

2. What guides the CIO's decisions and what techniques are employed?
3. Does the CIO organize the IT function and operate the core infrastructure and related services to serve the business? Could this be improved by:
   - Involving managers and functions in decisions related to IT priorities, projects and investments?
   - Managing the applications portfolio supporting business processes?
   - Recruiting and managing IT skills, expertise and people?
   - Developing and retaining IT project management skills?
   - Managing the suppliers of IT services and products?
   - Measuring and managing the company's IT investments?

Focus

4. Is the CIO focused on the key details necessary to develop the IT function's contribution to the business?
5. Are there adequate measures and performance criteria in place to measure the IT function's progress?
6. Does people's use of information and IT receive adequate attention and resources?
7. Is the use of information and IT by people affected by changes and new systems largely invisible to the CIO and business managers?

Glossary

Information orientation (IO)

Research at IMD business school identified three critical factors driving successful use of information. These three factors combine to provide an overall measure of information orientation (IO).

- *Information behaviours and values*.This is the capability of an organization to instil and promote behaviours and values for effective use of information. Managers need to promote integrity, formality, control, transparency and sharing, while removing barriers to information flow and promoting information use.
- *Information management practices*. Managing information involves sensing, collecting, organizing, processing and maintaining information.
  Managers set up processes, train their employees and take responsibility for the management of information, thus focusing their organizations on the right information. They take care to avoid (or at least minimize) information overload, improve the quality of information available to employees and enhance decision-making.
- *Information technology practices*. IT applications and infrastructure should support decision-making. Consequently, business strategy needs to be linked to IT strategy so that the infrastructure and applications support operations, business processes, innovation and decisions.

Enterprise resource planning (ERP) systems

ERP systems are designed to improve an organization's planning and the way that its business processes function. The advantages can be significant savings in time, expense, quality and human capital as previously vital but labour-intensive tasks such as planning, tracking and co-ordinating are automated.

The disadvantages arise from the ability of systems to comprehensively meet the evolving needs of an organization, and the way that it is used and maintained.

Customer relationship management (CRM) systems

CRM systems typically provide comprehensive details about customers, enabling organizations to make informed decisions, as well as serving customers and adapting to their changing needs. However, as with ERP systems, they are now, in many sectors, a competitive necessity rather than a source of competitive advantage.

Notes

1 M. Hammer, 'Reengineering work: Don't automate, obliterate', *Harvard Business Review*, July/August 1990, pp. 104–112.
2 N. G. Carr, *Does IT Matter?* (Cambridge, MA: Harvard Business School Press, 2004).
3 For a similar but earlier review of the challenges of the IT organization, see J. F. Rockart, M. J. Earl and J. W. Ross, 'Eight imperatives for the new IT organization', *Sloan Management Review*, Fall (1992), pp. 43–55.
4 For a review of the IT Project failure surveys, see Carr, *ibid.*, pp. 110–112.
5 Carr, *ibid.*, pp. 107–135.
6 See D. A. Marchand, W. J. Kettinger and J. D. Rollins, *Making the Invisible Visible: How Companies Win with the Right Information, People and IT* (Chichester, John Wiley and Sons, 2001).
7 D. A. Marchand, 'Extracting the business value of IT: It is usage, not just deployment that counts!', *Capco Institute Journal of Financial Transformation*, 11 (August 2004), p. 127.
8 Marchand et al., *Making the Invisible Visible*, *ibid.*, p. 24.
9 See, for example, D. A. Marchand, W. J. Kettinger and R. Chung, 'Citigroup's CEEMEA sales and trading unit: Rapid business improvement through effective use of information, people and IT'. IMD case no. IMD-3-1306, (Lausanne, Switzerland, 2004).
10 The capability of a CIO to contribute value to the business has long been viewed as essential for success. See, for example, M. J. Earl and D. F. Feeny, 'Is Your CIO Adding Value?', *Sloan Management Review*, Spring (1994), pp. 11–20.
11 See, for example, D. A. Marchand, R. Chung and K. Paddack, 'CEMEX: Global growth through superior information capabilities'. IMD case no. IMD-3-0953 (Lausanne, Switzerland: 2002) and D. A. Marchand, W. J. Kettinger and R. Chung, 'Dell's direct model: Everything to do with information'. IMD case no. IMD-3-1149, (Lausanne, Switzerland: 2004).
12 See R. Hunter and D. Aron, *From Value to Advantage: Exploiting Information* (Stamford, CT: Gartner Group. EXP CIO Signature Program, June 2004).
13 For further information about these examples see D. A. Marchand, 'How Effective is Your Company at Using Information?', *European Business Forum*, Winter (2001).
14 This view is persuasively presented by M. Broadbent and E. Kitzis in *The New CIO Leader* (Cambridge, MA: Harvard Business School Press, 2005).
15 See, for example, M. Earl and D. Feeny, 'How to be a CEO in the Information Age', *Sloan Management Review*, Winter (2000), pp. 11–23.

12 *The Chief Human Resources Officer – Delivering people who can deliver*

PRESTON BOTTGER AND
PAUL VANDERBROECK

When you ask, 'What's the purpose of an HR organization?' then the answer is to develop the talents and skill sets of your people and to drive the performance of the company. (CHRO, global US car manufacturer)

In the past decade, there have been strong calls for the chief human resources officer (CHRO) to be a very close partner to the CEO in the area of corporate strategy. This idea is of course very appealing to many HR people because it places the function at the centre of the business. But, to whatever degree that 'people are the key to business success', the reality is that HR is first and foremost a *service* function.

The CHRO has responsibilities for putting the right people in the right jobs with the right reporting relationships, at the right time, at the right cost. This is a service task.

Now, to supply the diverse people needs of the business, the CHRO must act on the requirements of the firm's business system: products, customers, competitors and the company's internal structure and culture. The methods used by the company to make products, serve customers and thereby create wealth are key determinants of the kinds of people to be recruited. And, the requirements of the business system must also drive the processes by which people are developed, motivated, retained and compensated.

As illustrated in Figure 12.1, it is the firm's business system that sets the parameters of the CHRO's role. It creates the necessity for certain key tasks to be accomplished. This in turn creates the need for people who possess the capabilities to carry out those tasks.

This adds up to a massive challenge for the CHRO. But the work is even greater than implied by the diagram. The human capabilities required by the business are not static. They are constantly evolving.

The portfolio of human capabilities that enabled the company to grow in the past might not help it *thrive* tomorrow, or even *survive*. So the CHRO must consider the emerging needs of the business system.

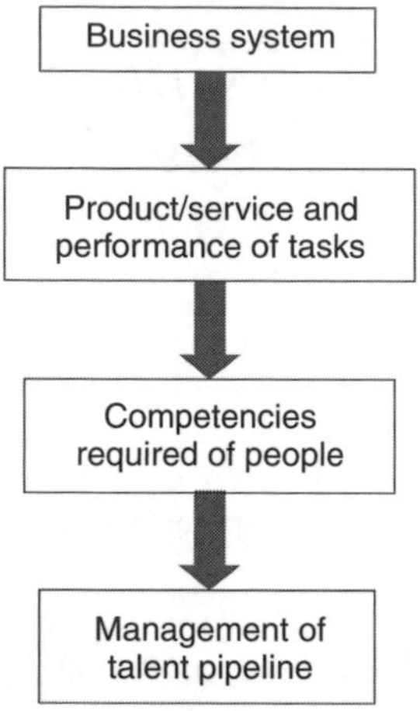

Figure 12.1: It all begins with the business model...

This sets up an ongoing mission for the CHRO that spans three overlapping roles.

- **Service provider** The CHRO must deliver on the technical aspects of the job, namely eight critical subprocesses underpinning the talent pipeline – this is the foundation of delivering people who can deliver (see Figure 12.3).
- **Change master** The CHRO must be the resident expert on the management of change. To support the evolving business model, he or she must be able to implement improvements in talent management, and critically in the organization's structure and culture. In addition, the CHRO must be capable of coaching other CXOs and line executives in the top team and below on how to implement 'projects for progress' in their respective areas.
- **Strategic contributor** The firm is subject to both continuous and discontinuous evolution in customer, product, workforce and financial markets. It is the CHRO's task to help anticipate how the firm's responses to these forces can best be handled by new capabilities and new processes. Also, he or she can contribute at a high level as trusted advisor to the CEO and other members of the senior team.

To fulfil his or her leadership role, the CHRO must master to all three aspects of the job, as shown in Figure 12.2.

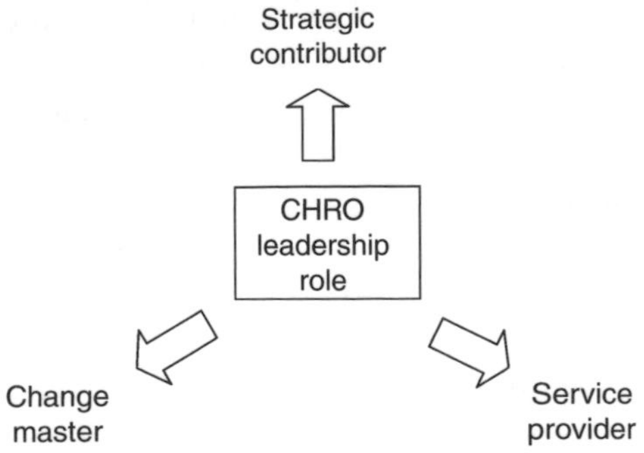

Figure 12.2: Three faces of the CHRO's leadership role

Before exploring these three facets of the CHRO's role in greater detail, we briefly consider how the role has evolved over the past decades.

The changing role of HR

The centralized management of employees' relationships with the company started as an administrative activity, initially handled by employment managers and later by personnel directors. In the early twentieth century, the focus was on administrative tasks of the employment of people, such as payroll processing and record keeping.

In the 1920s and 1930s, with the emergence of powerful unions, the personnel director's role grew to include industrial relations. Conflict-based relations between unions and employers were buffered to a degree by the presence of specialized mediators within the company. In some cases, the personnel director played a central role in large-scale negotiations. However, it was typically line executives, and particularly the CEO, who called the important shots in industrial relations.

In the second half of the twentieth century, as companies grew in size and complexity, the responsibilities of personnel directors expanded to include specialized activities, for example, training, workforce planning and the management of expatriates. The personnel function also took on responsibility for continuously adapting the company's policies and procedures to the many changes issuing from labour, tax, and social benefits laws. The head of personnel also had to decide what functions to outsource and what specialized staff to retain in-house.

By the late 1960s, the personnel director was firmly established as the key person responsible for managing 'the Deal' between the company and the individual. By 'the Deal' we refer to the economic exchange of work for financial and non-financial rewards.

At this time, a key aspect of the psychological component of this contract was the expectation of job security. But all that was set to change – as was the positioning and title of the personnel director.

In 1971, AT&T in the USA became the first company to create a position of senior vice president responsible for 'human resources'. This marked the first step in a broad transition, across most industries in most Western countries, from personnel management to human resource management. This transition was accompanied by three significant external developments.

- **Major downsizing and restructuring** From the first oil crisis in 1973 onwards, the European and US economies were painfully confronted with their productivity gap vis-à-vis the competition. Japan, other Asian countries, and, in some industry sectors, Latin American countries, were now producing manufactured goods of quality, price and service to beat US manufacturers.

  Western businesses were forced to re-examine their cost structures, the ways their people were deployed, the ways they used technology and the ways the firm was organized to serve the customer.

  Although these restructuring decisions were most often made by CEOs with their CFOs, responsibility for implementation often fell to the head of HR. In this process, the psychological contract of work-for-life was broken in many companies, not only in the USA, but in Europe. As a result, there was a decline in the reputation of HR as the guardian of employee interests at the top level of the company.
- **Reduced role of the unions** From the 1980s onwards, the power of unions in certain countries and industries was increasingly curtailed. And so, the profile of HR roles in the field of industrial relations was similarly reduced. The focus for heads of HR shifted from negotiating the collective bargain to introducing systems that tied individual performance to individual reward. To mark that switch, the term 'Industrial Relations' was often replaced by 'Employee Relations'.
- **The technological revolution** The 1990s saw further changes in the role of CHROs, provoked by the expanding applications of information technology. This influenced the way work was done, allowing

for more varied and sophisticated working arrangements, in networks and matrix structures, and across long distances. These shifts posed new challenges for HR. People now had to adapt or be trained to be members of loose and diverse teams whose members were separated by long distances and time zones, where following the 'team process' was in some cases now more valued than 'individual responsibility'.

Information technology also increased demand for highly mobile knowledge-workers. This resulted in intensified competition for staff, which required greater efforts by HR to sell the company to desirable new hires.

In addition, IT systems opened up new possibilities for managing data and keeping track of people, especially the details of their work experience, capabilities, and successes and failures. It also allowed outsourcing of certain administrative tasks that were previously the staple work of the HR function.

As a result of these wide and deep changes, executives within the human resources function had to become more and more business-knowledgeable.

Today, CHROs are expected to be fully fluent and *influential* in the language of the business system. They must bring a sharp business focus to all their activities. They are held to the same standards of accountability as other functional heads.[1]

Moreover, in some industries at least, the workforce *is* a critical competitive advantage. In companies where this is so, the most senior HR executive does have obvious strategic legitimacy. This has led to greater involvement by senior HR executives in top-level business discussions. In many firms, but not all, the head of HR has responsibility for leading a people strategy that is essential to the implementation of the firm's business system.

But, to be taken seriously as a strategic contributor, the CHRO must start with effective implementation of the HR foundations, as an excellent 'service provider'.

The service provider: managing the talent pipeline

Many HR textbooks and consultants have declared the arrival of the CHRO as an influential presence at the strategic table. Nevertheless,

The role of the workforce

In our observations of firms across many industries, we have seen evidence that in fact, the 'workforce' is not always super-critical to the economic performance of the firm. In firms with deeply embedded and long-standing presence in the market, with few competitors willing or able to invest in across-the-board rivalry, and with patient or sleepy investors, it seems that, beyond a few critical managers, 'good enough is good enough' as regards the workforce. While perhaps rare, this combination of factors does occur, and the firm does survive for a long time. Of course, finally, competitors do appear in some market segments, and the economic dominance of the original firm starts to decay.

many senior HR executives say to us: 'Always remember that human resources remains primarily a *service* function.' Indeed, one criticism by line managers is that some HR executives expect to contribute at strategy level, yet do not handle the basics effectively.

In my job I meet two different types of HR professionals. There are those who whine that they don't have a seat at the top table, but who don't really deserve it. Then there are the ones who are at the CEO's right hand. The latter seem to have truly understood that their job is to produce and retain management talent. Yet they haven't given up the traditional HR functions of recruitment, admin and so on.

(Editor of a global business journal)

In fact, technical mastery of the talent pipeline is the foundation of the CHRO's credibility. This entails ensuring that the right people are moved to the right jobs on a regular and well-planned basis.

The cost of getting this wrong can be significant, both financially and in human terms. For example, not having a replacement for a key position that suddenly becomes vacant can result in severe business disruption. Loss of momentum when top jobs are unexpectedly vacated can reduce revenue flows and upset cost-containment measures.

There is also the risk of putting the wrong people into key jobs. These risks are particularly high in the financial services sector where people costs represent a very high percentage of total expenses.

As a CHRO in the financial sector put it:

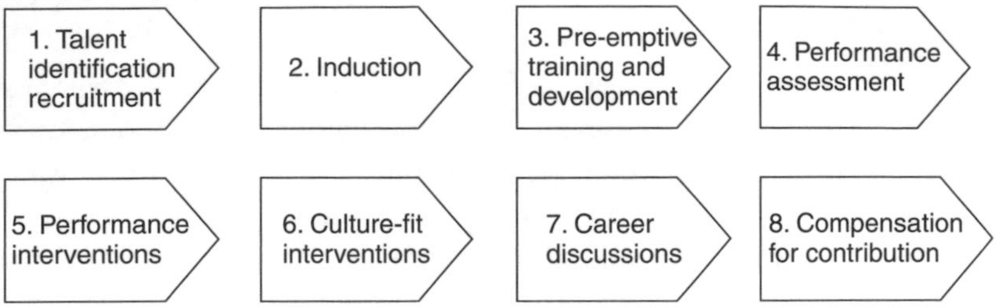

Figure 12.3: The talent pipeline

The biggest risk – and you see it time and time again – is the promotion into management of the best technical trader or underwriter, because these people are gurus in their field, sometimes with disastrous consequences, not only for the team, but for the individual.

The talent pipeline can be represented as a sequence of eight subprocesses, as illustrated in Figure 12.3. Some key elements of each of these are as follows:

Spot/recruit the raw talent

Spotting and recruiting raw talent requires identification of pools of candidates that match the needs of the business system, then selecting individuals who are most likely to fit with the firm's culture.

For example, a cosmetics and beauty products company seeks humanities and art design graduates. Here, the business system requires managers with a sense of the aesthetic and a desire to learn the business.

By contrast, a nation-wide building products firm seeks candidates with working class roots, with a 'hungry look in their eye' and with athletic and/or military background. In this case, the business model is best run by managers with an innate capacity to talk to and sell to building tradesmen, and with the energy and motivation for long work hours over many years.

The key to spotting and recruiting talent is not the method itself, but lies in ensuring that the method best supplies the people needs of the business model. The method must work, as measured by key indicators. For example, the method must reliably assess past short-term performance, the individual's agility to rotate to new assignments, and medium-term capacity and calibre to take on wider and higher levels of responsibility.

Induction

The entry-level recruits then need to be educated on the key success factors of the business system and their role within it. Some companies favour structured, classroom training, others a more informal walk around and 'get introduced informally' approach.

The type of approach is dictated by the clarity of the basic economic model ('how we make money'), the strength of the existing culture, the economic necessity of quick employee orientation, and the cost of retaining a person who is not working out.

One example, in the field of securities trading, is that new recruits might be paired with experienced traders, and trade in marginal currencies where bad decisions will 'not be fatal'. This highly structured, low-to-moderate risk, induction clearly represents an opportunity cost for the traders, yet accelerates the technical learning and assessment of culture-fit of the newcomers.

In essence, the CHRO must weigh the cost to the firm of structured induction versus the cost (and risk) of the person's simply learning on the job.

Pre-emptive training and development

Beyond the induction to the firm and its culture, training and development ensures that the employee has the capabilities necessary to get the job done.

Given the cost and time involved in training and development, the CHRO uses a return-on-investment approach. That is, systems are used to diagnose exactly who needs what training, and when, to support the business model. Also, the quality of the training and development must be evaluated and improved by measuring the learning impact of what has been delivered.

For example, in one international airline, the quality of customer care was found to be directly influenced by the technical knowledge and pleasant attitudes of front-line employees. This in turn was influenced by the quality of supervision. As a result, all supervisors were systematically trained in an in-house programme designed to improve their employee management skills.

Performance assessment

Performance assessment is a seemingly simple concept that typically follows an annual cycle. It is *seemingly* simple because it requires impartial judgment. But this is difficult to assure without tremendous effort and expense.

A high degree of training is required to reduce inconsistencies in approach. Either the indulgent boss rates everyone above average for fear of offending or demotivating employees; or the perfectionist boss rates everyone at or below average. For the rating numbers to carry useful meaning, an expensive and extensive teaching process must be implemented to impose commonality across raters, and sound judgement by individual raters.

For example, some companies have adopted a forced ranking system. This requires managers to identify, for example, their bottom 10 per cent and top 20 per cent of performers. As long as it is not only focused on reaching short-term objectives, but also on contributing to the future of the business system, such assessments can help companies to continuously raise the bar, while at the same time helping leaders to develop their staff for performance.

The CHRO must make robust benefit/cost judgements on methods for performance assessment, to ensure that performance crucial to the business model is assessed validly and fairly.

Performance improvement interventions

The purpose of performance improvement interventions is to provide experiences to help the person enlarge their capabilities. Such experiences range across job rotation assignments, executive education programmes, and 360-degree analysis with follow-up coaching.

At company level, the CHRO ensures that such programmes serve the business system and generally supplies the range of competencies required to get the job done. The focus should ensure that performance improvement interventions serve both short-term 'fixes', and longer term development of capabilities.

For example, a pharmaceutical company observed that one division was growing only at market average, despite product quality superior to competitors'. Improved training with more emphasis on leadership of sales teams was put in place. Next, all sales leaders and candidates for sales leadership positions, around the world, were put through a programme involving assessment centres, 360-degree feedback and leadership training.

The results were benchmarked both internally and externally and used to reorganize and focus the sales leader on key tasks. Subsequently sales/market share rose by 20 per cent.

Culture/fit interventions

Unlike interventions focused on job performance, culture/fit interventions are aimed at those who cannot or will not adapt to the company's culture. It is useful to put in place a process that provides individuals with early and forceful feedback. Thus the individuals have the opportunity either to adapt their behaviour or to leave the firm.

Mentoring by senior executives who are not direct bosses of the person, can prove a very effective tool. When this does not help, often, the only way is out. And actually, the sooner the better, both for the individual and for the company.

Yet culture/fit issues are rarely clear-cut. The CHRO might take into account that preserving a few people with non-traditional profiles and different perspectives – such as mavericks in a conformist culture or autocratic types in an informal culture – might be useful for the health of the company.

For example, a low-cost airline has a team-based, egalitarian culture, which is fundamental to the success of its business model. People need to chip in and help at all levels to solve problems when they arise. The company meticulously selects new individuals to fit this culture.

The leaders and key professionals in this company take care of business by taking care of relationships. This requires that people continue to fit the culture of the company and develop their interpersonal skills.

Career discussions and planning for the future

The CHRO takes the leadership in planning, quantitatively and qualitatively, what staffing the organization needs to reach its objectives. Specifically, the CHRO must supply the human resources needed to successfully implement the firm's business model.

For example, the private banking division of a global financial services organization discovered that it lacked succession candidates to meet the needs of its growth strategy, which involved a new business model of 'onshore private banking'. Thus it selected, based on specific leadership and performance criteria, a pool of high potentials.

A database was created to allow tracking of the individuals and for easy selection. The individuals were involved in keeping up-to-date their data and their development according to the competencies considered key to the implementation of the new business model.

At a company level, this system not only allows finding appropriate succession candidates, but also discovering competency gaps which need to be filled to have sufficient and adequate senior level manpower to realize the strategy. At individual level, one of the clear benefits is higher retention of key talent, because of increased attention and awareness of being developed towards competencies that are strategic to the firm.

On the job, smart HR policies enable firms to get better at rotating people through exciting and challenging assignments. These are aimed at energizing and developing the individual for greater responsibilities, while also serving the firm's needs to assign key talent to key tasks.[2]

Compensation for contribution: the deal

Each employee has an implied 'deal' with the company: the performance of tasks in exchange for extrinsic and intrinsic rewards. The CHRO is the overseer of this 'deal' from its inception to its conclusion.[3]

Firms expect a great deal from their employees, in terms of performance, commitment and mobility. So the CHRO must also be able to explain to people, 'Here's what's in it for you', in both tangible and intangible terms. It falls to the CHRO to be the best articulator, the best salesperson, of the nature of the exchange between the person and the firm.

Of course, the CHRO need not personally communicate with every person in the firm. But the CHRO does need to ensure that HR managers and professionals in all parts of the company are armed with persuasive arguments.

What are the key components of the deal, and, why is it a good deal?

In the 1990s, stock options were widely sold as the key to renewing executive loyalty in the face of increased mobility. They also had the advantage of increasing awareness among employees of shareholder value. But the crash of the stock markets, in the early 2000s, left many executives disenchanted with this system.

Today, CHROs are exploring how to recast the deal for a new generation of employees who often expect more than financial compensation. Increasingly, compensation can include a wide variety of lifestyle factors and interesting work.

For example, a supplier of software to the film industry was recently voted 'Best Place to Work', in spite of the highly-precarious nature of the work. Realizing that slow business periods could be very demotivating for high-level professionals, the company overhauled its compensation policies. It introduced guidelines allowing for individually-tailored approaches to compensation, benefits, and other rewards. People were free to leave. There were no 'golden chains' – there were no financial disincentives to early departures from the firm.

The deal became clearer and more flexible in order to keep people for whom it was a good deal and whose personal work rhythm fitted the business work rhythm.

The company's CHRO explained:

You retain individuals by providing a challenging, stimulating environment where they get to use their talents, grow their talents, and feel rewarded . . . A lot of companies have good talent. What differentiates the good companies from the great ones is that the great ones find a way to unleash that talent. It comes down to making an employee feel comfortable enough to use all his talents.

Increasingly, firms seek to offer greater flexibility in where time is spent: at company offices, working from home, or on the road. Indeed, even the city of residence can be negotiable. In some firms, where professionals and executives can spend several years essentially 'working around the clock', there are offers of extended 'sabbatical leaves', that is, several months' break to refresh oneself.

Of course, the CHRO must be able to devise good deals for the outstanding performers and key talents, but also for other employees. There is also the task to keep energized those who do not have the calibre or aspirations to move up the hierarchy, or to expand their responsibilities at the current job level.

Clearly, the management of compensation and benefits policies within the talent pipeline is one of the most important roles of the CHRO. Sometimes, company policy is to keep compensation information 'a secret'. But people are people, and they often spend energy trying to discover what 'deals' have been offered to or negotiated by their colleagues. Unfortunately, they can form an incorrect perception of what other people are receiving and that they are not receiving a fair deal. It is not necessarily how much people are compensated, but how fairly they feel they are treated in relation to colleagues in the company and peers in the market.

Dilemmas in managing the talent pipeline

The CHRO must confront a number of tensions and dilemmas when managing the talent pipeline. Examples are:

- What is good for the company is not always good for the individual. For example, from the firm's point of view, it might make sense to transfer an individual abroad. But such a move might clash with the individual's personal situation.
- There is a tension between focusing on the talent pool which is critical to the business model versus the remainder of the professional and executive workforce. In some cases, talent management for a select few reduces personal development and opportunities for the remaining employees. The result can be a silent war between 'haves' and 'have nots', with consequent arrogance on one side and cynicism on the other.
- A similar tension arises in matters of compensation. In some businesses there are wide differences between key employee compensation and everyone else. The CHRO is faced with answering: how does the company make everybody feel valued, not just the stars?
- Often, there is tension between focusing on the metrics and the numbers, versus resolving real people issues. Too often, the focus is on what can be measured by simple metrics; but greater benefits would flow if more effort were devoted to the hard work of developing shared language by which intangibles can be analysed, assessed and judged.

CHROs must fully master these technical demands and dilemmas of managing the talent pipeline, and demonstrate their ability to resolve the intrinsic tensions and dilemmas. They can then begin to exert their full influence as change masters and strategic contributors.[4]

The change master: advice and implementation

The first responsibility of the CHRO is establishing solid HR foundations. But competitive shifts, changes in customer demands, and technological developments require realignments and adaptations. As the people-expert, the CHRO has to play a central role in managing these efforts. The CHRO can guide colleagues on processes for introducing new initiatives into their areas. In particular, CHROs can assist their CXO colleagues as they:

- **Sell the need for change** Generally in the short run, people are better off by not changing, simply doing better what they were already doing. But this approach condemns the company to change only when a crisis hits. The CHRO can help line managers to build the case for change.
- **Analyse the likely obstacles and methods for dealing with them** Often, executives who expect strong resistance to change can trigger a self-fulfilling prophecy. Anticipating trouble, their behaviour can be so calculating that they end up nurturing the mistrust or hostility they feared.

  The real obstacles often lie elsewhere: not in the employees' inbuilt fear of change, but rather in the lack of explanation, selling, training, resources and support to assist the shift. The CHRO can alert colleagues to these dynamics and help them see the issues from the perspective of the people impacted by the changes.
- **Apply fair processes** Another key to gaining commitment to change is fairness. People can sometimes accept unfavourable (or even painful) outcomes far better if they perceive that the decisions were made fairly. In essence, did they get a say? Was the decision properly explained? And, are the rules of the new game made clear? CHROs are rarely the guarantor of employee jobs. But they can be guardians of fair and legal process within the company.

Much experience shows that respect for these principles promotes better acceptance and execution of change processes. The chance to influence the decision process and the right of appeal inspires many people to go 'beyond the call of duty'. They are more willing to engage in innovative actions, spontaneous co-operation, and creative behaviour on behalf of the company when implementing decisions.[5]

Simplifying the structure

A typical initiative, when the company needs to adapt to changing forces in its environment, is to reorganize the ways that roles and responsibilities are divided up, allocated and co-ordinated – that is, the structure. This is the system of allocating tasks and responsibilities to units, the people who head up the units, and how the work of these units is then co-ordinated. Structure is often represented by the boxes and lines sketched in the organization chart.

Over the past two decades, there have been widespread fundamental shifts in structural forms. Companies are now leaner, with fewer people at each level; and are often organized as much around processes as traditional functions.

A structural redesign can change the boxes on a formal organization chart. But this does not necessarily create the attitudes and capabilities of people to make the new structure work.

Flexible structures require people to work across functional boundaries and to work independently of hierarchy. Often, professionals and executives work on projects in which they must try to influence others who have greater formal status than their own. The maintenance of effective – if conflictful – interpersonal relations is sometimes more important than the maintenance of formal structures.

And so, in many companies, the focus of the CHRO's efforts has moved to create more flexibility in the individual's thinking about his or her job. Increasingly, the development of aspiring leaders is geared towards developing 'a matrix in the mind'.[6] This is aided by rotations, through functional and/or line responsibilities, as well as by a variety of project assignments, and by work experience in different geographical locations.

The strategic contributor: anticipating needs and facilitating major decisions

The suggestion that if you are enmeshed in the business you can't be cognisant of employees' needs is ridiculous ... I don't see the profession as a continuum with employee champion at one end and business partner at the other. It's HR professionals embedded in the business. (CHRO of UK bank)

As we have noted, there have been many calls for HR executives to take a 'seat at the top table' and become 'strategic partners with the CEO'. Many conferences, books and journals have been dedicated to the proposal that HR should have a greater role in driving the development of corporate strategy.[7]

But it seems that many HR practitioners remain unsure about this. One recent survey found that about one third of HR practitioners see themselves as a 'business partner', while most of the others aspire to become one.[8] Only 4 per cent responded that, in the future, they wanted to be an 'administrative expert', and one-third wanted to be a 'change agent'. The vast majority of CHROs *are* concerned about how to spend more time on strategic areas. But they concede that it is the activity where they spend the least time.

Another large-scale survey revealed that, in contrast to the grand proclamations, the amount of time spent by HR executives 'being a strategic business partner' has not actually increased over the past decade.[9] Moreover, line managers report that HR is far less involved in strategy than HR thinks it is.

These findings raise concerns. They suggest that some HR professionals have unrealistic views of their actual, versus perceived strategic, contribution. The idea seems to be that CHROs should shake off the shackles and move away from demeaning basic service work and get on with more important tasks.

However, what we see in companies is that the CHRO's strategic contribution is firmly built on the roles of service provider and change agent. Excellent performance in these two areas provides the foundations and the legitimacy for the CHRO to be heard on strategic matters.

Thus, to become a more effective strategic contributor, the CHRO must be effective in two ways: firstly, by anticipating the strategic must-wins of the firm. And secondly, by advising members of the CXO team and facilitating interactions among them.

The set of tasks formerly known as human resource services is now cast as a value chain of integrated processes and functions that are strategically positioned to help the organization compete. (CHRO, US retail chain)

Anticipating strategic needs

The CHRO must keep abreast of major demographic changes. These include shifts in education standards among university graduates, shifts in supply of job candidates with particular prior training and experience, and shifts in perceptions of the firm's attractiveness in different labour, consumer and financial markets.

The CHRO can have a significant strategic impact by articulating and upholding the firm's social responsibility model. This is especially so if the existing model seems to be at variance with prevailing public concerns. In many ways this is an extension of the CHRO's responsibility for managing 'the deal' that we discussed earlier. Attracting and retaining talent sometimes include offering an appealing vision of how the company sees its role in society.

Monitoring people trends

Similarly, the CHRO can contribute greatly to the firm by refining the people strategy to strengthen the foundation of the overall business system.

For example, a CHRO might notice that changing demographics indicate that a candidate pool, which is critical to the business, puts greater emphasis on flexible work hours, a feature that the firm does not currently offer. Successful companies are learning how to provide a 'workable mix' for those who are willing to work hard, but who also want time for family and personal interests.

The CHRO who is a strategic player identifies such trends and offers solutions that support the business model. He or she seeks to resolve tensions to work-life balance in ways that build the individual's commitment to the firm.

Assessing growth possibilities

In addition to monitoring external trends, the CHRO must also anticipate new requirements. The CHRO's input can be relevant to major moves – such as expanding into new markets, entering strategic alliances or acquiring other firms. One reason that such moves fail to yield the expected revenue gains and cost reductions, often has to do with badly managed people-challenges.

For example, if the company seeks to start an operation in an Eastern European country, the CHRO must discover where to get the right kinds of people and where to find employees who can quickly be trained to the right levels. They must uncover untapped local sources or networks of talent. Typically, this requires identifying reputable local consultants who can provide guidance.

The successful implementation of acquisitions and mergers depends greatly on how the people are handled. In one survey, the four top-ranked determinants of acquisition success were all related to people challenges: retention of key talent, executive retention, effective communication and cultural integration.[10]

By contrast, there is also evidence that assessments of culture are generally ignored until the financial deal is closed. One survey of

European executives closely involved in M&A activity revealed that assessment of cultural fit featured at the tail end of priorities. The importance of culture was eclipsed by the strategic and financial priorities of the dealmakers.[11]

Therefore, the CHRO's responsibility is to anticipate cultural challenges and to mitigate the consequent risks. Of course, this starts with a clear-eyed diagnosis of the company's own cultural attributes and idiosyncrasies. This helps to discern likely divergences with the target firm and to prepare methods for integration once the merger goes ahead.

Implementation of expansion plans

Another key issue for CHROs during major strategic decisions is *talent identification*. This especially applies to the target firm. The CHRO must assist line executives in assessing which individuals are critical to the success of the new business operations. The CHRO must be the expert on how these people can be reassured and retained, rather than alienated and lost.

The CHRO can also impact the success of a merger by advising on the selection of an effective integration manager and transition team. These developmental assignments serve as stepping stones into higher business leadership roles.

These types of appointments can be used as essential components of managing the talent pipeline. When the company seeks to apply its business system in new geographies, it needs to deploy its 'key cadre' to the front-line. These are the people who can transfer the firm's technology, methods and culture to other locations.

For example, one international retailer has created a dedicated start-up team to facilitate international expansion and keep up with the rapid rate of store openings. Each new store is planned and started by a temporary store start-up team, whose members arrive on-site about three months before the store's opening date. They prepare the opening, recruit and train the local staff, manage the opening, and stay for about a year before handing over the management of the store to the local staff.

For such efforts to succeed the company must identify and develop a pool of leaders and other professionals who can work easily in new locations with people of different cultures. These people must be loyal to the company rather than to any of its constituent parts.

It is costly and complex to develop and retain a pool of leaders capable of taking on such assignments. They must be able to deal with high levels of uncertainty – in terms of culture and people diversity, communication and language, organization, legal matters, distance and time, compensation, and strains on personal lives. These professionals must have a clear understanding of the firm's business and be able to react quickly to non-routine situations.

Clearly, this requires system-level design by the CHRO who must determine the key capabilities of these leaders. He or she must put in place systems to provide individuals with the critical support during the assignment and to leverage their experience on repatriation.

Once again, we see that the CHRO's strategic contribution is grounded in mastery of the technical details of human resource management. It is the CHRO's task to sell the importance of managing the talent pipeline to the business system, and then compete with CXO colleagues for scarce resources.

The trusted advisor

CHROs are well placed to make strategic contributions as extensions of their specialist people skills:

1 Through advice to the CEO on senior appointments;
2 Through monitoring and facilitation of CXO team dynamics.

Counsel on top-level appointments

The CHRO can be the CEO's natural partner in discussions regarding senior appointments. Also, it is often critical that the CHRO works closely with the Chief Communications Officer to control timing and information flow. Where external appointments are concerned, the CHRO is often the guardian of the decision process. The CHRO's role is to put in place robust methods to avoid some of the common traps in the area of unbalanced assessments of candidates.

It is rare to find a candidate who perfectly matches the selection criteria. Typically, candidates are outstanding on some required dimensions, but rate more modestly on others. And so, the selection decision involves a comparison of different sets of qualities. The big challenge for the CHRO is to help the selectors agree on which criteria really matter the most for the job.

Similarly with internal moves, the CHRO needs to diagnose a person's strengths and weaknesses, where and to what degree he or she is likely to succeed. Where the match between person and job is not perfect; the CHRO must assess what risks need to be managed. Sometimes in filling one position, the CHRO also needs to think about appointing a second person in a related role to fill capability gaps.

For example, we observed a multinational telecom company in which the business model involved setting up local operations in various countries. Getting the right people in the top jobs – the CEO and CFO – and determining incentives to keep them effective in their roles, was critical to success.

The quality of this CHRO's high-level contribution was based on his technical capabilities: in people selection; assembling the right pairs of CEOs and CFOs; deep appreciation of the requirements of the parent firm's business system; and critically, the ability to maintain a close working relationship with the CEO.

The CHRO in this company reported that he personally spent 60 to 70 per cent of his time working specifically on these CEO or CFO selections.

Facilitator of effective senior relationships

CHROs can sometimes contribute by assisting interactions within the CXO team. Applying their people skills, CHROs can play the role of 'process manager'.

For example, a new HR executive is brought in from outside to become a company's first Group CHRO. The firm is the result of a merger of two former competitors. The CEO has recruited the CHRO to help with the integration and to help build the senior team. The members of the new senior team are all members of the top teams of the former competitors.

One of the CHRO's jobs is to assist in harmonizing roles and responsibilities, and compensation. Some of the executives must surrender privileges that until now had been considered as given. At the same time, the CHRO must build a partnership with each team member to ensure that the integration will work. Great skill is required to facilitate co-operation while withdrawing privileges from some members of the team.

Of course, not all CHROs have the respect and acceptance of their CXO colleagues to work in this way. CHROs who have secured their credibility and influence based on outstanding service provision can be accepted as process facilitators. In this role, they help manage the decision processes of the top team.

The CHRO can hold up a mirror to highlight emerging tensions and counter-productive behaviours. This is risky work, and best handled by a highly skilled person. Credible CHROs can bring people together and help them deal with conflict or misunderstanding

Beyond this service to the team, the CHRO can be a trusted adviser to the CEO, notably on delicate top-level people issues. Any barrier to the functioning of the CXO team is a potential risk factor, which needs expert handling.

In the relationship between the CEO and the senior executives, the CHRO can help keep the CEO on his or her toes by forcing objective assessments of key executives. The CHRO can push back on the CEO to prevent a 'set-up-to-fail syndrome', which could keep a CEO from seeing the performance of this person in a true light.[12]

The influential role as trusted advisor is difficult to attain for CHROs. It depends greatly on the attitude of the CEO towards the human resource function and the CHRO as an individual. The CHRO might be faced with a major sales task: Demonstration of sustained competence and reliability in the way that HR serves the business system is an imperative.

The qualities needed to handle the tensions

To fulfil this dual role vis-à-vis the CEO and the top team, the CHRO must deal with inevitable tensions:

- How to be considered a trusted adviser by the individual senior team members, while assisting with the CEO's agenda. Certainly this is a dilemma for all CXOs. However, other CXOs deal primarily with business decisions. By contrast, the CHRO directly influences major decisions about people's careers – and this makes a big difference.
- How to deal with the personal and private issues of individual senior team members while maintaining a transparent relationship with the CEO?
- How to respond to the needs of individual internal clients, which might be inconsistent with the direction of the firm? For example, the sales manager might require an individual incentive system for the sales team, while the corporation as a whole favours team-based compensation.

To become a successful trusted adviser requires the CHRO's integrity, discretion and authenticity to be widely acknowledged throughout the company. Integrity, in this context, particularly means intolerance of behaviour that goes against the corporate values. The integrity of the CHRO can be an important model that encourages other CXOs to maintain high standards; especially to ensure that the company fulfils its side of the 'deal' with all employees.

Discretion entails knowing when to be transparent and when not. Having the confidence of the CXO team and showing that one can be trusted with confidential information is key to effective performance by the CHRO.

Authenticity, finally, requires being true to oneself and one's profession. A CHRO must express what he or she stands for, personally. The senior team expects high professional standards and a sparring partner of equal strength.

The CHRO must earn the reputation of a technically competent, personally courageous, and trustworthy colleague – and be seen as such by the CEO and all members of the CXO team.

Looking to the future

We do not see dramatic changes on the horizon for the future role of the CHRO. Whether or not the CHRO is a member of the top-most CXO team, the key success factors remain the same: managing the talent pipeline to match the company's needs; playing the role of change agent as companies re-structure; and playing the important role of strategic advisor when working with the CEO and CXO colleagues on top management human resources issues.

We can expect to see more executives from non-HR backgrounds moving into senior HR roles. This is for the simple reason that we noted in opening this chapter: the role of HR is to serve the business system. Executives who have had to manage operations and deliver results against real business challenges can bring the requisite understanding to ensure that HR does its job to a high level. HR is primarily a service function – an essential service function, but still a service function.

Assessing the role of the CHRO

The following questions are a starting point when assessing the role of the CHRO.

Purpose

1. How effectively does the CHRO:
   - Manage the talent pipeline to sustain the business model? Technically and in an integrated way?

- Work as a change agent in the organization?
- Perform as a strategic contributor by anticipating strategic needs and acting as a trusted adviser to the CEO and the senior team?

Direction

2. What guides the CHRO's decisions and what techniques are employed? Consider whether (and how) the management of the talent pipeline could be improved:
   (i) Talent identification & recruitment
   (ii) Induction
   (iii) Pre-emptive training & development
   (iv) Performance management
   (v) Performance interventions
   (vi) Culture-fit interventions
   (vii) Career discussions
   (viii) Compensation for contribution.
3. How does the CHRO perform as a change enabler to adapt the culture and the organization to the evolution of the business model?
4. How valuable is the CHRO in influencing strategic decisions concerning key executives' compensation, appointments and development?
5. How effective is the CHRO in facilitating and improving the interaction within the senior team?

Focus

On a day-to-day basis, to what extent does the CHRO:

6. Show authenticity, integrity and discretion when dealing with the various dilemmas and tensions?
7. Show exemplary behaviour when it comes to managing the talent pipeline within the HR functions?
8. Demonstrate role model behaviour for the entire organization?

Notes

1 J. Martin, *Making Partnership a Reality: A Global View of the State of the HR Function*, (London: Egon Zehnder International, 2005).

2 In developed economies, increasing salaries is losing its attraction to employers as a means to keep staff on board: Chartered Institute of Personnel and

Development, *Recruitment and Retention Survey* (2003). F. M. Horwitz, e.a. 'Finders, keepers? Attracting, motivating and retaining knowledge workers', *Human Resource Management Journal*, 13 (4) (2003), pp. 23–44.
3 Currently often coined under the term 'employee engagement', i.e. the measure of people's willingness and ability to give discretionary effort at work, the perception of the 'deal' and consequently influencing its perception by the CHRO, is of fundamental importance to an organization's productivity. Recently it has been shown that less than 80 per cent of employees in the US consider themselves 'fully engaged': *Towers Perrin Global Employee Engagement Survey*, 2005.
4 There is still a long way to go with regard to tying HR subprocesses to the business model, their integration and the quality of the subprocesses themselves: American Society for Training and Development, *The Human Capital Challenge*, ASTD White Paper (2003).
5 W. C. Kim and R. A Mauborgne, 'Fair process: Managing in the knowledge economy', *Harvard Business Review*, July–August (1997), pp. 65–76.
6 C. A. Bartlett and S. Ghoshal, *Managing Across Borders* (Cambridge, MA: Harvard Business School Press, 1989).
7 See most recently D. Ulrich and W. Brockbank, *The HR Value Proposition*, (Cambridge, MA: Harvard University Press, 2005).
8 Chartered Institute of Personnel and Development (UK), 'Where we are, where we are heading'. A survey of some 1200 HR practitioners, about 75 per cent in CHRO roles (2003).
9 E. E. Lawler and S. A. Mohrman, 'HR as a strategic partner: What does it take to make it happen?' *Human Resource Planning*, 26 (3) (2003), pp. 15–29. A recent study by McKinsey shows 'a troubling gulf between the needs of the business and the ability of HR to respond': E. Lawson, e.a., 'A dearth of HR talent', *The McKinsey Quarterly*, 2 (2005).
10 I. T. Kay and M. Shelton, 'The people problems in mergers', *McKinsey Quarterly*, 4 (2000), pp. 29–37.
11 D. Angwin, 'Mergers and acquisitions across European borders: National perspectives on pre-acquisition due diligence and the use of professional advisers', *Journal of World Business*, 36 (1) (2001), pp. 32–57.
12 J.-F. Manzoni, and J.-L. Barsoux, 'The set-up-to-fail syndrome', *Harvard Business Review*, March-April (1998), pp. 101–14.

13 *The Corporate Governance Officer – From company secretary to manager of governance processes*

ULRICH STEGER AND PRESTON BOTTGER

Over the last decade sound corporate governance has become a hot topic, as misconduct by senior executives rocked the business world and outraged investors. Increasingly, effective corporate governance contributes to a company's success, and the modern corporate governance officer (CGO) plays a key role in managing the process.

In this chapter, the authors outline the wide-ranging responsibilities of the CGO role. They go back to the roots of corporate governance to help us understand how the role has evolved and why there is a strong business case for sound governance structures and policies. Finally, they discuss the emerging challenges that will continue to shape the future role of the CGO.

The role of the corporate governance officer[1]

My predecessor was a lawyer, whereas I clearly have a strong business background. I studied business, then started working in our group's headquarters and then moved on to several management positions in foreign subsidiaries. Prior to my appointment as corporate governance officer, I worked on the post-merger strategy and integration of our biggest acquisition deal ever.

The reason the board chose me is simply that our company wants the board to have a strong strategic influence and more involvement in the day-to-day business.

(A CGO whose predecessor's title was company secretary)

The 1990s saw a degree of business expansion that was unprecedented. The combination of opportunities presented by new technologies, and the vastly-increased geographical scope and freedom in capital, product and labour markets led to remarkable risk-taking by investors and executives alike.

For a decade, stock market indices rose, apparently without limit, as investors and executives fed each other visions of unparalleled growth in wealth for all. Some even argued that historical instances of market collapse were just that: history. These optimists were sure there was no upper limit to the value placed on companies by investors who had the necessary imagination and courage.

Well, it appears that some of this optimism was not fuelled only by idealistic beliefs in new technologies and new freedoms in key markets. Indeed, some of it originated in malpractice and misrepresentation of important facts. In the wake of the stock market crashes of the early 2000s, it became clear that some senior executives in a remarkably large number of firms had cooked the books in spectacular fashion.

After years of illusion and delusion, there arose a critical mass of reforming opinion, from investors, politicians, public prosecutors and executives. This wave finally broke through the dream-like thinking that had dominated the actions of many investors and executives for the best part of a decade. Of course, there were many others who took advantage of the dreamers' exuberance and took their profits before the market collapse.

A key point came back into focus: in business, there must be minimum levels of empirical truth in reporting revenues and costs. Additionally, there must be minimum levels of realism in expectations of return on investment.

A great wave of counter-moves arose against the kinds of behaviour executives in companies and investment banks exhibited when they had misrepresented the truth of financial performance. Within a short time boards of directors and senior executives were held responsible for honest practice. Suddenly they had to implement new robust methods of corporate governance to protect not only shareholders, but their own interests as company fiduciaries.

Drastic measures had to be enacted and enforced if investors and the general public were to have renewed confidence in the institutions that make capitalist democracies workable and attractive. In parallel, we have seen the emergence, or expansion, of a very significant role in the CXO team: the Corporate Governance Officer.

What does the CGO do? We briefly list below the variety of tasks for which a CGO might be responsible. These tasks are determined by two main factors: the national and international legal jurisdictions that the company operates in, and policy choices made by the board to ensure that the desired messages are given both to internal executives and employees and to key external stakeholders.

A list of CGO responsibilities can include:

- **Facilitating governance processes** This involves helping the chair set the agenda, presenting management reports to the board and its committees, and ensuring that the board follows established procedures.
- **Supporting board meetings** The CGO is responsible for preparing board documents, drafting and distributing the minutes, and follow-up after the meetings.
- **Ensuring compliance** The CGO must ensure compliance with all internal rules and external laws and regulations applicable to the company. Compliance needs to become part of the company culture, and the CGO often spearheads this effort.
- **Shareholder management** This entails managing the entire process for the annual general meeting of shareholders, including recording and archiving minutes and keeping the shareholder register.
- **Integrating new directors** The CGO facilitates the integration of new, non-executive directors into the business and their role on the board. The CGO also assists with the ongoing training and development of directors.
- **Tracking key changes in the environment** The CGO must be able to read emerging pressures in the political and legal environment, and give the board and management early warning of changes that may affect the company.

Later in the chapter, we identify four types of CGOs, with varying degrees of responsibility in the above areas. But regardless of what category the CGO falls into, the demands on corporate governance are not static. Governance methods are subject to ever-developing pressures that will continue to shape the role of the CGO. As such, CGOs must be outward looking and forward looking, with flexible capabilities.

Historical influences on corporate governance

The topic of corporate governance and the role of the CGO raises some of the most critical questions in business. Namely, whom does the company serve and who controls its actions?

That is:

- Whose interests and rights are at stake when the firm does business?
- Who has control over what activities, and responsibility for what results?

- Who should benefit, in what ways and to what degree, from the fruits of the enterprise?

To appreciate the importance of the role, and the responsibilities of the present and future CGO, it is useful to examine several key trends in corporate history. In particular, we will explore developments in two major business arenas – the US and the UK.

Corporate governance in the US

In the early twentieth century it had become clear that senior executives in widely held US companies typically had greater control of the firm's strategic and operational moves than the shareholders.

Of course, shareholders own corporations. So it was expected that executives would work on behalf of the owners. However, with massive company growth, dilution of ownership and the consequent complexity in both management and ownership, it became increasingly difficult for shareholders to influence the company's directors, and the firm's operations.

Company owners started worrying about whether the system of separation of ownership and control could work in practice. This led to the conclusion that it was inadequate and inefficient for management to have fiduciary responsibility to shareholders.[2]

Although corporations in all growing economies were grappling with growth challenges, the relative power of executives over owners was greater in the US than elsewhere. The vast majority of US shareholders were interested in investment, not operational control of the firm.

Ownership became increasingly dispersed. And with this, shareholder control diminished, because few individual shareholders were in a position to influence the choice either of executives or of board members.

> ***Corporate governance deals with*** how senior management is controlled, how board decisions are made, and who influences the respective processes. Its main players are corporate supervisory and management boards, but external influences and stakeholders, i.e. stock markets, regulators or environmental interest groups, have become increasingly influential. ***Corporate governance should*** aim to establish clear structures of responsibility, accountability and transparency, and appropriate stakeholder representation.

This effect was less severe in other parts of the world, for example Northern Europe and Asia. This was because a single wealthy family, or a few main investors, owned the large firms. In addition, these firms tended to use bank loans to supply funding needs, not equity financing.

In the US, the CEO usually chaired the board. That is, one person controlled both the operations and the governance of the firm. This CEO-centred system allowed for quick, autonomous decision-making by senior executives, especially the CEO. With the CEO as chair, free to appoint his or her own choices to the board, the board rarely contradicted the chair. As such, the board had little impact on the company's business activities. It was often merely a rubber stamp to confirm CEO decisions.

Shareholder revolutions were rare. US investors had essentially put their trust in the market, not the board, to control senior executive decisions. With this trend, the notion of a 'market for corporate control' arose.

The theory was that bad management would lead to poor results, which in turn would mean a decline in share price. Shareholders would then leave the company by selling their shares, and new, knowledgeable and interested investors would buy shares and gain relative ownership control. When sufficient ownership was established, the new shareholders would remove the ineffective executives who were responsible for the share price decline.

This mechanism would correct the CEO's bad behaviour. CEOs would be forced to act in the interests of shareholders to protect their own position. This 'market for corporate control' was one of the drivers of the subsequent wave of mergers and acquisitions and hostile takeovers.

Other developments saw the rise of institutional investors, large pension fund managers and hedge funds. But these had little impact on executive power before 2000. While pension funds achieved considerable financial stakes in big companies, most assumed the role of 'outsiders looking in'. A notable exception is CALPERS, a California-based government employee pension plan that is one of the largest funds in the world and has a longer history of activism than most. General practice was that when share prices fell or bad news was in the press, pension fund managers quickly sold the poorly performing or unpopular stocks.

The share price, not the quality of corporate governance, was the critical factor in investment decisions. Later, hedge funds and leveraged buyout specialists became more powerful. But their reputation (which some recent studies have disputed) was for ownership decisions that focused on short-term financial performance, not the corporate governance system.

When these types of investors avoided becoming 'insiders', it was often because that would have limited their ability to trade shares. Generally, they were not represented on the board or involved in formal control of management, but times continue to change. If their interests were not considered, it could and has lead to lengthy and costly proxy fights. But while the rhetoric of 'shareholder value' did not change a great deal, as long as share prices were moving in the right direction, nobody objected.

Meanwhile, CEO salaries multiplied, mostly through generous stock options. One famous case is Disney CEO, Michael Eisner. In 1998, he was paid US$590 million, making him perhaps the highest-paid executive in corporate history to that time. Eisner himself, as chairman and CEO, was driven from Disney in a fury of shareholder activism and claims of mismanagement.

The US corporate governance earthquake

Then, in 2000 and 2001, came the dramatic failures of expectations of the dot-coms, and crashes in stock markets. These collapses deeply shocked investors. Stock price indices in technology and other sectors fell by 60 per cent and more. But adding to the pain of slumping asset prices was another disturbing element. Evidence began to emerge of widespread executive misconduct.

Under pressure to show results, or from greed, some executives had simply overstated revenues and hidden debt and costs. In some cases, company executives were aided by the external auditors. There were several high-profile bankruptcies, some resulting in criminal charges and convictions, the after-effects of which are still being felt several years later in late 2006.

This pattern of bad behaviour was not limited to upstart firms. It became clear that misrepresentation of important financial numbers extended to such icons of the US economy as AIG, WorldCom and General Electric. This added to the alarm of investors.

The negative consequences of these events, along with tensions about ownership versus control that had long been building, eventually reached unacceptable proportions. Stakeholder groups demanded radical changes to corporate governance practices. Politicians and zealous attorney-generals, seeing a bandwagon to jump on, pursued a number of high-profile cases with vigour. This resulted in a corporate governance earthquake – a dramatic shift in the way it was viewed and enacted.

In 2002, the Sarbanes-Oxley legislation was quickly pushed through the US Congress. This new law greatly changed accounting practices, corporate law and stock market regulations. As a result, in 2003 and 2004 alone, more than half of the S&P 500 firms were forced to restate their earnings. Many executives were called to testify in the subsequent criminal investigations and court proceedings.

There were prosecutions. In July 2005, in perhaps the most extreme case of corporate fraud of that time, former WorldCom CEO Bernard Ebbers was sentenced to twenty-five years in prison. Kenneth Lay, the former CEO of Enron, who may have matched Ebbers, did not live long enough to have his trials completed. He died on 5 July 2006, leaving many shareholders feeling that they had been robbed of justice.

A major awakening was now under way among US institutional investors, who began the process of improving the inspection and quality control of financial reporting. In particular, independent directors were installed as owner proxies. Powerful new audit committees, consisting only of independent directors, were set up to scrutinize top management behaviour and the financial details of companies. Additionally, independent directors now held all the seats on the all-important compensation and nomination committees.

Against strong opposition from some CEOs, investors moved to ensure that the roles of chair and CEO were separated. Often, as an intermediate step, one director would take the leadership of the group of independent directors, and thereby the power of the CEO.

Less than three years after the beginning of the crises, one-third of major companies in the US had separated the positions of chair and CEO.[3] This brought US corporate governance closer to the European model of checks and balances. This model was widely accepted as more appropriate for large firms with widely held ownership.

The situation in Europe

Historically, Europe had had many checks and balances in place. For example, the role of the supervisory boards in German companies was to scrutinize top executive behaviour. In most North European countries, one-tier systems were supported by a mandatory non-executive chair. In the UK and Ireland, company law ensured that the majority of board members were non-executive.

However, Europe had its share of corporate crises as well. Parmalat was a clear example with banks, company owners and even some suppliers and customers drawn into the scandal. But the problems did not extend as widely as in the US. The checks and balances of European governance systems, and the greater involvement of banks, prevented worse from happening. Nevertheless, in Europe and elsewhere, newly enhanced rules and regulations for corporate governance followed.

Special panels were set up, with the task of establishing high quality practices in codes of conduct. The basic idea was to 'comply or explain'. For example, there was no room for corporations to oppose moves such as ensuring the transparency of executive remuneration.

Boards gained new legal powers and were assigned new responsibilities, significantly increasing their importance. With this came massive changes for those responsible for corporate governance. In fact, boards had to reconsider the very basis of their methods for dealing with corporate governance. The task of understanding compliance, with all the new regulations, had become much more complex and intricate. As a result, boards had to invest in new capabilities.

In the wake of the corporate disasters, it now became clear to senior executives that investors, employees and customers alike would reward companies that implemented effective corporate governance practices. Both marketplace reputations and stock market valuations were influenced by perceptions of good versus bad governance.

Many companies created a CGO position, taking this opportunity to increase their market appeal. In doing so, they enhanced the scope of the former company secretary, who already had many of the responsibilities that were now emerging as mandatory. And company secretaries were most closely linked with the core of corporate governance – the board.

Additionally, companies, boards and even governments in greater numbers, facilitate whistle-blowing as a means to get more information on corporate impropriety. Increasingly there will have to be more dialogue between those people in positions to uncover corporate misbehaviour and those people who can do something about it.

The US corporate governance officer in practice

Example 1: American Express Company, US

In November 2003, American Express appointed Stephen P. Norman to the position of corporate governance officer, keeping his company secretary position. His task is the 'development and implementation of appropriate governance practices and formulating and recommending sound governance principles'.[4]

Example 2: Motorola, US

Patrick J. Canavan is senior vice-president and director of global governance at Motorola, and Secretary to the board committees on governance and nomination. In his role, he has provided consultation for the board of directors on issues of corporate governance, and consultation and advice for chair succession since 1990.

Example 3: Eastman Kodak Company, US

Laurence L. Hickey is chief governance officer and company secretary at Eastman Kodak. In this position since July 2003, he is responsible for the company's efforts on compliance and the identification and adoption of best practices in the field of corporate governance.

Example 4: SAP, Germany

In 2001, the German software giant passed its corporate governance principles that require the management board to appoint (in addition to a compliance officer) a corporate governance officer who must 'continuously develop the corporate governance principles and monitor compliance with them'[5], reporting directly to the supervisory board.

The UK system: The role of the company secretary (more on ICSA)

In the early 2000s, the UK had its share of executive malpractice that shook shareholder confidence. These problems also led to new rules for good practice. In fact it is in the UK that we find a long history of company law and practical guidelines designed to promote shareholder safety in corporate governance.

Certainly the Cadbury Report (1992) strongly influenced the behaviour of boards and senior executives. Even earlier than this, both legal requirements and public concern for quality in corporate governance had led to the codification of roles and responsibilities of a senior corporate officer called the *company secretary*.

The position of company secretary was first mentioned and described in the Companies Act 1948[6]. Demonstrating the importance of the role, the company secretary was positioned at the officer level.

Today, many countries, particularly those with UK-influenced legal systems (e.g. the US, Ireland, Australia, India) also legally prescribe a position of company secretary who has responsibilities both for acts of incorporation and for ongoing governance of the firm. The UK approach to regulations and guidelines for the company secretary role is widely regarded as both the forerunner in codification and an exemplary model.

There are no specific details in the Companies Act of 1948 on the tasks and responsibilities of a company secretary that would lead to comprehensive prescriptions for the role. As management responsibility is reserved for directors, the first assumption is that the company secretary's basic tasks are administrative.

In practice, the company secretary role is usually enhanced by an additional employment contract. This enhanced role is widely perceived as the one designated by UK regulation as the Companies Act. Other legislation also mentions expanded tasks a company secretary may have. For example, a company secretary may sign official documents on behalf of the company, which are then legally binding.

Depending on the size and nature of the company, the UK company secretary's tasks usually involve the actual writing (not setting) and distribution of directors' meeting agendas, compiling minutes of meetings and keeping statutory company documents.

In addition, the company secretary can be responsible for a variety of other responsibilities that are often detailed in the company's articles of association or the employment contract. These tasks generally include keeping company records (including transfer of share ownership and issuing of share certificates), the register of members, the register of charges, the directors' meetings and shareholder assembly minutes and providing them at the request of auditors or shareholders.

The position of company secretary in a public company (PLC) is subject to additional requirements. The directors must ensure that the company secretary has the necessary knowledge and experience and is properly qualified. Proper qualifications are, for example, a member of the Institute of Chartered Accountants (CA) or the Institute of Chartered Secretaries and Administrators (ICSA).

The UK's Combined Code of Corporate Governance[7] 1998 – to which compliance is a prerequisite for being listed on the London Stock Exchange[8] – states:

> All directors should have access to the advice and services of the company secretary, who is responsible to the board for ensuring that board procedures are followed and that applicable rules and regulations are complied with.

In the case of PLCs, therefore, the company secretary is also in charge of the process side of governance.

The ICSA recommends that the company secretary should be in charge of the integration of non-executive and newly appointed directors, to help them understand their responsibilities and the company's governance processes. They should also be in charge of managing the annual general meeting, keeping 'in touch with the debate on corporate social responsibility, monitoring all developments in this area and advising the board'.[9]

The corporate governance earthquake at the turn of the century brought further changes to UK regulations. These are likely to affect the CGO's future role: two more committees were established, an audit committee in 2002, and another on the role and effectiveness of non-executive directors in 2003.

In most other jurisdictions/countries, companies are free to set the rules and tasks of a company secretary, and the UK model widely serves as the basis for designating the responsibilities of the CGO. For this reason, most CGOs hold company secretary responsibilities. As this is the most common practice, we will focus on this type of CGO.

The CGO in practice: four types of roles

We have identified four major types of CGO role: chair's proxy, go-between, compliance ensurer and administrator. Depending on both the needs of a company and the maturity of the compliance officer's role and the current designee, executives and/or board members try to choose the style that best fits their company needs.

Before exploring the four roles, we look at aspects that are encompassed in all CGO positions. Legal requirements are one side of the CGO role. The other side is the business perspective. This is determined by the nature of the corporation and its strategy. Of course, the personality and character of the CGO can have a great impact as well. Nevertheless, two critical dimensions determine the CGO's role:

1 The positioning of the role, in terms of reporting line, strongly influences the CGO's tasks and responsibilities. There are two main options: the CGO reports either to the board or top management. And this usually means that he or she reports either to the chair or the CEO, respectively.

  Until recently, the CGO most often reported to the chairman's office, the board's office or the CEO's office. This positioning can be traced back to the 'secretarial' roots of the role. However, a growing trend is to locate CGOs in a separate corporate governance office. Because CGOs usually carry out a number of administrative tasks, it is important, in our opinion, to position the CGO as reporting to top management, preferably the CEO or the non-executive chair.[10]

  As part of the headquarters organization, the CGO is often seen to be in a direct reporting line to the CEO. When reporting directly to the chair, it is more difficult to predict how the position will be perceived. Even though the chair's office may be located at headquarters, it may be a detached unit.

2 The second critical dimension is the overall level of competence required. Competence strongly influences the CGO's role: either the CGO carries a high level of competences and more important tasks (going beyond compliance ensurance), or a lower level of competence. As a member of the CXO team and an employee of the company, the CGO must still have a strong knowledge of business conditions and wealth creation goals. Often, the CGO is there to point out the risks of non-compliance and not doing the 'right thing'.

  In any case, the level of competence goes along with the importance of the CGO's tasks and is therefore a useful indicator for the CGO's impact on the governance of the company.

Given the two reporting options – to the board or management – we now explore in more detail the four different types of CGO role (see

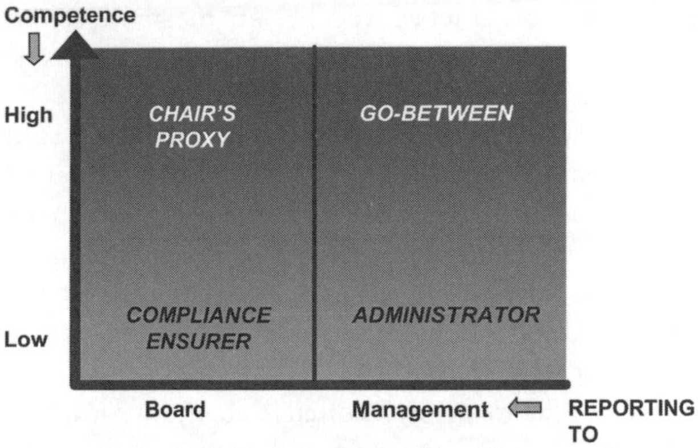

Figure 13.1: Types of corporate governance officers

Figure 13.1): that we have seen companies choose when appointing a CGO. While not all CGOs fall distinctly into one quadrant, we have found the following chart useful in helping CXO teams and boards to design a profile and reporting line for their ideal CGO.

Each CGO type has a relatively distinctive job description, distinctive tasks, and ultimately, has a distinctive impact on the company's corporate governance.

Chair's proxy

The chair's proxy has a high level of competence and reports to the chair of the board. If the chair is strong, this type of CGO will be a very important and influential person close to the helm of the company. He or she can even be 'the power behind the throne'.

Despite normally low-key behaviour, the chair's proxy is the eyes and ears of the chair. Given a strong trust relationship, the chair delegates the management of compliance and board information-gathering to the CGO. The chair's proxy is also in charge of more important board procedures, such as evaluating the board itself.

The person best qualified for this type of CGO role has often had a long, successful career in the company, with a strong record as a corporate lawyer, auditor or controller. In many cases this is the person's final career stage before retirement; they have already attained a position of respect in their company or industry. As such, this CGO has had extensive experience in the firm and could now be expected to demonstrate a high degree of independence. Even the most senior executives treat the chair's proxy type of CGO very respectfully, as he or she is often representing the board in the company.

The main task of this type of CGO is to organize effective board meetings. This is a far from trivial task. The CGO must ensure that all information is prepared and available to all board members, anticipate potential issues that may arise and alert the chair to them. He or she reviews all board papers in advance, to ensure the quality and completeness of the information, and often summarizes all relevant papers from external and internal auditors.

In addition, the CGO, as chair's proxy, is often in charge of formulating uncontroversial proposals in advance and sending them to the chair. Even without specific instructions, this type of CGO usually knows the reasoning that the chair and the board will use on an issue, what specific points to highlight and, most likely, how the board will vote. He or she is involved in the discussion and actual drafting of the agenda, and so can influence the topics addressed.

The power to influence the board's agenda is extremely significant. One CGO told us that to exercise his role as chair's proxy he sometimes had to contradict the CEO when setting the agenda:

> If we put this item at the end of the agenda, we will most likely have only a couple of minutes left, and the board cannot fully discuss this point. And this issue is much too important for a quick discussion and decision. We either have to work on this as one of the first and most important items, or postpone it until the next meeting.

Go-between

If a CGO has a high competence level and reports to top management, the position can be termed a 'go-between'. This type of CGO is a confidant of the CEO and has the task of 'managing the board'.

The go-between supplies the board with information, follows up on their requests and prepares the necessary board papers. Individual board members might call with specific requests or raise issues or concerns. By addressing their questions to the go-between, the board members expect they will be brought to the attention of the CEO.

The go-between is often a younger executive on a fast career track, and might also be in charge of other tasks, unrelated to corporate governance. The go-between's objective is to ensure that the board accepts proposals from the CEO and the management board/executive committee. In doing so, the go-between must be alert to emerging concerns, identify possible objections and alert the CEO about any forthcoming issues.

Normally, this requires the CGO to have an extensive network, especially if board members use their own staff to help them prepare for meetings. In most cases, the go-between must be responsive to informal feedback from board members rather than appear to be part of the inner circle of the CEO, as the latter might exclude him or her from noticing subtle signs.

During our interviews, one CGO told us:

When going around in the company, say to prepare for a board meeting, it is better not to have a CEO-signed letter or a formal chair request giving you authority to do this and that. Most people feel intimidated by it and end up not trusting you. Coming with no formal request at all makes cooperation easier.

The real authority of the corporate governance officer, though, comes from her/his personality and from explaining why a specific issue is very important now. You cannot rely on your hierarchical position for authority.

The go-between will also make sure that the CEO and other senior executives, especially the CFO, have sufficient direct contact with board members and the chair. The go-between controls process rather than content, so the responsible departments normally summarize external and internal auditor and financial reports.

Compliance ensurer

This type of CGO is assigned a lower level of competence and reports to the board (mostly the chair). The CEO and CFO take care of most of the interaction with the board. The compliance ensurer is typically a lower-level manager with legal expertise in the field of corporate governance.

In general, the CGO, as compliance ensurer, does not control or influence the preparation of board meetings or the process during the meetings. Instead, this CGO responds to individual requests, e.g. from the chair through the CEO, or directly from the chair's office.

Often, a vital part of the role is to keep records of board meetings and governance topics and to report internally on compliance issues. This involves documenting and summarizing all cases where the company has violated laws or regulations, or was prosecuted for non-compliance with internal rules.

Examples can include violations of codes of conduct, safety regulations or non-bribery rules. To be efficient, the compliance ensurer needs a wide internal network in areas such as internal auditing, health, safety, environmental departments and corporate communications.

Ideally, the compliance ensurer's network should extend to all divisions, and to key people in the company. If any forthcoming issues surprise the board before the CGO reports them, the result could be damaging for his or her career.

Administrator

The CGO, as administrator, reports directly to management and does not require a high level of competence. The administrator is a lower-level manager, often seconded to the chair's office from the corporate law department for a certain period.

As the name suggests, the tasks of this CGO are predominantly administrative. The administrator is not responsible for agenda setting, ensuring compliance or the quality of the information delivered to the board. He or she is only responsible for compiling the information for the board and supplying it in time.

Of all the CGO roles, the administrator comes closest to the basic company secretary described earlier. For example, in one board retreat that we observed, the company secretary, a young lawyer, did not participate in the meeting. Instead he waited outside for instructions from the chair, mostly on organizational issues.

We concluded the following distribution, based on extensive experience and involvement with boards: approximately 20 per cent of CGOs are chair's proxies, 40 per cent are go-betweens, 30 per cent are compliance ensurers and 10 per cent are administrators.

This is underpinned by the fact that boards often do not have full-time support staff. Instead, they have to rely on the CEO-controlled headquarters organization. In general, the majority of CGOs have high levels of competence, are influential and, for the most part, report to management.

The 40 per cent of companies that have compliance ensurers and administrators often have simply renamed their company secretary as CGO, without expanding the responsibilities. Over time, however, we expect this role to be enhanced and become more comprehensive, and so the percentage of administrators and compliance ensurers will most likely drop.

Case Study

The role of the company secretary at UBS AG, Switzerland

UBS arose from the merger of two major Swiss banks in 1998 and today has offices in 50 countries, employing more than 69,000 people worldwide. With a market capitalization of over $85 billion, UBS is one of the largest banks in the world. The company is listed on the Swiss, New York (NYSE) and Tokyo stock exchanges and operates under a strict two-tier board structure (Swiss Banking Law rule).

A speciality of UBS governance is that the Chairman and at least one vice-chairman of the board are full-time board members, without being members of the day-to-day executive management of the company.

The position of UBS company secretary as such was established in 1998, subsequent to the merger. Immediately after the UBS merger, the position was still administrative and 'secretary'-like. But in the following years, the tasks, competencies and organization of the company secretary's office became clearer and they were further enhanced, greatly influenced by the company secretary herself. In 2000, UBS acquired the US broker PaineWebber – significantly increasing both the scope and size of its business. Shortly before, UBS was listed as a 'foreign private issuer' on the NYSE and the company secretary's tasks were augmented considerably: legal expertise on US corporate law, capital markets and SEC regulation became indispensable.

The corporate governance earthquake began shortly after (around 2001) and its consequences were far-reaching: the Sarbanes-Oxley (SOX) legislation was passed quickly, and the SEC became much more active in controlling its listed companies. UBS was confronted with an increasing number of conflicting corporate governance rules between its Swiss domestic regulatory framework and the US requirements.

In one situation, the UBS company secretary had to alert her chairman and the board that the NYSE might not qualify one of the board members as 'fully independent' and therefore not accept him as a member of the compensation committee. The reason was the board member's ownership of the 'Alinghi' team, the winner of the 2004 America's Cup, for which UBS was the main sponsor.

After intensive negotiations, a solution was found: the UBS board declared its respective member 'independent' under Swiss law, moved him from the compensation to the nominating committee and disclosed this exception to the NYSE rules in its annual report.

Now, in the 'post-Enron' corporate governance era, the company secretary's quest is more for value-adding than trouble-shooting. In 2003, UBS moved the position further up the group hierarchy to the 'group managing board' – directly below the group's management board (called 'group executive board').

The company secretary is elected by the board of directors and reports directly to the chairman of the board, supported by two administrative assistants. Being a direct confidant of the chairman, the company secretary combines many competencies and reaches deep into the UBS group worldwide.

There are still national and local company secretaries, partly because they are required by law (e.g. in the UK or the US). These functions, however, are purely administrative and mostly positioned in the legal departments of subsidiaries. In particular, there is no reporting hierarchy to the group company secretary located in Switzerland.

With the growing importance of boards and corporate governance, the role of the company secretary at UBS has also grown.

The main and most value-adding tasks today are appropriate representation of corporate governance towards board and management, integrating the legitimate interests of company external stakeholders and meeting shareholders' information demands. For this, board agenda setting and board information management became crucial company secretary tasks. To allow the board to meet its strong UBS governance role, the company secretary maintains a group-wide network of contacts and sources information directly from all hierarchy levels in the group. Looking back, the company secretary noted:

> The company secretary at UBS is a powerful role: it is almost too much work for one person, but there is not enough room for a second strong character. So you have to be a tough maverick and still get along well with everybody.

The future of the corporate governance officer

Boards have become more important than ever before, and these changes have significantly influenced the role of the corporate governance officer. One CGO described it like this:

> My tasks and workload have greatly increased during the last years, not because I asked for more responsibilities, but because board work increased enormously. Before, it was not difficult to manage the board members' requests. Then corporate governance became more and more important for investors, and around 2000, everybody suddenly became aware of their personal responsibilities and liabilities as board members. Now they take this job seriously, and today even ordinary board members call me regularly throughout the year and ask for information or assistance.

Studies of board member opinions show that boards will continue to face pressures in three related areas:

1 Increasing scope of board duties;
2 Increased information flow to the board;
3 Greater demand for documentation of board processes and decisions.

All of this adds up to increased demands on individual board members. And because of these trends, the CGO can expect an increasingly-heavy and complex workload:

- **Increased workload of board members** The quantity and complexity of work has increased for every board member, including those already heavily involved (i.e. the chair). The main reasons are simply more board meetings throughout the year, more committee and preparatory work and more responsibility.
- **Increasing scope of board duties** Boards will continue to face more statutory duties. In addition, the work of monitoring and scrutinizing the performance of executives is increasing. If this leads to more departures of CEOs and CFOs, the board will have more work to ensure continuity of top management functions.
- **Increased information flow to the board** As boards have become involved in more issues, reporting to the board has increased. Not only is management providing extensive information to the board, the board members themselves are requesting more information and reports from the company.

- **Greater demand for documentation of board processes and decisions** The documentation of board meetings now reflects the detailed deliberations of every decision – only sound business judgment protects against shareholder lawsuits.

With these increased demands, boards will require higher levels of support. As a result, the role of the company secretary, or CGO, will continue to be elevated in terms of level in the hierarchy and number of support staff to support the function.

Of course, boards will wish to limit the growth of a new bureaucracy and avoid the growth of a large department of corporate governance employees. But the importance of legal compliance and its market appeal, along with the higher headcounts in corporate governance, do provide scope for new forms of turf war at the top of corporations.

We find three major areas where we expect companies to push the role of corporate governance: board information improvements, external and internal compliance management and managing governing processes. Some companies will adopt all three, others will cherry-pick depending on their needs:

Board information improvements

Our research in the field of board information reveals that board members feel the information they receive is:

- Backward-looking and untimely, instead of forward-looking and timely;
- Generated only internally (i.e. by the company) rather than externally;
- Delivered by old-fashioned channels.

Backward-looking

Board members feel that they lack enough timely, forward-looking information in order to influence the strategic decisions affecting the company. This is particularly true when it comes to market dynamics such as technology and product innovations or direct competitors. But the main issue is simply timing.

As stated by one CGO of a listed European financial services multinational:

Before announcing the quarterly financial figures, the board always met in our headquarters. The board came together on Thursday afternoon and the figures were always published early Friday morning. So when the board members arrived that evening, they were handed detailed documentation on all operations and figures for the past three months. Of course they were not able to work though all the documents before or during the meeting. And even if they had been able to, how could they have influenced anything when the quarterly financials were to be announced a mere twelve hours later!

Boards need to receive information with adequate time to review it thoroughly before decisions are made. Future issues of strategic interest, such as technology trends, also have to be brought to the early attention of the board. As more topics are placed on the agenda, board members are asking more questions in advance of meetings. This means more preparation time on the part of the CGO and an increase in workload and time commitment from each board member. As board membership continues to take more time, and non-compliance can result in penalties, fines or worse, we expect busy executives to decrease the number of board seats they hold.

Generated internally

Currently, senior management controls the gateway for information between the board and the company. More than half the board members we surveyed receive 100 per cent of their information directly from the company, particularly the CEO and other key officers.

This means that the people with the biggest interest in persuading the board to agree with their decisions are in charge of informing the board. It is still not common practice for boards to acquire information independently, from impartial, external sources. This raises the question of whether or not the information is unbiased.

Board members could acquire additional information from different channels, e.g. business line or department managers or the company's information system (MIS). By doing so, they would certainly receive different perspectives and opinions.

However, would board members be able to assess this information? And would they be able to put it into perspective without someone explaining the big picture? In one company, board members asked the CGO for detailed supplementary information, but when they received the extensive reports, they simply could not understand them. Certainly, the better option would be a board information infrastructure.

Electronic board libraries containing past board decisions or even comprehensive board information systems (BIS) with access to company databases do not exist for the most part. When it comes to board information sources, the bottom line seems to be, 'paper dominates and the source is the CEO'.

Delivered by old-fashioned channels

For boards to perform their crucial role, the CGO should be the gateway of information between the board and management, and guarantee that pertinent, unbiased information is forwarded to the board in time.

This might mean sending executive summaries to the board instead of extensive management or departmental reports. But it can also mean providing detailed information when necessary. For this, the CGO must ask the board to state its information requirements and priorities clearly. Then the CGO must deliver the information in a format that makes it easy for them to compare, visualize and store.

In very large companies, it can make sense to set up internal 'board information guidelines' which all information providers must follow. Easy access to external and internal sources should be provided. This alone will ensure that the board gets the big picture. It will also mean that board meetings, agendas and outcomes are in the best interests of the company and not the management.

Some companies have already created online board portals, which give easy access to a wide range of internal and external data. These portals also offer sophisticated software tools for data aggregation, comparison and visualization (as 'a picture's worth a thousand words').

External and internal compliance management

External compliance

The first task in ensuring compliance is managing external compliance. This means ensuring that the company adheres to external regulations and codes, e.g. from government authorities, regulatory bodies or stock exchanges.

A particular difficulty for boards of international companies is that they must comprehend and comply with national standards as well as international legislation, stock market rules and best-practice codes.

Once a company's business becomes international, there is a significant increase in corporate governance requirements. But the different legal requirements for each country are not always aligned, and can even be contradictory. For example, the US Sarbanes-Oxley Act requires that the audit committee be comprised of independent directors only, while German law requires that employee representatives make up half the board members.

In the case of a German company listed on the New York stock exchange, e.g. DaimlerChrysler, this could result in significant difficulties with the SEC. It is the CGO's responsibility to keep respective board members and managers informed in cases like these and to respond appropriately. In this case, it would be possible to negotiate exceptions with the SEC for countries such as Germany.

It is important that the CGO keeps abreast of the differences and forthcoming issues of law and corporate governance in all the company's markets, in order to operate successfully in this complex environment.

Internal compliance

The CGO must also manage internal compliance, which is just as important as external. Most companies have business guidelines, values or codes of conduct which they circulate to stock markets or other stakeholders. Even if there are no explicit guidelines, there are values that a company does or does not want to pursue. The CGO must be aware of these values and make sure that employees respect them. Often the CGO works through the internal audit department of a company for information on internal compliance.

In some cases, the CGO, in response to an environmental shift, may suggest to the board that an internal code of conduct be implemented before the impending shift becomes mandatory.

Managing the governance process

As we have stated, board work is becoming more complex now that the board is more involved in company affairs. The interaction between board members and senior executives has increased. Information must be prepared, coordinated and related to the overall responsibility of the board.

Risk management

Boards are now accountable for making sure that an effective risk management system is in place and that the identified risks are appropriately dealt with. This reaches far beyond the financial domain, and includes tax risks and technology risks. It also means having internal audits to detect fraud and corruption, checking legal compliance (e.g. in health, safety and environment), proper due diligence for acquisitions and so on.

What must be brought to the attention of the board?

The CGO must propose effective rules and criteria concerning the responsibilities of board committees. He or she must also clearly define what should be brought to the attention of the full board, and who should be presented with what information at what time. It is the CGO's job to make certain that board work remains transparent and the board members understand the necessary processes.

Managing conflict

The increased involvement of the board in the company and the more frequent interaction between board members and management means there will be more opportunities to disagree.

A key task for the CGO is to detect these situations early and deal with friction before it escalates. If there is a full-blown confrontation, the power struggle often dwarfs the issue, and it becomes more difficult to find a face-saving solution. If detected early, the CGO can alert the chair or CEO, or both, and propose further proceedings, or even alternative solutions to the dilemma. As one CGO remembers:

> Shortly after my appointment to the position, I was faced with a difficult situation: the CEO and chairman clashed during a board meeting on the issue of heavy board involvement in the company's day-to-day business. The differences were considerable and nobody dared interrupt their apparent conflict. I did not know what to do, so the other board members and I waited and watched. Today – with my experience and internal reputation – I know I should have talked to the other board members after the meeting to try to get them involved, e.g. as mediators. But it was a very intimidating situation, seeing these two powerful men in the boardroom – and so I did nothing.

Not usurping power

It is important that the CGO is not seen to be making decisions simply because senior managers are normally able and expected to do so. In managing the complex process of corporate governance at the highest level, the CGO must be careful not to appear to have assumed real power.

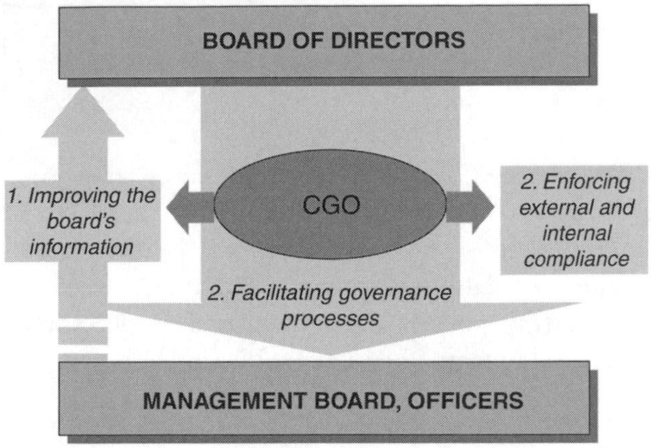

Figure 13.2: Strategic change drivers of the role of corporate governance officer

Yet there are occasional situations when it is appropriate for the CGO to exert influence, e.g. when supporting the board in its strategy discussions with management.

Figure 13.2 sums up the main factors and strategic change drivers that influence the CGO's work.

Conclusion

The business case for corporate governance has clearly grown as companies have grown, becoming more global and more complex. There is clear business value in having a well-functioning governance structure embedded into the corporate culture. For successful companies, sound corporate governance extends far beyond the legal dimension. It can be a source of competitive advantage for some and it is essential to board and company performance. The CGO plays a key role in championing the role that good corporate governance plays for all employees. Legal expertise can be bought if necessary, but not the mastery of a complex cultural process at the helm of a company.

Corporate governance will continue to be subject to continuous changes and external influences. In turn, this will continue to affect the role of the CGO in the future. As these changes cannot be foreseen, the CGO must remain forward-looking and flexible. Ensuring that companies practise sound corporate governance practices will lead to the ultimate goal of successful business performance.

Assessing the role of the CGO

Purpose

1. Ensures that the interests of owners are represented and protected in key board and management decisions;
2. Ensures that the interests of stakeholders beyond the owners are represented in key board and management decisions;
3. Ensures that company policies are upheld and as necessary reviewed and revised to match key stakeholder interests.

Direction

4. Ensures that in the management structure of the company there are clear lines of responsibility, accountability and transparency;
5. Provides consultation for the board on matters of best practice of corporate governance;
6. Provides monitoring to ensure compliance with principles of corporate governance;
7. As invited by the board, provides consultation on chair succession, and on structure of board committees.

Focus

8. Ensures the organizing of effective board meetings;
9. Ensures the quality and completeness of board papers, both in preparation for, and following board meetings;
10. Provides board members with critical information that is relevant to imminent board decisions and relevant for emerging board topics.

Notes

1 The diversity of the corporate governance officer role is also reflected in the name of the position: the title of the person in charge of corporate governance varies across companies and legislations and the tasks can also be in the hands of other positions. Other titles include general counsel, advisor to the chairman/CEO, board secretary, corporate lawyer, head of corporate affairs or head of

legal affairs. Some companies have created the position of chief ethics officer, who (unlike the corporate governance officer) is mostly in charge of code of conduct compliance only. Throughout this article, the term 'corporate governance officer' is used to refer to the full-time corporate position predominantly involved in board work and corporate governance. In some cases, the person might also be in charge of other, non-corporate-governance-related tasks as well (e.g. a head of legal affairs who is also corporate governance officer).

2 A. Berle and G. Means, *The Modern Corporation and Private Property*, (New York: Macmillan,1932).

3 R. F. Felton and S. C. Y. Wong, 'How to separate the roles of Chairman and CEO', *McKinsey Quarterly* 4 (2004), p. 12.

4 American Express Company, 'American Express Company appoints corporate governance officer', Press Release, 17 November (2003).

5 SAP, 'SAP's Principles of Corporate Governance', Version October 2005 (2005), p. 5.

6 The Companies Act of 1985 mandates that in all UK companies it is the board's task to appoint a company secretary. The company secretary and a director that runs the company's day-to-day business are the only two officer roles that UK company law dictates. Combining both offices is only allowed if there is more than one director running the company. But there may be more than one person running the company secretary's office in a so-called 'joint secretaries' office'. As the company secretary is positioned as an officer in the company, she/he may be held personally responsible for not complying with the Companies Act, the corporate articles of association or any other regulation to which the company is subject. This may also extend to a criminal liability.

7 The 'Combined Code of Corporate Governance' is the written and codified combination of the corporate governance recommendations of three UK investigative corporate governance committees – Cadbury (1992), Greenbury (1995), and Hampel (1998). The Combined Code was established by all UK stock exchanges as mandatory, beginning in 1998.

8 Mandatory compliance means there is a 'comply-or-explain' rule – leading to a factual 'comply' for every company, as most competitors 'comply' as well.

9 ICSA, 'Specimen job description for the corporate governance role of the company secretary', (2002), p. 1.

10 Alternatively, a corporate governance officer can report to an executive chair who is not CEO, but an ordinary officer. For the discussion of reporting lines in this paragraph, the use of the basic differentiation in board or management is more useful.

Institute of Chartered Secretaries and Administrators (UK) (ICSA), www.icsa.org.uk (UK Association of Company Secretaries).

Institute of Chartered Secretaries and Administrators (ICSA), *Duties of a Company Secretary – Best Practice Guide*, ICSA Guidance Note, London (1998).

Institute of Chartered Secretaries and Administrators (ICSA), *Reporting Lines for the Company Secretary*, ICSA Guidance Note 011101, London (2001).

Institute of Chartered Secretaries and Administrators (ICSA), *Specimen Job Description for the Corporate Governance Role of the Company Secretary*, ICSA Guidance Note 021001, London (2002).

Society of Corporate Secretaries and Governance Professionals (USA), www.governanceprofessionals.org (formerly known as 'American Society of Company Secretaries').

U. Steger, 'Beyond preventing crime – Where does corporate governance really add value?', *Perspectives for Managers*, 101(2003), pp. 1–4.

U. Steger and H. Krapf, *Corporate Governance in Global Companies – Content not Structure as the Main Driver* (Lausanne: International Institute for Management Development, 2003).

U. Steger (ed.), *Mastering Global Corporate Governance*, (Chichester: John Wiley and Sons, 2004).

International Secretarial Professional Associations: For a list of national organizations of company/chartered secretaries, log on to http://www.governanceprofessionals.org/sites.shtml

For more information on the IMD Global Corporate Governance Research Initiative and current projects, log on to www.imd.ch/research/projects/ or contact the author at steger@imd.ch.

This work focuses on publicly-listed companies (PLC) and their company secretaries. For corporate governance and company secretary implications in family business, see J. Ward, U. Steger, et al., *Unconventional Wisdom: Counterintuitive Insights for Family Business Success* (Chichester: John Wiley and Sons, 2005). Also, for an overview on corporate governance in private equity companies, see U. Steger and C. Frigast, 'Corporate governance in private equity companies: Can it add value?', *Perspectives for Managers*, 122 (Lausanne: International Institute for Management Development, 2005).

14 *The Chief Communications Officer – Leading strategic communications*

GORDON ADLER

In this chapter, the author describes the roles of the CCO: what they do, how they do it, and the choices they face. The CCO is responsible for strategic communications, the process by which a company aligns its communication with the company's strategy to enhance its strategic positioning and thereby better serve its customers.

The CCO's job is to orchestrate all the instruments in the company's communication battery (written and spoken media, symbols, and behaviour of members) to build competitive advantage for the firm. The technical heart of the job is managing an integrated communication system and being the in-house communications expert, but business skills such as project management, analysis and conceptualization also matter. Functional mastery, an understanding of strategy and change, and influence skills are vital for success.

The role of the chief communications officer

The profile of corporate communications has risen over the last decade. The spread of new technology and the speed of business change have made corporate communications a front-line position. The 'communications people' need to be able to react quickly to the latest crisis or opportunity. Gone are the days when time was a commodity. There is little time to prepare the latest CEO speech, the CFO's financial report or the latest corporate press release. The company's employees, shareholders, the media, governments and, most important, the customers are more impatient than ever – they want to hear the latest official company response to the company news of the moment, whatever it may be, whether financial results, a merger or acquisition, new product release, safety recall, competitors' actions, executive misconduct. The CCO never knows when the next newsworthy event will break: just be sure that it will, and it will require a clear, consistent and confident statement regardless of who ultimately delivers the message.

While not dealing with the latest crisis, many companies, taking up the call to focus on value, have oriented themselves more towards customers. This means that the entire organization needs to know more about its customers and other stakeholders, and communicate more effectively with them. The CCO's team is sometimes working hard behind the scenes to co-ordinate the company's arsenal to deliver messages, clearly and repeatedly, to the people who need to know. Often, however, corporate messages are not in fact co-ordinated; rather each CXO or their deputies feels as though they own the corporate messages coming from their area of responsibility.

But while value creation may sit at the top of most CXOs' agendas, the communications people are certainly not driving it in most companies. For all the progress made in theory, actual practice still lags a long way behind.

Contributing to this fact is the enduring misconception that communication is all about short-term action. It is thought by many that decisions about key shifts in the business system are reserved for other functions in the CXO team that deal, for example, with corporate strategy.

Despite the calls for communications specialists to take up the flag of 'strategic communications', too little has happened. No wonder: Internet access is growing, as is the power of pressure groups. Corporate complaint websites proliferate. New blogs appear on the Internet daily. Corporate journalism dominates the media. Consumers are better informed and more involved. Companies have no choice but to manoeuvre tactically.

Yet best practice suggests that communications should be central to strategy discussions, to enhance the firm's strategic positioning to better serve its customers. Companies should see communications as integral to setting strategy, not just to operations. And communications professionals should not only help implement strategy by communicating with key constituencies, but should also interpret the responses to inform future business moves.

Several studies reveal that these recommendations are still a long way from implementation. Many companies may have elegant business strategies, but they fail to articulate them well, either inside the firm, or to external stakeholders. Some companies, in fact, outsource many of their communications functions, leaving a junior colleague in a 'co-ordination' role rather than having a full-time member of the CXO team.

At best, communications departments do a good job of conveying whatever management tells them to, but they rarely take part in top management discussions. Nor do they have much say in discussions of company strategy. Yet sidelining communications professionals is not in the best interests of business.

The communications discipline itself must carry some of the blame for this state of affairs. It has often failed to rise above a traditional preoccupation with tactical methods of communication. Companies today ignore at their peril various informal postings on the internet about their products, financial results/predictions and their reputation as good global citizens (e.g. regarding the environment, how they treat employees and their general working conditions). Communications has often failed to address the big picture – the business system and the ways the company creates value, the transformations required to link a company's priorities with those of its customers. As a result, it has often excluded itself from taking part in strategic analysis and decision. Today's communications professionals must be well-rounded business executives, not just experts in traditional media such as writing or new media such as website traffic analysis.

Communications staff, particularly senior ones, are supposed to ensure that the company manages its communications effectively. They are also expected to help the company bond with its customers by linking strategy and messages. But how can they if they are not involved and have little say in strategy discussions?

The strategic view of communications yields important insights into the role that the communications function can and should play in a company that integrates communications into its business system.

This chapter looks at how the CCO can work hand-in-hand with CXO colleagues to focus the entire company on communicating with customers and other stakeholders. It asks how CCOs can make the *whole* business their focus and influence all company messages; not just those flowing from the top executives.

It reveals how strategy discussion is richer and execution is improved in companies where the people who communicate strategy are also involved in its formulation. And it shows how this involvement contributes to clearer articulation of the company brand, identity, reputation, messages, and a 'sustainable corporate story'.

This vision of the communications function demands that we look briefly at the state of the job now, the history of the function and the key challenges for the future. It also offers several tools that we recommend CCOs use to maintain the big picture of the business and to orchestrate all the company's communications. We recommend that communications moves from focus on tactics to focus on business strategy.

The scope of the job

It is clear that a vital part of strategy is the *communication* of strategy: inside the company and out, upwards and downwards, and among all stakeholders. The dividing line between business strategy and communications strategy may be blurred. Nevertheless, effective communication is one of the keys to operations and execution, and a central part of setting strategy and executing it.

In fact, some have argued that *everything* about an organization communicates messages. From product design to corporate culture and policies, media campaigns to press releases, company symbols to corporate charity – companies and their employees are communicating 24/7. As the old saying goes: 'One cannot not communicate.' A company sends messages even when it is silent. And when it is not silent, are the right messages being sent, and are they accurate and consistent?

So where does the CCO fit in? Of course, industries and companies have their own business systems and strategies, each a unique communications challenge. Overall, however, the CCO has to have a strategic mindset, making sure the content of messages lines up with the strategy.

The CCO's task is to enhance the company's position. The brief is simple to understand: make sure the company says the right things to the right people at the right time. And help make sure that the business system runs smoothly, projects succeed and the company achieves its purpose, short term and long term.

The CCO has the challenge of many jobs at once, and the balance of these jobs shifts daily. Of course, effective CCOs need to take tactical, short-term approaches to communication. They react to crises, write press releases and prepare top management speeches and presentations. They function as editors and writers, even ghost writers. They monitor short-term legal and financial angles. They keep investors and financial editors informed.

Also, effective CCOs must be strategic partners to top management, particularly the CEO. They work closely with senior executives to ensure that communication practices contribute directly to the company's strategy implementation. This also includes the top people in finance, marketing, human resources, the corporate governance officer and even board members.

CCOs know well the recent regulatory responses to corporate scandal at companies such as Qwest, Enron, Tyco, Global Crossing, Adelphia Communications, and even the venerable GE. By taking a long-term view, CCOs can ensure that the company has a sustainable, harmonious 'story'. CCOs must also consider their role in 'risk management' and co-ordinate with the CGO. Keeping colleagues on the CXO from saying the wrong things, especially in a public setting, is vital for both the company's and the individual's protection.

As chief messengers of the corporate 'big purpose', effective CCOs contribute to and then communicate the big decisions about major company commitments. These CCOs are far from the traditional editors and presentation specialists, taking instead a wide-ranging view of their role. In light of company strategy, they diagnose which messages have to get to which ears, for which purposes, by which channels in which vehicles, throughout the company and to key targets outside, including government agencies and regulatory authorities. Today, they are also responsible for responding to, or better yet fostering, an online presence for company news both formally and informally. And going beyond the mere online presence, a CCO may be asked to oversee – or even create – a presence in the form of multiple profiles at popular social networking and blogging sites like MySpace, YouTube, LinkedIn, Flickr or Xanga, to name only a few in the rapidly changing Web 2.0 world.

It is the CCO's responsibility to make sure that communications coming from everywhere in the company are aligned with and support the company strategy. The message to all constituencies must be harmonious. No matter where in the company a message comes from, it is the CCO's job to make sure it sounds as if it is spoken by the same 'voice'.

All too often, companies (and their CCOs) get caught up in short-term decisions and produce communications that are not strategic. Worse still, they can actually be inconsistent with the corporate strategy, or impede it. Think of Merck & Co. Inc.'s decision to wait until it was pressured to withdraw its arthritis and acute pain medication, Vioxx, from the market.

Many CCOs are indeed rewarded for short-term, tactical performance, such as getting good media coverage, an excellent photo-op for the CEO, or running a smooth press conference. They report last quarter's results, but they also have a responsibility for thinking about the results several years from now.

Yet understanding the 'strategic communications imperative' is no guarantee of success either. Unless this approach is embedded in the day-to-day communications of a company, its promise will be limited.

Other members of the CXO team often see communications as 'what the CCO does'. It is up to the CCOs to seek out CXO colleagues and senior executives and involve them. Their chief contribution here is providing crucial input in major transactions such as mergers, acquisitions or restructurings. Ironically, they must make sure that communications isn't owned exclusively by the communications department, only that its messages appear well coordinated.

Communications might be integrated as part of a formal structure, under one executive with clear reporting lines to other functions like marketing and public relations. But it can also be integrated through *informal* reporting relationships that the CCO nurtures outside the lines and boxes on the company's organization chart. Either way, communication is the job of everybody in the department, led by the CCO.

How can we think about the many tasks, methods, roles, competencies and personal qualities required by a CCO to execute all these tasks successfully?

Here is a list of what to look for in an effective CCO. Finding an executive who excels in half of these qualities is a tall order, and most large companies suffer from a lack of such talent.

Tasks and challenges	Orchestrate the company story: message management; media relations; government relations; employee and internal communications; brand gatekeeper; reputation manager; investor relations; financial, marketing and stakeholder communications; corporate identity.
Methods	Press releases; project planning; interviews; meetings (one-on-one meetings, town hall meetings); memos; newsletters; conference calls; events; speeches; philanthropy; lobbying; advertising.
Social roles	Message framer; reputation barometer and manager; senior manager confidante; message seller; social conscience of the company.

Competencies	Change and change models; broad general management skills: speak same language as senior management; good conceptual thinker and strategic analyst; persuasion skills; deep understanding of the business and strategy garnered outside the communications function or in formal education (MBA, EMBA); business communications expertise: writing, editing, public speaking, templates, standards; know the tools of the trade; crisis management; event management; media expertise.
Personal qualities	Tolerance of ambiguity; personal credibility; integrity; long-term view of the business; broad personal perspective, global thinker: widely read, up on current events; people skills: effective writer and speaker; fast on feet; stress resistant; media savvy; strong personal network, inside and outside company.

Traditional communications practice often attracts talent that is more 'word-oriented', strongly operational and tactical. These are the creative types, often graduates in English, marketing, or communication studies, who lack the necessary training and experience to contribute to discussions of business and management system effectiveness.

Strategic communication requires business knowledge and business experience. All too often, the communications job goes to managers who do not make the grade elsewhere, to the tacticians mentioned above who happen to speak or write well, or to a senior 'friend' of the CEO who will be loyal in orchestrating executive messages. Conversely, companies with effective CCOs have often recruited them from their own strategy or business development departments to focus on the corporate 'brand' or corporate 'identity'.

The challenge of recruiting CCOs is that the job is one of management's least appreciated, most-complicated and most-difficult to measure in terms of results. Few newly-minted MBAs show much inclination to go into communications. It is rarely seen as critical to the success of the firm's business system. It is big, woolly, unwieldy, soft and often thankless.

CCOs are asked to manage the corporate brand, build identity, boost reputation and run communications. Some companies combine the various communications functions in one CCO; others have a collection of top communications people, doing their best to work together formally or informally.

History: from propaganda to communications

The function of corporate communications has evolved over the decades from being a sales tool to becoming a form of dialogue with a company's most important stakeholders.

Along the way, a number of communication models have coalesced. All are still in use, in varying degrees. The CCO needs to be aware of them, see their advantages and pitfalls, and know which one best serves the company and management strategy, mission and values at any given time.

What we now call 'corporate communications' evolved from the field of PR. For many years, managers and management scholars commonly recognized only one business communication need: whether selling, telling, persuading or seducing, communication was about introducing products and services to the market. It was externally focused, top-down, customer-driven, and largely one-way.

But with the progress of technology and globalization, the pace of business accelerated. In the workplace, the idea of commitment replaced compliance. Knowledge and networking took centre stage. Management was suddenly much more about *processes* and *relationships* and less about formal structures. With these changes the one-way, one-dimensional view of communication started to give way to internally focused, employee-involving, two-way methods. Nevertheless, the purpose remained unchanged: sell more.

But then some highly publicized corporate crises put communications in the spotlight. There were Exxon's Valdez oil spill (1989), Shell's Brent Spar crisis (1995) and Coca-Cola's Belgian contaminated carbon dioxide problem (1999). Addressing these crises required more than the internal PR function and the help of outside consultants. Thus, in the fertile ground of public relations disaster, a new branch of the corporate communications function flourished, often called 'crisis management'.

Many global companies proclaim the value of integrated 'strategic' communications. Some get it right, but many do not. The ones who get it wrong lack a consistent strategy, or more specifically display a lack of effective strategy execution with communications not integrated through all parts of their worldwide operations.

As organizations get larger and more complex – more markets, customers, products, services, employees, suppliers, investors, and so on – the need for a consistent communication strategy becomes even more important. Why? Because it has to communicate to a diverse and rapidly growing audience where responsibility and decision-making authority has been dispersed.

Yet few companies communicate as effectively as they could. They still take a surprisingly short-term approach to communicating with their key constituencies, with the focus on limiting financial or legal vulnerability. Even as recently as a decade ago, it was widely believed by managers that PR added little value to company performance. And many are still using approaches that might have worked in the twentieth century, but are no longer very effective today.

One way to think about the new demands on corporate communicators is to look at four general models that have shaped its practice. Each model exhibits a different degree of power balance between the company and its stakeholders.

- **Propaganda model** The propaganda model, common in the nineteenth century, has the CCO manipulating the audience, using exaggeration and even direct falsehood. This approach can be characterized by a lack of interest in, even disrespect for, stakeholders' views. Needless to say, the CCO (most often backed by a CEO with the same thinking) who chooses this model today runs the risk of getting caught in a web of deceit.
- **Public information model** This model is a major shift from manipulating stakeholders to showing them respect. It is unacceptable for the company to ignore or try to fool stakeholders – they need to be informed. But the one-sidedness of the information prevents this model from being as neutral as it sounds. Even with the best of intentions, the company can censor what it decides to communicate, rarely giving the whole story. Still, this model can be useful for non-profit organizations, and government agencies and businesses.
- **Persuasion model** This model still suffers from an imbalance between the company and its stakeholders. Users of this model aim to influence by 'fair' means. Market surveys, for example, are open attempts at determining consumer needs and wishes. When the playing field is level, this is an effective, balanced approach. But the persuaders usually know more about how to achieve their intentions than customers and stakeholders. This model is the preferred choice of most marketing departments.
- **Two-way model** The two-way model aims to achieve mutual understanding and benefit. This is the great hope for the future that

textbooks heralded for decades, but has been slow to catch on. No wonder: it starts with the premise of company and constituents being on an equal footing and engaging in dialogue. But most communications experts agree that a level playing field where company and customers (as well as other stakeholders) engage in open dialogue is still a delusion.

These four models, with variants, have been practised over the last twenty years. The emphasis on one or other has shifted with changing times and company needs. Today, most CCOs use all four models. They talk about new areas of communications: reputation management or brand personality management.

Now, managers and researchers are taking an integrated approach to corporate communications. They also realize that they need to share control of defining both the issues and the 'truth'. Nevertheless, the reality of the CCO's job today is a far cry from the ideal.

The present: current preoccupations

Today's CCOs face many thorny challenges. The process of corporate communications has been likened to throwing a dart at a wall and then drawing a target around it. Managing messages and distributing them in ways that buttress corporate strategy is demanding. The information revolution has given people more channels of information than ever before. Speed matters – information takes less than ten minutes to zoom around the globe; bad news moves even faster, so to speak.

Further, in some industries, many companies have become more and more synonymous with the personalities of their CEOs ('personalization'). Think of Disney's Michael Eisner, GE's Jack Welch, Citigroup's Sandy Weill, The Body Shop's Anita Roddick. The CEO, some argue, represents 30 per cent to 40 per cent of the image of a corporation. Mistrust of balance sheets, auditor's reports and the ethical behaviour of corporations is growing. More than ever, the company 'personality' and targeted messages count. The challenge for the CCO is to turn a company's soft assets into hard assets.

Clearly, the CCO is vital as a kind of town crier. He or she also has to cope with unexpected crises where instant media interest leaves little time for thinking. While crisis management is an obvious drill for the CCO, management researchers otherwise do not seem to agree on what else companies should expect from their CCOs. Nor is there much consensus regarding how best to deal with the challenges.

Defining the job of the CCO is made more difficult by the diffuseness of the role in many companies. The job is viewed as an amalgam of company needs and the CCO's skills. In Europe, the term 'communication management' is common, while the term 'public relations' dominates US organization charts.

The list of titles for top communications people is long. A glance at the organization charts of *Fortune* 500 companies and job responsibilities reveals that each company puts a different emphasis on what is the same job, or divides it up differently.

Avon Rubber	Group Publicity Manager
British Airways	Director of Public Affairs
British Telecommunications	Director of Corporate Communications
GlaxoWellcome	Director of Group Public Affairs
Lloyds TSB	Head of Corporate Communications
W.H. Smith Group	Director of Corporate Affairs
Johnson & Johnson	VP, Public Affairs and Corporate Communications
FedEx	Executive Vice-President, Market Development and Corporate Communications
Dell	VP, Investor Relations and Corporate Communications
Coca-Cola	Director, Worldwide Public Affairs and Communications

At Home Depot, the senior vice-president of corporate communications and external affairs is responsible for global corporate communications, executive communications, associate communications, public relations, community affairs, events management, the Home Fund, and the Home Depot foundation.

Yet at Walt Disney what appears to be the same function, called senior vice-president of corporate communication:

> carries overall responsibility for both communications policies and strategic positioning of the Walt Disney Company and its diverse global business segments, but also chief spokesperson for Walt Disney Company and overseer of media relations and communication strategy.

A look at the individuals who hold these positions suggests that the jobs have been put together around them, to match their skills and special abilities. The role of CCO has been described as planner, watchdog, catalyst, communicator, savant, stimulant, strategic partner, coach, adviser and confidant.

One study found that companies with 'effective communication practices' show higher shareholder returns (nearly 50 per cent higher) and greater market value (nearly 30 per cent greater) over time.[1] It is surmised that at GE, the combined personality of Jack Welch and the 'myth' around the supreme measurement culture, fostered by business-school case studies and articles in the press, keep an additional $2–3 on the company's share price.

What's more, a lot of the writing about corporate communications trumpets its growing importance:

> over the past decade corporate communications has become recognized as one of the most valued strategic tools and has a crucial role to play in [. . .] the total business system.[2]

Nevertheless, in many organizations the function is still misunderstood and the job of the CCO is anything but clear-cut. Many European communications executives still struggle to attain *any* positions in strategic or operational management. Many CCOs work in a constant state of high stress and overload, moving from crises to crises. The advent of email, smartphones and the Internet has intensified the stress and demanded that CCOs be connected all the time. It is not uncommon to have family vacations, weekends and sleep regularly interrupted.

A few CCOs, by virtue of talent and personal performance, earn their seat at the senior executive table by the weight of their characters and the sway of their experience. At UNIXAS Optical, for example, the CCO is deeply involved in setting the communications strategy, but this is mainly because he has clearly demonstrated his understanding of the ins and outs of the business.

But sitting at the table does not mean partaking in the meal. CCOs are not always able to influence how other managers use information and communicate it to their constituencies. What is agreed in the executive conference room is often massaged by CXOs with differing opinions. The number of communications practitioners who *genuinely* contribute to strategy discussions appears to be small.

One study of the extent to which PR practitioners were involved directly in formulating and implementing corporate and business strategy exposed the main reason. It was found that strategy-making usually had a strong financial tendency, focused on achieving financial goals, or was about highly technical or operational matters.

In either case, the study found:

> it would be inappropriate to expect public relations to contribute to decisions about highly complex financial matters. Indeed, the high complexity of technical issues served as a kind of 'barrier to entry' for public relations participants.[3]

People who manage communications often know little about real management and cannot speak the language of business beyond the superficial. As a result, they are often excluded from management decisions. At the highest levels, they are also excluded from strategy discussions.

CCOs therefore often operate one step removed from the mainstream process of strategy formulation – as a kind of secondary function. They counsel and advise senior management about communications-related matters, but they are rarely invited to comment upon the overall 'fit' of the business units in the company portfolio.

The challenge for the CCO who seeks to make a greater contribution is first to conceptualize the position and then put it into operation.

The remainder of this chapter offers ways to think about the key challenges of strategic communications: crafting a sustainable corporate story, integrating the various communications functions to serve that story, building a communications plan to make it all happen, and mastering the right personal capabilities to bring it all to fruition.

The future: the strategic communication imperative

In many companies the output of communications specialists and managers (marketing communications, press relations, investor relations, and employee communication) results in a mish-mash of messages – anything but a coherent story.

The following case gives an indication of the room for improvement that often exists in firms:

> One of the world's largest mobile network providers – we will call them 'Mobile 1' – was operating in a highly decentralized manner.

Its communications departments were spread over five continents and six sectors. Group discipline was lacking. There were contradictions in the company image that the group was presenting to the outside world.

Branding and public relations initiatives were confusing employees, analysts, investors, journalists and customers alike. A new CCO was called in to integrate the communications functions into one entity that focused its first efforts on corporate branding and strategic communications objectives.

The new CCO standardized the structure and processes of the various communications functions. The aim: to make sure the combined effect of all public relations activities around the world would portray a uniform, contradiction-free corporate story.

Not only did this change make it possible for the new CCO and his team to coordinate communications for all target groups, which enhanced the group's international profile, but it also brought a reported 30 per cent reduction in communications costs.

When viewed overall, the company was sending fragmented, sometimes conflicting messages. Many companies are aware of this danger, yet still fail to organize a coherent 'story'. Many of these inconsistencies could be ironed out if their CCOs could be involved earlier or had a stronger mandate and support. The strategic process is normally an ongoing, ever-changing blend of formal and informal interactions, and the CCOs need to be 'in the mix'. How else can they understand the strategy well enough to communicate it?

Little has been written about *how* to integrate communication with strategy development and implementation. In fact, very little attention has been given to the links between strategy and communication in the articles appearing in the flagship journal for business communications, the *Journal of Business Communications*.[4]

When strategy books mention communication, they focus on organization structure and processes, and the allocation of resources. The focus is on *implementing* strategy – making sure that the strategy is communicated and works well, and that objectives are met. Management books sparsely analyse communicative processes and structures; communication books sparsely analyse managerial processes and structures.

If the role of corporate communications in strategic decision-making is mentioned at all, it is viewed either as meeting largely tactical needs, basically supporting marketing strategies, or as merely the communicator of business messages, rather than as the identifier and interpreter of key communications issues at the stage of strategy formulation.

CCOs can learn from companies which do ensure that communications are aligned with company strategy and are fully integrated, even among widely dispersed offices and divisions.

Shell, FedEx, Dell, PepsiCo, Tetra Pak, Compass Group and Securitas all involve their top communications people in strategy discussions, and communicate their strategy to varied constituents with the aim of getting them to 'buy in'. Their senior managers are involved in communications, and can align their own communications with the company's strategy and implementation.

To move beyond short-term approaches, CCOs of large, international companies need to help integrate communications in whatever way fits best, find ways to involve senior management, take a broad perspective, gain personal credibility, and make sure they have the skills needed to understand the company's business.

For full effect, the CCO must ensure that all communications to all groups through all channels, are all consistent with one another and are tailored to an agreed objective that furthers the company strategy. CCOs have two major tools at their disposal for achieving these aims.

Tool #1: The company story

Companies have various ways of aligning communications. One practical approach is for CCOs and their executive colleagues to view the company as having its own 'story'; it is a hallmark of their culture. The company story must convey originality, or uniqueness; it is often built around the ideals of a great founder or a strong sense of purpose, business, social or otherwise. Great companies are distinguished by stories as idiosyncratic as they are. And companies that communicate well, know their stories. These companies stay 'on message'.

An effective CCO knows the company story, can tell it and where necessary refine it. Knowing how to create this story and articulate it to others is a big step forward. But often, companies struggle to decide what exactly their story is. Even more difficult to define and control is the role of top management in creating and furthering the company story.

How can a CCO and other CXOs focus everybody on the story that helps customers and employees understand, and be attracted to, the company? This requires that all communications with customers and other stakeholders are, first and foremost, simple and clear (but not overly simple or general).

A company seeking to develop a story might need to revamp its approach to the communications function. In many companies, this function is effective at getting the traditional benefits of press releases, investor conferences and so on. But the company story is unlikely to take hold unless all top executives are brought along.

The difficulty of the switch to more strategic communication implied by the company story should not be underestimated. Anyone who has tried to make a clear, engaging presentation, and have the message stand over time, knows this.

Creating the company story cannot be entrusted solely to the CCO's department. At this level, questions of strategy might not seem very important. But the key messages that make up the story need to reflect company strategy, so the CCO must lead top management through an exercise of asking the right questions.

Achieving clarity in all the elements of a story requires intense debate. So, top management must be involved. They will have to explain the story to the people who work for them, so the story can pass on down the chain.

Company story guideline

1 Strategy
  a Does everybody inside the company understand the business model and its objectives?
  b How can we make sense of and describe what we're doing day-to-day?
  c Can we describe the business model so that both employees and customers can understand it?
2 Positioning
  a What are our product/market choices?
  b How will we articulate them?
  c Have we considered all key stakeholders?
3 Identity: actual and desired
  a What is the identity of our company to internal and external stakeholders? The CCO must be familiar with the many measurement tools available.
  b What influence do certain aspects of our identity have on our performance?
  c To what degree have all constituent parts of the company agreed on our key messages?

4 Reputation
   a What is the reputation of our company?
   b How will we measure our reputation?
   c What is the influence or correlation of reputation (positive or negative) on our performance?
   d What factors influence our reputation most strongly and how can we improve?
5 Brand
   a What is our brand? What is its added value?
   b How can I orchestrate our internal decision making with an endorsement of the corporate brand at the business unit level?
6 Corporate story: write, revise, validate
   a What are the key promises that our company makes?
   b What support will 'prove' these claims?
   c What are our most important messages?
   d In what 'tone of voice' will we tell our story?
   e How compelling is our story?
   f How well does it capture our identity, reputation, brand and messages?
   g Have we involved top management, marketing, human resources, and communications?
   h Does everybody inside the company know the story, share it, and believe in it?
7 Implement the final version of the sustainable corporate story
   a How will we apply the story to all forms of communication?
   b Who must be involved for the story to get out?
   c Who will be the gatekeeper of the story?
8 Monitor
   a How will we measure whether our story works?
   b How will we recognize success?
   c How often will we revisit our story?

To answer these questions, the CCO must ensure that the approach is spread widely throughout the CXO team. If it is to be adopted broadly, many people in the company need to take part in data gathering and analysis. Results of the exercise need to be shared.

For a company story to take hold, the CCO must lead a process that is consistent over a long period of time. This exercise should never be a one-off. It should be part of the company's regular marketing communications work, internally and externally. It needs to be honed, refined and strengthened; repeated often but not over-used. It certainly needs the support of the CEO. The story-building exercise should be built into the regular marketing planning cycles, and revising it, with changes in the key messages, should become part of all communications plans.

Tool #2: The functional integration matrix

The CCO is responsible, with the CEO and CXO colleagues, not only for articulating the company story, but getting it across to everyone that matters. The CCO must harmonize all forms of communication, simplifying overall policies, making them more consistent, and orchestrating the company story, symbols, and behaviour of staff.

In other words, the CCO is also the chief message integrator. He or she defines the company's various communications and their objectives, delineates the primary and secondary target constituencies, and chooses the channels. A useful way to think about this task is to use the matrix shown in Table 14.1.

Once the CCO has integrated the communications functions, he or she will need to draw up strategic plans for any major company change or initiatives, whether mergers, acquisitions, redundancies, divestitures, etc. When the communications strategy is unclear – or unarticulated – the communication plan is poor, and the results will be unclear roles, insufficient follow-up, and mixed messages to stakeholders. Or worse, the corporate communications plan will be ignored and each major functional area will build their own.

For this, the matrix outlined in Table 14.2 can be helpful.

The communications plan is the heart of the work of company communication. It supports the company's overall communications goals, which helps spread the company story. These goals need to be measurable, for this is the only way to judge how effectively the company is executing the plan. It is the road map by which the CCO, as leader, orchestrates the communication of key messages, through defined channels to specified audiences for a clearly articulated purpose.

The plan is a living document, since it essentially frames all media activities, including all internal and external communications, but it also clarifies the company's strategic priorities, target constituencies, resources and communications assignments.

The central challenge of a communication plan is execution. This is obvious when you have a major change, bad or unplanned news

Table 14.1: *Sample functional integration matrix*

Comms functions	Objectives	Target constituencies Primary	Target constituencies Secondary	Channels
Media relations	Public relations Crisis management	Media	All constituencies	Press releases Interviews COO
Employee relations	Internal consensus building	Employees	Customers Family	Town hall meetings, memos, newsletters, video, webcasts, conference calls, web logs (blogs) CEO, HR, CCO
Financial communications	Transparency Meeting financial expectations	Investors	Analysts Media	Conference calls Press conferences CEO, CFO, CCO
Community relations	Image building Reputation enhancement	Communities	NGOs Media	Events Speeches Philanthropy CEO, CCO
Government relations	Regulatory compliance Meeting social expectations	Regulators	Media Customers	Lobbying efforts One-on-one meetings CCO, CEO, gov affairs officer
Marketing communications	Driving sales Building image	Customers	All key constituencies	Advertising Promotions
Stakeholders communications	Image building Meeting expectations	Main stakeholders	Secondary stakeholders	Main stakeholders
Competitor communications	Information sharing	Competitors	Customers of competitors	Press releases Media collateral

Table 14.2: ***Sample strategic communication plan***

Audience/Target Who to	Purpose Why	Key messages What	Vehicles How	Timing When/How often	Responsibility Who from
Middle managers	Buy-in Understanding Dialogue New skills	New roles New methods Personal impacts	Meetings: CEO and senior management Training	Launch: week 1 Define frequency	CEO Senior managers Training department
Employees	Buy in Understanding Dialogue New skills	New roles New methods Personal impact	Meetings with managers Training	Launch: week 1 Define frequency	Managers Training department
Customers	Information Awareness	New methods Service impact	Meetings with sales reps	Launch: week 1 Define frequency	Managers Training managers
Shareholders	Information Awareness Support (votes)	Service impact Financial impact	Written information from CEO and CFO	Launch: week 1 Define frequency	CEO & CFO
Community	Information Awareness	Service impact Financial impact	Press releases	Launch: week 1 Define frequency	CEO

coverage, or a merger to manage. The difficulty is not so much articulating the purpose, messages, audiences and channels, but clarifying who does what, who says what and how, and how things will be done.

Managers might believe that by withholding information, they can ensure that the news only goes through official channels. But since the advent of the Internet, trying to withhold information is a pointless exercise. It is a fact of business life that employees, and any other interested persons, know more than ever before.

To execute the plan, the CCO obviously needs to understand the company mission and vision, values and beliefs, and strategic goals. These elements must inform or shape every communication decision. But creating and executing such a plan requires that the CCO and communications team get critical elements right:

1 Know each target audience, internal or external, and how to reach it;
2 Have research into past communications to these audiences;
3 Articulate the messages to be delivered;
4 Clearly define the materials to be produced;
5 Get the resources;
6 Have a written project management plan, including crisis control plan and an evaluation or 'after action review' aspect.

A new set of skills for the CCO

Views about the future tasks and capabilities of the CCO are fast converging. A recent Wyatt Watson study in more than 100 UK public and private sector companies is a good example.[5] Here is what emerged:

- The three most important competencies for managers and directors responsible for internal communications are:
  1 Strategic thinking (77 per cent);
  2 Internal communication practice (61 per cent);
  3 Change management (55 per cent).
- Possessing practical skills like writing, speaking and research are no longer viewed as adequate. Now, it is essential for anyone working in the field to understand business and strategic issues. CCOs and other practitioners need to be able to grasp business issues quickly, and understand them well enough to explain them to a wider audience.

Clearly, in addition to the competencies that have been traditionally associated with the profile of CCOs, the additional demands call for new skills. The CCO needs to understand change and know how to influence people. While the CCO and communications team have to deliver on their key responsibilities, the function should also be offering greater consistency, change management, coaching and mentoring support.

The CCO thus increasingly needs to develop the right communication behaviours and also help the senior team develop its own communications effectively. Here the added value is more advice than delivery. At the level of the CCO, the nature of the communication job changes – communications people lower down take care of execution and bring the functional skills (although the CCO should also have those skills).

The skills required here, as represented in Figure 14.1, are strong consultancy skills, knowledge of change management, and expertise in the psychology of change. This involves very strong coaching skills, knowledge of different communication models and how to implement them effectively.

Mastering the traditional communications methods

One of the CCO's main tasks is to be an advocate for professional communication management. It may seem obvious that the CCO needs to be master of the communication plan (see Table 14.2 above), but many CCOs do not know how to manage projects well enough to communicate big changes or co-ordinate large, multi-divisional communications campaigns.

The CCO should play a strong role in identifying the right vehicles for particular communications: emails, webcasts, videos, memos, speeches, town hall meetings, face-to-face meetings, electronic message boards or chat rooms, interactive web sessions, training sessions, press releases, posters, and any future medium.

Whatever the choice of vehicle, the CCO must aim for consistency: the more consistent the set of communications, the more credible the story.

The CCO needs management skills to lead the communications department. He or she needs capable people who have the freedom to make the right decisions swiftly, but it is important to make sure they don't spend all their time responding to one crisis after another or re-creating the message.

The CCO, who knows the big picture, needs to guide employees in a directive, top-down way. This way, actions and decisions will be guided

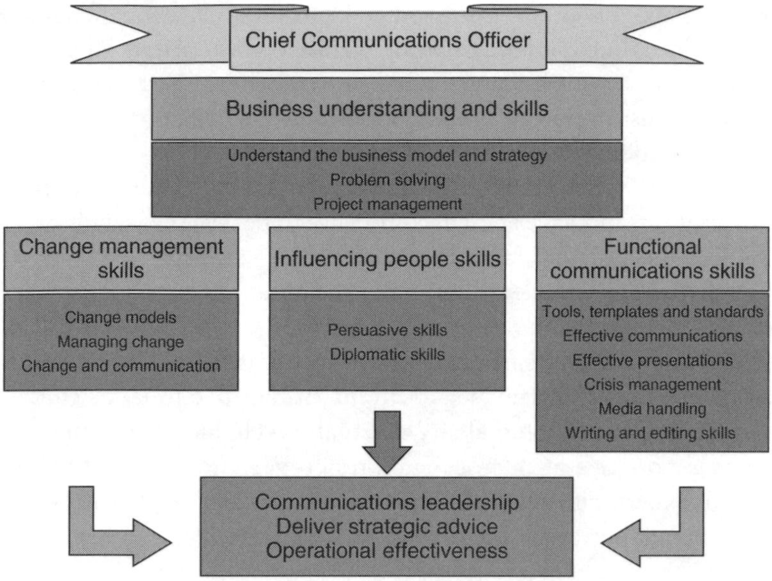

Figure 14.1: The skills of the CCO

not by whatever seems to be expedient, but by what the CXO team has agreed is best for the company and its customers.

It is the CCO who should oversee the formulation of messages, set up the delivery channels, create the opportunities for communication, and conduct events. Nevertheless, to get around the pitfall of low employee commitment, senior managers need to make it clear from the outset that they take final responsibility for communication efforts, just as they carry the ball for any major change effort.

Business understanding and capabilities

The CCO is the company's communication leader, providing *strategic* advice and contributing directly to *operational* effectiveness (see Figure 14.1). For this, the CCO needs, above all, to understand the nuts and bolts of the company's business. Gone are the days when the CCO could be merely an accomplished communicator – today's business challenges are far too complex. To wield influence, today's CCO requires a deeper understanding of the business than ever before.

The chief communications function also requires stronger business skills than ever before, such as analysis, problem solving, strategy, and project management. The CCO of a liquid food packaging company, for example, does not need to be an engineer, consumer packaging or a supply chain expert, but understanding the concerns and challenges of engineers, customers and supply chain managers will improve the company's communications.

CCOs need to understand the business well enough to take part in the conversation, and have enough confidence to believe that senior executive colleagues should take their advice. They also have to be strong enough to change the view of the CEO and senior managers that the role requires little more than functional expertise.

Here the focus shifts from a concern for single-shot communication campaigns, and crisis management to sustained efforts to educate, involve, and engage internal and external stakeholders. Thus the CCO is acting more as a facilitator than a results generator. He or she is the resident expert, playing in the inner circle and positioned as the expert on all communications issues, as shown in Figure 14.1.

Change management skills

Communication is an important part of any successful change, whether merger, acquisition, downsizing or reorganization. Communicating clearly, consistently and believably can boost a company's chances of success. Nevertheless, a 2001 survey of change implementers found that they ranked communication as among the most problematic issues they had to deal with.[6]

The CCO will usually have his hands full trying to support company change. He will need to forge close ties between the *change* and *communications* strategies.

In any change effort, the CCO must work to keep the channels of communication open. This may be difficult. By the time senior management sets a direction, they may believe that communicating about it is not as important as making the actual changes. But it is precisely now that more open communication is needed to help implement the change and sell the ideas to those people not in the decision-making team. People have questions, worries, anxieties, and if they feel they are being heard or considered, it is more likely they will stay aligned.

It is not enough for the CEO to tell people about the planned changes in an email, often drafted by the CCO. The CCO, working with the CEO and top management team, must get the co-operation more widely and be seen to 'deliver' the message personally.

First, people need to know about the change, and then they need to understand the impact on their work. The CCO must make sure, as Table 14.2 above shows, that all communications to stakeholders describe the rationale for the change, people's new roles, and the benefits that can be expected for employees, customers, shareholders and the company.

The CCO must build credibility to communicate change, and so he or she needs to build a high profile, since they will need both visibility and status. They should report directly to the CEO.

Influencing skills

One common role for the CCO is serving as strategic advisor to the CEO or top management team. A CCO has to manage expectations upwards and downwards. This requires skills in negotiation and influence.

The CCO has to earn a reputation for openness, frankness and honesty. This is time-consuming, especially for a CCO new to the position. But the investment is more than rewarded by employee engagement and top management support. Failure to manage expectations can lead stakeholders to hold unrealistic expectations, followed by dissatisfaction and cynicism.

To be influential, the CCO can play four *roles*: conceptualizer, counsellor, coach and executor. To fill all these roles, the CCO will need some basic competencies: influencing skills; the ability and willingness to share knowledge; multi-tasking; and putting the client, internal or external, first. If necessary, supporting the chief marketing officer, the CCO might even serve as the internal customer advocate, since he or she will have, through work on the company story, a deep understanding of the customer's expectations and desires.

The CCO must be a **conceptualizer**, developing plans to communicate and maintain relationships with various groups of stakeholders, mainly to gain public trust. In this role, the CCO is concerned mostly with broad business topics through other internal and external groups, and with public opinion as a whole. The aim is the flawless execution of company mission and strategies.

The effective CCO must be a **counsellor**. He or she analyses the changing values, norms and issues of society, of company culture and in the markets, and discusses these with members of the organization. He or she counsels other members of the organization, particularly top management, to make sure that they express the company vision/

mission, story and strategy accurately and honestly. He or she also counsels them on the use of communication guidelines, policies and standards.

At the same time, the CCO is a **coach**. He or she works to educate members of the company to communicate competently, in order to serve the company strategy (which the CCO works to ensure is aligned with market and societal demands). In practice, this is a common role: the CCO serves as an internal coach to the CEO and other top managers, often preparing them for major communication events.

But the most common role in large, international companies is **executing**. The CCO, or team, prepares the means of communication in order to help the organization formulate its specific communications practices. But in execution – the measure of all business effectiveness – the CCO needs the expertise of any executive, managing against targets, deadlines and measurements.

What is next?

Given the huge costs caused by poor communication, it is surely time for many companies to rethink the position of the CCO. The life of the CCO is getting more and more complicated and unpredictable. This is particularly the case with so much media converging on the Web, and the Web itself making company information (and dis-information) more readily available than ever before to a widening audience of journalists, investors, competitors and customers.

A solution lies in seeing the CCO as a full member of the CXO team. The CCO should not be chiefly concerned with editing the CEO's speeches and drafting press releases. He or she needs to join CXO colleagues at the strategy table, and keep the big picture. The position will be different from company to company. There is no single prescription. But, it should be understood by all CXO members that a well-orchestrated communications strategy (often stewarded by the CCO) will yield better results both at the bottom line and in the minds of all stakeholders.

In most companies the effective CCO will put together the company story. He or she will comprehend the business model as well as the CEO; will identify the most important stakeholders and constituencies; and communicate key moves such as mergers and acquisitions, restructuring, and new products going to market.

This will involve working out the implications of each strategic issue for each of the stakeholders (for example, employees may feel confused or threatened by changes brought about by mergers that could make them redundant).

Out of all this, the CCO will formulate the company's communications strategy. Firstly, this means deciding what needs to be communicated to solve the problem or take advantage of an opportunity presented by a strategic choice. Secondly, it means developing a strategy communications plan around the communications goals and leading the communications team. Thirdly, it also means steering the company clear of too much communication, saturating the audience with too many messages. In a world in which companies are trying to build relationships with individual customers, involving them in designing and improving products, the ability, noted above, to gauge the right message for the right people, knowing how to 'filter' or highlight what is important to each audience, is becoming more and more important.

Life for the CCO, at least in some companies, is better than ever. A number of CCOs we have worked with at IMD now sit at the strategy table. Most have gained higher status as they are increasingly seen as *business* experts, not merely *communications* experts.

Assessing the role of the CCO

The following questions provide a starting point when assessing the role of the CCO.

Purpose

1. Does the CCO effectively help diagnose and then articulate corporate objectives and then influence others – inside the department and out – to see and understand those objectives?
2. Does the CCO articulate effectively how individual and team efforts will contribute to realizing those objectives?

Direction

3. Does the CCO diagnose, articulate and influence others in choosing how best to accomplish the objectives?

4. Does the CCO lead the orchestration of a 'sustainable company story' – including managing internal identity, external reputation, co-ordinating the various tasks of communication, and corporate branding – that is aligned with company vision/mission, strategy and objectives?
5. Does the CCO effectively manage the joint communications efforts of the company?

Focus

6. Does the CCO ensure that internal communications tasks are properly organized internally?
7. Does the CCO ensure that there are internal agreements about who is responsible for what, and especially about the commonly agreed-upon company story?
8. Does the CCO lead company efforts to build a story through the common efforts of top management, the human resources department and the communications department?

Business knowledge

9. Do communications initiatives have a significant business impact?
10. Does the CCO use communications plans to solve business problems?

Effective communications plans

11. Does the CCO match various approaches to various communications needs (print, face-to-face, email, etc.)?

Change champion

12. Does the CCO build support for company change initiatives?
13. Does the CCO effectively deal with the obstacles typical to communicating change?
14. Does the CCO, in co-ordination with CXO colleagues, use effective tools and approaches to communicate change?

Clear and compelling communicator

15. Does the CCO effectively present company strategy and management conclusions and recommendations?

16. Does the CCO use effective research techniques to plan, pilot test, and measure and analyse the effectiveness of company communications?

Project manager

17. Does the CCO deal effectively with changing plans and the challenges of implementation?
18. Does the CCO effectively lead the company communications team?
19. What role does corporate communications play in your organization?
20. How do you evaluate the contribution of corporate communications to your business success?
21. How do you measure its performance?

Perhaps the CCOs of the future will be running more integrated, higher status, better resourced departments than their 2005 counterparts. Perhaps they will take up the mantle of leadership that this most complex function demands and offers. If so, they stand a chance of weaving communications into the essential fabric of the company.

Glossary

Blog (web log)
A blog is a website where entries are made in journal style and displayed in reverse chronological order. The term 'blog' is derived from 'web log'. 'Blog' can also be used as a verb, meaning *to maintain or add content to a blog*. Blogs often provide commentary or news on a particular subject, such as food, politics, or local news; some are more like personal online diaries. A typical blog combines text, images, and links to other blogs, web pages, and other media related to its topic. An important part of many blogs is the ability for readers to post comments. Most blogs are textual although some focus on photographs (photoblog), videos (vlog), or audio (podcasting).

Communications plan (-ning)
Communication planning (creating a communications plan) is about figuring out how to communicate important messages to key

stakeholders of an organization effectively. Communication planning, while often overlooked, is an important business function that can become urgent; for example, in change management situations where communication can counter the anxiety triggered by organizational changes, or in crisis management such as the Tylenol scare or the Union Carbide Bhopal incident.

Communication plans may focus internally or externally. For example (1) internal: rolling out a new benefit programme to the employees, or external (2) informing shareholders about a new stock or product offering. Elements of communication planning include: communicating company vision, philosophy, and information. Key concerns of communications planners are credibility, key messages, channel, audience, timing, effectiveness.

Corporate communications

Corporate communications can be described as the orchestration of all the elements of an organization's identity, in such an attractive, realistic and truthful manner as to create or maintain a positive reputation for groups with which the organization has an interdependent relationship (often referred to as stakeholders) for creating a competitive advantage. Corporate communications can involve management communication, organizational communication and marketing communication. It thus means facilitating information and knowledge exchanges with internal and external groups and individuals that have a direct relationship with an enterprise. It is concerned with managing a company's communications from the standpoint of sharing knowledge and decisions from the enterprise with employees, suppliers, investors and partners. Here are a few examples: enterprises use annual reports as corporate communications tools to convey information related to results, processes and relationships. Corporations use electronic and print newsletters to share corporate diversity hiring practices and information on new hires. Organizations use corporate Intranets to create communication platforms to formalize processes, share policies, news and other information vital to employees.

Corporate or Company Story

The corporate, or company, story is the commonly-agreed-upon story that colours and shapes all forms of a corporation's communication. Corporate stories are important in three ways. They increase the distinguishing power of an organization. They simplify the orchestration of communication. And third, building a story through the common efforts of top management, the human resources, marketing and communications departments may create a bond among these people and other employees that increases their enthusiasm to live and share the story.

Ghostwriter

A ghostwriter is a writer whose work is credited to another. Ghostwriters are often employed by celebrities to write autobiographies. Many politicians and top managers, even those with refined writing skills, employ ghostwriters to compose letters and speeches for them.

Internal communications

Internal communications includes all communication inside an organization. It may be informal or a formal function or department that provides communication in various forms to employees. The 'products' of internal communication can include Intranet, newsletters, emails, blogs, and surveys. Effective internal communication – which can be said to be 'downward, upward and horizontal' – is a vital means of addressing organizational concerns. Good internal communication may help increase job satisfaction, safety, productivity and profits, and decrease absenteeism, grievances and turnover. Good communication helps to establish formal roles and responsibilities for employees.

Social networking site

A social network is a social structure made of nodes, which are generally individuals or organizations who are connected through various social familiarities, ranging from casual acquaintance to close familial bonds. The term was first coined in 1954 by J. A. Barnes (in: *Class and Committees in a Norwegian Island Parish, Human Relations* 7, pp. 39–58). The maximum size of social networks tends to be around 150 people (Dunbar's number) and the average size around 124 (R. Hill and R. Dunbar, *Evolutionary Ecology* 16 (2002) pp. 579–593). Research in a number of academic fields has shown that social networks operate on many levels, from families up to the level of nations, and play a critical role in determining the way problems are solved, organizations are run, and the degree to which individuals succeed in achieving their goals. Thus, a social networking site is one of many Internet applications to help connect friends, business partners, or other individuals together using a variety of tools. These applications, known as online social networks are becoming increasingly popular.

Soft assets

Soft assets in a business include human resources (people, skills and knowledge) and intangible assets (for example information, brands, reputation, intellectual property and goodwill). Soft assets are hard to value and are not usually reflected in the books of account, nor are they typically subjected to periodic inventory.

Stakeholders

The term stakeholder has two distinct uses in the English language. The traditional use, in law and notably gambling, is a third party who temporarily holds money or property while its owner is still being determined. In the last decades of the twentieth century, the word 'stakeholder' as used in management became more commonly used to mean a person or organization that has a legitimate interest in a project or entity. This use of the term arose together with and due to the spread of corporate social responsibility ideas, but there are also utilitarian and traditional business goals that are served by the new meaning of the term.

In discussing the decision-making process for organizations – including large business corporations, government agencies, and non-profit organizations – the concept has been broadened to include everyone with an interest (or 'stake') in what the entity does. This includes not only its vendors, employees, and customers, but even members of a community where its offices or factory may affect the local economy or environment. In this context, 'stakeholder' includes not only the directors or trustees on its governing board (who are stakeholders in the traditional sense of the word) but also all persons who 'paid in' the figurative stake and the persons to whom it may be 'paid out' (in the sense of a 'payoff' in game theory, meaning the outcome of the transaction).

Web 2.0

The phrase 'Web 2.0' refers to one or more of the following. The transition of websites from isolated information silos to sources of content and functionality, computing platforms serving web applications to end-users. A social phenomenon that embraces, that generates and distributes Web content itself, characterized by open communication, decentralization of authority, freedom to share and re-use, and 'the market as a conversation'. More organized and categorized content, with a more developed deep-linking web architecture than in early forms of the Web. A shift in economic value of the Web, possibly surpassing that of the dot-com boom of the late 1990s. A marketing term used to differentiate new web-based firms from those of the dot-com boom. The resurgence of excitement around the implications of innovative web applications and services that gained a lot of momentum around mid-2005. Proponents of the Web 2.0 concept say that Web 2.0 differs from Web 1.0 in that it moves away from static websites, the use of search engines, and surfing from one website to the next, towards a more dynamic and interactive World Wide Web.

Notes

1 Watson Wyatt's Communication 2003 Return on Investment Study™.
2 R. Dolphin and Y. Fan, 'Is corporate communications a strategic function?', *Management Decision*, 38 (2000), pp. 99–106.
3 D. Moss, G. Warnaby and A. J. Newman, 'Public relations practitioner role enactment at the senior management level within UK companics', *Journal of Public Relations Research*, 12 (2000), pp. 298–9.
4 P. A. Argenti and J. Forman, 'The communication advantage: A constituency-focused approach to formulating and implementing strategy', in M. Schultz, M. J. Hatch and M. H. Larsen (eds.), *The Expressive Organization* (Oxford: Oxford Books, 2001).
5 Watson Wyatt's Communication 2003 Return on Investment Study™.
6 L. K. Lewis, 'Communicating change: Four cases of quality programs', *Journal of Business Communication*, 37 (2000), pp. 128–55.

15 *The SBU President – Perhaps the best job for the CEO-in-training*

JONATHAN LACHOWITZ AND
PRESTON BOTTGER

No discussion of the top leadership team of a global company would be complete without a mention of the role of the strategic business unit (SBU) president. Much like the State of California in the United States has the world's tenth largest economy, when compared to country economies, many global companies have business units whose turnover would put them well into *Fortune's* Global 500 largest companies

In this chapter, the authors explain how the SBU president's role works within a global organization's top leadership team. They explore the role of the SBU president, as distinct from other CXOs, and how this position has unique leadership challenges that differ from company to company.

The role of the strategic business unit president

Working for three years as the head of our company's largest business unit was the best training I could imagine for the challenges I faced when I became the company's CEO. As the SBU President I was responsible to my boss [the CEO] for the P&L of the business unit, but each month I would receive this huge allocation from 'corporate' for all of the central 'services'. That was one of the first things I changed upon becoming CEO, I took responsibility for corporate overhead into the CEO's office and made sure the SBU Presidents focused only on their business units and what they could directly control. It saved a lot of time and discussion. I of course delegated much of the corporate overhead responsibility to the other CXOs, they could no longer just allocate their costs around the businesses, but rather they had to answer to me and our CFO.

(CEO and former SBU president of a large global manufacturing company)

As companies grow and expand organically, or through mergers and acquisitions, they often become unwieldy to manage. Products within the same company may range from light bulbs to aircraft engines to television media and it often does not make sense to merge operational and functional organizations even though everyone works for the same company. General Electric has been largely credited with pioneering the strategic business unit concept as an answer to how to best manage a large diversified company.

Strategic business unit presidents often have a large responsibility, much bigger in fact than many of the other CXOs. A business unit may have tens of thousands of employees, have offices in scores of countries and make up a large percentage of the company's turnover. The SBU presidents often wield far-reaching power, commensurate with their responsibility. They are often included in the CXO team, with an office in the corporate headquarters *and* an office at the business unit headquarters.

The SBU president may also have a staff that mirrors the CEO's staff, with their own CFO and heads of marketing, sales, operations, HR, communications, and so on. In these cases, the SBU president is in fact a CEO of the business unit, but also part of a larger corporate leadership team.

Since the 1980s a popular view in large companies has been that decentralized management is better than centralized management. The thinking was that proximity to the 'business', customers, manufacturing, suppliers and employees makes management more responsive. As business units became identified as stand-alone entities the most successful SBU presidents were those who built up businesses, often at the expense of acting in the best interests of the whole corporation.[1]

It is vital for the CXO team, and in many cases the board, to encourage the development of:

> ... enterprise leaders – people who can deliver differentiated value by bringing the total resources of their companies to their customers. In order to link strategy to leadership development, they must be able to answer three questions: What are the key elements of the enterprise leader's job? Why is learning to lead at the enterprise level such a difficult challenge? And what can companies do to identify and develop enterprise leaders?[2]

However, the scope of this chapter is not how a company develops SBU presidents as CXO leaders; it is rather focused on the challenges from the perspective of the SBU president in the first person. We will explore in more depth the challenges and responsibilities facing the SBU president, but first we will describe the two primary forms of business unit structures within a larger global corporation.

Strategic business unit forms

In one of its purest forms, a corporate structure with SBUs has a tiny headquarters, consisting of only a few people (sometimes fewer than ten) and each business unit president is left with full responsibility and autonomy to run the business. In less pure forms, an 'SBU President' may only have global responsibility for sales and marketing or even only manufacturing, depending on the nature of the business. In this form, corporate and shared-service centres attempt to fill many of the gaps that the SBU is not responsible for. The worst cases (or best opportunities) are where boundaries of responsibility are unclear and there is a lot of overlap between centralized and business-unit responsibilities. In this case, a company is normally ripe for reorganization and a cost-savings drive.

Based on our experience, it is more common for large global companies to have a sizeable corporate headquarters, even when they have several SBUs. SBU presidents often have global P&L and responsibility, and their own functional and operational leadership teams. They may be responsible for all corporate functions as well as operations in their business unit. The SBU president and his or her team may also be involved in financing the operations, legal and insurance matters, lobbying governments, the environment and, really, everything from A to Z that concerns the business. In this case, the SBU president is more or less the CEO of the business unit (often carrying the CEO title), but instead of reporting to the board, he or she will often report to the CEO or perhaps the COO, depending on the structure of the leadership team.

Another form of SBU is when the business unit acts as primarily a sales and marketing operation. The SBU president is responsible for selling a distinct set of products but instead of being responsible for the entire P&L, they are only responsible down to the operating income level. This means that they are responsible for sales, most aspects of the cost of sales and expenses incurred by their business unit, but the other elements further down the P&L are the responsibility of the corporate headquarters. In these set-ups, transfer pricing often becomes an item of contention.

If the company manufactures its own products, the manufacturing may be embedded in a business unit, may be a separate business unit or may be controlled directly from the CXO team. Some companies have large and extensive manufacturing operations, selling internally to some companies in the corporate umbrella, and also externally to other customers or even competitors.

One of the main challenges facing large companies is deciding what functions to centralize (in corporate headquarters) and what functions to leave in the hands of the operational business units or 'the field'. 'Cost pressure' or 'quality improvement' is normally the driver for most such projects, while strengthening an executive's powerbase is another primary driver. Major projects and restructuring are often undertaken, normally with management consultants in tow (with their rubber stamps), to centralize or decentralize functions and responsibilities. At the end of one of these rounds, a new or newly restructured SBU will often emerge, with a rising star at the helm.

Where business units are used, the corporate form can be a result of blending history with strategic design. Companies with many diverse products and product lines are often strategically divided into business units. This makes the units themselves easier to manage and easier to sell if they no longer fit in the company's portfolio. Companies that have made many acquisitions often re-organize along business unit lines, again for management efficiency.

Sometimes the division or reorganization of a company into business units is seamless with all interested parties understanding the logic; at other times, it is part of a painful restructuring where both leaders and staff may lose their jobs or have less or different responsibilities. The SBU president's role is not as firmly grounded as that of the CEO. The business unit may have been created to make a big position for a rising star. Equally, the business unit may as easily be collapsed into another business unit, leaving one SBU president without a job.

The structure of a company's business units and how they were formed is unique to each company, but the roles of the SBU president, as part of the leadership team, tend to be more uniform. In the following sections we will focus more on the leadership role.

The purpose of the SBU president

The SBU president is in charge of running one, normally distinct, part of a company. In some cases the SBU president is akin to a CEO, in other cases, the SBU president is more like the CMO or the CSCO. When a company is large and diverse, the SBU president's role is to be an executive in charge of a separate operating part of the company, having burdens and responsibility delegated from the CEO or others in the leadership team. Often, the business unit is a truly independent entity and could be split away from the parent company with little noticeable effect on the employees, customers and suppliers.

When a company has very distinctive products and businesses, and is also significant in size and geography, the role of the business unit president can help to keep a company well organized and focused. Employees will often associate themselves more with the business unit than with the company, and in many cases this is useful for the business.

Some companies take great pains to explain 'strategy' to their employees, but the fact is that a large majority of employees do not have the capacity, interest or time to deal with strategic issues on a corporate level. By dividing companies into smaller pieces it is often easier to stay focused on customers, quality, service and the competition. Organizations that are too large and disorganized will become vulnerable.

The SBU president must be a global business manager, responsible for strategy and business co-ordination. The overall responsibility is to grow profitably and leverage the company's scale for efficiency and competitiveness.[3] The SBU president is in fact the chief wealth creator in the company. Operationally, he or she is responsible for a business portfolio that generates sales and expenses.

Well-run business units can bring significant top and bottom-line growth to a company's financial statements. In good times, the SBU president is a company hero and often rewarded generously for a strong financial contribution. Conversely when sales growth flattens or falls, the SBU president is often the scapegoat and can easily be sacrificed by the top leadership team in order to try to reverse the fortunes of a struggling business.

While part of the SBU president's role is taking some burden from the CEO (and other CXOs), it is often also a developmental role for a budding CEO. Business units are often created, or made larger, to test internal candidates' abilities and potential to ascend to the top job. When the board is involved in CEO succession planning, as most boards should be, they will often compare the best internal candidates with each other and external candidates.

The SBU president's leadership role

The word 'executive' is operative in describing the typical SBU president. The SBU president often wears two very distinct leadership hats. To the members of the business unit they are in charge of, the president is the leader, the boss, the CEO. Employees in the organization often more associate themselves with their SBU president than with the CEO; their loyalties are to the business unit. But the other distinctive hat SBU presidents wear is as a corporate executive or corporate officer. In this sense the SBU president is normally a very senior executive and must also represent the view of the corporate headquarters to the business unit employees. The success of many corporate initiatives hinges on how or whether the SBU president supports them.

In this role, the SBU president, while wielding considerable influence, is often a 'go-between', representing the customers and the SBU employees to the other corporate executives, or playing a lobbying or influencing role when it comes to corporate policies. The SBU president must also be the champion of the leadership team and sell corporate policies to the business unit employees.

This can be a delicate balancing act. The SBU president will often take the blame in front of CXO colleagues when a corporate initiative (e.g. from finance, IT or human resources) is not going smoothly in 'their' business unit. The CXO function will often complain about not getting enough support from the 'business' when it comes to implementing a new IT system, a new reporting requirement or a new HR policy.

On the other hand, when the corporate headquarters sends a new directive, programme, initiative or requirement to each of the business units, SBU presidents have to be there to explain why and how the decision was made. They also need to align the SBU's leadership team and employees to accept these new directions from headquarters.

Despite being operational in nature, we find that many SBU presidents spend a considerable amount of time in meetings, trying to influence other executives, rather than concentrating on running their business. The entire CXO team must be aware that the SBU president's job should be to concentrate on a profitable segment of the business and should also be aware of how their 'corporate initiatives' should really be helpful or necessary globally before becoming a requirement.

The SBU president's challenges

The SBU president wears two distinct hats.

1 As the head of a business, the SBU president is the top executive, often with a management/leadership team of direct reports that will closely mirror a CXO team.

2 When the SBU president is part of the company's CXO team, he or she is one of several team members often reporting directly to the CEO and sometimes to another CXO, such as a CSCO, COO or even the CMO.

The SBU president, as an enterprise leader, faces several challenges. One is that the culture of an organization often favours the SBU's business objectives over the enterprise as a whole. A second significant challenge is that companies tend to promote 'experts' based on the company focus, engineers in manufacturing companies, marketing experts in product-driven companies and technology wizards in high-tech companies. Even if the SBU president is excellent in one specific area, he or she may not have the overall leadership qualities necessary to ascend beyond the business unit. A final challenge is that reward systems are often skewed to favour the business unit's operational objectives over the corporation needs. This is often a source of internal conflict for SBU presidents.[4]

The SBU presidents' most significant challenge is balancing their roles and their time as CXOs and president. As CXOs they will be part of a team that makes company-level strategy, starts and supports global initiatives and leads the corporation on its strategic mission. As president of the SBU, the primary focus is often on the profitability of the business unit, focusing on keeping customers satisfied and keeping a quality mindset in the organization.

Corporate overheads and central initiatives often cost the business unit time and money. How then does an SBU president decide between lobbying for what may be good for the company (or one of the CXO colleagues) and not for the business unit? These are the same types of tough decisions that a CEO is required to make. The answer almost naturally comes down to how the SBU president will be rewarded for performance; and what the likelihood is that the stance on the issue will affect career progression. Designing a balanced scorecard or other framework for evaluating the performance of an SBU president *is* a balancing act, and one that the CEO and CHRO should not take lightly.

In addition to divided loyalties, perhaps the next biggest challenge SBU presidents face is how to divide themselves between their business units and their responsibilities to the CXO team and its members. SBU presidents have a very different, and much more operational, role to most of the other CXOs; this is often a recipe for conflict.

The SBU president and their colleagues on the CXO team

Depending on the structure of a company's top leadership team, SBU president(s) may or may not be members. It often depends on the size and number of SBUs, their relative size compared to the entire corporation and whether the CEO feels it is appropriate to have SBU presidents as part of the company's leadership team. SBU presidents in some companies are only invited to sit at the top leadership table when they become the heir-apparent to the sitting CEO. In many companies, where SBU presidents are not part of the formal leadership team, they still wield considerable influence in the company and may have as much or more relative power and influence compared to other CXO team members.

The SBU president will often interact with most if not all of the members of the CXO team and often in not the friendliest of manners. The relationship between CXOs and the SBU president is often tense because many companies fail to clarify the boundaries between 'corporate' areas of responsibility and business unit areas of responsibility. There is often a sense of competition between the field and the head office. There is also the very real prospect that there is competition between some of the CXOs and the SBU president to become the next CEO of the company.

In the case of one food packaging company we have worked with, there was a corporate department in charge of global marketing and at the same time the company's largest business unit had a large marketing staff both in headquarters and dispersed throughout the world. The relationship between these organizations was often tense. It was not clear who was responsible for what activities, the employees in the field felt under constant bombardment from 'central marketing initiatives' from both HQ organizations and in the end there was a lot of overlap. The CMO and the president of the SBU were constantly at odds. The SBU president wielded a lot more power since over 60 per cent of the organization reported to him. It was not until the company was forced by management into a restructuring that many of the duplicate functions were eliminated and the CMO's staff was usurped by the marketing function in the large business unit.

Not all SBU presidents are so powerful. Around the CXO table, they have to defend the results of their SBU, and often take the heat when their SBU is seen to be unco-operative with a particular request from other corporate departments. On the other hand, SBU presidents can also bring a sense of reality to the corporate headquarters and the leadership team.

The SBU president often interacts with key customers and suppliers as well as employees all over the company and this 'field' experience is weighed heavily (and often too heavily) when making central decisions. Sometimes a good anecdote from the field, an exception rather than the norm, will be enough for the SBU president to scare off an initiative or request from a CXO colleague (that may cause more work in the SBU).

Perhaps the one position, besides the CEO, that holds significant influence over the SBU president is that of the CFO. The CFO is often acutely aware of the SBU's performance through the regular financial reporting, audit reports and general compliance issues. The CFO is often in the position to cut SBU presidents down to size if they act too much like corporate cowboys.

The conflict and compromise that characterize the SBU president's role are in fact an excellent way to experience the issues that CEOs will need to deal with, or resolve, in their role. Again, another reason why the SBU president is an excellent training ground for future CEOs.

The future of the SBU president's role

Mergers, acquisitions, divestures and new business ventures continue at a fast pace among the world's large and medium-sized corporations. The emphasis on geographic and organic growth, with product extensions and, really, at any cost, is demanded by CEOs and shareholders alike. The SBU president's role is not likely to change significantly over time. The number of SBU president positions globally will likely increase rather than decrease.

This is good news for those who aspire to the top job at the CXO table. CEOs are leaving public companies at a record rate and a record high of 1,478 American CEOs left their positions in 2006 according to a recent Watson Wyatt study. Many times, employees or outsiders are 'shocked' when a business unit president is appointed to the top job. They are often not as well known by regular employees in the company and externally. However, the SBU president is the ideal training ground for the aspiring CEO. We believe this is a natural accession.

SBU presidents can often make the leap directly to CEO both in their own company and in another corporation. It is their unique experience, when compared to most of their CXO colleagues that best prepares them for the job. They are both operational and already part of the CXO team. The experiences they bring to the table managing an entire business and a team of business unit executives is often just what the board of directors is looking for when they choose the next chief executive officer.

Assessing the role of the SBU president

The following questions provide a starting point when assessing the role of the SBU president.

Purpose

1. How effectively does the SBU president:
   - Manage the responsibilities and profitability of the business unit?
   - Act as a good corporate leader and strike an effective balance between the SBU and the corporate headquarters?
   - Manage their own team of business unit leaders?
   - Drive quality and customer satisfaction through the business unit's culture?

Direction

2. Does the SBU president provide transparent real-time information for internal decision-making and governance purposes or do they shield information and problems from the CEO and the other CXO colleagues?
3. Effectiveness: Does the SBU president do and say the right things? Are they a model of corporate citizenship making it clear that they could ascend to the CEO's office or do people see them as having reached the pinnacle of their talent and abilities?
4. Efficiency: Does the SBU president do things at the right cost, balancing the needs of the business unit with those of the company? Can they think beyond just the business unit? In particular, does the SBU president lead by example?
5. How well does the SBU president combine and balance operational excellence with dynamic support for the company's overall

strategic direction and priorities? Are they able to wear several hats and to balance their CXO and business unit responsibilities?

Focus

6. How well does the SBU build and develop a winning team? Could some of their team members ascend to CXO roles?
7. Does the SBU president effectively manage performance and support corporate objective and initiatives – again, managing by example? Or do they defend the way that 'their' business unit does things and look at their people as an exception and not having to follow corporate guidelines? Is the SBU president a team player?
8. Does the SBU hire team players with high capacities – people who work with other business units and the corporate headquarters as well as other people in the business unit?
9. Is the SBU president able to voice their opinion to the board and CEO? Are they a strong leader who could go further or do they rely on the support and the strength of the CEO and other CXO members to drive their SBU.

Glossary

The field

Company employees working in operations that include manufacturing, marketing and sales, more or less anyone who works directly with customers and suppliers and is not located in the company headquarters is part of the 'field'. This term is normally used in juxtaposition with 'corporate' which refers to corporate headquarter functions.

Operating income

This is the line on the profit and loss statement (income statement) that contains all of the operational income and expenses. It normally excludes financing income and expenses, corporate overheads (sometimes), taxes, dividends and a host of miscellaneous items.

P&L – profit and loss

When SBU presidents are said to have P&L responsibility, it means that they are responsible for the financial results of the business they are managing. In the same way that the CEO is responsible for the total company's P&L, the SBU president is responsible for the business unit.

SBU – strategic business unit

A strategic business unit is an organization within a company. It may be a full operating company within a company (e.g. NBC, National Broadcasting Corporation, is an SBU at General Electric.). An SBU may also be limited in scope. For example, the sales and marketing of all of a company's products globally may fall within the responsibility of global sales and marketing, an autonomous or semi-autonomous business unit.

Transfer pricing

Transfer pricing is the internal pricing level between two business units or companies within the same corporate structure. Transfer pricing levels are often decided based on where (in which country) it is most efficient to have income for tax purposes. Often, transfer pricing does not reflect the actual cost of sales or market price of a product. This can be a point of contention for SBU presidents since their P&L is affected by the transfer price level and more often than not leads to a lower operating profit. Companies often compensate for this by making an operational P&L that adds this profit back to the performance of the business unit to give a more true picture of profitability.

Notes

1 D. A. Ready, 'Leading at the enterprise level', MIT *Sloan Management Review*, 45 (3) (Spring 2004), p. 87.
2 *Ibid.*, pp. 87–88.
3 C. A. Bartlett and S. Ghoshal, 'What is a global manager', *Harvard Business Review, Best of HBR, 1992*, August (2003), pp. 1–4.
4 Ready, 'Leading at the enterprise level', pp. 90–91.

16 *CXOs and the Line – Serving the internal customer*

PRESTON BOTTGER, PAUL VANDERBROECK AND JEAN-LOUIS BARSOUX

The focus of the people at headquarters is on big, multiyear projects and strategies with dubious relevance to our perception of reality.

(Business unit manager, global consumer goods firm)

To wrap up our exploration of the leadership work of the CXOs, we now turn our attention to their relationship with line managers.

The big challenge for all CXOs is to contribute their functional expertise to points where business actually occurs. So, before moving onto section 3 of the book, we review some key factors that limit the impact of CXOs out in the business units.

CXOs exert their influence through the line executives – the heads of strategic business units, divisions, regions, and countries. Indeed, a defining characteristic of CXOs as a group is that their functional expertise is only as useful as their ability to influence their line colleagues.

Paradoxically, the line often resists their 'help'. So the big challenge for CXOs is to build credibility and productive relationships with the people in the revenue-earning sectors of the business.

CXOs must be aware of how line managers perceive them – and the emotional burden that comes from being seen as costs – and to find ways of dealing with it.

The collaboration of CXOs and line managers within the senior team is discussed in chapter 20. Here, we describe why the relationship between CXOs and operational leaders is often strained. Then we discuss steps for creating more effective collaboration.

Why line managers hate CXOs

What operations managers want from the CXO colleague is service. This service should lead to high-quality, fast and real results. Results mean meeting the operational manager's business goals. The CXO's expertise is taken for granted. The operational manager expects a high-performance, results-focused mindset from the CXO.

Unfortunately, it does not always work out that way. Often, the CXO's role as service provider to the line is overshadowed by the CXO's other role as initiator and upholder of company policies – a dilemma we revisit in chapter 20.

The structure of the situation creates tensions and resentment and CXOs often suffer from a poor image with their line colleagues. The remark *'We're from headquarters and we're here to help . . .'* is a well-worn joke among business unit managers.

As one SBU president summed up the problem with CXOs:

They are too close to the seat of power and too far from the point of sale.

This sweeping criticism covers a multitude of perceived sins. More concretely, CXOs are regarded as:

- *Over-controlling*: CXOs exercise a policing function on behalf of the CEO, and are sometimes suspected of relishing this role. They want to be informed of everything, and perhaps over-control local practices.
- *Bureaucratic*: CXOs are perceived to be administration-minded rather than entrepreneurial. They are seen as more concerned with pursuing an abstract headquarters agenda than a making-a-sale agenda.
- *Remote*: CXOs are overly concerned with the requirements of their own professional domain and out of touch with the business realities – the pace of business action, the threat of competitors, the fickleness of customers and the immediacy of profit and loss considerations.
- *Interfering*: Their studies, visits and unsolicited advice are often seen as unhelpful and disruptive. Line managers believe that they have better things to do.
- *Non-value-adding*: They request information and reports, the value and purpose of which mostly eludes the line. CXOs are often viewed as and sometimes called *cost centres*.
- *Unreceptive*: Line managers out in the business units often feel that their concerns are not welcomed by CXOs. They tend to think that they have insufficient influence on the initiatives that come out of headquarters.
- *Unaware*: CXOs often appear to have little understanding of local conditions and the need for adaptability, so they often come across as insensitive. In the words of one regional manager:

The HQ tends to be rigid and methodical, emphasizing process and a global approach, while ignoring country-to-country differences.

- *Domineering*: Headquarters' staff are criticized for having a 'supply-side mentality' and imposing policies that make little sense to line managers.
- *Playing politics*: Typically, with an office located near the CEO's, CXOs are often thought to be more concerned with impression management than providing service. Sometimes CXOs are viewed as having access to privileged information and are suspected of withholding it from the line.

Again, we emphasize that this litany of accusations is heavily driven: firstly, by the physical distance between the managers in the field and the CXOs at HQ (which blinds them to local requirements); and secondly, by the responsibility of CXOs to uphold consistent corporate practice while also trying to provide a service.

A further source of frustration for the operational units is that they are captive customers of the services provided by the CXO – even when CXOs do not have the expertise they need.

Some companies try to remedy this by setting up a market, where certain CXO areas become 'profit centres'. That is, the CXOs have to show that their service is better or cheaper than can be supplied by an external provider. In some cases, the CXOs can even sell their services outside the company.

Though attractive in principle, few companies have been able to make this set-up work effectively. For the line managers, it adds the cost and hassle of going through a tendering process. And for the CXOs, it is a distraction from the company's primary business. Plus, it adds administrative costs caused by the necessity of internal transfer payments.

Given the difficulties in implementing a structural solution, the onus is on CXOs themselves to bridge the gap. In the next section, we consider how CXOs can build more productive relationships with line managers.

Connecting with the line

Given the structural tensions stemming from their very different responsibilities and roles, CXOs have difficulty winning the confidence of line managers. And without that confidence, the CXO cannot contribute meaningfully to the operational leader's part of the business.

To facilitate the situation, some large companies have separate CXO structures for divisions or business units, to provide a more customized service.

Such structural arrangements can help, but they cannot remove the root cause of the problem. Connecting with the line is a matter of mutual respect and trust. And these are difficult to establish. But a number of measures can help to transform perceptions of the staff functions from cost centres into value adding units.

The key idea is that the CXO is there to enhance the line manager's performance. Providing an ongoing high-level service requires a high-quality relationship.

As in any provider-customer relationship, CXOs can build their credibility with line managers in three ways: firstly, by getting the basics right; secondly, by providing real solutions, *now*; and thirdly, by investing for the long term.

We look at each of these below.

Good foundations

CXOs can build their credibility with line managers by identifying more clearly what both parties want to achieve, and by helping line managers reach their business goals.

Put the client's business imperatives at the top of the agenda

CXOs must ask the line managers what they want and do not want. To understand their needs and priorities better, CXOs must meet regularly and face-to-face with their internal clients to update their understanding of their client's business context. They should also visit their clients' customers. Discussing and clarifying needs will curb the CXO's 'supply-side mentality'.

Ensure mutual expectations are understood and agreed

It is easy to bore line managers with function-specific jargon. Deliverables and features of CXO solutions, systems and processes should be specified. But at the same time the costs and benefits need to be spelt out in a way line managers understand – preferably in terms of facts and figures. Line managers need to see where the added value is for them.

Deliver on commitments

CXO credibility follows reliability and consistency in their performance. This is true for any business relationship, but is critically so in a service relationship.

Specify the business reasons

When CXOs want something from the line manager, they should remember that *they* are the service providers. So, while it may be more expedient to invoke the authority of the CEO, they must do a thorough job of explaining the business purpose. Line managers will want to know *why* they are investing the effort. The CXO must explain the added value for the company as a whole, without forgetting the specific benefits for the line manager's part of the business.

Think first

When introducing policies or initiatives, CXOs need to identify who will be most affected by their project, as well as who will be most or least supportive. As with any change project, CXOs must target their influence efforts at the opinion leaders and quick adopters – to build momentum for a wider push.

Providing solutions

The crux of the service relationship is that the CXOs must create value for the line manager. They must provide real solutions to immediate problems and deliver superior service to help the line manager be successful. Here are some suggestions.

Be a troubleshooter

CXOs can make themselves the line manager's trouble shooters, providing fast and robust answers within their area of expertise. Solving material and immediate problems for line managers earns credibility and goodwill. If it can be done without telling the CEO, it also builds a partnership.

For example, a small Japan-based unit of a Swiss firm complained about quality problems on a new high-tech piece of machinery. The head of the local business unit passed on the complaint to the Swiss-based CTO, half-expecting a defensive reply. Instead, the CTO dispatched the designer of the equipment out to Japan. In two days, the problem was solved.

The designer returned with ideas to improve the machine design. And the customer was so impressed by the attention that he publicly praised the manufacturer at the next meeting of the Japanese industry association.

Bundle CXO expertise

CXOs will sometimes realize that the line manager's problem spans several functional areas, beyond the CXO's immediate expertise. This provides the CXO with the opportunity to position him or herself as the orchestrator of various CXO inputs to offer a complete solution. Engaging a line manager together rather than individually shows respect for the line manager's time. It also pinpoints the orchestrator as a high-level service provider and the go-to person at HQ who can really bring solutions to the line.

Leverage network contacts

CXOs have a view over the entire organization. Their contacts, as well as their knowledge of initiatives, resources or talent in other parts of the company, can be of great value to line managers. The extensive network of CXOs may be particularly valuable to line managers when they have to run a company-wide project.

Investing for the long term

Beyond providing solutions now, the CXO must lay the groundwork for broader, more long-term relationships. There are a number of ways to do this.

Propose and manage staff-line exchanges

High potentials from the CXO talent pool can be given broadening assignments with the line, and vice versa. It is the best way for CXO staff to gain understanding of what is going on in the business. They will return to their function as ambassadors for the line.

Conversely, line managers are always short of good assignments for high potentials. They will welcome the CXO's offer to create meaningful assignments for their high potentials. Such functional experience serves as a preparation for general management roles.

Propose and facilitate pilot projects

Line managers are often reluctant to volunteer for pilot projects of company-wide initiatives. Offering their own areas for a pilot may be seen as a risky move by certain line executives. After all, a new initiative is always time-consuming. And, it may not even be pursued once the pilot has been completed. But there is also a big upside that the CXO can sell. First, it is the best way to get the line manager's specific needs considered. It is also an opportunity to turn the piloting line manager's specific solution into a group standard. Participating in a pilot can be a useful way of getting the benefit of high-level expertise.

For example, the chief human resources officer of a global financial services group was asked to introduce a global recruitment process. She sold the idea of sponsoring and piloting the project to the head of a newly created division, with urgent recruitment needs.

HR experts from head office linked up with the division's own head of HR and senior managers to identify the specific needs. The CHRO also called upon the CIO and the CMO. The group's Intranet was adapted to help run the recruitment process. The CMO designed an employee brand and a marketing strategy to support the recruitment effort.

The immediate target of recruiting hundreds of top professionals worldwide was met, to the great satisfaction of the division head. The recruitment process was successfully rolled out, significantly upgrading the quality of selection. And in the process, the CHRO created a lasting relationship with the head of the new division.

Create allies

The CXO must engage in a purposeful campaign to create allies out in the field. Of course, CXOs do this by providing immediate solutions, by inviting contact and feedback outside official meetings.

But CXOs can also give line managers access to their informal pathways of communication and influence, particularly their inside track to the CEO. This can help line managers to gather support and push through their projects. CXOs can, of course, go further by adding arguments from their own areas of expertise to reinforce the line manager's standpoint.

Clearly what we propose here is that CXOs take all available steps to build credibility in a situation where they have little formal authority over the line and where there are many reasons why the line could resent or ignore their inputs.

To transform a captive customer into a willing collaborator, the effective CXO takes responsibility for all aspects of the relationship. Fruitful and productive collaboration does not entail compromise. It typically requires clarity about who is the service provider and who is the client. Even if the CXO is acting on behalf of the CEO, the line manager should still be treated as an important client.

Looking back at earlier chapters, we have seen that each of the CXOs confronts a huge set of tasks. There is a lot of work involved in simply running the function. What we have surveyed in this brief concluding chapter of section 2 is the additional work required to be influential out in the business units where resources are earned and costs are incurred. Now, we go on to the final section of the book, where we add yet another layer of challenge for the CXOs, namely how they work together to create wealth.

Note

1 See, for example, C. Chan and N. B. Holbert, 'Marketing home and away: Perceptions of managers in headquarter and subsidiaries', *Journal of World Business* 36 (2) (2001), pp. 205–21.

SECTION III

The CEO and the Leadership Team – Pulling it all together

17 *From CXO to CEO – The weight of accountability*

JEAN-LOUIS BARSOUX AND
PRESTON BOTTGER

Becoming the CEO is a big change. It's less glamorous than it looked from below and it's a lot more pressure. There's more work and more responsibility. As a CXO, I knew all that, but I never realized how many expectations there were from directors, shareholders and customers – not to mention the responsibility I feel for our 16,000 employees. (CEO, insurance company)

In this third and final section of the book, we shift attention from the individual business functions to the task of ensuring that they work together in productive ways. We examine this challenge in two stages: first, by exploring the job of the CEO; then by setting out the tasks that must be handled by all CXOs to ensure productive teamwork at the top.

To describe the work of the CEO, we begin in this present chapter by examining the *background* to the greater responsibilities faced by CEOs compared to other CXOs. Then in the following chapter, we set out the key *details* of the CEO's job.

The CEO: many people to influence, and it's lonely work

A typical CEO wears many hats on any given day. Typical daily agenda items include: attending board meetings, CXO team meetings, one-to-one discussions with CXOs and other subordinates, giving and receiving updates on company activities and results, meeting with key customers and suppliers, and generally guiding the firm forward.

The CEO's time is generally the bottleneck resource in the company. Time management is critical and setting the daily agenda for efficiency carries much greater weight than for other executives of the company.

The CEO is constantly engaged in the leadership role: words and actions are watched carefully by many stakeholders and assessed for meaning and implications.

We often hear CEOs describing their role as 'lonely'. Inside the company no other person faces the same magnitude of accountability that encompasses the CEO's role. The CEO is the ultimate decision maker, the ultimate holder of responsibility. Outside the company, the CEO may be able to share ideas and experiences with other CEOs, but on home turf, often there is no one in whom to confide.

A very distinctive job

The job of the CEO is simply much greater than that of any other CXO. The CEO is the leader of leaders. Being part of a chain of command – even when one is responsible for a large function, division or business unit – is different from being at the top. The chief executive officer is the highest ranking operational employee of the company. Every word, action and decision of the CEO carries enormous weight; the position of CEO is, in important ways, greater than the person who occupies the office. The burden of responsibility is unlike any other position.

Furthermore, unless the CEO is also the majority owner of the company, he or she has great responsibilities but is not all-powerful. The CEO is sandwiched in between many, often competing, constituencies: owners and the board on top, all of the company's employees below, and externally, the customers, suppliers, government agencies, the court of public opinion and all other ultimate stakeholders. The CEO's role is powerful, but less so than often imagined.

The distinctiveness in the CEO's job responsibilities arises from the much greater scale, variety, complexity and sheer pressures of the job compared to any of the subordinate roles. Not only does the CEO's responsibility extend across all of the corporate functions, it also covers the entire breadth of the firm's business operations, which often span many products and many countries.

The CEO's role is greater than those of other CXOs in many aspects that include: managing the CXO team, defining CXO boundaries, being a board member if not the chairman, with responsibility for the entire business system: economics, social impact, current operations, innovation, the structural design and the culture.

Managing the CXO team

One of the first and ongoing responsibilities for the CEO is to build and maintain the right CXO team. CEOs approach this task in their own way, depending on their and their company's unique circumstances. Member selection is one of the critical factors to the overall success of the top executive team whose job is to devise and implement company strategy.

In selecting executives for the CXO team, the CEO will assess candidates on the basis of their functional knowledge, leadership qualities and past performance against objectives. The CEO's effectiveness and reputation will be strongly determined by the CXO appointments and removals – and so careful consideration must be made for each change to the team.

A key task of team management is to define the boundaries of responsibility for each CXO team member. Sometimes, the CEO might be called on to resolve conflicts where unclear boundaries or overlaps exist. The CEO is the ultimate decision maker, and lack of decision can be worse than making a less-than-perfect decision. Related to the definition of boundaries is also determining the CEO's own responsibilities and pet projects. These choices determine what can and must be delegated to each CXO.

The CEO's personal time management and the use of highly capable administrative support can make an enormous difference at this level. The CEO's efficiency, decision processes and delegation processes are all key defining factors in the successful performance of the entire business system, including of course the CXO team itself.

Custodian of the culture

The culture of a company is also largely created and maintained by the CEO and the actions he or she endorses and prohibits. If lavish travel expenses, company parties and 'idiosyncratic' bonus packages are the norm for top executives, we would not be surprised to find throughout the company people spending big on the company's account.

Of course, if the CEO is famously cost-conscious, driving a modest car, and not allowing employees to accept so much as a cup of coffee from vendors, we can expect employees to be much more cost-conscious. But the exemplary behaviour of the CEO does not necessarily drive out corruption – as the daily business media continue to report.

Strategic and operational responsibilities

The CEO is often a member of the board of directors and in many cases (especially in the United States) is the chairman of the board. The board of directors of a company has many key roles to play, above the operational responsibility of the CXO team. The CEO's role as a board member tends to consist of high-level company strategy (including mergers, acquisitions and divestitures), review of quarterly financial results, independent review of the auditor's results, key remuneration decisions for all employees, and more recently an even stronger role in compliance with regulations.

Finally, the CEO is truly responsible for effective implementation of corporate strategy. Whether the CEO comes from a marketing and sales, finance, operations, technology or other background does not matter, company strategy must be owned by the CEO. The CEO's legacy will be defined by a number of factors not least of which is how well and successfully the company's strategy was implemented.

CEOs are confronted with additional pressures to perform well in the short term or risk being driven out of office by demanding owners and/or shareholders. In addition to the previously discussed 'standard' roles that are different from the other CXOs', problems and opportunities that the CEO confronts come in complicated packages. Tasks at the CEO level typically contain elements from several different functional areas and often impact several business units.

Always new challenges

As we see, to a far greater extent than other CXOs, the CEO is likely to face tasks outside his or her zone of past experience – whether functional, business or geographical.

It is this vast array of challenges that can encourage new CEOs, possibly overwhelmed by the challenge, to focus on those areas they are most familiar with. They start doing the job they know best – that of someone reporting to them.

For example, in one international toy company, the CEO's persistent meddling actually led to the joint departures of the highly regarded CSCO and the marketing chief.

In addition to internal company issues, there is a complicated range of external demands on the CEO's time. All the external constituencies discussed in the previous chapters – notably key customers, strategic suppliers, alliance partners, the board, not to mention the shareholders, the analysts and the press – feel entitled to a share of the CEO's attention.

Far from enjoying freedom and autonomy, the CEO is answerable to many authorities. One newly promoted CEO observed:

> As CXO, you need to be there whenever the CEO wants you ... [But now as CEO] if Nokia wants to see me, I have to go to Finland.[1]

There is also the size and diversity of the work-force for which the CEO is responsible. Decisions that CEOs are called upon to make can have far-reaching consequences for many thousands of employees and their families. The human and financial stakes are higher. As the CEO of a media group put it:

> The decisions you take are invariably the most difficult of all, affecting people's livelihoods and the firm's profitability.[2]

All this adds up to a lot of pressure. More things can go wrong, on a larger scale, especially in domains the CEO does not fully master. Compared to other CXO positions, the CEO role is far more exposed. If the company underperforms or fails to execute in any given domain, the wrath of the board, the customers, the employees, the shareholders, the media and even at times the general public is directed at the office, and the person, of the CEO.

The CEO is the leader of the CXOs, the final decision maker, the chief of chiefs, the head of the company. Most CXOs do not have what it takes to make the jump to CEO and in fact many CEOs, once in their role, fail to be successful in moving a company forward. In the remainder of this chapter we characterize the different role perspectives a CEO can choose to adopt as he or she undertakes the mighty step from CXO to CEO.

CEO roles

Imagine the CXO team departing from a leadership meeting. The CEO will return to a job that is significantly different from his or her CXO subordinates'. The previous chapters have explained the roles each of the CXOs typically play, and the following chapter will delve into specifics of CEO tasks. Here, we offer a 'role perspective' to show how the CEO's job is indeed distinctive.

There are many ways to describe the weight and complexity of the CEO's job. One approach is to categorize the job in terms of the main business tasks, as in the next chapter. Another angle is to consider the main competencies or capabilities required. Yet another is to describe the desirable personal characteristics and qualities of the person who holds the position.

These various perspectives are complementary and all should be used at different times to get a full appreciation of the scope and responsibilities of the position.

In this chapter, we present a *role* perspective on the work of the CEO. We have found this perspective helpful in demonstrating the difference between leading a function and leading the entire company. It also offers some telling insights about activities which an aspiring CEO might add to his or her experience base.

Here, we describe the work of the CEO as an integrated set of five generic roles:

- **Originator** The CEO's responsibility is to establish and maintain a competitive basis for the company by initiating or backing large-scale programmes.
- **Designer** The CEO's responsibility is to design the means and methods – that is, the structures, processes and a supporting culture – by which to enact the winning competitive model.
- **Energizer** The CEO's responsibility is to ignite and fuel people's enthusiasm to drive the business system – not just within the top team but throughout the organization.
- **Integrator** The CEO's responsibility is to synthesize the many contributions from all parts of the firm and to bring people together in pursuit of opportunities or to solve problems.
- **Protector** The CEO's responsibility is to shield the firm – its economic and human assets – from disruptive external forces such as takeover bids or legal and environmental crises.

The different CXO jobs described in previous chapters involve varying degrees of exposure to these CEO roles. As we examine each of these CEO roles in turn, it will become clear why some functions have more difficulty than others in developing credible candidates for CEO positions.

Originator

As chief originator, the CEO will mark his or her time at the helm of the company by launching big initiatives that are actually driven by other CXOs.

Of course, leaders surround themselves with people who are often smarter or better qualified than themselves. In that sense, the CEO might not be the most creative personality in the group. Nevertheless, the CEO is ultimately responsible for the creation of new ideas and new directions. He or she needs to *emphasize those factors that are critical*, even if the ideas happen to come from others. The key point here is that the CEO must determine what is needed most and where emphasis needs to be placed.

Providing a competitive focus for the organization requires decisions and actions in two dimensions, which are often brought together in corporate mission statements: the economic dimension and the social responsibility dimension.

1 *The economic model*: The CEO must articulate the economic imperatives, i.e. what it takes to succeed profitably in this business and where the company needs to be heading to distinguish itself from the competition. The CEO must ensure that all managers know which business units, product lines and major customers are the most profitable today and how this competitive landscape will look in the future.

   This includes the kinds of acquisitions, divestures and alliances that might be necessary to become or remain a leading player in the markets where the CEO chooses to compete. The CEO must get these factors right or else the company's future may be in jeopardy. Yet developing a great business plan or model does not in itself necessarily elicit commitment or support from the employees.

2 *The social responsibility model*: Often, the CEO must explain a wider corporate purpose, something in addition to making money. The social responsibility dimension expresses the company's desire to do the right things – in terms of valuing its employees, benefiting its customers, respecting the environment – while pursuing the firm's economic model.[3] Many employees want their company to be a good corporate citizen, to have a social conscience. It helps employees stay committed to their jobs and to the company.

Which CXOs get good experience as originators?

Of course, all CXOs must be originators in the general sense of seeing things from a greater perspective and guiding the processes for getting solutions to drive the company forward.

But in terms of understanding what drives the business, the CFO, CMO and CSCO often have the best grasp of the sources of economic value across the firm's activities. The CFO and CMO must have a clear picture of *where* the company makes money. The CSCO must be clear on *how* the company transforms raw material, labour, supply chain and other inputs into products and services that drive the company's profitability.

To be effective members of the leadership team, all CXOs must have one eye on the day-to-day running of the company and another eye on the future. Depending on their current focus and job responsibilities, some CXOs may have more time to focus on the future than others.

Perhaps the most important decisions a CEO makes in the originator role is when to start a major company activity and how to garner the necessary support. This may be a change in company strategy, a cost-cutting drive, a major organic expansion or an important acquisition. Whether they are ultimately led by one of the other CXO team members or spearheaded by the CEO, big change programmes and their subsequent successes or failures are most often what define the tenure of the CEO.

Designer

The CEO, as chief designer of the company, guides the CXO team members in their decisions and ultimately shapes the future of the company.

CEOs in the role of originator articulate the strategic positioning and purpose that captures people's imagination. But the CEO must also ascertain that the means and methods are in place to ensure the implementation of the business model. When CEOs are in their designer role, they are reshaping the company, at the highest of levels, in order to sustain competitiveness and future profitability.

While the typical CEO does not have the time to get into detailed design issues, he or she does have the ultimate responsibility for overarching and broad design decisions.

This starts with the design of the physical structure. The company must have the right configuration to deliver on the strategy. Businesses, offices and factories may be consolidated or closed, manufacturing or back office functions may be centralized or outsourced and even relocating the company headquarters may be necessary to realign the company for the future. These are all major decisions that a typical CEO will face in the role of chief designer.

Design changes will not only affect physical structures. They may also require changing the assignment of responsibilities and reporting relationships so that they support people in working towards those strategic goals. The engineering of cultural changes in a company also starts with effective design.

For example, if the company seeks to lead the industry in customer service, then employees must be recruited and/or trained to deliver it consistently and effectively. They must be rewarded for excellence in customer satisfaction. Systems are required to measure customer feedback and management processes. New reward structures need to be implemented and are required to sensitize the entire firm to the importance of customer satisfaction. Customer-facing staff must receive the managerial and back-office support they need. Thus, design often implies major decisions about where to commit resources.

Which CXOs get good experience as designers?

Most CXOs have faced major resource allocation decisions and tough choices, forcing them to redesign their organizations. But some functions offer more scope for implementing organization-wide systems.

The CFO is charged with translating corporate goals into systems of management, measurement and control – and creating the checks and balances to make sure targets are met and financial communication is clear and compliant. The CSCO oversees the supply chain and is likely to have the most complete understanding of the need to align processes across functions. Effective design is crucial to the CSCO.

Meanwhile, the CIO is likely to have installed integrated systems (enterprise resource planning) that cut across functions, notably finance, sales, purchasing and logistics. Such projects not only provide insight into the dependencies across functions, but also promote valuable experience with the mechanics of driving large-scale improvement projects and dealing with resistance to change.

Energizer

As chief energizer, the CEO has the role of engaging, motivating and mobilizing all the firm's employees.

Leaders do this by personal example; where actions speak louder than words, and each action is followed closely by a wide audience.

A CEO's own intellectual, emotional and physical vitality serves to convey and spread his or her sense of excitement and engagement. The CEO's personality and the weight of enthusiasm he or she puts behind each goal or initiative will be felt well beyond the top executive offices.

Leaders also energize others through their words: by cultivating a sense of togetherness, by expressing their confidence in their collective ability to achieve challenging goals, by identifying the mental inhibitors, and by highlighting examples of success. The CEO might employ tactics of optimistic excitement, fear, sense of purpose and destination – all towards energizing people to meet the goals of the company strategy.

The capacity to energize others is also grounded in the CEO's personal capabilities and dispositions. Verve and eloquence can obviously help to galvanize people into action. And more understated qualities such as persistence, empathy and intensity can further contribute.

But energizing an entire company also requires a great degree of multi-functional knowledge and credibility.

For example, one technology giant appointed a marketing heavyweight as CEO to help boost its brand. Though high on personal energy, enthusiasm and confidence, and successful in repositioning the brand, the CEO was forced out after five years. The CEO never quite succeeded in energizing a dominant group of engineers who continued to see the CEO as 'just a marketer . . . more PowerPoint than patents.'[4]

This kind of challenge will only get greater in the future as labour markets for skilled employees continue to tighten, especially with the aging of the baby boomers. A major competitive element in retaining talent will be the CEO's ability to create the right – energizing – kind of work environment.

As the CEO of an investment bank put it:

I am increasingly thinking about our competitors as anyone, no matter what industry, who is competing with me to hire the best people.[5]

An 'energizing environment' entails offering people the opportunity to work on breakthrough projects which feature the powerful mix of: 'never-been-done-before'; a major stretch but do-able in terms of performance goals; clear social and human benefits beyond the economic value-added; and for the implementers, financial rewards that fully and fairly reflect the scale of the investors' capital gains.

One key tactic for energizing people is to engage them in work by which they not only benefit in career and financial terms, but also by giving them a sense of contributing to social concerns beyond their own personal well-being. Many highly talented people have such aspirations.

The CEO as the chief energizer is, like an actor, always on stage. People are always watching, listening and interpreting each word, each action and each decision. The CEO's own level of commitment and enthusiasm for achieving corporate objectives are key ingredients for success. Each CEO leaves a mark on the company culture, especially through the ways that he or she energizes and orchestrates the company's employees to move in harmony and with the necessary speed.

Which CXOs get good experience as energizers?

Some functions provide broader platforms for exercising the CXO's energizing talents. For example, CXOs with a large staff, such as operations or marketing/sales, often confront big challenges in terms of energizing the front-line workforce. By contrast, CXOs such as the corporate governance officer and the CCO only have to contend with small staffs and are unlikely to ascend to the CEO's position without other, more broad-based experiences.

In other respects, the heads of HR, communications and marketing, with their view on the outside world and sensitivity to public perceptions, have a better appreciation for what the business means and what role it plays in society. As a result, they might have more idea of how to appeal to key stakeholders, especially current and prospective employees.

Yet, the HR and communications chiefs may have difficulty convincing others that they truly comprehend and can act on the business tasks. By contrast, the CTO, for example, should have ideas about where the company needs to be heading in terms of emerging changes in product or process technology. And, as the Web forces the rewriting of business systems, the CIO may have special insight into new methods for the company to sell to, and serve its customers.

In some types of business, faith in the technological credentials of the CEO is critical to connect with and energize the core talent – be it software developers in IT companies or researchers in drug companies.

Integrator

In the role of chief integrator, the CEO can bring together people, ideas and resources like no other person in the company. Integrating and synthesizing company resources in new ways enables the CEO to wield tremendous power in driving the organization.

Of course, integration of the company's activities is in part accomplished through the structure, processes and the nurturing of a strong culture. But not everything can be achieved through business systems.

When individuals have been energized into action, different initiatives will arise and these need to be aligned. Some efforts may duplicate or contradict one another. It falls to the CEO to decide which ones to pursue and which to abandon, in order to retain focus.

As a CEO in the software sector put it:

> Innovation comes from saying no to 1,000 things to make sure we don't get on the wrong track or try to do too much. We're always thinking about new markets we could enter, but it's only by saying no that you can concentrate on the things that are really important.[6]

The CEO, the person at the apex of all of the company's activities, is uniquely positioned to spot potential synergies between different units. The CEO can foster relationships among people who may not be aware of their mutual interests in a particular opportunity. It is the CEO's job to see the big pieces and to try to make sure they fit together effectively.

The CEO as chief integrator is ambassador and master of introductions. The CEO can often bring together different or competing parts of the organization. Through diplomacy and force he or she can bring together diverse sub-units and use their combined efforts to achieve the company's strategic objectives. Often it is through the CEO's wide network that partnerships and teams can be assembled to take advantage of diverse skill sets and tackle business challenges.

Which CXOs get good experience as integrators?

The integrator role clearly requires interpersonal abilities such as persuasion and conflict management skills. One might expect the CHRO to support the CEO in this. As discussed in chapter 12, the CHRO often plays the role of process manager within the executive team, and is likely to be accustomed to monitoring and facilitating the interactions of colleagues. But critically, the integrator role also requires the capacity to make the difficult trade-offs that are the province of the CEO.

The finance function provides some exposure to such dilemmas in that the CFO must always be looking at both the big picture and the details. Similarly, the CSCO is concerned with making operations seamless and establishing continuity. In fact, the high-performing CSCO not only gets daily experience in integration for efficiency purposes, but often has to drive change projects for innovation purposes.

If we consider the network aspect of integration – having a strong network, knowing who can do what and combining people from different areas – then the CHRO role provides a useful platform. The CHRO gains an overview from attending training programmes and evaluation committees. But effective HR people also make it their business to have developed personal relationships with rising talent within the company and many others besides.

Protector

Finally, the CEO is the chief protector of company assets – both tangible and intangible, people, processes and technology – from today's threats and tomorrow's risks.

Companies are constantly under threat: competitors, thieves – from the petty to the industrial secret level – the media, regulatory bodies, natural catastrophes, over-zealous lawyers, and even the company's own employees and customers, can at some time pose a serious threat to the company's interests. The list of shocks that a company can face is long and the employees of the company depend on the CEO to direct them on how to overcome difficult challenges. The way in which a CEO projects the company's response is a key factor in how the organization responds and moves past each major challenge.

Also, for employees to maintain their full attention on value-adding activities, they often must be shielded from outside threats and distractions. The CEO's protective role is about managing the external environment, reducing risk and uncertainty. A strong leader at the helm, ready to protect the company from significant threats, is often required to give confidence to the workforce.

CEOs do this in a proactive way through their relations with key external constituencies (big clients, suppliers, shareholders, analysts, journalists, banks and insurance companies, and other stakeholders). The aim is to build and preserve the company's reputation and its business capabilities.

CEOs can build optimism through their internal communications – especially by putting setbacks and negative events into perspective.

For example, a major oil company was receiving a lot of adverse press coverage regarding a problematic investment in Siberia. The CEO reassured employees by reminding them that although it was a strategic investment, it nevertheless represented only a tiny fraction of the company's overall interests, should it need to be written off.

And of course, CEOs can absorb uncertainty by declaring and committing to a clear course of action when conditions are volatile. As the CEO of a computer services firm put it:

I'm the guy in the organization . . . who says, 'Okay, we've talked through this enough. Let's do it and see what happens.' By taking on the risk, I free the organization to act.[7]

Which CXOs get good experience as protectors?

Some members of the CXO team can assist the CEO in dealing with certain kinds of threats. In handling demands from key outside constituencies, three CXOs stand out:

The CFO has close links with the financial community (shareholders, creditors, bankers and analysts). These constituencies can be friendly or adversarial. Running a tight ship financially can protect the company on many fronts and create a feeling of security both inside and outside the company. Many CFOs have ascended to the CEO chair with an excellent ability to manage risks and protect the company's interests.

The CCO who is used to handling the media and exercising judgement in determining what, when and how important information should be released, is accustomed to protecting, or more often defending, the interests of the company. The CCO is often the 'spin master' and is charged with responding to difficult questions and putting the best face on the company even during difficult times.

The CGO and the top legal counsel, who deals frequently with regulatory authorities, serve as primary protectors of the company. The CGO and top legal counsel tend to get recognition only when things go terribly wrong. However, their day-to-day tasks are to diagnose, imagine and prepare for a myriad of eventualities and to defend the company's interests. Writing guidelines, ensuring the company employees follow policies and obey the law and contracting with insurance companies and law firms are only some of the important protective roles the CGO fulfils.

Other functions, such as R&D and manufacturing, tend to have less experience of managing *any* of these key stakeholders, but their role in protection is important too. Designing and making high-quality products that consistently perform as specified are important in avoiding problems with customers, consumer watchdogs and government agencies.

On the other hand, none of the CXOs will have experienced what can be termed the 'weight of accountability' associated with the position of CEO.

For example the head of one bio-technology company recalled a momentous decision to compete head-to-head against the biggest player in the industry. The decision was reached after informally polling his executives at a cocktail party.

Looking back, he reflected: 'If it hadn't worked out, I wouldn't be sitting here.'[8]

The CEO as the chief protector sometimes has to play a superhero role when a company is facing major adversity. Whether it is an attack from the competition, the press, the financial community, regulatory authorities or even special interest groups, the way in which the CEO handles the role as chief protector is an important signal to the firm's employees as well as the outside world.

The CEO knows that when defending the company from a significant external attack, words and actions will be observed and assessed very carefully by stakeholders, possibly from around the globe.

Bridging the gap: from CXO to CEO

Functional leaders learn to lead functions, not whole companies. The five-role framework used above serves to highlight the gap between the two levels.

Some CXO positions clearly provide more relevant CEO-type experiences than others. Yet, even rotation through all the CXO roles would leave a CEO candidate short of the full repertoire of experience needed to perform well as a CEO. He or she would be missing the all-important operational experience as well as the task of being ultimately responsible for all corporate functions.

To acquire additional skills, companies put their CXOs in charge of a business or large projects that allow them to develop their P&L responsibilities in preparation for the top job. One former CFO who had gone on to become a successful CEO recognized the critical importance of having had a chance to run a division first:

> You need a stepping stone to understand how a business operates and to lead people from multiple disciplines.[9]

The reverse is also true. P&L-tested leaders may be given stints as CXOs to round out their corporate HQ experience and enhance their strategic perspective. Indeed, in some companies, certain functional roles have become *de facto* developmental roles – notably the positions of CSCO, CFO, CMO and in some cases CIO – as part of the grooming for the top job.

Yet ultimately, no combination of assignments quite prepares an individual for the special job circumstances – the demands, the diversity of business challenges, issues and relationships – that constitute the work of the CEO. An exception perhaps is the experience of being CEO of another company. But even success in one business environment is no guarantee of success in a new environment.

In the next chapter, we move from these background considerations of the challenges facing CEOs to specific details of leading and managing the company.

Notes

1 S. Barr, 'The view from there', *CFO Magazine*, 17 (11), 1 September (2001), p. 92.
2 M.Kennett, 'View from the top', *Management Today*, June (2005), pp. 38–47.
3 P. Bottger, 'Leading on the run: How to do it right', *IMD Perspectives for Managers*, September (2003), pp. 1–4.
4 A. Lashinsky, 'Now for the hard part', *Fortune*, 18 November (2002), pp. 56–65.
5 J. E. Garten, *The Mind of the CEO* (New York: Basic Books, 2001), p. 183.

6 P. Burrows, 'The seed of Apple's innovation', *BusinessWeek Online*, 12 October (2004).
7 N. G. Carr, 'On the edge: An interview with Akamai's George Conrades', *Harvard Business Review*, May–June (2000), pp. 119–25.
8 P. Hemp, 'A time for growth', *Harvard Business Review*, July/August (2004), pp. 66–64.
9 S. Barr, 'The view from there', p. 92.

18 *The Chief Executive Officer – Orchestrating the whole*

PETER LORANGE

[As CEO] you have to choose which broad areas you will focus on at any given moment . . . Obviously, a variety of altitudes exist within each of these areas. Moving nimbly in and out of these areas and at different altitudes in each is crucial to leadership success, particularly in times of growth and uncertainty. (CEO, biotechnology company)[1]

The CEO, as the top boss, is ultimately responsible for all the tasks and results surveyed in the chapters to date.

He or she must drive and embody the imperatives of quality, talent and learning, outlined in section 1. He or she is accountable for all the functional decisions covered in section 2 and on how to apportion resources across the functions. He or she must also reconcile the preoccupations of the CXOs with those of the business leaders in operations, where the money is made. It is the CEO who sits on top of the revenue stream and the cost stream.

More generally, the CEO must cater to the needs of the firm's many stakeholders, most notably the shareholders, the customers, the company's top executives and other employees, the board of directors, and suppliers.

These many activities can be grouped into four broad sets of issues on which the CEO must focus:

- Growth issues;
- Cost issues;
- Internal issues; and
- External issues.

Before examining these in detail, we will consider how the CEO role has become both more complex and more publicly scrutinized over time.

Evolution of the CEO role

Both macroeconomic forces and the accomplishments of a small number of highly influential corporate leaders have influenced the evolution of the job of CEO. Beginning long before the title of chief executive officer existed, early founder-entrepreneurs often ruled their companies with an idiosyncratic, sometimes dictatorial style.

Public ownership created a separation between ownership and management, with ownership traded publicly on one or many global exchanges. To ensure stockholders' interests were looked after, many firms implemented a two-tiered hierarchy that persists today. On the first tier is the board of directors elected by the shareholders of the corporation. On the second tier is the senior executive group hired by the board of directors.

By the 1930s, a rising class of professional executives was running corporations, accountable to a widely dispersed group of shareholders. These early presidents or managing directors, epitomized by Alfred Sloan of General Motors, introduced a management system marked by hierarchies of responsibilities and control. Management became less top-down, and more open to influence by competence.

By the 1960s, companies were growing much larger and more complex, with diverse businesses comprising a single corporate entity. CEOs trained in finance – an example was ITT's Harold S. Geneen – imposed the rigours of quantitative analysis on the management of large corporations.

The 1970s was an era of inflation, fuel shortages and intensifying competition. Macroeconomic forces drew the attention of CEOs outward, and many became influential at the level of government policy. The title of chief executive officer gained widespread usage and reflected the expansion of the role to statesman-like activities.

The 1980s were notable for two reasons: the rise of the institutional investor with the power to usurp the CEO, and the emergence of the celebrity CEO. Lee Iacocca's turnaround success at Chrysler drew unprecedented media attention. Similar was Jack Welch's unwavering focus on stock price and the internal determinants of stock price, namely, eliminating unprofitable businesses, and fat processes and structures.

The IT revolution propelled youthful entrepreneurs, CEOs like Bill Gates and Steve Jobs, onto the cover of *Fortune* magazine. A few CEOs became household names: Donald Trump and Ted Turner in the US; Richard Branson and Alan Sugar in Britain; Bernard Tapie in France. And the media-infatuation with CEOs grew without limits through the 1990s.

Also, the early-1990s saw GM's CEO Robert Stempel ousted by the board, after the company posted massive losses. It was a strong signal of the power now wielded by big institutional investors. This trend gathered pace as the decade unfolded – and eventually gave rise to the expression 'CEO churning' as CEO tenures were dramatically shortened.

As the CEO job became increasingly risky, incumbents and aspirants demanded higher compensation and exit guarantees. But progressively, the public grew disenchanted with the enormous severance packages awarded to CEOs who had driven value out of their companies.

A spate of corporate scandals in the early 2000s converged with the bursting of the dot-com bubble. This fuelled public cynicism regarding CEO pronouncements and general trustworthiness.

These events severely tarnished the image of the chief executive position and led to increased regulatory scrutiny. They also ushered in calls for a more discrete and disciplined style of business leadership. These developments added to the CEO's ever-expanding list of responsibilities. We now explore these in greater detail.

Growth issues

Maximizing shareholder capital is widely regarded as the top priority of the CEO. The two basic routes to value maximization are through growth – that is increased revenues – and through cost reductions.

Growth, as the cornerstone of maximizing shareholder capital, can be pursued through a combination of both acquisitions and internally generated expansion. In the early 1990s, there was a huge upsurge in acquisition-driven growth, particularly across industry and geographical borders.

Yet the difficulty of securing anticipated returns from synergies has engendered a healthy conservatism among many boards of directors, cautioning against too much growth through acquisition. Coupled with this, the costs of acquisition candidates have risen significantly. Thus, to a much larger extent today than just a few years ago, the focus has shifted to internally generated growth.

Internally generated growth

The CEO's task is to maintain focus on growth by:

- Exploiting the firm's core strengths by which value is created for customers: for example, can these strengths be leveraged, by expanding into new geographic markets and customer segments?
- Broadening the existing platform of strengths and so growing the business: what new technologies can be added, to develop additional products or services around the current offerings?
- Communicating constantly about growth, especially organic growth: how best to shape external perceptions, and also to maintain internal momentum and to raise collective expectations?

The big challenge with internally generated growth is to see business opportunities before they are obvious to competitors. The customer is a good place to start. Often, the CEO and senior executives become so specialized or busy that they forget that their chief inspiration for growth actually comes from the customer.

Of course, the customer will always be on the move, always changing, leading to new opportunities as well as new threats. To maintain focus on growth the CEO must stay in close contact with customers. Internally generated growth initiatives are unlikely to survive unless they are based on valid understanding of specific customer needs, and driven and legitimized by the CEO.

Thus, links to the customer are vital for the effective CEO. More specifically, the CEO must encourage exchange with leading customers, those who are the most advanced users and opinion setters. This forces the firm to try new initiatives and to set the platforms for future growth.

For example, the CEO of an information storage company established twice yearly 'customer councils'. These were intensive two-day gatherings of the company's top engineers and fifty to sixty leading-edge customers. This method allowed the company to pinpoint products and features that would address future customer priorities. The idea was to extract product requirements from customers, to test existing concepts, but also to determine what customers 'want first'?[2]

Beyond helping to identify customer needs as the drivers of internally generated growth, the CEO has three ways of influencing the firm's growth patterns and priorities:

- By determining which strategic projects to back for growth. This requires picking a few central projects. Then, the CEO must pump resources into them so they can develop them faster and pre-empt competition from catching up or taking the lead. Clearly, this implies distributing financial resources. And, more significantly, often it implies enforcing the specific allocations of management time and energy.
- By maintaining a strong decision focus in driving growth, rather than procrastinating and creating doubt. Decisions must be made and debates closed so that growth initiatives can move ahead.

  As one leading European CEO put it:

> Somebody has to take responsibility and say, 'Okay, this is it. This is what we are going to do.' Otherwise you just have a lot of fun in discussing things – and nobody takes the ball and carries it. It's all very well passing it around in a circle. But somebody, at the right point in time, has to grab it and run.[3]

- By balancing long-term and short-term points of view in both top-line and bottom-line growth, both sales and profits. When a new growth project is launched, it typically must aim for 'low-hanging fruit' to generate the necessary immediate cash flows. It also must build a long-term position with customer groups, to generate a more distant pay-off.

  For example, when approaching many developing markets, it is clear that the majority of the customers tend to be young but less affluent. They need to be part of the growth equation, but with a longer-term focus. In parallel, the more affluent, older consumers must be addressed to create the shorter-term balance in the overall growth strategy.

Acquisition-driven growth

Currently, the pendulum has swung away from pursuing growth primarily through acquisitions. But acquisition still remains an important complement to internally generated growth.

It is possible to distinguish between two types of acquisition. One extends established strengths by acquiring new market positions relating to the business the company already has. The other type provides a new platform for growth, not directly related to present strengths. Obviously, the former type of acquisition tends to be less risky, easier to manage and less expensive than the latter.

Acquisitions make heavy demands on the CEO and top executive team. They must meet regularly and frequently to discuss potential challenges, to assess progress and to air emerging problems. The aim is not only to secure value from the current acquisition, but also to develop a process for doing it better next time.

For example, ISS, one of the world's largest facility service groups based in Denmark, specializes in acquisition-driven growth. Typically, it makes more than forty purchases a year, most of which are relatively modest 'bolt-ons'. A key lesson that has emerged from this experience is that it is critical to quickly integrate the new acquisition into the ISS operating mode.

ISS changes the brand name of the acquired firm and insists on adoption of ISS's processes, both for business development and for steering the economic model. And, if the acquired executives feel that they cannot work within the new ISS mode, they are replaced.

Clearly, this hands-on integration requires strong coordination among the various CXOs and close attention to learning. Underlying this approach is the understanding that the specific execution method in each case is very much a matter of quick learning from experience. It requires flexibility, pragmatism and, above all, speed.

While ISS has developed a very sophisticated process for integrating new acquisitions, the CEO and senior executives remain mindful that executive time and energy must also be dedicated to internally oriented growth. External growth must not completely supplant internal growth.

Cost issues

Since the 1980s, there has been ever-growing pressure on CEOs to generate steadily increasing earnings.

If opportunities for top-line growth were limited, then to improve profits, CEOs were expected to wage war on costs. And so, the implementation of large-scale efficiency initiatives was added to the list of CEO responsibilities. Numerous company-wide efforts were launched as part of the drive to eliminate costs and help companies meet earnings targets. These included re-engineering, ERP, downsizing, restructuring and outsourcing.

In the process, cost management has come to be regarded as the painful alternative to revenue growth. If the firm cannot grow its revenues profitability, then it must become leaner. That way the company can still satisfy shareholder expectations regarding earnings and/or pass on cost savings to customers.

In reality, the CEO must focus on costs *all the time*, not just when growth stalls. The challenges of working smarter, developing better processes, finding ways for multitasking within one's organization will always be part of the CEO's agenda. Fiefdoms and silos must be broken down, barriers removed and new, better ways of working have to be developed and embedded in operating processes.

At the same time, the CEO must ensure that the new ways of working do not create new rigidities and other dysfunctions. Cost savings in one area must not result in false economies by simply displacing costs to another area. These are ongoing challenges.

In one classic failure, the reorganization of a company's sales force along industry lines was implemented before the sales representatives had been retrained. The expectation that product specialists could now sell all of the company's products and services led to acute dissatisfaction and losses among both customers and staff. These results precipitated the CEO's removal.

The control of costs also requires that cost-saving improvements in one function are aligned with and supported by changes in the other functions. It is the CEO's responsibility to take a system-wide view, and ensure implementation of the required alignment and mutual support.

So far, we have considered cost issues in a general way. Now we focus more closely on two tasks that can dominate the CEO's agenda: specific cost-cutting programmes and outsourcing operations.

Cost-cutting programmes

Cost-cutting programmes have become an integral part of the CEO's responsibilities. Such programmes often deliver temporary gains in efficiency that help firms meet their earnings targets. But they rarely lead to sustained improvement in the firm's competitive position. There are two ways that CEOs can help cost-cutting initiatives provide a better platform for growth:

Preserving core capabilities

Some costs can be removed without an immediate impact on profit. The first targets for cost cutting are often those units whose output is invisible in the short run, but which contribute to the long-term growth or survival of the firm.

A good example was the decision of an incoming CEO in the airline industry to kill a customer-monitoring unit as part of an efficiency drive, at a time of record profits. In doing so, he cut off the flow of feedback from the passengers. This delayed recognition of the fact that the efficiency programme was inflicting irreparable damage on the airline's hard-won reputation for excellence in customer service.

Another risk is associated with applying the same cost-cutting measures (such as budget cuts or layoffs) evenly across the board. While this 'cookie cutter' approach has the advantage of simplicity and equity, it confuses the issue of which costs are critical to the company's existing and future competitive positions.

It is part of the CEO's responsibility to weigh the trade-offs between different cost-reduction options. The CEO must lead the debate on the difference between 'good costs' and 'bad costs' – and to reduce costs in such a way that critical prevention or innovation capabilities are not lost.

Preserving morale

Many cost-cutting programmes involve pain for employees – notably in terms of layoffs, relocations or salary freezes. This can make it very difficult, once the medicine has been applied, to rekindle innovation and growth.

The cost cutting might have damaged trust in management and loyalty to the company. Employees can feel demoralized and anxious about their own future, having seen colleagues depart, voluntarily or not. These employees might now have reservations about contributing the ideas, energy and commitment needed to capitalize on new market opportunities.

The CEO can help by ensuring that painful measures are counter-balanced by hopeful measures – and that employee's understand *why* they are making sacrifices.

For example, at the same time as implementing plant closures at Nissan, CEO Carlos Ghosn also announced a significant increase in the budget and headcount of the R&D function. Nissan people knew that the falling sales problem was largely related to uninspiring designs. By channelling cost savings into product development, Ghosn laid the platform for the auto firm's dramatic and sustained turnaround.

Outsourcing internationally

The major cost and efficiency challenge for CEOs today involves outsourcing activities to Asia (especially China and India), Europe (Romania, Bulgaria, etc.) and the Americas (especially Mexico and Central America). In these regions, manufacturing can be dramatically cheaper. And, certain services, such as call centres and software development, can be successfully carried out at low costs. In some cases, parts of HR, marketing and even R&D can be moved outside the firm.

The global economy is changing the way CEOs think about their organizations and their value chains – and about which particular core capabilities actually do drive competitive advantage within their industries. This puts pressure on CEOs to assess rigorously each of the operations to determine where the firm has sufficient scale and differentiated skills and where it does not.

In some cases, to maintain competitiveness, the CEO and the executive team have no option but to close significant activities in high-cost regions, possibly even in the company's home country. Operations are moved to low-cost areas, where new competencies will have to be built up.

The CEO of a German industrial giant recently observed:

> Six Chinese engineers cost as much as one American or German engineer. And they work 2,600 hours per year. So how do you deal with this? I don't have the answer, but in my opinion, the risk of not being there is higher than the risk of being there.[4]

Different industries are hit by this trend at different rates. In some, it remains a peripheral issue – with a focus on 'what could be farmed out?'. In other industries the core discussion is shifting to 'what *must* remain?' For CEOs, even in mid-sized companies, such discussions are becoming inescapable.

The role of the CEO in these offshoring and outsourcing decisions is *first*, to ensure that the costs and benefits are properly weighed up.

Crude salary comparisons of like-profile employees in two locations can fail to account for major issues. These include the costs of managing the relationships complicated by cultural, language and legal differences, the risk to reputation (through underperformance), the danger of opportunistic behaviour (protection of intellectual property) and the likelihood of creeping costs as demand for qualified labour in that part of the world begins to outstrip supply.

Even if the business advantage is too compelling to ignore, the CEO will also have to deal with the human implications of offshoring decisions – namely the fear and anxiety created in those directly affected *and* in those who remain.

For those directly affected, the first question will be: 'What will happen to me?' The CEO has a responsibility to create some options for these people, in terms of training, in terms of helping them find other jobs and in terms of financial compensation. The survivors will be watching closely how fairly their colleagues are treated: 'Today it was them, but tomorrow it could be us.'

The survivors will be more interested in the question: 'Now what?' Here, the CEO must explain the decision against the wider perspective and explain how the offshoring of non-core activities can help to boost the core activities and secure remaining jobs.

For example, the offshoring of manufacturing frees capital for investment in new infrastructure or to scale up R&D. This helps the company stay ahead of the commoditized competition. Or, it allows the company to take on more of a systems integration role, drawing on low-cost inputs (hardware, software, systems and processes) from scattered locations.

The point underlying both international outsourcing and cost-cutting programmes is that they are more palatable when the savings generated are clearly linked to corporate growth and to new opportunities for the people who remain involved.

Internal issues

A company's culture is built in countless subtle, covert and overt ways. Of course, the CEO has major impact by his or her decisions on structure and systems. But the CEO's impact is also felt through his or her everyday pronouncements or actions – as well as silences or inactions.

Is he or she visible within the company? Is taking calculated risks rewarded ... regardless of the outcome? Who is disciplined, for what, and how? What behaviours are tolerated, or rewarded? Each of these sends signals.

Ensuring that business decisions – whether for growth or cost reduction – are executed requires shaping of this internal context. In the effort to develop a proactive culture and to mobilize employees to enact the strategy, the CEO has to work at two levels: on the immediate CXO team and on the workforce as a whole.

Mobilizing the CXO team

Many of the top team issues are dealt with in the next chapter, but the CEO's specific challenge in developing a proactive culture is to ensure that the CXOs work together in pragmatic and interactive ways and not in independent silos.

This requires making sure that business initiatives are being backed by all, and that individual CXOs are not withholding their support. Some might sit on the fence, to see how things go before committing themselves. Such political safety-seeking within the top team will extinguish efforts to develop a culture of innovation and learning.

For example, Eric Schmidt, when he was appointed as CEO of Novell, had to eradicate a ubiquitous practice known as the 'Novell nod':

> People would sit in a room, listening to someone talk and nodding in agreement. Then, as they left the room, they'd all say to one another, 'That was the stupidest thing I've ever heard.' I'd see that kind of behavior constantly.'[5]

The CEO's responsibility is to make sure that the real discussion happens *during* the meetings and not *afterwards*. He or she must create an environment where learning can take place around the table, where different functional perspectives are exchanged and confronted, and where problems and their solutions get aired in the same forum.

Of course, there is built-in bias among the members of the top team to avoid upsetting the boss. This puts the onus on the CEO to demonstrate a capacity to face dissonant information. In fact, the CEO must encourage individuals to bring it forward.

These discussions must be based on facts, not just opinions. But the CEO also has to push for action on new initiatives – and might sometimes have to ignore calls for more analysis, more planning or more testing. At some point, the discussion has to give way to action, with experimentation providing the momentum and learning for ongoing improvement.

At that point, the CEO has to ensure that the entire top team rallies behind the initiative. The CXOs will have to sell it on to the troops, so that they themselves can 'get on board'.

Now, there is only so much that a CEO can do to bring existing team members together. To deal with resistance, the composition of the team might require reshaping. This might involve changes in who reports directly to the CEO. If the CEO sees significant shifts in the competitive landscape, then certain CXO roles might be upgraded or downgraded. It can also involve actual changes in personnel, with particular attention to covering the CEO's own areas of weakness.

When bringing in fresh blood, the CEO must get the right workable mix of fit and diversity. One, the CEO must pick senior executives with whom he or she feels personally comfortable, and who command respect and trust within the organization. But secondly, it is important to recruit people who bring fresh insights and who can challenge the team's existing orthodoxies. Companies might not have to look externally for suitable candidates. They just have to look outside the existing top team.

The CXO team plays a more important role today than ever before. The high degree of complexity and specialization and the intense focus on performance make the expertise in the senior ranks crucial to a company's success. And exploiting that talent is the CEO's job.

Often, the business press heaps praise on CEOs for insights or decisions that were actually developed by the leadership team. The leader's merit, in these cases, is in knowing how to attract the right people, and how to back a good idea when hearing one.

It is critical to understand that the culture of the company is set by the behaviour of top team. Corporate headquarters can too easily set an example of a negative culture. This is particularly the risk if they are seen as too bureaucratic, too cautious, too political, or too far removed from the business reality of the customer.

Establishing a close-knit and single-minded top management team is a good start to creating a proactive culture. But front-line employees also need to be persuaded to move in that direction.

Mobilizing the troops

Most companies capture only a fraction of the energy and ideas available to them internally. Capturing more of that value has become a competitive necessity. It is the CEO's role to create an environment that helps employees perform and come forward with ideas.

Everyone must understand that their real responsibilities are larger than their formal authority; that things get done when employees see they must be done, based on their own initiatives. There is no room for the excuse that it is 'not part of my job'.

To encourage large groups of front-line employees to be more proactive and innovative, CEOs must take action on three broad fronts: systems, structure and processes.

Systems

Changes to corporate systems may need to be signed off by the CEO. But they are more the province of the individual CXOs and have already been covered in the earlier chapters.

Examples include: HR systems that help shape individual and collective behaviour through training, performance measurement and reward; financial systems that dictate the levels of budgetary discretion that might or might not encourage responsiveness and experimentation; IT systems that determine the quality and availability of information on which to make decisions or detect unexpected causal relationships.

Structure

CEOs typically must be directly involved in decisions about organizational structure. While the structure of the company might not actively encourage innovation, it can easily get in its way. Thus, changing the focus of the structure – from geography to business or from centralized to decentralized – is often part of the effort to invigorate a company and make it more enterprising and responsive.

But structural initiatives do not have to be large-scale affairs. There are other ways to remove barriers to the upward flow of ideas.

In one highly successful case, in the auto industry, the CEO created ten cross-functional teams that looked at various aspects of the firm's operations. The teams were staffed by up-and-coming executives and were given ten weeks to come up with recommendations.

This initiative helped to break down the paralysing boundaries between functions and to instil faster and more open communications. These cross-functional teams were not disbanded until their recommendations had been implemented.

Other examples of management methods that function in parallel with the existing structure include task forces, which the CEO can set up to look into on-going or emerging challenges; as well as pilot projects which can be used to test new approaches.

Processes

CEOs have a wide variety of process mechanisms at their disposal. They can bring people together on a regular basis for learning and exchange across functional boundaries or business units.

For example, one of the world leaders in the catering industry organizes a bi-annual fair where the company's 18,000 operating units get a chance to showcase and view internal examples of innovation and best practice.

At an individual level, the CEO can also establish processes for interacting directly with employees, such as skip-level meetings, 'coffee talks' or 'town hall' meetings.

For example, the CEO of an international electronics distributor convenes regular forums where people can speak up:

At least once a month . . . I gather people at one of our sites; no managers are allowed. I start every meeting by saying something like 'This is your company. Tell me what's wrong with it.' I get amazing feedback. And then I promise to deal with the feedback in two weeks or less. We don't always do what people want: companies aren't democracies. But people know that we haven't just heard their criticisms – we've dealt with them.[6]

Beyond creating opportunities for learning and removing blocks to action, the CEO must provide stimulus. Establishing processes for getting out in front of employees and interacting with them candidly is part of establishing the CEO's personal credibility and creating trust.

External issues

As the public face of the company, many of the demands on the CEO's time are driven by external constituencies. Some of these have long featured prominently among the CEO's concerns: notably, shareholders and analysts, the unions, customers and suppliers, government agencies and regulatory authorities.

Others are more recent additions, such as joint venture or alliance partners, journalists, NGOs, activists (consumer advocates, environmentalists, special interest groups) and local communities. Some are part of the value chain, in that the company formally transacts with them. Others can be better described as social constituencies.

What characterizes all of these constituencies is that they have grown more demanding in their expectations. A possible exception is the unions, which do not generally have the same clout as they once had. Significantly, the term IR continues to dominate the CEO's agenda, but where it once stood for Industrial Relations, it now stands for Investor Relations.

These stakeholders do not all require the same level of CEO attention. But none can be neglected. Dealings with many of these constituencies are in fact handled in conjunction with various CXOs – for example, the media (CCO), investors (CFO) and the unions (CHRO). These have been discussed earlier in the book.

But the one constituency that commands the CEO's special attention is the board. Clearly, the task of working with the board could also be regarded as belonging to the previous section on internal issues. But changes in the expectations of the board have shifted its positioning vis-à-vis the organization.

It is worthwhile here to recall some key themes about boards that were surveyed in chapter 13. As we saw, boards of directors were once seen as advisors to management. They were unlikely to challenge the CEO openly – and were typically staffed by people handpicked from among the CEO's own social or business circle.

But with the rising activism of institutional investors, boards of directors have found themselves thrust into a new role. They are now held responsible for how well management runs the business and are increasingly engaged in monitoring management and even firing CEOs.

Boards have become increasingly independent entities. They are often responsible for establishing their own governance guidelines and selecting their own new members. They sometimes meet without the CEO – and not just to plot the CEO's removal! With a clear mandate to represent the interests of the shareholders, the board is now less of an advisor to the CEO and more of a boss.

This does not mean that the relationship has become adversarial. It is simply not as cosy as it once was. Of course, the danger is that the increasingly cautious stance of boards – driven in large part by earlier corporate excesses and transgressions – may impinge on the firm's responsiveness and risk-taking.

This puts the onus on the CEO to educate the board and to keep it informed, as it can no longer be expected to 'rubber stamp' management decisions it does not fully understand or support. To help the CEO, the board needs to know where the company is and where it is heading.

As the CEO of a fast-growing biotechnology company explains:

> It's tempting to go to the board meeting and say, 'Here are the results, here's how we're doing against budget, here's ... here's ... here's ... Any questions? Thanks a lot.' But it's crucial that the board is thinking with you ... because if you don't have the board with you, you can't seize opportunities as they come up.[7]

To diagnose where to focus their external efforts, CEOs need to consider two dimensions. One dimension is the potential impact on the firm of the various external stakeholders. The other dimension is the extent to which the groups are aligned with the firm's objectives.

CEOs must devote most of their energy to those stakeholders who have a high impact on the firm – perhaps engaging a relatively unreceptive regulator to find common ground or consolidating existing ties with a key supplier.

At the same time, the CEO must pay attention to possible changes among the less important stakeholders. New external issues are emerging all the time. For example, a range of social, economic and environmental topics have started to penetrate CEO agendas. And it is important for CEOs to monitor these shifts which can have a big impact on the business.

Balancing the tensions

As highlighted in this chapter and the previous one, the distinctiveness of the CEO's role lies in the breadth of issues for which he or she is responsible.

The CEO is the bridge between the operational issues and the functional issues. The CEO is also the point of intersection for the divergent and often contradictory concerns emanating from multiple constituencies – both internal and external.

This pivotal role requires constant juggling between time frames and levels of focus or abstraction. It demands rapid switches of attention between areas, but also the ability to make connections between issues across units and to draw the organization-wide conclusions.

In this respect, the CEO is constantly balancing opposing forces. This calls for a capacity to maintain a dual focus. One, CEOs need to be thinking about leveraging existing resources; two, they *also* need to be developing new ones.

There are many other instances where CEOs must manage balance. For example, they must be concerned with satisfying customer needs *and* anticipating them; growing the top line *and* the bottom line; focusing on long-term *and* short-term considerations; encouraging compliance (safety, health, environment, ethics) *and* business focus; building organizational resilience *and* flexibility; cultivating focus *and* responsiveness; and developing entrepreneurship *and* accountability.

Of course, the CEO does not face these dilemmas alone. But it is the CEO's task to restore the balance when the emphasis is swinging too far in one direction.

Although it is often presented as an individual challenge, leading the firm is very much a collective leadership challenge. The CEO has the responsibility to optimize the talent and expertise residing within the team. The CEO must ensure that the sum of the parts is greater, not less, than the whole.

The next two chapters examine how the CXO team can be part of the solution, rather than part of the problem.

Notes

1 P. Hemp, 'A time for growth', *Harvard Business Review*, July/August (2004), pp. 66–74.

2 P. Hemp, P. Lyman and H. R. Varian, 'Managing for the next big thing', *Harvard Business Review*, January(2001), pp. 130–9.

3 J. S. McClenahen, 'Nokia's Jorma Ollila wants to unwire the world', *Industry Week*, 20 November (2000), pp. 38–44.

4 T. A. Stewart and L. O'Brien, 'Transforming an industrial giant', *Harvard Business Review*, February (2005), pp. 114–22.

5 B. Fryer, 'Leading through rough times', *Harvard Business Review*, May (2001), pp. 116–23.

6 A. Muoio, 'The truth is, the truth hurts', *Fast Company*, April (1998), pp. 93–99.

7 Hemp, 'A time for growth', pp. 66–74.

19 *Relations Among CXOs – Competing priorities spell trouble*

JEAN-LOUIS BARSOUX

Trying to push through a technology project, the CTO said of his marketing colleagues: 'If they find facts to support their view, they grab it at face value. Anything that contradicts their view, they put through a micro-fine sieve.' The head of marketing reciprocated by saying, 'If they don't like the data, they say it is flawed and go on their merry way . . .'[1]

We have surveyed the important types of CXO positions, culminating with the CEO. In this chapter and the next, we turn our attention to how well, or poorly, the incumbents work together.

In this chapter, which is more conceptual in its treatment of topics than previous and future chapters, we explore the critical twin challenges of CXO conflict and cohesion, both good and bad. This sets the platform for the following chapter, which examines important real-life challenges: both for CXOs working together, and in working with line colleagues as part of the top team.

Combining different perspectives

In examining the various CXO functional roles, the previous chapters have diagnosed the distinctive objectives, responsibilities, challenges, relationships and time orientations that characterize the different functions.

These distinguishing features mean that CXOs in different areas develop different scanning and information processing systems. In other words, they tend to *notice* and filter out different data relating to technologies, products, markets and people. And, even when they look at the same information, they will tend to *interpret* it idiosyncratically, each seeing different implications in it.

Thus, the positions that various CXOs hold on business issues are likely to reflect their distinctive role-influenced responsibilities. How the business operates, what is happening in the environment, what actions

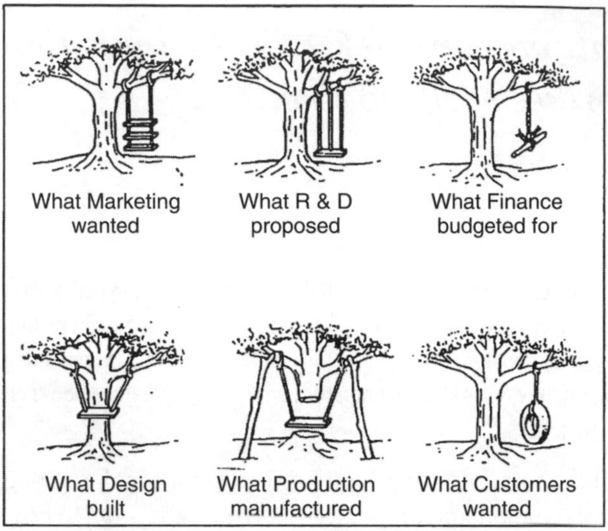

Figure 19.1: Functional myopia

will lead to success and their own role within the company – CXOs' views on these questions are strongly determined by their current functional role and work history.

Figure 19.1 is a familiar sight in many offices and is a light-hearted way of showing how CXO views can be over-determined by their functional background.

Now, these different 'understandings' or conceptual frames can be essential to corporate success. It is particularly important from a diagnostic perspective to bring diverse expertise and information to bear on key strategic issues.

The combined standpoints of the CXOs are more likely to reflect the complexity of the competitive environment than a single view. Their specific training and functional preoccupations alert them to different weak signals, concerning particular threats and opportunities. These lead to different interpretations and insights about how to capitalize on opportunities.

It is not so much the case of blind men touching different parts of the elephant, and coming to different conclusions about the type of creature before them. Actually, it is more like witnesses of an incident, where each sees a *complete* story but from a different angle.[2] And while this phenomenon offers the possibility of deeper understanding and more sophisticated responses, it also increases the opportunities for differences of opinion and conflict.

Beyond silo thinking

Though an overused term, 'silo thinking' is a good description of a real impediment to collective effectiveness. Yet the remedy can generate more problems than the condition itself.

To capture the full value of their divergent insights, CXOs must work together. They must develop a better understanding of how their own silo relates to other silos. They must deal proactively with the inevitable misunderstandings and consequent mistrust that will stem from their functional differences.

A heightened sense of unity and identification with the group encourages CXOs to keep their own preoccupations in perspective, *and* to consider the bigger picture. This increases their commitment to the leader, to the CXO team and to the company.

These are highly desirable outcomes in the pursuit of top team effectiveness.

However, in their bid to connect, build rapport and look for agreement on productive action, members of the top team can fall into another trap. They can start to confuse co-operation with avoiding disagreement. And the danger is that in reaching for social cohesion, the group walks away from all conflict. Members start to devote more energy to making sure they do not fall out, than they do to critical or analytical thinking.

While team member comfort might be served, team performance can suffer. Evidence from high-level corporate- and public-policy failures highlights the negative consequences of *too much* group cohesion.[3] Effective decision-making is undermined in four ways:

- **People stop thinking critically** High cohesion can create an unquestioning atmosphere where independent critical thinking is not encouraged. Group objectives and options tend to go unexamined and conformity reigns. Group pressures to conform can even persuade people to distrust the evidence of their own eyes.[4]
- **People have critical thoughts, but do not voice them** Group members withhold their doubts or objections in case they provoke threat or

embarrassment. They go along with decisions despite their misgivings because they do not want to seem disloyal or to let the group down.

- **The group suppresses critical comments** Certain members take it on themselves to protect the group and the leader from adverse information that might upset the group harmony. Warning signals that contradict the dominant thinking are discredited. Dissenters are pressured not to speak out against the group's assumptions, plans or commitments.
- **The group is over-confident** The lack of internal challenge comforts the group members in their illusion that they are right. A sense of superiority weakens group vigilance to external signals. Nor does the group bother testing its conclusions on outsiders who might have different values, priorities and viewpoints.

The effects of these dysfunctions are predictable. They generate complacency, shallow thinking, flawed reasoning and poor decision-making. The resulting decisions are likely to be unnecessarily risky because they ignore obvious threats. And when members are reluctant to speak their minds but want to be seen as cohesive, they can even end up making collective decisions that none of the individual members believes is right.[5]

Thus, the dangers of conflict from silo thinking are matched by the dangers of defective decision making from too much cohesion. To find a path between these two risks, CXOs need a sound appreciation of the role of conflict in effective top team dynamics.

Good and bad conflict

Conflict in management teams is not necessarily an indicator of dysfunction. To be more precise, there are two types of work conflict: task conflict and relationship conflict. These have been found to have very different influences on top team effectiveness.

Experience tells us that task-related conflict can be particularly valuable. When CXOs discuss and challenge each other's diverse perspectives, it typically clarifies opinions about complex topics. Disagreements concerning the business tasks or the process of addressing them are often very useful. This is because they lead to more thorough and creative discussion of alternative courses of action and avoid premature closure on decisions.[6]

Debate is critical in surfacing relevant information and shaping effective courses of action. Many studies show that such interaction promotes desirable outcomes of productive innovation, performance and improvement.[7]

By contrast, relationship-related conflict is generally unproductive and detrimental to performance.[8] It focuses on personal likes and dislikes that are separate from or peripheral to the work itself. It often generates negative emotions such as anger, fear and frustration, as well as defensive attitudes and behaviours such as suspicion and impatience.

Low trust and the resulting faulty communication discourage information sharing among team members. And, contradictory views will be suppressed for fear of further antagonizing others. Inevitably, this impairs reflection, joint decision-making and purposeful implementation.

On the face it, the way forward seems fairly clear-cut. Top teams should try to gain the benefits of task conflict while avoiding the costs associated with relationship conflict. CEOs should encourage productive conflict and discourage destructive conflict.

The trouble is that the two are easily confused. Personalities and issues become entangled. Two CXOs with different knowledge bases, different cognitive grids for assessing issues and different priorities can view one another's central concerns as peripheral, if not meaningless.

Idiosyncratic views based on a distinctive functional background can be mistaken for political views, based on one's personal career needs. Similarly, when one CXO makes comments about another CXO's area it can be perceived as a personal attack. It is seen as a challenge to the other's professional competence or credibility – rather than as feedback or as constructive debate. Recalling one such incident, an executive commented:

> She was trying to sort something out in [her area] and turned around and said to myself and one of the other staff that she did not get enough support from us with her job . . . I guess that upset us . . . and . . . we confronted her and because we were very upset, it became intense after that point.[9]

It is not always easy to dissociate discrepant professional views from interpersonal incompatibilities. *What* is said is always important. But *how* it is said, and especially the recipient's inference about *why* it is said, can obscure the factual content of the message.

Participants can feel bruised or offended by poorly expressed or poorly managed task conflict. What starts as a conflict over issues can either be misattributed to relationship conflict, or can escalate into interpersonal conflict.[10]

The matter of role conflict is so important to effective collaboration that it is worthwhile exploring a specific case. Here, we select a CXO conflict that is endemic to manufacturing companies and well documented: the often antagonistic relationship between marketing and manufacturing.

Marketing versus manufacturing

The relationship between the manufacturing and the marketing functions is frequently critical to the firm's performance.[11] It is also often 'the focal point of much more frequent and heated disagreement than occurs between other pairs of functions'.[12]

There are good reasons for these disagreements. A fundamental difference in outlook between the functions stems from their different contributions to revenue and profit. Whereas the main objective for marketing is to increase revenue, production is often mainly responsible for reducing costs. The two objectives are often in conflict.

For example, the marketing function wants a wide range of products to satisfy customer demand and increase sales. By contrast, the production function wants long production runs and narrow product offerings to increase economies of scale and reduce changeover times.

Marketing wants to promise quick delivery times and to respond instantly to unexpected surges in demand. But for manufacturing, this implies maintenance of large inventories, which increases holding costs. Table 19.1 categorizes some of the other 'hot spots' between the two areas.

Now, in addition to conflicting goals, there is also a high level of interdependence. Marketing is the key link between manufacturing and customers. From the manufacturing perspective this means that a lot of bad news arrives via the marketing function. The challenges of new product requirements, pressures to increase flexibility or lower costs, and sudden changes in demand patterns are communicated to manufacturing by the marketing unit. And it is easy to start confusing the message with the messenger.

For its part, manufacturing must acquiesce to these customer demands and market opportunities, or else be perceived (both internally and externally) as intransigent and unco-operative. These tensions can derail essential information exchange and create misunderstandings.

Table 19.1: ***Areas of potential conflict between marketing and manufacturing***

Area of conflict	Marketing objective	Manufacturing objective
Managing diversity		
1. Product line length/breadth	Many and complex models	Few and simple models
2. Product customization	Customer specifications	'Stock' products
3. Product line changes	Product changes immediately; high risk	Planned, only necessary changes; low risk
Managing conformity		
4. Product scheduling	Constant change	Inflexible
5. Capacity/facility planning	Accept all orders	Critically evaluate 'fit' of orders
Managing dependability		
6. Delivery	Immediate: large inventory	As soon as possible: no inventory
7. Quality control	High standards	Reasonable control

Source: Crittenden et al, 1993[13]

Each function can see the other as a key barrier to achieving its objectives. And when parties see their goals thwarted by others, they are inclined to view these others in a negative light.

Conflict becomes personal

The underlying structural tensions can be intensified by differences in the personal and educational profiles of those drawn to those functions. When added to differences in work norms, these can affect their respective approaches to problem solving and work, their preferences for orderliness or spontaneity. For example, it has been noted that executives from different functions favour different tactics and contexts when trying to influence their peers.[14]

Such differences can promote labelling and stereotyping. The chief of marketing's love of customers and the chief of manufacturing's love of schedules and systems become easy targets for caricature. The head of marketing can easily be seen as 'eager to please', 'all talk' or 'disconnected from reality'. Likewise, the head of manufacturing can be regarded as 'inflexible', 'risk averse' and 'out of touch with where the company has to go'.

Once such labels are activated, the parties are likely to start misinterpreting constructive initiatives or debate. They can be seen as efforts by others to expand their power or to score points. Such misinterpretation can deepen personal mistrust and resistance to the other party's perspective or recommendations.

Also, the parties are likely to make negative inferences about what the other is 'up to', and then to act on these assumptions. This ignites yet another round of conflict, and sets up a self-reinforcing process.

For example, over-optimistic market forecasts can lead manufacturing to question marketing's competence and to downgrade those forecasts unilaterally. But when this becomes known, marketing is likely to inflate subsequent forecasts still further.

Such lack of trust can lead to second-guessing, delayed decision making and under-communication that generate further problems. These can easily be pinned on the unhelpful attitude of the other party and may be put down to stubbornness, political scheming, secretiveness, self-importance and parochialism.

Each party sees the problem from its own perspective and is reluctant to give ground. The stock response from manufacturing to marketing is that 'it can't be done'. Marketing becomes fed up of manufacturing's 'no can do' attitude and intensifies the pressure on manufacturing to get its way. The adversarial relationship becomes entrenched.

Pretty soon, all issues are personalized. The two CXOs are at loggerheads and incapable of seeing beyond the fact that the other person has a difficult personality.

But others also get dragged into the conflict. The negative feelings and rivalries cascade down throughout both functions – and impair strategy implementation. They also radiate out to the other functions.

For example, meetings become arenas for finger-pointing and disparaging comments. Other CXOs are forced to choose camps or risk getting caught in the crossfire. The group dynamics suffer as positions become polarized.

In other cases, the warring parties may 'agree to disagree' but CXO meetings become muted affairs, involving mere information exchange, as no one wants to trigger hostilities. The real discussion happens in pairs as rival CXOs manoeuvre for the CEO's ear.

Building on this examination of the corrosive effects of friction between two CXOs, we now broaden the discussion to consider how such clashes might be of particular concern to the top team.

How top teams differ from other teams

The top team differs from cross-functional teams further down the structure, most notably by its composition, the demands of the task and its duty to set the example.

Composition

Functional differences are likely to be a sharper source of conflict at the top, for the simple reason that the top team often includes the widest mix of functional representatives.

Of course, the CEO can reduce the number of CXOs on the top team. The CEO can also favour direct reports with similar occupational backgrounds, such as engineers, economists, accountants or scientists, depending on the sector.

As noted earlier, this may make for easier consensus, but will also create certain blind spots for the top team. The *content* gains, from broader expertise, have to be weighed up against the *process* losses, from more disagreements.

Those quarrels can be magnified by the personalities involved. More than other teams, the top team is composed of ambitious individuals. As heads of major staff functions, CXOs are institutional leaders in their own right. Indeed, most of them will have got to where they are on the basis of their abilities to *lead* rather than *participate* in effective teams.

Moreover, the status of the CXOs within the team will vary depending on their importance to the business model – and this can introduce additional tensions, as explored in more detail in the next chapter. So the make-up of the team is one source of conflict, but so is the nature of its activities.

Demands of the task

Compared to other cross-functional teams, the team at the apex faces more complex and intense work challenges.

The decisions made by the top team have important implications for resource allocation, and the high stakes involved may make the deliberations especially passionate and vocal. Indeed, that discord is likely to be amplified by the pressure coming up from the CXOs' own constituencies.

High pressure and stress have well-known distorting effects on people's judgments about others. When executives lack the mental bandwidth for processing information about others, they tend to rely more heavily on stereotypes and are quicker to label.

In addition, when trying to make sense of the negative behaviour of colleagues, overstretched executives are also more inclined to discount the influence of the situation. Instead, they exaggerate the responsibility of the person – what is technically labelled as *fundamental attribution error*.[15]

Such biases increase the likelihood that healthy disagreement is misinterpreted. CXOs will be tempted to blame the opposition of colleagues on self-interest and personal ambition, when their views are in fact driven by differences in outlook stemming from their differing CXO positions.

As pointed out in the next chapter, these role tensions are further complicated by the presence of divisional and geographical heads in the top management team. Besides introducing another set of conflicting objectives and responsibilities, these line managers often hold unfavourable opinions of the value of staff functions, as pointed out in chapter 16.

Setting the example

Beyond technical reasons, there are also important symbolic reasons for the CXOs to strive to work effectively as a team.

This is because the top executive team serves as the company's model of how a team should operate. When the relationships among CXOs or between the CXOs and the CEO are not working, it sets up a dysfunctional example for the rest of the company to emulate. And that can be very costly.

All the talk about team management and the team-based culture will seem very hollow, and actually will be corrosive to morale, if the CXO group cannot model the right behaviours in their dealings together.

As we have shown in this chapter, it is not only conflict that has to be managed, but also agreement.

Teams are not an ideology

Now, in this chapter and the next, we are exploring challenges for executives in the company's topmost positions, as they attempt to integrate and energize the entire firm. Inevitably then, we have used and will continue to use the language of teams and teamwork.

But we want to be clear that our point is *not* that CXOs should decide everything as a team. Some issues require the team's combined input, but many others do not.

In fact, we often hear managers complain that they are involved in too many meetings and group discussions that do not concern them. Sometimes it is not clear why the particular meeting is being held. Nor are all participants sure of their role in the meeting. They are also puzzled why certain others are present. And, when we ask managers for their estimate of time wasted in meetings, the bidding starts at 50 per cent, and quickly climbs higher.

Thus, we wish to emphasize that we regard teams as a methodology. They are a way of getting high-quality and workable decisions under certain conditions. They are not ends in themselves. They are not an ideology.

Following this somewhat conceptual treatment of team issues, we move to the practical challenges of teams.

Notes

1 S. Kaplan, 'Framing contests: Micro mechanisms of strategy making in the face of technical change', MIT Working Paper, April (2005).

2 D. Dougherty, 'Interpretive barriers to successful product innovation in large firms', *Organization Science*, 3 (2) (1992), pp. 179–202.

3 I. L. Janis, *Groupthink: A Psychological Study of Policy Decisions and Fiascos* (Boston: Houghton Mifflin Company, 1982).

4 S. E. Asch, 'Effects of group pressure on the modification and distortion of judgments', in G. E. Swanson, T. M. Newcomb, and E. L. Hartley (eds.), *Readings in Social Psychology* (New York: Holt, 1952), pp. 2–11.

5 J. B. Harvey, 'The Abilene Paradox: The management of agreement', *Organizational Dynamics*, 17 (1) (1988), pp. 17–43.

6 K. M. Eisenhardt, J. L. Kahwajy, and L. J. Bourgeois, 'How management teams can have a good fight', *Harvard Business Review*, July–August (1997), pp. 77–85.

7 A. C. Mooney and J. Sonnenfeld, 'Exploring antecedents of top management team conflict: The importance of behavioral integration', *Academy of Management Proceedings* (2001), pp. 11–17.

8 A. L. Simons and R. S. Peterson, 'Task conflict and relationship conflict in top management teams: The pivotal role of intragroup trust', *Journal of Applied Psychology*, 85 (1) (2000), pp. 102–11.
9 O. B. Ayoko, C. E. J. Härtel and V. J. Callan, 'Resolving the puzzle of productive and destructive conflict in culturally heterogeneous workshops', *International Journal of Conflict Management*, 13 (2) (2002), pp. 165–90.
10 A. C. Amason and H. J. Sapienza, 'The effects of top management team size and interaction norms on cognitive and affective conflict,' *Journal of General Management*, 23 (4) (1997), pp. 495–516.
11 R. Hayes, S. Wheelwright and K. Clark, *Dynamic Manufacturing* (New York: John Wiley, 1989).
12 R. H. Hayes and S. C. Wheelwright, *Restoring our Competitive Edge: Competing Through Manufacturing* (New York: John Wiley, 1984).
13 V. L. Crittenden, L. R. Gardiner and A. Stam, 'Reducing conflict between marketing and manufacturing', *Industrial Marketing Management*, 22 (1993), pp. 299–309.
14 H. G. Enns and D. B. McFarlin, 'When executives influence peers: Does function matter?' *Human Resource Management*, 42 (2) (2003), pp. 125–142.
15 Z. Kunda, *Social Cognition* (Cambridge, MA: MIT Press, 2001), p. 295.

20 *The Top Team – From executive group to executive team*

JEAN-PHILIPPE DESCHAMPS

On the first day of the retreat, one of the business line guys piped up, 'If you, support-function guys, would just do this . . .' The CEO said, 'Hang on. We're all part of this company. If you're going to sit in this room and work on this team, you've got to drop this "we" and "they" . . . This is a collective effort.' People got the message, and this has turned into a real team. CXO, global motor company[1]

To support the CEO effectively, CXOs must often engage in combined action.

This chapter considers some of the obstacles to the pursuit of an integrated and coherent corporate agenda. We pull together some of the previous themes and propose ways of surmounting the barriers to collective action that are built into the social system.

Building on points made earlier in chapters 16 and 19, we can identify four practical challenges for the CEO, and for the CXOs in their work to support the CEO:

- Handling the effects of the inevitable informal hierarchy within the top team, particularly when this pits CXOs against their line colleagues;
- Ensuring that CXOs find the right balance between supporting their line colleagues and enforcing corporate-wide policies in their functional area;
- Encouraging CXOs to broaden their thinking to act as full members of the top executive team;
- Aligning the work of all CXOs with the entire corporate agenda.

Before exploring these four tasks in greater depth, it is useful to clarify the composition of the corporation's top team. This book focuses on the CXOs, the heads of the corporate functions. But the CXOs contributions to the top team, of which they are members, are also influenced by their relationships with two other categories of senior executive.

A multi-layered team

In most large corporations, the topmost executive group consists of three different types of executives.

1 The business heads

These are entrusted by the CEO to lead an integrated piece of the corporation's business, be it a group of divisions (for very large corporations), or a single division or business unit.

Business heads are directly accountable for the profits and losses of their businesses. As chief executives in their own right, they must set direction, integrate their functions and be the ultimate decision makers in their domain. They generally campaign for full control over the various functions they need to support their business, be it marketing, R&D, finance and control or human resources.

In some companies, heads of business units behave as powerful barons, particularly if their business contributes significantly to company sales or profits. Being judged on their business results, they tend to emulate the CEO's behaviour, particularly when they know that the next CEO may come from their ranks.

2 The market heads

Their mission is to represent and optimize the company's business in a particular market, generally a cluster of geographical areas, industry segments or channels.

In most global corporations, which calculate profits horizontally (by business) and vertically (by market), market heads share profit and loss responsibilities with the business heads. But generally, their power is based on their direct control over the corporation's customers, often via a network of market companies.

Their level of influence generally depends on whether the corporation is mostly customer-driven, in which case they have a prime position, or technology/product-driven, in which case the business heads typically have greater power than the heads of markets.

Market heads often focus on marketing and selling the products that are developed and produced elsewhere in the corporation. But they can also play a significant role in product specification, development and local manufacturing. In the latter case, their power base is obviously very important.

3 The CXOs

Whereas the first two groups are line executives, the third group comprises the corporate heads of functions, whose leadership roles were covered earlier in this book. They are the promoters and guardians of the corporation's functional knowledge and expertise, the instigators of its functional policies and procedures, and they are counsellors to the CEO in their functional domain.

With these brief descriptions as background, we can now explore the main challenges facing the CEO and CXOs as they combine to lead the company.

The 'pecking order' challenge

In most companies, an informal hierarchy in the top executive team is inevitable. It is typically the result of three entrenched organizational tendencies.

- Firstly, there is the usual dominance of 'line' over 'staff', which was outlined in chapter 16. Business line managers have an in-built advantage when it comes to getting the CEO's attention. They are the executives who drive the revenue and cost systems and their businesses involve large numbers of people. CXOs rarely, if ever, have such responsibilities and the consequent power bases.
- Secondly, there will be differences in status among CXOs themselves. In particular, the business model will largely determine the relative visibility of the various CXOs. For example, CFOs will tend to have high standing in firms driven by stock-market imperatives, while CT/ROs will tend to be more influential in technology-driven companies.
- Thirdly, the CEO's own background and experience can confer privilege on certain functional areas. Some chief executives are more capable and therefore more comfortable dealing with executives in the functions where they themselves 'grew up' and developed their professional mastery. In contrast, other CEOs will favour functions where they see a gap in their capabilities and might tend to rely excessively on the opinions of those CXOs.

Many factors can determine the power base and level of influence of a CXO. It starts obviously with internal ones, such as the perceived performance of the function under his/her jurisdiction. A sterile R&D pipeline will inevitably weaken the position of a CT/RO with his/her business colleagues. And respect for the CIO is weakened when IT applications are consistently delayed, budgets are exceeded and the standardization of hardware and software remains a dream.

External factors can also determine the pecking order. A change in the firm's business model can affect CXO power. For example, consider the outsourcing of a large part of the manufacturing load and the consequent divestment of many plants. These actions will clearly weaken the status of the chief manufacturing officer, particularly in companies where prestige is closely linked to payroll size. Similarly, the break-up of a large corporate R&D centre into decentralized labs in the business units may induce the chief technology or research officer to feel, rightly or wrongly, a sense of lost influence.

Sometimes, a potential loss of status can have a negative impact on CXO team cohesion. A CXO whose status is eroded might be inclined to focus more effort on self-preservation than on contributing to the team's and the company's objectives.

Such pecking order effects are perhaps inevitable. But they need not be destructive. However, there are two situations where the functioning of the top executive group as a team will be negatively affected.

Firstly, the compensation system might lead CXOs to behave in parochial fashion. This can happen if they are measured primarily on narrow functional performance indicators rather than on a diversified balanced scorecard.

Secondly, the CEO – consciously or unconsciously – might encourage or tolerate a strong, rigid official hierarchy that invites turf battles and excessive politicking, or other unproductive uses of executive energy.

Of course, each CXO will fight for a share of the CEO's attention. This can be healthy and useful, but it must be managed so that the benefits are fully realized.

Certain functions are clearly more important to the business model than others. Typically, the CEO will recognize the reality of these differences and will act to reduce petty status-mongering. This requires particular sensitivity and skill on the part of the CEO who must build a culture where the CXOs all feel that their input is valued, even if their contributions do not carry equal weight.

To further dispel perceptions of favouritism and promote co-operation, the CEO can allocate comparable time slots for individual functional and operational reviews with each CXO, while giving privileged access to joint cross-functional reviews.

Similar to the point made in chapter 4, the CEO can also assign the CXOs to projects or task forces outside their existing or previously experienced domains. Beyond broadening their experience, such measures also promote the sense of equity in contribution to the corporate purpose. In addition, these assignments can reduce the sense of predictability inherent in the hierarchy. For example, it might happen that the CMO, who is being groomed for the CEO role, always gets the high-profile projects; or that the CFO necessarily always heads up finance-related initiatives.

Finally, another dilemma for the CEO in managing the team is the difference in rewards among CXOs. Clearly, market forces will determine base salaries, depending on the importance of the function. But it might be in the company's interests, and that is in the CEO's interests, to use bonuses to recognize important contributions from the less prominent functions.

The 'balancing act' challenge

As mentioned in chapter 16, all CXOs find themselves in the delicate situation of facing two conflicting objectives.

On one side, they must set and enforce policies, rules and guidelines to preserve the standards of their own functions in support of the general corporate interest. Now, these regulatory and policing actions will inevitably interfere with the freedom of executives in running their business units, R&D departments, computer centres and market organizations. And so it can make CXOs extremely unpopular in the line organization.

On the other side, CXOs must support the performance of line executives by providing specialized resources, methods or simply advice.

This dilemma is not an easy one to manage. Many CXOs may find themselves pushed to one side or the other. When their policing role prevails, they are accused of rigidity and of being impervious to the needs of the line's business. When they lean the other way to support businesses, they can be accused by others, in staff and corporate roles, of indulging the desires of line executives and neglecting the fundamentals of their function, or of broader corporate necessities.

Of course, the CEO is often caught in the same dilemma: whether to reinforce strict corporate guidelines or to explore possibilities for a different way of doing things locally. On occasion, the CEO can demand that the CXOs uphold corporate discipline. Yet – and we have seen this happen minutes later in the same meeting – the CEO can also show sympathy to a particular line executive who argues for more freedom from corporate constraints in order to meet targets.

Such conflicting messages can create confusion. This again illustrates that at high executive levels, the key task is often to balance opposing policies and goals, as stressed in chapter 18.

To resolve such dilemmas, the CEO has a decision to make. The fast and simple option is to discuss the problem with individual executives one-to-one. But the risk is that the side-deals that result from such discussions can breed resentment among those who believe they have been ignored or abandoned.

The alternative is for the CEO to push for such matters to be discussed openly in team meetings. While time-consuming, this method often leads to more permanent solutions as there will be pressures for fair-dealing, and everybody gets the same message at the same time.

In practice, CEOs typically employ a mix of the two solutions and the main question is which approach they tend to favour. Ultimately, it comes down to the kind of culture the CEO wants to promote – a culture focused on time efficiency or a culture that encourages collegiality.

The 'narrow thinking' challenge

Contrary to what might be expected, it is at the top of a company that we often find the least diversity of experience. It is in the top team where we often see the largest investment in the past and the greatest reverence for industry dogma.[2]

This is particularly the case for CXOs who have often spent many years moving up the ranks by developing their functional expertise. They become both proprietary about their own domain and uncomfortable pushing back on colleagues in other functional domains. A rebuff by another more knowledgeable colleague can lead to an embarrassing and costly loss of face. Such confrontations can escalate into corrosive tit-for-tat hostilities between CXOs, as described in chapter 19.

So, the team at the top often falls well short of its potential because the CXOs, like the business heads, are cautious about stepping into each other's territory. The result is still more work for the CEO. He/she must sort through individual CXO proposals and select a course of action without knowing in advance if it will be fully supported by all members in the top team.

As the CEO of a global computing company once put it:

> It's okay to spend a lot of time arguing about which route to take to San Francisco when everyone wants to end up there, but a lot of time gets wasted in such arguments if one person wants to go to San Francisco and another secretly wants to go to San Diego.[3]

When initiatives are adopted against the unspoken reservations of others in the team, then the prospects for implementation are weakened. And, the costs go beyond those of incomplete commitment.

As highlighted in chapter 6, breakthrough thinking and innovation are best served by candid exchange of opinions, offbeat insights, the application of one science to another. This happens most reliably when CXOs are willing to set aside functional expertise and to challenge one another.

Developing this sense of collective responsibility requires great effort from each of the CXOs. They need to be clear on how their own domain contributes to overall performance. And they must know enough of the other functions' roles and capabilities to develop a holistic view of company performance.

For technical and emotional reasons, it is helpful if the issues and priorities of each CXO are laid out explicitly and recognized as legitimate by the CEO and other members of the team. Only then can competing priorities and potential conflicts (for example, over scarce funding) be openly discussed. This is never easy, but transparency offers a better chance of finding superior and mutually acceptable solutions. Or, at least, it can promote equitable trade-offs that, over time, add up to an acceptable situation for all involved.

Attaining such openness also requires the active support of the CEO, who must acknowledge the risks involved for individual CXOs and remind them of the benefits. In practice, the CEO might be quite content to operate through a set of one-to-one relationships with the CXOs. When there is no 'team', it becomes difficult to effectively oppose the chief executive – a situation that the CEO might favour.

Yet it is frequently in the interests of both the CEO and the CXOs to form a real team to avoid the traps of autocratic rule or paralysis by fiefdom. Three measures can help promote this objective of joint responsibility.

1 A simple approach, when setting the agenda for team meetings, is to frame agenda topics in terms of corporate requirements. Each CXO can then be asked to contribute in terms of what his/her function can bring to solving corporate problems and exploiting opportunities. By contrast, it is best to avoid agendas that work their way through each of the functional topics. This method, which treats functional factors as isolated issues will encourage individual CXOs to defend their own areas rather than to seek corporate-wide solutions.

2 Another way forward is to combine very different supervisory responsibilities. This might involve allocating either geographical or business-line responsibilities to a particular CXO.

   Some companies go even further and radically shuffle the functional responsibility allocation. For example, a marketing chief can be asked to supervise information technology, the heads of technology and operations can swap responsibilities or the CFO can take over human resources.

   These moves blur the very notion of a specialist CXO job and encourage functional chiefs to behave as full members of the top executive team. Such approaches are common in some European countries, notably in Germany and Switzerland.

3 An alternative to reshuffling functional responsibilities is to shift from a traditional functional or business unit organization to a process-oriented organization. Organizing by process brings three major functional integration benefits, besides its main efficiency advantages.

   Firstly, and by definition, corporate processes are cross-functional. Allocating process-coaching responsibilities to CXOs obliges them to behave in a cross-functional mode.

   Secondly, since there are several processes to be steered and coached, interdependencies will grow among the top team, reinforcing the team spirit.

   Thirdly, because process performance is generally more measurable than functional performance, CXOs can be evaluated on their objective contribution to overall business performance.

Structural remedies can therefore help CXOs to raise their sights beyond their immediate functional concerns and to move towards the goal of greater company-wide alignment.

The alignment challenge

To help the company add up to more than the sum of its parts, members of the top team must be on the same wavelength and be working towards the same corporate objectives. In other words, they need to be aligned at the levels of overall purpose, strategic direction and daily focus.

Alignment with the company's sense of purpose

The starting point for a fully aligned organization is that CXOs share, intellectually and emotionally, their company's declared purpose, that is its mission and values, its core ideology, its reason for being.

Some companies – such as Johnson & Johnson and Medtronic, both in the healthcare industry – are known for maintaining a very strong and vivid expression of their big purpose. Their mission statements and lists of values are not just adornments in the annual report. They pervade the behaviour of most employees throughout the company. And, they influence management decisions and actions in all functions.

By contrast, many companies do not make the effort to define their purpose beyond very general business-goal statements, such as providing satisfactory returns to their shareholders, meeting customers' needs and taking good care of their employees.

In the absence of a compelling and unifying sense of purpose, CXOs and other top managers are left to rely on personal principles and values to guide their decisions. This does not help alignment across the functions.

A powerful way to promote cross-functional alignment is to reformulate the corporate vision and mission as a top team, under the direction of the CEO. This will build common and agreed purpose within the team, and consistency of action when CXOs return to their own functions, and the whirlwind of everyday business.

Now, leadership often requires the effective communication of a story.[4] And, it is helpful if members of the top team can develop their stories together, such that the individual CXOs can then share similar stories with their own constituencies. Indeed, in discussing the implications of the corporate story for their own departments, CXOs and their staff can develop both the concepts and details, and produce clear mission statements that apply to their particular functions.

Alignment with the company's direction

In addition to alignment on the high-level mission, CXOs must develop commitment within their own staff to the company's business strategy. However, CXOs might not be very familiar with the details of all strategies of the business units of the firm. These are often defined by business and market heads without CXO input.

For example, the chief human resources officer is often excluded from business review meetings. Likewise, the CFO is rarely involved in discussions of marketing strategy. At best, this leads to sub-optimization of the company's resources. At worst, it can result in policies or decisions within the functions that conflict with the chosen strategic direction.

Even if CXOs generally agree with the corporate mission, they will often want to influence their colleagues' understanding of what constitutes a successful business strategy. Typically, they will stress the importance of their own domain. For example, the CIO will tend to argue that business success depends on the firm's ability to use information.

Clearly, it is at least partly rational for CXOs to try to shape the corporate strategic agenda according to their own functional view. They are pursuing a genuine desire to enhance the company's success. But this process is not exempt from self-serving politics. The thinking is often like this:

> If I can convince the CEO and the rest of the team that our business performance will be enhanced through greater contribution from my own function, then I will be entitled to a higher share of resources. And my contribution will attract increased recognition and reward.

An effective way to promote alignment in direction at the top is to engage in strategy workshops. Led by the CEO, these workshops typically include the heads of the business units and the CXO team. Working through the business issues from a variety of perspectives is helpful in providing top executives with a shared understanding of key investment and directional decisions.

In such workshops, the task of each CXO is to define how their function's resources, combined with those of other departments, can best support the business. More particularly, there will be discussions about how to reinforce existing activities versus pursuing new revenue streams. These debates open up a special role for the CXOs. Precisely because they do not have business unit responsibilities, they are well placed to discuss the interests of new and established businesses in a less partial way than their line colleagues.

Alignment with the company's focus

It requires strong and sustained effort by the CEO and CXOs to communicate their priorities in ways people can understand and act upon.

High-performing companies typically devote considerable resources, notably executive time, to ensuring that each employee fully understands what is needed to achieve the critical few objectives. Employees are then better able to focus their personal efforts to contribute towards those objectives.

Such focus can be achieved when the top executive team agrees on a set of specific, prioritized high-leverage actions. These specific projects are sometimes referred to as 'must-win battles'.[5] The priorities should be few, but compelling enough to mobilize all energies over a sufficient period of time towards achieving the firm's objectives.

'Must-win battles' will vary greatly across companies depending on their strategic objectives and situations. Some will focus on business restructuring or performance improvements; others on market penetration or market recapture; yet others on internal staff mobilization for a change in mindset or the development of new resources and competencies. When these battles have been defined, they can be turned into priorities, and so influence CXOs' agendas and set the focus for each function.

The alignment challenge, then, is for the ***CEO and CXOs to build a shared and agreed mindset***. This can best result from careful orchestration of the interactions among CXOs.

Yet, as explored in chapter 19, the pursuit of cohesion can also limit team effectiveness. That is, the final twist in the alignment challenge is that the more that the CXOs embrace a common vision, values and objectives, the higher the danger of uncritical and dangerous consensus.

This risk, and the blind spots that it creates in the way senior executives look at their environment, can be reduced if the CEO forces the top team to remain open to external input. This was discussed in chapter 4 as part of the general treatment of the imperative of *learning*.

In vibrant and effective top teams, it is common to see external experts regularly invited to enrich internal discussions, to bring new perspectives and to challenge the comfortable top executive consensus.

Again, we see that the need to operate as a team grows not from ideology but from principles of creating outcomes that benefit the firm's stakeholders.

In concluding this chapter, we can briefly restate the purpose of this third section of the book. What we have shown is that it is through the efforts of the CXOs in joining forces, in going beyond their own areas of responsibilities, that they enable the firm's business system to maximize its wealth-creating potential.

Notes

1 K. Hammonds, 'How do we break out of the box we're stuck in?', *Fast Company*, November (2000), pp. 260–8.

2 G. Hamel, 'Strategy as revolution', *Harvard Business Review*, July–August (1996), pp. 69–83.

3 K. M. Eisenhardt, J. L Kahwajy and L. J. Bourgeois, 'How management teams have a good fight', *Harvard Business Review*, July–August (1997), pp. 77–85.

4 H. Gardner and E. Laskin, *Leading Minds: An Anatomy of Leadership* (New York: BasicBooks, 1995).

5 P. J. Killing, T. Malnight and T. Keys, *Must-Win Battles* (London: FT Prentice Hall, 2005).

Conclusion

21 *Summary: the CXO Challenge – Wealth creation by the executive team*

PRESTON BOTTGER AND
JEAN-LOUIS BARSOUX

I don't have to take all the decisions. In fact, in the new world of business, it can't be me, it shouldn't be me, and my job is to prevent it from being me.

(CEO, international technology-services company)[1]

This closing chapter brings together the primary ideas explored in the three main sections of the book. Our organizing theme is the idea introduced in chapter 2 that the goal of business leadership is to create wealth – financial and material, human and social – in the face of external developments that are never entirely foreseeable. With this in mind, we have explored the tasks that comprise purposeful contribution by members of the top executive team, the CXOs.

A key challenge for the company's top leader, the CEO, is to create a CXO team that can successfully carry out this wealth-creating mission. Actually, this challenge is repeated at all levels of leadership in the company: leaders must nurture teams that must produce results – on the basis of which further wealth-creating goals can be pursued.

We now revisit the three main sections of the book: The business imperatives, the functions of the CXOs and the CEO's view. For companies to prosper, facing as they do non-predictable shifts in their environments, their CXOs must:

- Strongly influence the actions of people working around them to put their energies in the pursuit of the firm's economic and other goals. This can be achieved by an ongoing campaign that employs the methods of mission, process, structure and culture. Essential components of these campaign methods are: nurturing and managing talented people; putting into practice the lessons of experience; and instilling the ethos of quality-mindedness.
- Maintain in current operations, the high degrees of *purposefulness*, *directional decision-making*, and *focus* in implementation, with the guiding principle of incessant improvement, whether this be in daily

incremental steps, or in major step-function innovations; and with all of this informed by and fully serving broader and longer-term corporate goals.

- Contribute to the company's wealth-creating mission as a member of the topmost team, working around, with and for the CEO. Each CXO should be fully capable of explaining the firm's strategy in comprehensive terms, and be able to explain to people within their own functions how best they can contribute to the implementation of this strategy. As members of the senior executive group, CXOs must both collaborate effectively with one another, and confront, even compete with, one another, all in the quest for high-quality results for the firm.

Perhaps the reader finds these three sets of challenges to be not very exciting. However, this is one of the key messages of the book. Success, both within each of the business functions and for the entire company, consists mostly in doing what it is clear must be done, doing it well and building a platform, rich in resources, to meet tomorrow's unknowable challenges.

Often, we hear from seasoned executives that too much human energy is wasted reinventing wheels, chasing fads, and pursuing exciting and novel ideas. These executives say: 'The methodology for creating wealth is not a mystery. It is well understood. We just must do what we must do.'

Perhaps the real mystery is why people, alone and collectively, omit to take the obvious steps that would ensure success. Leaders and leadership teams are sometimes sidetracked from paying attention to the decisions, implementation methods and details that would lead to desired results. This presents a dual challenge: to maintain purpose, direction and focus when it is easy to be distracted by interesting alternatives; and to have the discipline to stand aside occasionally from busy-work to check if current patterns of activity are indeed wealth-creating.

Therefore, to finish this book, we present a set of reminders about effective methods of leadership, not magic; it is about maintaining management attention to accomplish important and essential purposes.

Building capability for wealth creation

In section 1 of the book, we focused on the fundamental business imperatives in business leadership. These are the capabilities, methods and mindsets that all CXOs must develop to help the firm respond effectively to challenges of today and tomorrow. Along with the essential leadership methods implied in the concepts of mission, process, structure and culture, we especially highlighted the importance of the management of talented people and learning from experience.

Talent

Wealth-creating capacity, in the context of ever-evolving threats and opportunities in the environment, requires major investment in people. CXOs must create and manage large pools of managers and other professionals who can sense and respond to opportunities and problems. These people must have a context of understanding that allows them to see the significance of what is happening and to devise methods to capitalize on opportunities, and overcome threatening challenges.

The chief means of developing talented people to handle the unexpected is to expose them to a wide variety of stretching experiences, and to ensure that this helps them to see things from emergent perspectives, not just their earlier learned beliefs. It gets them used to dealing with the unexpected, forcing them to embrace and resolve novel problems.

More generally, senior executives must find and promote people who can deal well with conflict, who can face reality, debate constructively, and fight to win, because changes in external circumstances and uncertainty about what these changes will lead to, inevitably generates disagreement among those involved. And, the more capable the people, the greater the potential for disagreement.

Learning

To deal with emerging, unforeseen circumstances, CXOs must be able to question their existing beliefs, and devise and implement new methods to deal with new tasks. We saw in chapter 4 that people often have difficultly seeing matters anew while doing their day-to-day jobs. To make sense of faint or confusing signals, to develop new responses and initiatives, CXOs and their teams must be capable of breaking the pattern of their regular activities. They must step away from the accustomed daily work environment and re-evaluate their methods and goals from different perspectives.

CXOs must also set up systems to detect emerging signals about key developments in the firm's business system: for example, in customer concerns, product quality, supplier behaviour, investor sentiment. Then they must ensure that both confirming and distressing information are appropriately amplified and transmitted to the people who must react to the concerns. Critical information is all too often known 'in the system', just not by the managers who must formulate a response and make a decision. High-speed consideration of an issue, decision-making, and subsequent CXO leadership of the consequent new initiative is often vital for corporate effectiveness.

CXOs must follow through on decisions for improvements; first, by finding creative ways of testing out ideas on a small scale before committing large resources in an irreversible way; and second, by adjusting the surrounding systems – that is, structure and processes – to fit in with and support the new practices. These are vital reflexes for CXOs who want to turn breakthrough thinking into wealth-creating activities.

Quality

A quality mindset which is firmly established within the CXO team and which permeates the firm's culture prepares people in the company to deal with uncertainty. Instilling a quality focus requires CXOs to do more than just say the right things; they must also do the right things, visibly and consistently.

Quality focus provides a shared language for CXOs to recognize debate and decide on wealth-creating strategies and activities. A quality mindset gets people focused on the necessity, and the pleasures, of doing things that have lasting value, and perhaps even have attributes of beauty. Quality-mindedness also gets people to pay attention to facts and effective and efficient actions. Waste of time and money is recognized and minimized when a company has made quality the centre of its core values. It provides methods for diagnosing upside opportunities and for reducing, if not eliminating, weak processes by which human energy and other resources are wasted.

In other words, companies that are quality focused respect current goals and implementation methods *and* they maintain the abilities to question existing practices and to see emerging opportunities and threats. Fact-driven discussions help to protect professional debates against possible fogging by personality clashes or turf-inspired blindness, of the kind described in chapter 17.

This protection promotes the robust assessment of the meaning of information and the benefits and costs of possible new courses of action. In turn, this assists strategic decisions on where to make major investments of resources.

Thus executive commitment to quality, learning and talent makes for a culture that is always on its toes, taking initiatives and ready to respond to unexpected events. The more that people are thinking about and acting on these essentials, the better the firm's capacity to spot and react successfully to whatever challenges they face as they pursue the creation of high-quality wealth.

Leading within the function

Section 2 of the book set out the tasks and methods by which individual CXOs must lead within their functions. Effective leadership within the function typically requires finding the right mix of three arenas of purposeful activity:

1 Managing current operations.
2 Preparing for change, and implementing projects that accomplish the required transitions.
3 Ensuring that these two remain in harmony with, and contribute to, the overall company strategy. Again, these three sets of activities are aimed at the goal of wealth creation under continuing unpredictable changes in the external environment.

Managing current operations

To deal with unexpected events, the firm's people must be ready to devise clever counter-moves and initiatives under crisis conditions. The firm is best prepared to handle new opportunities and threats when its current operations are running efficiently and smoothly so that it is not in 'catch up' mode when the unexpected happens.

Firms are best prepared for responding to crises and for intentional transitions when individuals, and the firm's systems, are up-to-date, when they both excel at current operations and can deploy managerial attention to the external environment. To keep the company's systems fully up-to-date, CXOs must regularly review existing projects and discard those that have lost their significance in competitive advantage and the creation of wealth.

Stripping out non-essentials provides more resources to respond forcefully to unexpected developments. It frees up managerial attention, allowing CXOs to remain in a vigilant state, for fast responses when the need occurs. By making sure that current operations are running to high-quality standards, CXOs can generate reserves of capabilities and assets that allow the firm to take a hit and to bounce back.

From results today to results tomorrow

A recurring theme in section 2 is the need for the individual CXOs to take a broad corporate view with an eye on the future. Daily results represent the creation of wealth using the existing model. By contrast, the longer-term view is concerned with where and how the firm will create tomorrow's wealth. This aspect is concerned with identifying possibilities that might be the basis of future capital generation.

Each CXO must be capable of engaging in such strategic explorations. Of course, to get from the present state to the future state, CXOs must design and oversee improvement projects. Within their functions, they must convert the choices that emerge from strategic conversations into a mission, with supporting processes, structures and a culture that will produce high-value results.

Often, these efforts to develop new capabilities compete for resources with on-going efforts to extract results from existing capabilities. This reinforces the need for ruthlessness in weeding out non-value-adding activities that might deprive innovative efforts of financial and intellectual resources; and of letting go of 'old favourites' that are declining in productive value.

Critically, CXOs have to work together to make this happen. To manage progress in the face of emerging, unforeseeable obstacles, the firm must be able to alter its course quickly; and this requires concerted and co-ordinated action within the CXO team.

Purposeful CXO collaboration

Section 3 of the book explored the CXOs' relationships with one another and with the CEO, and as members of the leadership team. It has been a common piece of advice over the past forty years that executives should conduct their daily work, indeed make all decisions, within groups, and that they should avoid unilateral decision making. Consequently, we often hear from executives that much time is unnecessarily spent in group meetings.

Pragmatically, the CEO must often take the lead in managing uncertainty and cut through the confusion by making decisions and setting direction. There are certain dangerous corporate challenges in which safe passage, or the securing of major benefits in a brief moment of opportunity, are best led from the front by a highly competent CEO.

By contrast, there are other cases where the necessary leadership must be exercised, visibly, by the CXO team as a team. When there is uncertainty about goals and the methods for achieving them, confrontation among multiple viewpoints is likely to enhance the technical quality of decisions and the prospects for effective implementation.

In such situations, effective teamwork is certainly not the result of individuals surrendering their personal wills or denying their comparative strengths in the interests of consensus. On the contrary, it requires that all members remain very alert for indications of both corporate peril and corporate opportunity, in which their personal contribution of expertise and effort will be critical for team success.

This kind of effective combined effort is very different from notions of teamwork as harmonious, co-operative activities, without conflict or competition among members. Teamwork frequently consists of conflict and confrontation to find the best methods to accomplish the right goals.

Dealing with the unexpected often involves conflictual interactions. Executives are vitally concerned about their own success, their turf and their careers. They also have different role-determined ways of analysing business issues. As highlighted in chapter 17, CXOs therefore must act to minimize the unhealthy kinds of relationship conflicts while managing the healthy kinds of task conflicts, and avoid slipping into unhealthy cohesion.

Given the many obstacles to effective CXO collaboration highlighted in section 3, we repeat here the point that teamwork is best regarded as a method, not an ideology. CEOs have to be judicious in declaring that a particular issue is a CXO team task. For CXOs, time spent in group discussions, especially working on 'other people's problems', can be seen as time that would be better spent attending to their own jobs. As suggested in chapter 18, this is especially true for those CXOs low in the pecking order, whose opinions often carry less weight.

Spending too much time on group activities that do not actually require the presence of all participants can nurture scepticism about the value of combined efforts, and the boss's real intention. Thus, poor use of CXO time in pretend teamwork can create more problems than it solves. There are many issues that, rightly, should be dealt with by a sole CXO; and, some that are best decided by the CXO and CEO together. Then, there are deliberations and decisions that can be best handled by the CXO team. It is useful if the CEO and the CXO team diagnose and agree which classes of decisions are best handled by individuals, pairs or the group.

Teamwork, yes: but individuals make the difference

In the business media, stories typically focus on individual leaders. This is understandable because brief sound bites, and even 1,000-word print articles, can rarely capture and communicate the full complexity of corporate life.

The reality is that CEOs, indeed all leaders at all levels, face severe limitations on what they can accomplish alone. Building a loyal and competent CXO team that can handle the broad range of challenges facing the company is a key to business success. For example, in chapter 17, we suggested that CEOs should cover five critical roles: originator, designer, energizer, integrator and protector. In practice, it is best if CEOs assemble a team that can handle the combination of these five roles.

The CEO's task is to devise a highly robust management system comprising the necessary mission, structure, processes and culture, staffed by talented people, to accomplish the business objectives, whatever difficulties might arise. In the words of the former CEO of one of the world's most respected airlines:

> Leadership always matters, but it matters most when technology disrupts and fear kicks in. Any fool can hand out stock options and keep his team together when the market is hot.
>
> But real leadership means keeping the team focused when fear is a force ... The ability to command is still important, but the ability to build unit cohesion among team members is what matters most. In a networked world, the edge goes to the most cohesive team.[2]

However, what we also see in highly effective executive teams is that each member, each CXO, is continuously diagnosing what his best contribution could be, alone or in action with colleagues, and then doing what must be done. Sometimes, cohesion must be disrupted, by a lonely single voice, so that empirical validity in the team's thinking can be re-established. Sometimes, individual preferences must be overridden or extinguished, because actually, cohesive teamwork is the very factor most necessary to secure the greater good.

Wealth-creating teamwork is the result when each member makes his or her best possible personal contribution. Magical team-level creativity is very rare; it simply does not occur without high-quality, high-contributing individual members. CXOs must be the role models of wealth-creating behaviour for all members of the company, by showing individual leadership *and* by demonstrating teamwork.

Notes

1 N. Farris, 'Everything I thought I knew about leadership is wrong', *Fast Company*, April (1996), pp. 71–79.

2 Cheong Choong Kong, CEO of Singapore Airlines. Cited in J. Ellis 'Many things matter, and here's what matters most', *Fast Company*, June (2001), pp. 74–85.

Index

Page numbers in *italic* indicate Glossary items